AF446323

Garnet and Gold!
History of Florida State Seminoles Football

Text Copyright © 2025 by Steve's Football Bible, LLC
{6th Edition}

All rights reserved. No part of this publication may be reproduced, stored, or transmitted in any form or by any means, electronic, mechanical, photocopying, recording, scanning, or otherwise without written permission from the publisher. It is illegal to copy this book, post it to a website, or distribute it by any other means without permission.

The information in this book is for educational and entertainment purposes.

Information sourced from but not limited to: Associated Press, NoleFan.org, Seminoles.com, New York Times, and Wikipedia.com

ISBN: 9-798201918-18-7

Disclaimer: This book is not authorized or approved by any Football team or league

College Football History Books available at www.stevesfootballbible.com

Introduction

My love of College Football began in 1966. As a 7-year-old kid I remember watching the Notre Dame-Michigan State "Game of the Century". Next, I remember the 1967 USC-UCLA game and O.J. Simpson weaving through the UCLA defense for the winning touchdown with 6 minutes left in the game. I remember the 1968 Rose Bowl, Indiana vs USC. Who was this Indiana team that went to the Rose Bowl over my beloved Minnesota Golden Gopher's?   I attended my first college football game in 1971. Michigan vs Minnesota at Memorial Stadium on the Campus of the University of Minnesota. My Aunt Roberta took me. I was hooked after that. The Golden Gophers were defeated that day 35-7 by the Wolverines. George Honza of the Golden Gophers scored the only touchdown that day on a pass from Craig Curry. Ironically, I met Mr. Honza in January of 2017 while officiating a basketball game. Growing up in a rural farming town {Alden} in southern Minnesota, as a youth I spent a lot of my Saturdays in the fall watching ABC Sports College game of the week.

This book is for all the College Football fans, casual or diehard, historians or those who just plain love the College game. I hope everyone enjoys it.

Steve Fulton

Contents

Pro Football History Books available at <u>www.stevesfootballbible.com</u>

Florida State Seminoles

The team is known for its storied history, distinctive helmet, fight song and colors as well as the many traditions associated with the school. Since 1977, the Seminoles have only had four losing seasons (2018, 2019, 2020 & 2021).

Florida State has won three national championships, 18 conference titles and six division titles along with a playoff appearance. The Seminoles have achieved three undefeated seasons, finished ranked in the top four of the AP Poll for 14 straight years from 1987 through 2000 and completed 41 straight winning seasons from 1977 through 2017; from 2012 through 2014, the team won 29 consecutive games, tied for the twelfth-longest winning streak in college football and tied for the longest winning streak in ACC history. The 1999 team received votes from ESPN as one of the top teams in college football history. From 1982 to 2017, the Seminoles went to a Bowl game each season. The team has produced three Heisman Trophy winners: quarterbacks Charlie Ward in 1993, Chris Weinke in 2000 and Jameis Winston in 2013. The Biletnikoff Award, presented annually to the top receiver in college football, is named for Florida State hall of famer Fred Biletnikoff. Other awards won by Florida State players include the Walter Camp Award, the Maxwell Award, the Davey O'Brien Award, the Lombardi Award, the Dick Butkus Award, the Johnny Unitas Golden Arm Award, the Lou Groza Award, the Dave Rimington Trophy and the Bobby Bowden Award. Florida State coaches have been honored with the Bobby Dodd Coach of the Year Award, the Walter Camp Coach of the Year Award, the Home Depot Coach of the Year Award, the Broyles Award, and the Paul "Bear" Bryant Award. Many former Seminoles have gone on to have successful careers in the NFL.

The program has produced 219 All-Americans (45 consensus and 15 unanimous) and 250 professional players. Florida State has had six members inducted into the College Football Hall of Fame, three members inducted into the College Football Coaches Hall of Fame and four members inducted into the Pro Football Hall of Fame. The Seminoles have the tenth-highest winning percentage among all college football programs in Division I FBS history with over 500 victories. Florida State has appeared in 48 postseason bowl games and ranks ninth nationally for bowl winning percentage and fourth for bowl wins. The Seminoles' archrivals are Florida, whom they meet annually in the last game of the regular season, and Miami; both games are considered among the greatest rivalries in college football.

Bobby Bowden Era

Under head coach Bobby Bowden, who came to Florida State from West Virginia, the Seminoles became one of the nation's most competitive programs, greatly expanding the tradition of football at Florida State. The Seminoles played in five national championship games between 1993 and 2000, and claimed the championship twice, in 1993 and 1999. The FSU football team was the most successful team in college football during the 1990s, boasting an 89% winning percentage. FSU also set an NCAA record for most consecutive Top 5 finishes in the AP football poll – receiving placement 14 years in a row, from 1987 to 2000. The Seminoles under Bowden were the first college football team in history to go wire-to-wire (ranked first place from preseason to postseason) since the AP began releasing preseason rankings in 1936. On December 1, 2009 Bowden announced that he would retire from coaching after the Seminoles' game on New Year's Day 2010 against West Virginia, Bowden's former team, in the Gator Bowl. His legacy has led to the creation of two awards in his honor, the Bobby Bowden Award, an award presented to college football players, and the Bobby Bowden National Collegiate Coach of the Year Award, an award presented to college football coaches.

In the late 1980s and throughout the 1990s, the Seminoles had 14 consecutive seasons with 10 or more wins and a top four finish, with a record of 152−19−1 between these years (11 of their 19 losses were decided by seven points or less), and one of the best home records of the era. FSU's accomplishments in these 14 seasons included eleven bowl wins, nine ACC championships, two Heisman Trophy winners, and two national championships.

Traditions

Osceola and Renegade

Osceola and Renegade are the official symbols of the Florida State Seminoles. During home football games, Osceola, portraying the Seminole leader Osceola, charges down the field at Bobby Bowden Field at Doak Campbell Stadium riding an appaloosa horse named Renegade, and hurls a burning spear at midfield to begin every game. The Seminole Tribe of Florida officially sanctions the use of the Seminole as Florida State University's nickname and of Osceola as FSU's symbol.

Sod Cemetery

For Florida State Football, "sod games" and the Sod Cemetery have been a rich part of the Seminoles college football history, commemorating many of the greatest victories. Away from home and against the odds, Florida State sod games represent the most difficult battles on the football field. The Sod Cemetery stands as a tribute to those triumphs. There are currently 103 pieces of sod in the cemetery.

In 1962, as the Seminoles completed their Thursday practice in preparation to face Georgia at Sanford Stadium, Dean Coyle Moore – a long-time professor and member of FSU's athletic board – issued a challenge: "Bring back some sod from between the hedges at Georgia." On Saturday, October 20, the Seminoles scored an 18–0 victory over the favored Bulldogs. Team captain Gene McDowell pulled a small piece of grass from the field, which was presented to Moore at the next football practice. Moore and FSU coach Bill Peterson had the sod buried on the practice field as a symbol of victory. A monument was placed to commemorate the triumph and the tradition of the sod game was born. Before leaving for all road games in which Florida State is the underdog, all road games at the University of Florida and all ACC championship and bowl games, Seminole captains gather their teammates to explain the significance of the tradition. Victorious captains return with a piece of the opponent's turf to be buried in the Sod Cemetery inside the gates of the practice field. In recent years, as the Florida State program has been successful, games of significance regardless of whether the Seminoles are the underdog, can be designated a "sod game." This most recently occurred in 2013 when the Seminoles traveled to Clemson, South Carolina in what was called the biggest game in ACC history. The Seminoles defeated Clemson, 51–14, in what was the biggest margin of victory in Clemson's Memorial Stadium.

Marching Chiefs

The Marching Chiefs is the official marching band of the Florida State Seminoles. The band plays at every home game as well as at some away games (Clemson, Miami, and Florida) as well as any Championship or Bowl game. There are upwards of 470 members in the band, holding the distinction of being the world's largest collegiate marching band.

War Chant

The Seminole War Chant was first used in a 1984 game against Auburn. The chant was started in FSU's Marching Band – The Marching Chiefs, originally by members of the percussion section. The melody is based on the 1960s cheer, massacre. The chant has also become associated with the tomahawk chop. The War Chant would be adopted by the Atlanta Braves when FSU football alumnus Deion Sanders joined the team and has been used ever since. Craig Day began the Chop at now-defunct Fulton County stadium in response to UF Gator fans doing the Gator Chomp every time Deion came up to the plate.

Honored jersey numbers

No.	Name	Position	Career
2	Deion Sanders	CB	1985–88
9	Peter Warrick	WR	1995-1999
10	Derrick Brooks	LB	1991–1994
16	Chris Weinke	QB	1997–2000
17	Charlie Ward	QB	1989–1993
25	Fred Biletnikoff	WR	1962–1964
27	Terrell Buckley	CB	1989–1991
28	Warrick Dunn	RB	1993–1996
34	Ron Sellers	WR	1966–1968
50	Ron Simmons	DT	1977–1980
55	Marvin Jones	LB	1990–1992

College Football Hall of Fame

Seven FSU players and three coaches have been inducted into the College Football Hall of Fame.

Name	Position	Career	Inducted
Ron Sellers	WR	1966–1968	1988
Fred Biletnikoff	WR	1962–1964	1991
Darrell Mudra	Coach	1974–1975	2000
Bobby Bowden	Coach	1976–2009	2006
Charlie Ward	QB	1989, 1991–1993	2006
Ron Simmons	DT	1977–1980	2009
Deion Sanders	CB	1985–1988	2011
Derrick Brooks	LB	1992–1994	2016
Mack Brown	Coach	1972–1973 (player)	2018
Terrell Buckley	CB	1989–1991	2019

Pro Football Hall of Fame

Four former Seminoles have been inducted into the Pro Football Hall of Fame

Name	Position	Career	Inducted
Fred Biletnikoff	WR	1965–1978	1988
Deion Sanders	CB	1989–2000, 2004–2005	2011
Derrick Brooks	LB	1995–2008	2014
Walter Jones	OL	1997–2008	2014

National Awards

Chic Harley Award	Archie Griffin Award	AP Player of the Year
1993 – Charlie Ward, QB	2013 – Jameis Winston, QB	2013 – Jameis Winston, QB
Davey O'Brien Award	**Manning Award**	**Kellen Moore Award**
1993 – Charlie Ward, QB	2013 – Jameis Winston	1991 – Casey Weldon
2000 – Chris Weinke, QB		1993 – Charlie Ward, QB
2013 – Jameis Winston, QB		
Johhny Unitas Award	**Sammy Baugh Trophy**	**Jim Brown Award**
1991 – Casey Weldon	2000 – Chris Weinke, QB	2015 – Dalvin Cook
1993 – Charlie Ward, QB		
2000 – Chris Weinke, QB		
Paul Warfield Award	**John Mackey Award**	**Dave Remington Trophy**
1999 – Peter Warrick	2014 – Nick O'Leary	2013 – Bryan Stork
Jim Thorpe Award	**Jack Tatum Trophy**	**Lombardi Award**
1988 – Deion Sanders	1991 – Terrell Buckley	1992 – Marvin Jones
1991 – Terrell Buckley	2016 – Tarvarus McFadden	2000 – Jamal Reynolds
Bill Willis Trophy	**Butkus Award**	**Jack Lambert Trophy**
1997 – Andre Wadsworth	1987 – Paul McGowan	1992 – Marvin Jones
2000 – Jamal Reynolds	1992 – Marvin Jones	1994 – Derrick Brooks
Lou Groza Award	**Vlade Award**	**Bobby Bowden Award**
1998, 1999 – Sebastian Janikowski	2013 – Roberto Aguayo	2010 – Christian Ponder
1999 – Sebastian Janikowski	2014 – Roberto Aguayo	
2008 – Graham Gano		
2013 – Roberto Aguayo		
Bobby Dodd Award	**Walter Camp Award**	**Home Depot Award**
1980 – Bobby Bowden	1980 – Bobby Bowden	1980 – Bobby Bowden
Broyles Award		
1996 – Mickey Andrews, DC		
Paul "Bear" Bryant Award	**Bobby Bowden Award**	
1980 – Bobby Bowden	1980 – Bobby Bowden	

Heisman Trophy Winners

| Charlie Ward - 1993 | Chris Weinke - 2000 | Jameis Winston -2013 |

Conference Awards

ACC Player of the Year	**ACC Offensive Player of the Year**	**ACC Defensive Player of the Year**
Charlie Ward (1992, 1993)	Charlie Ward (1993)	Derrick Brooks (1993)
Danny Kanell (1995)	Danny Kanell (1995)	Derrick Alexander (1994)
Andre Wadsworth (1997)	Thad Busby (1997)	Peter Boulware (1996)
Chris Weinke (2000)	Chris Weinke (2000)	Andre Wadsworth (1997)
Jameis Winston (2013)	Jameis Winston (2013)	Darnell Dockett (2003)
Jordan Travis (2023)	Jordan Travis (2-23)	Björn Werner (2012)
ACC Rookie of the Year	**ACC Offensive Rookie of the Year**	DeMarcus Walker (2016)
Tamarick Vanover (1992)	Jameis Winston (2013)	
Travis Minor (1997)	Deondre Francois (2016)	**ACC Defensive Rookie of the Year**
Chris Rix (2001)	**Jacobs Blocking Trophy**	Myron Rolle (2006)
Jameis Winston (2013)	Clay Shiver (1994,1995)	Xavier Rhodes (2010)
Deondre Francois (2016)	Tra Thomas (1997)	Ronald Darby (2012)
Brian Piccolo Award	Tarlos Thomas (2000)	**ACC Coach of the Year**
Dan Footman (1992)	Brett Williams (2001,2002)	Bobby Bowden (1993, 1997)
Sam Cowart (1997)	Rodney Hudson (2008,2009)	Mike Norvell (2023)
Corey Simon (1998)	Cameron Erving (2013, 2014)	
Chris Weinke (1999)	Roderick Johnson (2015, 2016)	
Anquan Boldin (2002)		
Chris Thompson (2012)		

All-Americans

Year(s)	Name	Position	Year(s)	Name	Position
1964	Fred Biletnikoff	WR	1999	Jason Whitaker	OL
1967–1968	Ron Sellers	WR	1999	Sebastian Janikowski	K
1979–1980	Ron Simmons	DL	1999	Peter Warrick	WR
1983	Greg Allen	RB	2000	Tay Cody	CB
1985	Jamie Dukes	OL	2000	Snoop Minnis	WR
1987–1988	Deion Sanders	CB	2000	Jamal Reynolds	DE
1989	LeRoy Butler	CB	2003	Alex Barron	OL
1991	Terrell Buckley	CB	2004	Alex Barron	OL
1991-1992	Marvin Jones	LB	2010	Rodney Hudson	OL
1993	Charlie Ward	QB	2011	Shawn Powell	P
1993	Corey Sawyer	CB	2012	Björn Werner	DL
1993	Derrick Brooks	LB	2013	Lamarcus Joyner	S
1994	Derrick Brooks	LB	2013	Bryan Stork	C
1994	Clifton Abraham	CB	2013	Jameis Winston	QB
1995	Clay Shiver	C	2014	Roberto Aguayo	K
1996	Peter Boulware	DE	2014	Tre' Jackson	OL
1996	Reinard Wilson	DE	2014	Nick O'Leary	TE
1997	Sam Cowart	LB	2015	Jalen Ramsey	CB
1997	Andre Wadsworth	DE	2016	Dalvin Cook	RB
1998	Sebastian Janikowski	K	2016	DeMarcus Walker	DE
1998	Peter Warrick	WR	2023	Jared Verse	DL
1999	Corey Simon	DL	2024	Alex Mastromanno	P

Biletnikoff

Brooks

Warrick

Bowl Games

12/30/2023	#5 FLORIDA STATE	vs	#6 GEORGIA	3	63	L	Orange Bowl
12/29/2022	#13 FLORIDA STATE {10-3}	vs	OKLAHOMA {6-7}	35	32	W	Cheez-It Bowl
12/31/2019	FLORIDA STATE (6-7)	vs	ARIZONA STATE (8-5)	14	20	L	Sun Bowl
12/27/2017	FLORIDA STATE (7-6)	vs	SOUTHERN MISS (8-5)	42	13	W	Independence Bowl
12/30/2016	#10 FLORIDA STATE (10-3)	vs	#6 MICHIGAN (10-3)	33	32	W	Orange Bowl
12/31/2015	#9 FLORIDA STATE (10-2)	vs	#14 HOUSTON (12-1)	24	38	L	Chick-Fil-A Peach Bowl
1/1/2015	#2 FLORIDA STATE (13-1)	vs	#3 OREGON (13-1)	20	59	L	Rose Bowl (National Semi-Final)
1/6/2014	#1 FLORIDA STATE (14-0)	vs	#2 AUBURN (12-2)	34	31	W	BCS Championship
1/1/2013	#13 FLORIDA STATE (12-2)	vs	#16 NORTHERN ILLINOIS (12-2)	31	10	W	Orange Bowl
12/29/2011	#25 FLORIDA STATE (10-4)	vs	NOTRE DAME (8-5)	18	14	W	Champs Sports Bowl
12/31/2010	#23 FLORIDA STATE (9-4)	vs	#19 SOUTH CAROLINA (9-5)	26	17	W	Chick-Fil-A Peach Bowl
1/1/2010	FLORIDA STATE (7-6)	vs	#17 WEST VIRGINIA (9-4)	33	21	W	Gator Bowl
12/27/2008	FLORIDA STATE (9-4)	vs	WISCONSIN (7-6)	42	13	W	Champs Sports Bowl
12/31/2007	FLORIDA STATE (7-6)	vs	KENTUCKY (8-5)	28	35	L	Music City Bowl
12/27/2006	FLORIDA STATE (7-6)	vs	UCLA (7-6)	44	27	W	Emerald Bowl
1/3/2006	#23 FLORIDA STATE (8-5)	vs	#3 PENN STATE (11-1)	23	26	L	Orange Bowl
1/1/2005	#16 FLORIDA STATE (9-3)	vs	WEST VIRGINIA (8-4)	30	18	W	Gator Bowl
1/1/2004	#9 FLORIDA STATE (10-3)	vs	#10 MIAMI (11-2)	14	16	L	Orange Bowl
1/1/2003	#16 FLORIDA STATE (9-5)	vs	#4 GEORGIA (13-1)	13	26	L	Sugar Bowl
1/1/2002	#24 FLORIDA STATE (8-4)	vs	#15 VIRGINIA TECH (8-4)	30	17	W	Gator Bowl
1/3/2001	#2 FLORIDA STATE (11-2)	vs	#1 OKLAHOMA (13-0)	2	13	L	Orange Bowl
1/4/2000	#1 FLORIDA STATE (12-0)	vs	#2 VIRGINIA TECH (11-1)	46	29	W	Sugar Bowl
1/4/1999	#2 FLORIDA STATE (11-2)	vs	#1 TENNESSEE (13-0)	16	23	L	Fiesta Bowl
1/1/1998	#4 FLORIDA STATE (11-1)	vs	#10 OHIO STATE (10-3)	31	14	W	Sugar Bowl
1/2/1997	#1 FLORIDA STATE (11-1)	vs	#3 FLORIDA (12-1)	20	52	L	Sugar Bowl
1/1/1996	#8 FLORIDA STATE (10-2)	vs	#6 NOTRE DAME (9-3)	31	26	W	Orange Bowl
1/2/1995	#7 FLORIDA STATE (10-1-1)	vs	#5 FLORIDA (10-2-1)	23	17	W	Sugar Bowl
1/1/1994	#1 FLORIDA STATE (12-1)	vs	#2 NEBRASKA (11-1)	18	16	W	Orange Bowl
1/1/1993	#3 FLORIDA STATE (11-2)	vs	#11 NEBRASKA (9-3)	27	14	W	Orange Bowl
1/1/1992	#5 FLORIDA STATE (11-2)	vs	#9 TEXAS A&M (10-2)	10	2	W	Cotton Bowl
12/28/1990	#6 FLORIDA STATE (10-2)	vs	#7 PENN STATE (9-3)	24	17	W	Blockbuster Bowl
1/1/1990	#5 FLORIDA STATE (10-2)	vs	#6 NEBRASKA (10-2)	41	17	W	Fiesta Bowl
1/2/1989	#4 FLORIDA STATE (11-1)	vs	#7 AUBURN (10-2)	13	7	W	Sugar Bowl
1/1/1988	#3 FLORIDA STATE (11-1)	vs	#5 NEBRASKA (10-2)	31	28	W	Fiesta Bowl
12/31/1986	FLORIDA STATE (7-4-1)	vs	INDIANA (6-6)	27	13	W	All-American Bowl
12/30/1985	#18 FLORIDA STATE (9-3)	vs	#19 OKLAHOMA STATE (8-4)	34	23	W	Gator Bowl
12/22/1984	#15 FLORIDA STATE (7-3-2)	vs	GEORGIA (7-4-1)	17	17	T	Florida Citrus Bowl
12/30/1983	FLORIDA STATE (7-5)	vs	NORTH CAROLINA (8-4)	28	3	W	Peach Bowl
12/30/1982	FLORIDA STATE (9-3)	vs	#10 WEST VIRGINIA (9-3)	31	12	W	Gator Bowl
1/1/1981	#2 FLORIDA STATE (10-2)	vs	#4 OKLAHOMA (10-2)	17	18	L	Orange Bowl

1/1/1980	#6 FLORIDA STATE (11-1)	vs	#5 OKLAHOMA (11-1)	7	24	L	Orange Bowl
12/23/1977	#19 FLORIDA STATE (10-2)	vs	TEXAS TECH (7-5)	40	17	W	Tangerine Bowl
12/27/1971	FLORIDA STATE (8-4)	vs	#8 ARIZONA STATE (11-1)	38	45	L	Fiesta Bowl
12/30/1968	#19 FLORIDA STATE (8-3)	vs	LSU (8-3)	27	31	L	Peach Bowl
12/30/1967	FLORIDA STATE (7-2-2)	vs	#10 PENN STATE (8-2-1)	17	17	T	Gator Bowl
12/24/1966	FLORIDA STATE (6-5)	vs	WYOMING (10-1)	20	28	L	Sun Bowl
1/2/1965	FLORIDA STATE (9-1-1)	vs	OKLAHOMA (6-4-1)	36	19	W	Gator Bowl
12/13/1958	FLORIDA STATE (7-4)	vs	#19 OKLAHOMA STATE (8-3)	6	15	L	Bluegrass Bowl
1/1/1955	FLORIDA STATE (8-4)	vs	TEXAS-EL PASO (8-3)	20	47	L	Sun Bowl
1/2/1950	FLORIDA STATE (9-1)	vs	Wofford (11-1)	19	6	W	Cigar Bowl

Stadiums
Centennial Field {1947-1949}

Florida State began to play at Centennial Field during the team's 1947 season and would continue to play there for the following two years (1948 and 1949).

Doak Campbell Stadium {1950-present}

The stadium, named after former school president Doak Sheridan Campbell, hosted its first game against the Randolph-Macon College Yellowjackets on October 7, 1950 with the Seminoles winning the game 40–7. At that time the facility had a seating capacity of 15,000. Doak Campbell Stadium, with its original capacity of 15,000 in 1950, was built at a cost of $250,000. In 1954, the stadium grew to a capacity of 19,000. Six thousand more seats were added in 1961. During the Bill Peterson era (1960–70), the stadium was expanded to 40,500 seats, and it remained at that capacity for the next 14 years. Since that time, the stadium has expanded to almost 83,000, largely due to the success of the football team under head coach Bobby Bowden coupled with the ever-growing student body. It now is the second largest football stadium in the Atlantic Coast Conference (ACC).

Aesthetically, a brick facade surrounding the stadium matches the architectural design of most of the buildings on the university's campus. In addition to the obvious recreational uses, The University Center surrounds the stadium and houses many of the university's offices as well as The College of Motion Picture Arts, The Dedman School of Hospitality, and The College of Social Work. The field was officially named Bobby Bowden field on November 20, 2004 as Florida State hosted intrastate rival Florida. Florida State has been recognized as having one of the best gameday atmospheres in the country, and Doak Campbell Stadium has been named one of the top stadiums in college sports.

Doak Campbell Stadium has been a great home field advantage for the Noles. Florida State is one of only three schools that can boast a decade home field unbeaten streak. The Seminoles never lost a home game from 1992–2001, a total of 54 games, and have completed 23 undefeated seasons at their home stadiums, including 21 at Doak Campbell. The record crowd for the stadium is 84,431; set during a game against the Notre Dame Fighting Irish on October 18, 2014.

Rivalries
Florida-Florida State Rivalry

The Florida Gators are the main rival of the Florida State Seminoles. Florida State and Florida have played each other 64 times, with **the Gators holding a 38–28–2 advantage through the 2024 season**. After the arrival of Bobby Bowden in 1976, the Seminoles compiled a record of 24–21–1; the rivals share a record of 10-10 against each other since 2000. The game alternates between Florida's home stadium, Ben Hill Griffin Stadium at Florida Field in Gainesville, Florida and Florida State's home stadium, Bobby Bowden Field at Doak Campbell Stadium in Tallahassee, Florida.

Florida State-Miami Rivalry

The rivalry dates to 1951, when the Miami Hurricanes defeated the Seminoles 35–13 in their inaugural meeting. The schools have played uninterrupted since 1966, with **Miami leading the series 36–33 through the 2024 season**. Florida State holds a 10–7 advantage since the Hurricanes became a conference foe in 2004. During the 1980s and 90s, the series emerged as one of the premier rivalries in college football. Between 1983 and 2013, the Hurricanes and Seminoles combined to win 8 national championships (5 for Miami, 3 for Florida State) and played in 15 national championship games (1983, 85, 86, 87, 89, 91, 92, 93, 96, 98, 99, 2000, 01, 02, 13). The rivalry has been popular not only because of its profound national championship implications and the competitiveness of the games but also because of the immense NFL-caliber talent typically present on the field when the two teams meet. The famous 1987 matchup featured over 50 future NFL players on both rosters combined.

The rivalry is a television ratings bonanza, accounting for the two highest rated college football telecasts in ESPN history. The 2006 game between Miami and FSU was the second most-viewed college football game, regular season or bowl, in the history of ESPN, averaging 6.33 million households in viewership (a 6.9 rating). It trailed only the 1994 game between Miami and FSU, which notched a 7.7 rating.

Florida State-Virginia Rivalry {Jefferson-Eppes Trophy}

The Seminoles also have a rivalry with the Virginia Cavaliers. Florida State and Virginia compete for the Jefferson–Eppes Trophy. The two schools have played for the trophy since its creation in 1995. It has been awarded a total of 19 times, with FSU receiving it 14 times (FSU vacated its 2006 win). **The Seminoles hold the all-time advantage 14–4 through the 2023 season**. Because of conference expansion, the teams no longer play annually; the teams last met in 2019.

The Jefferson–Eppes Trophy is awarded to the winner of the Florida State–Virginia game. This game was played annually from 1992 through 2005, but since the conference split into divisions, the teams meet twice every six years. Florida State has been awarded the trophy 15 times.

1947 Florida State Seminoles

In its first and only season under head coach Ed Williamson, the team compiled a 0–5 record and was outscored by a total of 90 to 18. The team played its home games at Centennial Field in Tallahassee, Florida. In September 1947, the Florida State College for Women became coeducational, was renamed Florida State University, and announced that it would field a football team, though it had no plans to compete with the University of Florida "for some time to come." The 1947 team was Florida State's first football team since 1904, after which Florida State became a women's college. Ed Williamson served as both athletic director and football coach and vowed to develop "a 'well rounded athletic program' without particular emphasis on football or any other single sport." In five games during the 1947 season, the team gained only 687 yards from scrimmage. The team completed 32 of 87 passes for 400 yards and 14 interceptions. "Red" Parrish was the team's leading rusher with 111 yards. Fullback Kenneth McLean led the team with 105 yards of total offense (105 rushing yards, 45 passing yards).

Home games were played at Centennial Field

9/27/1947	Florida State	vs	STETSON	6	14	L
10/4/1947	Florida State	@	Cumberland	0	6	L
10/11/1947	Florida State	vs	TENNESSEE TECH	6	27	L
10/18/1947	Florida State	vs	TROY STATE	6	36	L
10/25/1947	Florida State	vs	JACKSONVILLE STATE	0	7	L
Coach: Ed Williamson			**Season Record >>**	18	59	**0-5**

Schedule Source: Steve's Football Bible LLC

Selected game(s) highlights

STETSON

The Seminoles hosted the Hatters at Centennial Field in front of 8,000 fans in their first game ever. Charlie McMillan caught a touchdown pass from Don Grant to give the Noles' a 6-0 halftime lead. Stetson rallied in the 2nd half with two touchdowns to defeat FSU, 14-6. The Noles' offense was held to 111 yards.

Cumberland

Hampered by wind, rain and mud, a Cumberland University football squad eked out a 6 to 0 victory over a visiting Florida State. The game's only score came in the second quarter when Bernard Hicks took a 10 yard pass from Brown Braley on Florida State's 20 yard line and cut across the gridiron for the only marker of the game. Both teams dropped the slippery, heavy ball numerous times. The hometown team recovered three of its five fumbles, while Florida State regained six of its 11 bobbles. The passing was as numerous, and as bad, as the fumbling. Florida State made 11 attempts, completed three and had two intercepted. The Bulldogs tossed 16, completed six, and saw Florida State grab three. In the last quarter Florida State made its bid for a score moving up to the Cumberland 25 yard line, but there the Bulldogs held them for downs.

TENNESSEE TECH

The Seminoles hosted Tennessee Tech at Centennial Field before over 5,000 fans. The Tech defense held FSU to 105 total yards, including only 5 yards rushing. Tech took a 27-0 lead into the 4th quarter. Billy O'Steen scored from 2 yards out for the Seminoles lone touchdown in a 27-6 defeat at the hands of the Eagles.

TROY STATE

Troy State jumped to a 24-0 halftime lead before a Thanksgiving Day crowd of over 3,000. Troy State ran back two intercepted passes for touchdowns, passed for two touchdowns and ran for two touchdowns as they rolled to a 36-6 victory over the Seminoles. Leonard Melton scored from 1 yard out for the Seminoles lone touchdown.

JACKSONVILLE STATE

The Jacksonville State Teachers College Gamecocks maintained their place among the nation's unbeaten with a first period scoring march that gave them a slim 7-0 win before over 3,500 fans at Centennial Field. The Seminoles held the Gamecocks to 199 yards while managing 178 yards of total offense on the day.

1948 Florida State Seminoles

1948 was Don Veller's first year as Florida State's head coach. The Seminoles went 7-1 on the season and were Dixie Conference champions. In 1948, the Dixie Conference was formed with nine schools: Florida State, Howard, Lambuth, Mercer, Millsaps, Mississippi College, Oglethorpe, Stetson and Tampa. Five of the schools had football teams: Florida State, Millsaps, Mississippi College, Stetson and Tampa. The Dixie Conference did not allow scholarships, but they allowed freshmen and transfers to play. FSU had all four of its football conference opponents on it's 1948 schedule.

Dixie Conference Champions						
Home games were played at Centennial Field						
10/2/1948	Florida State	vs	CUMBERLAND	30	0	W
10/9/1948	Florida State	@	Erskine	6	14	L
10/16/1948	Florida State	@	Millsaps	7	6	W
10/23/1948	Florida State	@	Stetson	18	7	W
10/30/1948	Florida State	vs	MISSISSIPPI COLLEGE	26	6	W
11/6/1948	Florida State	vs	LIVINGSTON STATE	12	6	W
11/13/1948	Florida State	@	Troy State	20	13	W
11/20/1948	Florida State	vs	TAMPA	33	12	W
Coach: Don Veller			Season Record >>	152	64	7-1

Schedule Source: Steve's Football Bible LLC

Selected game(s) highlights

CUMBERLAND

The Seminoles hammered out a 30-0 triumph over an outclassed Cumberland University Bulldog team before 6,500 fans in Centennial field. FSU had 426 yards of total offense while holding Cumberland to 133 yards. Ken Mclean and Red Parrish each ran for two touchdowns, with McLean rushing for 146 yards and Parrish rushing for 111 yards.

Erskine

The Seminoles traveled to Anderson, SC to play the Erskine. Clarence Lowery scored twice for Erskine as they held off the Seminoles in a 14-6 victory. Ken Mclean scored the lone FSU touchdown, which gave the Noles' an early 6-0 lead. Erskine rolled to 420 yards of total offense, with 358 yards on the ground.

Millsaps

Florida State came from behind with a 52 yard touchdown drive and a perfect point from placement by Joe Crona to knock the Millsaps Majors from the ranks of the undefeated teams with a 7-6 victory. Buddy Strauss scored from 10 yards out to give the Seminoles the lead, which they made stand up for the rest of the game.

Stetson

Florida State traveled to Deland to play before a Stetson homecoming crowd of 4,500 fans that was highlighted by an action packed first half that provided all the scoring and most of the thrills. Buddy Strauss scored from 2 yards out to start the scoring. Trailing 7-6, Ken McLean threw a 19 yard TD pass to Red Parrish, that was followed by Ted Hewitt's 99 yard interception return for a touchdown to give the Seminoles an 18-7 lead that stood up for the final score.

MISSISSIPPI COLLEGE

The Seminoles rolled to a decisive 26-6 triumph over Mississippi College before a crowd of 6,000 fans in Centennial Field. The Choctaw's led 6-0 after the 1st quarter, then FSU poured it on. Red Parrish caught a 53 yard TD pass from Ken McLean and then followed it up with a 40 yard touchdown run. Buddy Strauss scored from 1 yard out in the 3rd quarter and Whitey Urqhuart scored from 1 yard out in the 4th quarter to seal the win for the Seminoles.

LIVINGSTON STATE

The teams were tied 0-0 at halftime and FSU trailed 6-0 after the 3rd quarter, but finally broke through a stubborn Livingston State College defense in the fourth period and pounded out a 12-6 victory over the tiring Tigers in a rough and tumble tilt before 5,000 fans in Centennial Field. Ken McLean ran for two 4th quarter touchdown to rally the Seminoles to victory.

Troy State

The Seminoles traveled to Dothan, AL on a 4 game winning streak. The Seminoles struck through the air late in the fourth period to break a 13-13 deadlock and take a 20-13 victory over the Troy State Red Wave before a slim crowd of 1,500. Norman Eubanks caught a 24 yard TD pass from Walter Foy for the winning touchdown. Ken McLean and Red Parrish ran for short touchdowns earlier in the game to give the Noles' a chance to win.

TAMPA

Florida State University Seminoles rumbled to the Dixie Conference's championship by trampling the Tampa Spartans 33-12 before a colorful homecoming crowd of 7,000 in sun-drenched Centennial Field. The Noles' rumbled to 512 yards of total offense and five different players scored in the win. Ken McLean, Bo Manuel and Ralph Chaudron ran for touchdowns. Norman Eubanks caught a 35 yard TD pass from Whitey Urhquart and Ernie Reddick caught an 18 yard TD pass from Chaudron to cap the scoring for FSU.

1949 Florida State Seminoles

1949 was Don Veller's second year as Florida State's head coach. The Seminoles went 9-1 on the season and were Dixie Conference champions again. They played Wofford in the Cigar Bowl in Havana, Cuba.

Dixie Conference Champions							
Home games were played at Centennial Field							
9/24/1949	Florida State	vs	*WHITING FIELD*	74	0	W	
10/1/1949	Florida State	@	**Mississippi College**	33	12	W	
10/4/1949	Florida State	vs	*ERSKINE*	28	7	W	
10/15/1949	Florida State	@	*Sewanee*	6	0	W	
10/22/1949	Florida State	vs	**STETSON**	33	14	W	
10/29/1949	Florida State	@	*Livingston State*	6	13	L	
11/5/1949	Florida State	vs	**MILLSAPS**	40	0	W	
11/12/1949	Florida State	@	**Tampa**	34	7	W	
11/19/1949	Florida State	vs	*TROY STATE*	20	0	W	
1/1/1950	**Florida State**	vs	**WOFFORD**	19	6	W	Cigar Bowl
Coach: Don Veller			Season Record >>	219	59	9-1	

Schedule Source: Steve's Football Bible LLC

Selected game(s) highlights

WHITING FIELD

A crowd of around 6,800 fans watched the Seminoles roll relentlessly up and down Centennial field as they scored in every period to set a new modern high-scoring mark for the school. Buddy Strauss ran for two touchdowns, Ralph Chaudron returned a punt 75 yards for a touchdown and ran 15 yards for a touchdown and Ernie Reddick ran 15 yards for a touchdown, returned an interception 20 yards for a touchdown and caught a 55 yard pass from Dick Peterson for a touchdown to lead the Seminoles.

Mississippi College

The Seminoles rumbled over Mississippi College's Choctaws 33-12 with a power packed running attack headed by fullback Buddy Strauss. Strauss ran for 161 yards and a touchdown and threw a 9 yard touchdown pass to Ted Hewitt. Ken McLean, Red Parrish and Dick Peterson all ran for touchdowns.

ERSKINE

The Seminoles slammed over three quick touchdowns in a scoring burst early and raced on to a 26-7 triumph over Erskine's Flying Fleet before a crowd of 6,800 fans in Centennial Field. In a short space of 10 plays, beginning late in the first period and running over into the early minutes of the second quarter, the Indians took advantage of every break to score three touchdowns that clinched the decision. Dick Peterson started the flurry when he pounded over right guard from two yards out to climax a 50 yard march. Loren Maltby recovered a Fleet fumble on the 37, and two plays later Walter Foy swept right end for 32 yards and a touchdown. Maltby recovered another fumble on the 29 yard line on the first play following FSU's second touchdown and Peterson cracked over right tackle from 3 yards out for the score. Red Parish accounted for FSU's final score, running around left end for 14 yards on a reverse.

Sewanee

Florida State punched out a fourth period touchdown to defeat the University of the South (Sewanee) 6-0 in a game played in the fog. Red Parrish scored from 18 yards out for the lone Seminoles touchdown. The Seminole defense held Sewanee to 86 yards of total offense.

STETSON

Florida State rolled over the Stetson Hatters 33-14 in a decisive show of power staged before an estimated crowd of 7,500 at the Gator Bowl in Jacksonville. The Seminoles scored twice in the second period and three times in the third quarter to take a commanding 33-0 lead that stood up until the fading minutes of the final quarter when the Hatters struck for two quick scores against the Seminole reserves. Five different Seminole players scored touchdowns and the defense held the Hatters to 77 yards of total offense.

Livingston State

Florida State's hope for a perfect season was ended by a big, tough Livingston Tiger team halted the Seminoles' undeafeated march at 11 straight games by snatching a 13-6 decision. The Tigers put together a pair of touchdowns in the second and fourth periods to offset the Seminoles' lone tally by Walter Foy in the third period. The Seminoles were outgained 263 yards to 187 yards.

MILLSAPS

The Seminoles mauled Millsaps' undermanned Majors 40-0 before a gala Homecoming crowd of around 7,500 in Centennial Field. FSU ground out 271 yards running and added another 132 yards through the air. They held the Majors to 21 yards of total offense, which included minus 34 yards rushing. Red Parrish ran for a touchdown, caught a touchdown pass and threw a 22 yard TD pass to Chris Banakas. Dick Peterson ran for a touchdown and threw two touchdown passes, one to Ted Hewitt and one to Red Parrish.

Tampa

A shivering crowd of around 4,000 fans saw the Spartans turn in their best game of the season against the heavily favored Indians before going down under the weight of superior manpower, 34-7, and a succession of breaks which the Seminoles quickly cashed in. FSU concentrated all its scoring in two periods, the second when they scored three times, and the fourth when they added their final two TDs. In between those two flurries Tampa punched across its only score in the third period. The running Red Parish and an effective passing game operated by Buddy Strauss and Dick Peterson either scored or set up four of the Indians five touchdowns. Parish picked up 101 yards in 13 carries, raced 20 yards for one score, 22 yards to the two to set up another, and kept the attack moving with additional jaunts of 14, 36 and 19 yards.

TROY STATE

The Seminoles fired a quick three touchdown burst at a stunned Troy State team and rode safely in to a 20-0 victory over the Red Wave before a chilled crowd of around 4,000 fans in Centennial Field. Red Parish passed 37 yards to end Chris Banakas for the first score. Dick Peterson accounted for the last two touchdowns, ramming over from the eight, then slicing off tackle from the three. Parrish ran for 122 yards.

1949 CIGAR BOWL

Florida State wasn't given much of of a chance against the Wofford Terriers, who were established as 14 point favorites, but the Seminoles pounded the burly South Carolinians into submission and scored a surprising 19-6 upset victory in the fourth annual Shrine Cigar Bowlgame played before around 14,000. Buddy Strauss ran for 132 yards and a touchdown, and Red Parrish scored two touchdowns to lead the Seminole attack.

1950 Florida State Seminoles

1950 was Don Veller's third year as Florida State's head coach. The Seminoles went 8-0 on the season and were Dixie Conference champions again. It was the first undefeated season at Florida State. The second game, a victory against Randolph–Macon, was the first game played at Doak Campbell Stadium.

Wayne Benner {B} {Cleveland Browns} and Bill Driver {B} {Cleveland Browns} were selected in the 1951 NFL draft.

Dixie Conference Champions						
Home games were played at Doak Campbell Stadium						
9/23/1950	Florida State	@	Troy State	26	7	W
9/30/1950	Florida State	vs	RANDOLPH MACON	40	7	W
10/7/1950	Florida State	vs	HOWARD	20	6	W
10/14/1950	Florida State	@	Newberry	24	0	W
10/21/1950	Florida State	vs	SEWANEE	14	8	W
10/28/1950	Florida State	@	Stetson	27	7	W
11/4/1950	Florida State	vs	MISSISSIPPI COLLEGE	33	0	W
11/11/1950	Florida State	vs	TAMPA	35	19	W
Coach: Don Veller			**Season Record >>**	219	54	**8-0**

Schedule Source: Steve's Football Bible LLC

Selected game(s) highlights

Troy State

Florida State opened its season with a 26-7 victory over Troy State Teachers. FSU started rolling early in the first quarter after Dick Wade's punt was blocked on the Troy 13. FSU drove to a first down on the 2 and Tom Brown went around left end for the score. Ernie Huggett's kick was good. A 34 yard pass from Dick Peterson to Brown brought Florida State its second touchdown. Brown ran 15 yards for the touchdown. Late in the second quarter, Mike Sellers drove five yards over left guard and then 24 inside right tackle for the third touchdown. Huggett's kick was blocked a second time. James Arnold blocked his second punt in the third to set up Florida State's last touchdown when Dick Turk scored from 1 yard out.

RANDOLPH-MACON

Florida State romped to t 40-7 before a record crowd of 9,676 fans. Mike Sellers ran for 110 yards and two touchdowns. Dick Peterson, Dick Turk and Nelson Itailiano ran for touchdowns and Eddie Gray caught a 25 yard touchdown pass from Dick Peterson to cap the scoring for the Seminoles.

HOWARD

Florida State had to pull out all the stops and take advantage of a couple of breaks last night to score a 20-6 triumph over the Howard College Bulldogs in Doak S. Campbell Stadium. A crowd of 5,537 fans saw the lightly regarded invaders from Birmingham bottle up the heavily favored Seminoles in the first quarter and then take a 6-0 lead in the opening minutes of the second quarter. Two third period touchdowns which climaxed drives of 60 and 59 yards and a 30 yard power exhibition by fullback Mike Sellers in the third period were the blows that finally broke the Bulldogs' backs. Sellers scored from 1 yard out each time and Nelson Italiano scored from 1 yard out for the Seminoles.

Newberry

The Seminoles overcame the effects of numerous penalties, a wet field, and a gallant Newberry College effort to fashion a 24-0 triumph. FSU punched over a score in each of the four quarters, while keeping the Newberry attack well bottled up with a hard-charging line and an alert secondary. Nelson Italiano threw for two touchdowns and ran for one to lead the offense. Eddie Gray caught an 80 yard TD pass and Clint Thomas caught a 20 yard TD Pass. Dick Turk scored from 1 yard out to cap the scoring for the Seminoles.

SEWANEE

The Seminoles had to struggle and then pull out all the stops in a second half comeback to subdue a stubborn Sewanee team 14-8 before a record Homecoming crowd in Doak S. Campbell Stadium, while an estimated crowd of 12,033 homecoming fans watched. Ted Hewitt returned an interception 54 yards for a touchdown and Nelson Italiano ran 13 yards for a touchdown for the Seminoles. Italiano added 85 yards on the ground.

Stetson

Florida State punched and pounded Stetson's Hatters into submission in a 27-7 triumph that left most of a record crowd of 6,000 stunned at Municipal Stadium in Deland. FSU shot off to a 13-0 lead in the first four minutes, scored again on a beautiful 57 yard pass play at the end of the first half and then had enough left for one final touchdown thrust in the fourth period. Nelson Italiano threw two touchdown passes, one to Bill Driver for 15 yards and one to Harold Bringger for 57 yards. Mike Sellers ran for two touchdowns and the Seminoles outgained the Hatters 376 yards to 198 yards.

MISSISSIPPI COLLEGE

Florida State continued their unbeaten march blasting Mississippi College out of their path 33-0, before a chilled crowd of 5,000 in Doak S. Campbell Stadium. Harry Bringger caught two touchdown passes from Nelson Italiano and Mike Sellers and Dick Turk ran for touchdowns. Cliff Powell caught a 16 yard TD pass from Gary Folsom to cap the scoring for the Noles.

TAMPA

Florida State exploded for three lightning like touchdowns in the space of four minutes and eight seconds of a fast and furious fourth quarter in Campbell Stadium to bury the Tampa Spartans' hopes of an upset by a 35-19 score. The game was tied 13-13 when the Seminoles put the game away on a Harry Bringger 34 yard TD pass from Nelson Italiano, a 27 yard TD run by Italiano and Wayne Benner's 11 yard return of a blocked punt for touchdown. Mike Sellers ran for one touchdown and Bringger caught a 27 yard TD pass from Italiano in the first half.

1951 Florida State Seminoles

1951 was Don Veller's fourth year as Florida State's head coach. The Seminoles went 6-2 on the season and it was the beginning of the longstanding rivalry with Miami. The Hurricanes won the first meeting by a score of 35–13.

1951 was the first year FSU offered scholarships to their athletes because of that, in the spring of 1951 FSU withdrew from the Dixie Conference. Roy Thompson {B} {Cleveland Browns} was selected in the 1952 NFL draft.

Home games were played at Doak Campbell Stadium

9/29/1951	Florida State	vs	TROY STATE	40	0	W
10/6/1951	Florida State	@	Miami	13	35	L
10/13/1951	Florida State	vs	DELTA STATE	34	0	W
10/20/1951	Florida State	vs	SUL ROSS STATE	35	13	W
10/27/1951	Florida State	vs	STETSON	13	10	W
11/3/1951	Florida State	@	Jacksonville Navy	39	0	W
11/10/1951	Florida State	vs	WOFFORD	14	0	W
11/17/1951	Florida State	vs	TAMPA	6	14	L
Coach: Don Veller			**Season Record >>**	188	72	**6-2**

Schedule Source: Steve's Football Bible LLC

Selected game(s) highlights

TROY STATE

Florida State opened the season hosting Troy State and rolled to a 40-0 victory. Mike Sellers and Ronnie King each ran for two touchdowns. Dick Turk ran 4 yards for a touchdown and Bob Whitmer caught a 14 yard pass from Nelson Italiano to close out the scoring for the Seminoles. FSU had 375 yards of total offense while holding the Red Wave to 8 total yards.

Miami

In the very first meeting between the two schools, FSU traveled to Miami to visit the Hurricanes in just the second game of the year for both teams. The tone was set early as Miami jumped to a 28-0 lead at halftime. During the start of the second half, FSU got the ball and marched down the field scoring a touchdown cutting the deficit to 21, but Miami was just too much as the very next possession Miami flew down the field for their fifth touchdown of the game, giving Miami the lead at 35-7 after three. FSU would score one more time in the fourth quarter, but missed the extra point, wide right. Neither team scored again as Miami beat FSU, 35-13.

DELTA STATE

Sparked by Nelson Italiano, who set a new Seminole passing record of 191 yards gained on seven completions, Florida State struck through the air last night to defeat Delta State Teachers 34-0 before a slim crowd of 5,308 in Doak S. Campbell Stadium. Italiano ran 1 yard for a touchdown to go along with his two touchdown passes. Bob Whitmer caught a 28 yard pass from Gary Folsom and Preston Bradley ran 5 yards for a touchdown. Earl O'Neal and Curt Campbell caught Italiano's TD throws. The Noles had 360 yards of total offense.

SUL ROSS STATE

The Seminoles sloshed to a 35-13 triumph over the Texans before a scant, rain-coated crowd of 1,969 fans in Doak S. Campbell Stadium. A three-touchdown explosion in the second period in the space of six minutes and 22 seconds blew the ball game apart after the battling Lobos had clawed out a 13-7 margin in the first period. Mike Sellers ran for two touchdowns and returned a blocked punt 11 yards for a touchdown. Nelson Italiano ran 40 yards for a touchdown and Curt Campbell returned an interception 30 yards for a touchdown for the Noles.

STETSON

The Seminoles surged back with a second half assault to squeeze by a spirited Stetson Hatter squad, 13-10, before a record Homecoming throng of 13,701 in overcast Doak S. Campbell Stadium. Mike Sellers scored from 3 yards out and Preston Bradley blocked and returned it 7 yards for a touchdown to give the Noles a comeback victory.

Jacksonville Navy

Florida State fired a six-touchdown salvo into an overmatched, under-conditioned Jacksonville Naval Air Station and shot the futile Flyers down, 39-0 before a slim, shivering crowd of 1,732. Dick Turk ran for two touchdowns and Curt Campbell caught two touchdown passes from Gary Folsom to lead the Seminoles. Mike Sellers added a touchdown run and Tommy Brown returned a punt 58 yards for a touchdown. The Noles defense held the Flyers to 115 yards of total offense.

WOFFORD

Florida State's hard charging defensive line held Wofford's Terriers completely at bay yesterday as the Seminoles scored a 14-0 win before a crowd of 5,666 fans at Doak S. Campbell Stadium. The Seminole defense limited the Terriers to 42 yards on the ground. Curt Campbell caught a 27 yard pass from Nelson Italiano and Dick Turk ran for a touchdown for the Seminole points.

TAMPA

A record Tampa University crowd of around 12,000 saw the Spartans hand the Seminoles their second loss of the season. Vince Chicko and Gene King, and a hard-running fullback, Jim Mathis, combined with some fierce line play by the Spartans to fashion a stunning upset victory. Chicko scored Tampa's first touchdown in the first period on a 75 yard punt return, and Mathis scored the second and clinching TD on the first play of the fourth period with an 18 yard reverse run. Nelson Italiano scored FSU's lone touchdown in the third period with a 35 yard slash off right tackle

1952 Florida State Seminoles

1951 was Don Veller's fifth year as Florida State's head coach. The Seminoles went 1-8-1 on the season. Florida State boosted the value of its athletic scholarships to rival as much as the Southeastern and Southern Conference teams are allowed by their rules to give.

No Seminole players were selected in the 1953 NFL draft.

Home games were played at Doak Campbell Stadium

9/27/1952	Florida State	vs	LOUISIANA TECH	13	32	L
10/4/1952	Florida State	vs	LOUISVILLE	14	41	L
10/11/1952	Florida State	vs	VMI	7	28	L
10/25/1952	Florida State	@	NC State	7	13	L
11/1/1952	Florida State	vs	STETSON	6	6	**T**
11/8/1952	Florida State	vs	MISSISSIPPI SOUTHERN	21	50	L
11/15/1952	Florida State	vs	FURMAN	0	9	L
11/22/1952	Florida State	@	Georgia Tech	0	30	L
11/29/1952	Florida State	@	Wofford	27	13	W
12/6/1952	Florida State	vs	TAMPA	6	39	L
Coach: Don Veller			**Season Record >>**	101	261	**1-8-1**

Schedule Source: Steve's Football Bible LLC

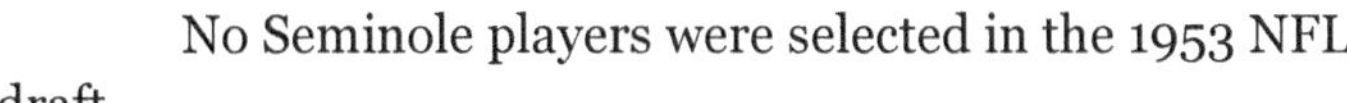

Selected game(s) highlights

LOUISIANA TECH

With a line that dominated the FSU lines all night, and a set of backs who chewed yardage out of the middle and around ends, the Bulldogs rocketed to a 32-0 lead before the stunned Seminoles could strike back for two TDs in the fourth period on a five yard blast through the middle by Nelson Italiano and a 20 yard pass from Roy Thompson to Ronnie King.

LOUISVILLE

The Louisville Cardinals rumbled to a 41-14 victory over Florida State University last night before a crowd of 10,636 that included 1,622 "Band Day" performers. Fullback Jim Williams battered the Seminoles into submission on the ground and quarterback **Johnny Unitas** passed them dizzy in the air, the Cardinals rolled up the highest score any team has racked up against Florida State in its six seasons. Williams had 143 yards rushing and scored three times. Unitas put on the finest passing show ever staged in Campbell Stadium. He completed 15 out of 21 for 195 yards and three touchdowns. Al Woodham ran 34 yards for a touchdown and Roy Thompson ran 3 yards for a touchdown for the Seminoles points.

VIRGINIA MILITARY

Two long passes completed behind the Seminole defensive left half, a short 17 yard punt and two fumbles were the mistakes that cost FSU against the colorful Keydets. Nelson Italiano ran 1 yard for a touchdown to the Noles a 7-0 lead, but it was all VMI after that, as they cruised to a 28-7 win over FSU. The Keydets outgained the Seminoles 374 yards to 234 yards.

NC State

A 70 yard return of an intercepted pass by all-Southern Conference halfback Alex Webster on the first play of the fourth period gave the North Carolina State College Wolfpack a hard-earned 13-7 victory here today over an injury-riddled Florida State University football team. A homecoming crowd of only 6,000 was present to see the tilt. Stan Dobosz ran 10 yards for a touchdown to give the Seminoles an early 7-0 lead, but the Wolfpack battled back and held the Noles offense scoreless in the 2nd half. The Wolfpack outgained the Noles 318 yards to 184 yards.

STETSON

An underdog Florida State fought Stetson to a 6-6 tie before 10,000 fans at the Tangerine Bowl in Orlando. FSU scored first in the second quarter, moving 44 yards in six plays with freshman fullback Stan Dobosz getting the last two yards at the middle of the line. Stetson stormed back in the third period, speeding 86 yards in 12 plays with freshman Billy Odom getting the last 45 when he broke off right tackle and outraced the Seminole secondary to score standing up.

MISSISSIPPI SOUTHERN

Mississippi Southern exploded for six touchdowns and a safety in the first half, then cruised to a 50-21 triumph over Florida State University before a slim crowd of 5,020 fans in Doak S. Campbell Stadium. Ronnie King caught a 6 yard pass from Nelson Italiano to tie the game at 7-7, but it was all Mississippi Southern after that. King caught a 6 yard TD pass from Bobby Fiveash for the other Noles score.

FURMAN

Florida State's best all-around performance of the season wasn't good enough to overcome mistakes and breaks and give the Seminoles their first victory of the season yesterday as Furman's Purple Hurricane punched out a 9-0 triumph before a slim Homecoming crowd of 8,096 fans at Doak Campbell Stadium. Gene Pedrick's nine yard dash inside right tackle for a touchdown on the quarterback option play in the third period, and Gus Pringels' 10 yard field goal in the fourth quarter were all the scoring that the Purple Hurricane needed as FSU failed to score for the first time in 41 straight games.

Georgia Tech

Georgia Tech struck for 4 lightning touchdowns and a safety in the first and third periods and coasted to a 30-0 triumph over an outmanned Florida State. A crowd estimated at 25,000 saw the Ramblin' Wreck take a 16-0 lead in the first half and tacked on two quick TD's in the opening minutes of the third period while on the way to their tenth victory of the season and their 24th win in a row without a defeat. The Noles were held to 171 yards of total offense.

Wofford

Florida State mixed a powerful running game with two touchdown passes to come from behind and defeat Wofford 27-13 for their first victory of the season. Wofford and the 3,500 freezing fans that turned out, got a small consolation in Jack Abell's pass catching as he grabbed four catches for a season total of 56 to break all existing pass receiving records in U.S. College football. After spotting the Terriers a 7-0 lead in the first period, FSU struck back for two TD's in the second period on Nelson Italiano's six yard run off tackle for one score and his 28 yard pass to Stan Dobosz for a second. Hitting again in the third period, FSU sent Bobby Fiveash off left guard for an 11 yard score, then came back for a fourth and final TD on a 26 yard pass from Fiveash to "Crazylegs" Al Woodham. The Noles offense rushed for 299 yards on the ground.

TAMPA

Vince Chicko bolted 54 and 38 yards for touchdowns on punt returns to lead Tampa University to a 39-6 football victory over Florida State at Doak Campbell Stadium. Al Leathers punched over for two touchdowns and Tom Spack and Bob Boucher each counted once as Tampa scored in every period to achieve its second straight victory over FSU in the bitter intra-state rivalry. The game was played before fewer than 4,000 fans. Bobby Fiveash scored from 18 yards out for the lone Seminole touchdown.

1953 Florida State Seminoles

Tom Nugent, the creator of the I formation, became head coach and led the team to a 5–5 record. Nugent joins FSU for the same money - $8,000 per year - and under the same terms that Veller guided the Indians. There is no coaching contract between Nugent and the school, he is hired on a professional basis with his salary supplemented for the additional chores of coaching the football squad.

Bobby Fiveash {RB} {San Francisco}, Tom Feamster {T} {Chicago Bears} and Bill Mote {T} {New York Giants} were selected in the 1954 NFL draft.

Home games were played at Doak Campbell Stadium

9/25/1953	Florida State	@	Miami	0	27	L
10/3/1953	Florida State	vs	LOUISVILLE	59	0	W
10/17/1953	Florida State	vs	ABILENE-CHRISTIAN	7	20	L
10/24/1953	Florida State	@	Louisiana Tech	21	32	L
10/31/1953	Florida State	vs	VMI	12	7	W
11/7/1953	Florida State	@	Mississippi Southern	0	21	L
11/14/1953	Florida State	vs	FURMAN	7	14	L
11/21/1953	Florida State	vs	STETSON	13	6	W
11/28/1953	Florida State	vs	NC STATE	23	13	W
12/5/1953	Florida State	@	Tampa	41	6	W
Coach: Tom Nugent			**Season Record >>**	183	146	**5-5**

Schedule Source: Steve's Football Bible LLC

Selected game(s) highlights

Miami

Seminoles gave a tough University of Miami team all the football it could handle for the better part of two quarters, but the Hurricanes added two touchdowns in the second half to shutout FSU, 27-0. Jimmy Lee Taylor had six tackles and two assists, caught three of the four passes that FSU completed, for 45 yards. Bob Crenshaw had four tackles and 10 assists. **Lee Corso** survived the mammoth pressure of being starting quarterback. He held the reins very well until he was hurt - a slight concussion. It may have been coincidence, but FSU's stock started falling along about the time Corso was injured. The Seminoles were held to 175 yards of total offense.

LOUISVILLE

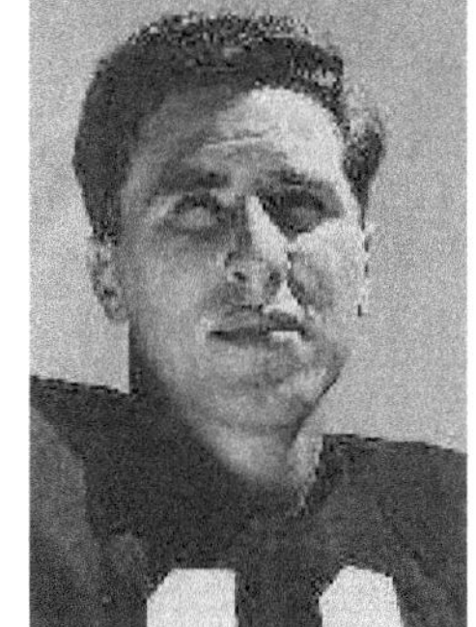

The Cardinals won the coin toss, and it was all downhill after that as the Seminoles steamrolled to a 59-0 victory. Bobby Fiveash continued his superb play, scoring three of the nine touchdowns. Stan Dobosz scored two, Billy Graham, **Lee Corso**, Junior Metts and Carl Grenn got one apiece. Harry Massey impressed with his quarterbacking. He started the game, guided FSU to its first two scores. Lee Corso played more than Massey, however. Corso's running on the option play was the best weapon of the game. FSU set a new school record for yards rushing with 397. The Seminoles' total offensive yardage was 544, despite having 100 yards assessed in penalties. Jarring tackles caused Louisville to fumble eight times, and FSU recovered five of them. Corso carried 10 times for 73 yards to head the individual ground-gaining figures. His touchdown, however, came on a 59 yard punt return.

ABILENE-CHRISTIAN

The Seminoles contributed to their own downfall with a leaky pass defense, an erratic punting game and costly fumbles. FSU's secondary was faked out of position repeatedly. Abilene came from behind to do it. FSU struck quickly for seven points on a Bobby Fiveash 10 yard TD pass from Harry Massey, before the visitors got warmed up well. They tied it on a 30 yard pass from freshman ace Leondous Fry to end Von Morgan midway the second quarter. It was Morgan's fifth touchdown grab of the season. They went ahead on a 75 yard run by fullback Gene Boyd a couple of minutes after the second half opened. And they polished things off with a final six points with seconds remaining to make the final score, 20-7.

Louisiana Tech

A 21 point second half output by Florida State fell short for the Seminoles as Louisiana Tech team won a hard-earned 32-21 verdict in a wild offensive game. Trailing 26-7 as the 4th quarter began, the Seminoles scored early in the quarter and then again minutes later on a 52 yard pass play from quarterback Leonard Swantic to Jimmy Lee Taylor. It was then 26-21 with eight minutes 30 seconds left. FSU gambled for the lead but Tech's Milford Andrews intercepted a Swantic pass at the Seminole 45 and raced over for the final score with 35 seconds left. Jimmy Lee Taylor caught a 25 yard TD pass from Harry Massey to cut the Tech lead to 14-7 early in the 3rd quarter.

VIRGINIA MILITARY

Freshmen halfback Junior Metts and tackle Bob Barber helped propel Florida State's Seminoles to a 12-7 upset of Virginia Military Institute's outplayed Keydets. Metts ran for 111 yards in nine carries, scoring once, and punted five times for a 34.1 average. Barber was credited with 10 tackles and six assists in his first major turn at tackle. Billy Graham scored from 1 yard out for the other Seminole touchdown.

Mississippi Southern

Mississippi Southern struck for three sudden touchdowns and tumbled Florida State's Seminoles 21-0 here tonight before a shivering Homecoming crowd of 11,000 in Hattiesburg. FSU filled the air with passes, completing 9 of 23 for 158 yards. Five interceptions by Southern stalled repeated Seminole bids. The Noles were held to 48 yards on the ground.

FURMAN

Florida State's offense was cut to a slow fizzle by 115 yards in penalties, fell 14-7 to Furman before a disappointing and disappointed crowd of 7,000 at Doak Campbell Stadium. Russ Sutton broke Seminole hearts midway the third quarter when he returned a kickoff 82 yards to pavethe way for the winning touchdown on a Bobby Dellinger 3 yard run, after FSU had battled 72 hard-earned yards to tie the game at 7-7. Sutton scored on a 5 yard run in the first quarter for a 7-0 Furman lead. Harry Massey scored from 1 yard out for the Seminoles lone touchdown.

STETSON

Florida State managed two touchdowns, one on a Stan Dobosz 3 yard TD run and a Buck Metts 3 yard TD run, enough to hold off Stetson University, 13-6. Metts ran for 85 yards and had 37 yards receiving to lead the Seminoles.

NC STATE

Florida State pounded out a 23-13 victory over North Carolina State in a rugged battle saturated with fumbles and passes. A slim crowd of 5,000 at Doak Campbell Stadium saw some interesting football. Four of the game's five touchdowns came after recovery of opponent's fumbles, the fifth followed a pass interception. And a safety that gave FSU an early 2-0 lead came from a fumble. Jerry Jacobs recovered three of the fumbles for the Noles. FSU had its best passing day of the season, hitting 13 of 28 for 144 yards. Harry Massey completed 6 of 17 and two touchdowns. **Lee Corso**, hit on four of five and Bobby Fiveash on two of two. Jimmy Lee Taylor, set a new school record for yardage gained on pass receptions, hauling in three for 47 yards and running his season's total to 377 on 20 catches. Fiveash caught a 2 yard TD pass from Harry Massey and ran 2 yards for a touchdown. Taylor caught a 19 yards TD pass from Massey.

Tampa

Florida State flexed their muscles and closed the 1953 football season with a 41-6 mauling of the University of Tampa. The Seminole defense bottled up Tampa's attack and the Spartans netted only 85 yards on offense, including 26 yards rushing. Tampa vainly filled the air with passes but completed just eight out of 22 throws and FSU came up with five interceptions. Bobby Fiveash ran for 141 yards in a dozen rushing tries and scored twice. **Lee Corso** had two interceptions to lead the defense. Buck Metts, Billy Graham, and Ronnie King had rushing touchdowns and John Griner returned an interception 85 yards for a touchdown.

1954 Florida State Seminoles

Tom Nugent was the head coach in his second year at Tallahassee and led the team to an 8-4 record. The Seminoles were invited to the Sun Bowl after the season to play Texas Western {UTEP}. The schedule gives FSU major college ranking for the first time by virtue of five opponents on the NCAA major college list.

FSU led the nation's major and small colleges in throwing touchdown passes during 1954 with 19. Nineteen of FSU's 39 touchdowns the past season were scored through the air. Quarterback Harry Massey tossed 10 of them.

Tom Feamster {T} {Los Angeles Rams} and Bill Proctor {OL} {Cleveland Browns} were selected in the 1955 NFL draft.

Home games were played at Doak Campbell Stadium

9/18/1954	Florida State	vs	GEORGIA (6-3-1)	0	14	L	
9/25/1954	Florida State	vs	ABILENE-CHRISTIAN	0	13	L	
10/2/1954	Florida State	@	Louisville	47	6	W	
10/9/1954	Florida State	vs	VILLANOVA (1-9)	52	13	W	
10/16/1954	Florida State	@	NC State (2-8)	13	7	W	
10/23/1954	Florida State	@	Auburn (8-3)	0	33	L	
10/30/1954	Florida State	vs	VMI (4-6)	33	19	W	@ Lynchburg, VA
11/13/1954	Florida State	vs	FURMAN (5-5)	33	14	W	
11/20/1954	Florida State	@	Stetson	47	6	W	
11/27/1954	Florida State	vs	MISSISSIPPI SOUTHERN	19	18	W	
12/4/1954	Florida State	@	Tampa	13	0	W	
1/1/1955	**Florida State**	**vs**	**Texas Western (8-3)**	**20**	**47**	**L**	**Sun Bowl**
Coach: Tom Nugent			**Season Record >>**	277	190	**8-4**	

Schedule Source: Steve's Football Bible LLC

Selected game(s) highlights

GEORGIA

Florida State University Seminoles threw a healthy scare at Georgia before a record 19,401 at Doak Campbell Stadium. The Bulldogs perked up a sputtering offense for first and last quarter touchdowns and a 14-0 victory. Jimmy Harper struck erratic sparks for the Bulldogs, scored the first touchdown, and passed for the second to Matthew Arthur for a 24 yard TD, but mistakes and penalties canceled several budding bids. Harper threw 10 times, completed six but FSU intercepted a pair off him and two more off his back-up, Dick Young. **Lee Corso** caught 2 passes for 36 yards and **Burt Reynolds** caught one pass for 33 yards.

ABILENE-CHRISTIAN

The Wildcats scored in each of the first two quarters, then sat back and let FSU play itself out in the second half. FSU's offense, confined to a net total of 27 yards in the first half, finally got going in the latter portion of the game but fell short, despite 3rd quarter penetrations to the Abilene three and seven. Abilene shutout the Seminoles 13-0. The Noles were held to 141 yards of total offense.

Louisville

Billy Graham spurred FSU's early game with runs and pass interceptions and had the distinction of scoring the first touchdown of the campaign for the Seminoles. Graham, and most of the other regulars, sat on the bench much of the way as Coach Tom Nugent used his entire squad of 40. Louisville managed to make it interesting in the first quarter and it was 7-6 after 15 minutes. But the Seminoles raced away with three second quarter touchdowns, tacked on two more in the third, one in the fourth on the way to a 47-6 rout of the Cardinals. No Seminole scored more than one of the seven touchdowns. An alert FSU defense accounted for four interceptions. Louisville hauled in three FSU strays. The Seminoles hopped on two Cardinal fumbles. FSU held to the ball, fumbled not at all. For the first time, FSU was playing against a team with Negroes in its lineup. Three of them - center Andy Walker, halfbacks George Cain and Leonard Lyles - were starters. Harry Massey, Len Swantic, Ronnie King, **Burt Reynolds**, Tom Feamster and Vic Prinzi scored touchdowns for the Seminoles. FSU rolled up 478 yards of total offense and held Louisville to 152 yards of total offense.

VILLANOVA

Florida State's Leonard Swantic, cut loose an unbelievable aerial barrage and mercilessly pounded Villanova University, 52-13. More than 8,000 fans attended Doak Campbell Stadium. FSU led 13-7 at halftime, then unleashed a rapid fire 39 point second half splurge. 27 came in the final quarter. Swantic completed 13 of 17 for 226 yards, three touchdowns. For good measure, Swantic ran one over. Tom Feamster caught three touchdown passes and set up another with a 15 yard catch at the one. Billy Odom and Ted Rogrigue ran for touchdowns while John Griner and Buck Metts hauled in touchdown passes. **Lee Corso** caught two passes for 47 yards.

NC State

Bogged down by their own mistakes for half the game, Florida State Seminoles hung to the clutch passing arm of Quarterback Harry Massey for a 13-7 victory over North Carolina State. A chilled crowd of 9,000 at Riddick Stadium stuck to their seats as FSU came from behind with third and fourth quarter touchdowns, then held off a desperate Wolfpack counterattack. NC State took a 7-0 lead in the first period on an Eddie West 2 yard run, with a 33 yard dash by Fullback Tom Langston setting it up. Jimmy Lee Taylor caught an 8 yard TD pass from Harry Massey and Billy Graham caught a 3 yard TD pass from Massey for the winning touchdown.

Auburn

Jim Pyburn led Auburn's powerful Plainsmen to a 33-0 rout of an outgunned Florida State at Cliff Stadium before over 15,000 fans. Pyburn turned two passes into 28 and 65 yard gains, setting up one touchdown at the three and scoring on the longer reception. He blocked a punt, helped pave the way to another TD with a nine yard run on an end-around and was stalwart on defense. **Burt Reynolds** led the Noles with 62 yards rushing.

VIRGINIA MILITARY

Victor Prinzi passed for three touchdowns and ran for one to lead Florida State's on-again-off-again Seminoles to a 33-19 triumph over a fighting Virginia Military Institute team before over 7,000 fans in Lynchburg. With the game tied 13-13, In a total of five FSU offensive plays running into the fourth period, Prinzi passed four times. Three went for touchdowns on 53, 55 and 45 yard plays. Ronnie Schomburger caught the two longer ones, John Griner the other. It was 33-13 before VMI knew what hit them. Prinzi finished with 153 yards passing, all on those 3 completions.

FURMAN

Harry Massey completed 15 of 22 passes for 196 yards and **Lee Corso** ran 14 times for 75 yards, caught seven passes for 87, and scored three touchdowns as the Noles rolled over Furman, 33-14. **Corso** was also superb defensively. He made a tackle that caused a fumble that paved FSU's first touchdown and he intercepted his fourth pass of the season. The game, after the first couple of minutes, was not in doubt. FSU which found a scoring key early in each quarter, skipped to a 20-0 lead midway the second quarter, boosted it to 26-0 before Furman finally scored.

Stetson

Florida State worked the passing arm of Harry Massey to pave an early two-touchdown lead, then turned its ground troops loose to do most of the rest as the Seminoles assured their best season since 1951 by walloping an outmanned Stetson University, 47-6. **Lee Corso** ran 6 yards for a touchdown, Vic Prinzi ran 25 yards for a touchdown, **Burt Reynolds** ran 5 yards for a touchdown and Buck Metts ran 78 yards for a touchdown. Tom Feamster caught a 19 yard TD pass from Massey. Billy Odom returned a punt 80 yards for a touchdown and Jerry Jacobs returned an interception 19 yards for a touchdown for the Seminoles scoring.

MISSISSIPPI SOUTHERN

FSU rolled up an astounding 200 yards against the Eagles defense. A fired up defense held Southern's touted runners to 163 on the ground as the Noles upset Mississippi Southern, 19-18 before over 6,700 fans at Doak Campbell Stadium. Southern turned desperately to George Herring's passes but, though he hit Hub Waters for two touchdowns, he completed only seven of 24. Southern struck first after Carl Bolt returned the opening kick 73 yards. FSU replied rapidly for a 6-6 tie on Harry Massey's 20 yard pass to **Lee Corso**. Southern vaulted back led 12-6 at the half. Billy Graham put FSU ahead early in the third quarter with a 31 yard run. The margin was quickly upped to 19-12 on Massey's 22 yard TD pass to Tom Feamster. Southern's final score, on the second payoff pitch of Herring to Waters, was in vain. Joe Holt blocked the extra point kick attempt to preserve the Noles victory. Feamster caught his 26th pass of the campaign, breaking the school record of 24 set by Curt Campbell in '52.

Tampa

The Tampa Spartans fought favored Florida State to a second half standstill, but Harry Massey had led the Noles to two early touchdowns under his passing arm and the Seminoles hung on for a 13-0 victory. Multiple fumbles hobbled both sides. FSU was further staggered by 80 penalty yards. Massey, who passed for his ninth and tenth touchdowns of an 11-game season, collaborated with **Lee Corso** on a 28 yard scoring play, then kicked a point that provided a 7-0 lead in the first couple of minutes. Buck Metts picked his way with a Massey pass through a mass of Spartans on a 47 yard TD reception in the second quarter.

1955 SUN BOWL

Harry Massey scored on a 1 yard touchdown run to give the Seminoles an early 7–0 lead, set up by a 25 yard kickoff return and a 48 yard rush both by **Lee Corso**. After Florida State lost both Corso (on a collision) and the ball after an ensuing punt, the Miners took advantage, scoring on a Rusty Rutledge touchdown catch from Jesse Whittenton to make it 7–7 after one quarter. In the second, the Miners exploded for 27 points. Whittenton ran for a touchdown run from 7 yards out to make it 13–7. Bob Forrest scored on a 45 yard touchdown run to make it 20–7. Whittenton threw his 2nd touchdown pass to make it 27–7. He then threw a pass to Rutledge from 16 yards out to make it 34–7 at halftime. Forrest scored once again to make it 41–7 Miners. The Seminoles finally responded with a Len Swantic touchdown pass to make it 41–13 (after the kick was blocked). Whittenton made it 47–13 on his 2 yard touchdown plunge. In the fourth quarter, the only score was on a Larry Massey touchdown pass to make it 47–20. Future actor Burt Reynolds rushed for 35 yards on 7 carries for Florida State. Whittenton went 7 of 13 for 138 yards and three touchdowns passing and two touchdowns on 13 yards (on 8 carries) rushing in an MVP effort.

1955 Florida State Seminoles

Tom Nugent was the head coach in his third year at Tallahassee and led the team to a 5-5 record. Florida State University's rapid climb in the national football picture reached a climax in Chicago when the Seminoles were classified as a major power in football by the Football Writers' Association of America.

Lee Corso led the team in rushing with 463 yards, was second on the team with 13 catches, led the team in punt returns with a 14.3 average and tied for the team lead with 3 interceptions. Jerry Jacobs {G} {Pittsburgh Steelers} was selected in the 1956 NFL draft.

Home games were played at Doak Campbell Stadium

9/17/1955	Florida State	vs		NC STATE (4-5-1)	7	0	W
9/30/1955	Florida State	@		Miami (6-3)	0	34	L
10/8/1955	Florida State	vs		VIRGINIA TECH (6-3-1)	20	24	L
10/15/1955	Florida State	vs		GEORGIA (4-6)	14	47	L
10/22/1955	Florida State	@	#13	Georgia Tech (9-1-1)	0	34	L
11/5/1955	Florida State	vs		VILLANOVA (1-9)	16	13	W
11/11/1955	Florida State	@		Furman (1-9)	19	6	W
11/19/1955	Florida State	vs		THE CITADEL (5-4)	39	0	W
11/26/1955	Florida State	@		Mississippi Southern	6	21	L
12/3/1955	Florida State	@		Tampa	26	7	W
Coach: Tom Nugent				**Season Record >>**	147	186	**5-5**

Schedule Source: Steve's Football Bible LLC

Selected game(s) highlights

NC STATE

Len Swantic gambled his way to one bright moment that brought Florida State a 7-0 victory over North Carolina State in the football opener at Doak Campbell Stadium before over 15,000 fans. Held at arm's length all evening long and never inside N.C. State 20, the Seminoles won it with six minutes left when Swantic fooled an entire team with a superb bit of fakery, then passed to giant end Tom Feamster for a touchdown on a 49 yard play. With inches to go for a first down. From the "I" formation, Swantic stepped back, hid the ball behind him as a fullback slammed the middle. Feamster was all alone at the 32 when Swantic hit him, and nobody had a chance to stop him.

Miami

The heralded Hurricanes hung a 34-0 defeat on Florida State before 42,363 people, the largest crowd ever to see Miami play an opening college game in the Orange Bowl. The Hurricanes mixed telling passes with a brutal running attack. FSU's offense never had a chance and the Seminoles turned only three first downs, one by running. The Seminoles were outgained 356 yards to 126 yards.

VIRGINIA TECH

Billy Odom pumped some last quarter vigor into the Florida State football team, but his fast work was not quite enough as Virginia Tech squeezed out a 24-20 decision. Behind 21-0 going into that final period, FSU got off the floor when Odom ran 39 yards to set up a touchdown at the nine. Vic Prinzi scored from the one. A couple of minutes later, after VPI had moved the margin to 24-7 on Frank Webster's field goal from the 19, Odom took a kickoff and zipped 89 yards to score. With 2:05 left in the game the Seminoles got their third TD. **Lee Corso** sparked a 59 yard push, then took the ball across from three yards out.

GEORGIA

Held to a 13-7 halftime lead, the Georgia Bulldogs rushed away with a trio of third quarter touchdowns and continued to 47-14 win over Florida State at Doak Campbell Stadium. The Bulldogs pulled out front early. FSU bobbled the kickoff and Georgia's recovery left only 40 yards between the Bulldogs and a touchdown. Wally Butts manipulated four quarterbacks in and out. Each succeeded at least once. Dick Young, who leads the country in passing yardage and touchdowns, via passing, hit on five of six throws for 69 yards and one touchdown. Wendell Tarleton was an ace for the winners, scoring Georgia's first two touchdowns, on a 2 yard sweep and on a 29 yard pass from Young. He also set up Georgia's fourth TD with a pass interception. Len Swantic notched both FSU touchdowns on runs of 12 yards and one yard.

Georgia Tech

For 28 minutes, Florida State threw a monkey wrench into Georgia Tech's high-geared football machine. After which the Ramblin' Wreck cranked up and drove to a 34-0 victory. 30,000 Grant Field folks looked on with respect as the Seminoles checked well regarded Tech on seven points until two minutes before halftime. At the midway mark it was 14-0. Tech racked two quick touchdowns in the third quarter, had to wait until the final half minute for its fifth and final one. Tech ran twice as many plays as the Noles and outgained them, 442 yards to 135 yards.

VILLANOVA

Florida State hung on for 16-13 decision over Villanova in a rather weird game of breaks and mistakes. Behind much of the way, the Seminoles had a 4th quarter winner when Leo Baggett swiped the ball from Villanova quarterback Bill Magee's hands and fell across the goal, a yard away from the point of the thievery, for six points. Ham Bisbee provided FSU with its first points in the 2nd quarter, crashing through to ground would-be punter Nick Sapienza behind the Villanova goal for a safety. FSU moved to a 9-7 halftime advantage on quarterback Vic Prinzi's 6 yard run a minute before halftime. Villanova took a 7-0 lead early in the second quarter on a penalty paved drive of 61 yards, climaxed by Davey Parr's smash from the one. And the Wildcats went back in front, 13-9, in the third quarter when Magee sliced 64 yards with an intercepted pass. **Lee Corso** ran for 107 yards on 21 carries for the Noles.

Furman

Behind 6-0 two minutes before halftime, Florida State finally got untracked with a Joe Holt 1 yard touchdown to pull even at 6-6 going into halftime. Billy Weaver ran 11 yards for a 3rd quarter touchdown and **Lee Corso** ran 5 yards for a touchdown to seal the game in the 4th quarter as the Noles held on for a 19-6 victory. The Seminoles had 251 yards rushing on the day.

THE CITADEL

Buck Metts and Billy Odom ran wild to lead the Seminoles to a smashing 39 to 0 win over The Citadel Bulldogs before 15,756 cheering Homecoming fans at Doak Campbell Stadium. Metts scored three times in the first half as FSU built up a 19-0 halftime lead and Odom quickly took the wind out of the Cadets' sails with a 46 yard touchdown scamper soon after the second half gun sounded. Len Swantic and Ted Rodrigue contributed the other two scores, both on short runs. FSU rolled up 385 yards on the ground and passed for 130 yards. The Citadel team never posed a serious scoring threat and only twice entered FSU territory. The only time the Cadets got inside the FSU 35 was in the waning minutes of the game when a series of desperation passes carried them to the 26 where the game ended with Billy Weaver intercepting a pass by Cadet Quarterback Bob Miller.

Mississippi Southern

Florida State dropped a clear cut 21-6 decision to Southern in Hattiesburg and were hampered by being with Buck Metts who missed the game due to an injury suffered in practice. Southern's George Herring's 37 yard pass to Harold Clark paved the first touchdown, which Harvey Seligman cashed in from the three. Fred Smallwood's 62 yard run was the big blow in the drive for a second score that Lawrence Meeks tallied from the four to provide a 14-0 halftime lead. Dallas Whitfield's 38 yard runback of a pass interception laid the ground for Herring's 29 yard touchdown pass to end Curry Juneau. Billy Odom scored from 2 yards out for the lone Seminole touchdown. The Noles were held to 50 yards rushing.

Tampa

Scoring touchdowns in each quarter, Florida State had things its own way as it closed out Tampa, 26-7. FSU scored in succession on Buck Metts' 5 yard plunge, Len Swantic's 12 yard sweep, **Lee Corso's** 9 yard pass to Ham Bisbee, and Corso's 1 yard run. **Corso** led the ground corps with 54 yards rushing.

1956 Florida State Seminoles

Tom Nugent was the head coach in his fourth year at Tallahassee and led the team to a 5-4-1 record.

Lee Corso led the team in passing with 369 yards and 5 touchdown passes. **Corso** finished 2nd on the team in rushing, 356 yards, to Bobby Renn, who had 596 yards rushing. **Corso** led the team in punt returns with a 14.6 average and tied for the team lead with 2 interceptions.

Corso was named an Honorable Mention All-American by the Associated Press. Ron Schomburger {OL} {Washington} was selected in the 1957 NFL draft.

Home games were played at Doak Campbell Stadium

9/22/1956	Florida State	vs		OHIO	47	7	W
9/29/1956	Florida State	@		Georgia (3-6-1)	0	3	L
10/6/1956	Florida State	vs		VIRGINIA TECH (7-2-1)	7	20	L
10/13/1956	Florida State	@		NC State (3-7)	14	0	W
10/20/1956	Florida State	vs		WAKE FOREST (2-5-3)	14	14	T
10/27/1956	Florida State	@		Villanova (5-4)	20	13	W
11/2/1956	Florida State	@	#9	Miami (8-1-1)	7	20	L
11/10/1956	Florida State	vs		FURMAN (2-8)	42	7	W
11/17/1956	Florida State	vs		MISSISSIPPI SOUTHERN	20	19	W
11/24/1956	Florida State	@		Auburn (7-3)	7	13	L
Coach: Tom Nugent				**Season Record >>**	178	116	**5-4-1**

Schedule Source: Steve's Football Bible LLC

Selected game(s) highlights

OHIO

With Lee Corso wheeling deftly in his new role as quarterback, and Bobby Renn dealing from a fast-running deck, Florida State poured it on Ohio University, 47-7, at Doak Campbell Stadium. It was the most points ever scored against an Ohio U. team under Coach Carroll Widdoes. It was the first opening-game setback in Widdoes' nine seasons with the Bobcats. The crowd of 18,312 - one of the largest turnouts in FSU history - saw the Seminoles let loose a balanced attack that brought three touchdowns on the ground, three via air and another on a pass interception. **Lee Corso** was the game's leading rusher on 104 yards in 13 carries and hit on three of five passes for 51 yards. Renn scored twice, on a 15 yard run and a 35 yard runback of a pass interception. Other FSU touchdowns were added by Ham Bisbee, on a 25 yard pass from Len Swantic, Buck Metts from four yards out, and Billy Weaver on an 8 yard end sweep.

Georgia

Ken Cooper kicked a 36 yard field goal with 1:30 left in the game to give Georgia a narrow 3-0 victory. It was the longest in Sanford Stadium history and 25,000 predominantly Georgia fans screamed their appreciation. With a minute and a half left, FSU threatened to ruin Georgia's home opener. Billy Odom burst through for a 34 yard sprint to Georgia's 40 in the closing 10 seconds. But time shut the Seminoles out after one more play.

VIRGINIA TECH

Virginia Tech finally put away from Florida State with two third quarter touchdowns that sent the Seminoles to 20-7 defeat. FSU stayed in the game during the first two periods, coming from behind to tie it up at 7-7 two minutes before halftime when Rodrigue threw 15 yards to Bob Nellums for the score. Tech answered right away in the second half when they marched 65 yards to another TD. Fullback Bobby Conner scored from the one. Minutes later Tech got their third touchdown. Ray England paved the way with a 27 yard punt return to the FSU 38. Two plays later, Jimmy Lugar sailed a 34 yard pass into the arms of Nick Mihales as he crossed the goal line.

NC State

Florida State used the twinkling feet of **Lee Corso** for two 2nd half touchdowns for a satisfying 14-0 victory over surprised North Carolina State at Riddick Stadium. NC State had the ball for only 40 offensive plays, and most of those came late in the game when FSU had the game wrapped up. FSU ran or passed 74 times, ran up 17 first downs to its opponent's six. NC State intercepted a pair of passes, recovered three FSU fumbles that kept the Seminoles from an even bigger victory margin. **Corso**, completing five of 10 passes and running up 108 yards rushing in 10 carries, cracked things open in the third quarter when he weaved 35 yards to score. Early in the final period, **Corso** set sail with a punt 62 yards to the NC State 10 yard line. Three plays later, Vic Prinzi passed eight yards to end Bob Nellums for a second TD.

WAKE FOREST

Racked by the rolling rushes of big fullback Bill Barnes, Florida State had to struggle from behind twice to earn a 14-14 tie with Wake Forest in the rain at Doak Campbell Stadium in front of over 14,000 homecoming fans. **Lee Corso** scored from 1 yard out to tie the game at 7-7 and Buck Metts scored from 1 yard out to tie the game at 14-14. FSU outgained the Demon Deacons 241 yards to 157 yards.

Villanova

Bobby Renn tore through Villanova's defense for 124 yards in 18 carries. Twice he helped nip Wildcat threats with fumble recoveries. And twice he quick-kicked beautifully, getting off 49 and 46 yard boots to pin the Wildcats deep in their own territory, as the Seminoles handed Nova a 20-13 defeat. The game drew over 42,000 fans at Villanova's Municipal Stadium. FSU scored its first touchdown in four plays, with Vic Prinzi sweeping around end from nine yards out. The second score came on Ted Rodrigue's 29 yard pass to Bob Nellums in the end zone. **Lee Corso's** 9 yard pass to Joe Holt in the end zone moved FSU in front 20-7.

Miami

The unbeaten Hurricanes, ranked #9 in the nation, repeatedly stymied FSU's upset-designed offensive strategy with a hard charging defense in their 20-7 victory over the Seminoles. Brilliant passing by Bonnie Yarbrough riddled the Seminoles in the first half. Miami led 13-0 at the midway point and extended the margin to 20-0 before the Seminoles got their one and only on **Lee Corso's** two yard run with three minutes remaining. All FSU had to cheer about was Bobby Renn's extraordinary punting. Renn kicked four times for an average of 53. Buck Metts chipped in with two punts that averaged 46 apiece.

FURMAN

Florida State clobbered Furman into 42-7 submission in front of over 9,000 fans at Doak Campbell Stadium. Lee Corso and Len Swantic passed for two touchdowns apiece. Bobby Renn scored two. Corso was at his best, passing for 51 yards and running for 87 more. He hit five of eight throws. He got those 87 running in just nine carries, including one for 57 yards. Renn ripped off 119 yards in 16 runs and caught four passes for 49. Swantic, completed four of five passes for 89 yards. Ted Rodrigue connected on three of four as the Seminoles ended with a showing of 12 completions in 17 attempts.

MISSISSIPPI SOUTHERN

Behind 13-0 before, Mississippi Southern fought back furiously as Florida State's slightly stunned the Eagles by a 20-19 score, ending Southern's 14 game winning streak. Dallas Whitehead missed the game tying extra point for Southern with 2:44 left in the game. Buck Metts got the Seminoles on the board first with a 38 yard interception return for a touchdown. Jerry Philp caught a 6 yard pass from Len Swantic and Bobby Renn caught the game winner, an 11 yard TD pass from Swantic.

Auburn

Fired by the sizzling runs of Bobby Renn, Florida State rose on this cold Saturday afternoon to give Auburn's touted Tigers all the football they could handle before finally yielding, 13-7. **Lee Corso** quarterbacked the Seminoles in place of injured QB Len Swantic and completed 2 of 4 passes for 28 yards. The Tigers Bobby Hoppe ran for 90 yards and Tommy Lorino ran for 69 yards to lead the offense. Red Phillips caught a 62 yard TD reception from Howell Tubbs and Jim Walsh added a 3 yard TD run for all of Auburn's points.

1957 Florida State Seminoles

Tom Nugent was the head coach in his fifth year at Tallahassee and led the team to a 4-6 record. Bobby Renn led the team in passing yards {263} and total yards {680}. Fred Pickard led the team in rushing yards {463}

Home games were played at Doak Campbell Stadium

9/21/1957	Florida State	vs		FURMAN (3-7)	27	7	W
9/28/1957	Florida State	@		Boston College (7-2)	7	20	L
10/5/1957	Florida State	@		Villanova (3-6)	7	21	L
10/12/1957	Florida State	vs	#13	NC STATE (7-1-2)	0	7	L
10/19/1957	Florida State	vs		ABILENE-CHRISTIAN	34	7	W
10/26/1957	Florida State	vs		VIRGINIA TECH (4-6)	20	7	W
11/8/1957	Florida State	vs		MIAMI (5-4-1)	13	40	L
11/16/1957	Florida State	@		Mississippi Southern	0	20	L
11/23/1957	Florida State	vs	#2	AUBURN (10-0)	7	29	L
11/30/1957	Florida State	@		Tampa	21	7	W
Coach: Tom Nugent				**Season Record >>**	136	165	**4-6**

Schedule Source: Steve's Football Bible LLC

Selected game(s) highlights

FURMAN

Held scoreless in the first quarter, FSU struck for three quick touchdowns in the second period. After Furman trimmed the score to 20-7 by halftime, FSU answered with a third quarter TD. FSU's payoffs came, in succession, on Bobby Renn's 1 yard plunge after an 82 yard drive, Bob Nellums' recovery in the end zone of an abortive punting effort, Ted Rodrigue's 33 yard pass to Clare Bagnell, and Renn's 4 yard pass to Nellums. Furman got its only touchdown just before halftime when Billy Baker passed 13 yards to Ray Siminski. It was set up at the FSU 33 when a punt was muffled, and Furman recovered.

Boston College

Boston College, spurred by the superb passing of Don Allard, earned a decisive 20-7 triumph. Allard 12 of 18 passes for 147 yards. Boston College fumbled the kickoff and Troy Barnes recovered for the Seminoles at the 24. But the Seminoles set a pattern of futility with the opportunity that plagued them the rest of the game. They got no further than the 21, and it was to be their deepest penetration until the fourth quarter was almost gone. Behind 7-0 at halftime, a 20-0 deficit was on the scoreboard by the time FSU, led by the passes of Ted Rodrigue, at last scored. The touchdown came on Rodrigue's 23 yard pass to Ron Schomburger. It climaxed a 74 yard drive.

Villanova

With the three straight losses to FSU, the Wildcats finally handed the Seminoles a loss, beating FSU 21-7. Villanova scored in the second quarter on John Daniels' run from the two after a 62 yard march and on Grazione's 61 yard pass to Rick Sapienza. FSU narrowed things to 14-7 early in the third period when Henderson threw a 14 yard pass to Ron Schomburger in a fourth and one situation. But Villanova got its 14 point advantage back in a hurry with fullback Jack Devereaux pounding across from the two following a 55 yard drive.

NC STATE

When all was done, a 46 yard pass from Ernie Driscoll to Dick Christy that was the difference. It came 10 seconds before halftime. The Seminoles were outgained by the Wolfpack, 377 yards to 216 yards.

ABILENE-CHRISTIAN

A Doak Campbell Stadium crowd of 15,300 watched as the Seminoles raced away from previously unbeaten Abilene Christian College by a surprising 34-7. Operating at quarterback for almost the entire game, Bobby Renn deftly manipulated FSU to a 21-0 lead at halftime. Renn ran for 150 yards in 14 carries and scored the game's first touchdown on a 52 yard run. Bob Nellums ran 20 times, gained 72 yards, scored twice, once on a 45 yard pass play. FSU had to punt only once, that the first time it had the ball. The Seminoles chiseled out 383 yards rushing. They hit on only two of 11 passes, but it didn't matter. Stan Dobosz ran 2 yards for a touchdown and Pappy Rozman ran 5 yards for a touchdown.

VIRGINIA TECH

In the first minute and a half of the second quarter, FSU struck for back-to-back touchdowns within 10 playing-time seconds of each other. First score came when Bobby Renn hit Ron Schomburger for a 51 yard touchdownpass. Nine seconds later, trying to run from its 1 yard line, Tech fumbled and tackle George Boyer covered the ball in the end zone for touchdown #2. FSU's first offensive play in the last half was a record breaking one. Fred Pickard ran 80 yards off tackle for the Seminoles' third TD.

Miami

The Seminoles led 7-6 at halftime, but then the wheels came off in the 2nd half as Miami unleashed a blitzkrieg of scoring to beat the Noles, 40-13. Joe Plevel scored three of Miami's six touchdowns on a 5 yard pass from Curci, a 3 yard run and a 5 yard run. Curci passed six yards to Phil Gaetz for another. Bill Sandie scored on a 2 yarder and Byron Blasko scored one from three yards out. FSU's first score came on Bob Nellums' 1 yard push after a 66 yard drive and Joe Majors' 45 yard pass to Bill Kimber in the last quarter.

Mississippi Southern

Backed up by Florida State for the first 20 minutes, Mississippi State struck for two swift second quarter touchdowns and was almost the whole show from then on as it crunched out a 20-0 victory over the Noles. The crusher was a 57 yard run by Bobby Lance for Southern's first touchdown. Less than a minute later, Southern grabbed a fumble at the FSU 27 and tallied again in seven plays, with Bo Dickinson scoring from seven yards out. The Seminoles were outgained 385 yards to 135 yards, hardly a prescription for winning.

AUBURN

Auburn traveled to Tallahassee to play the Seminoles at Doak-Campbell Stadium. The Tigers rushed for 201 yards, led by Billy Atkins who ran for two touchdowns. Lamar Rawson and Tommy Lorino each had TD runs as the Tigers romped to a 29-7 victory.

Tampa

Florida State ground out a 21-7 victory over Tampa. Bobby Renn, held to 59 yards in 20 runs, scored twice for the Tribe, on runs of one and two yards. Fred Pickard, big wheel for FSU in this one with 100 yards in 13 carries, got the other from eight yards out.

1958 Florida State Seminoles

Tom Nugent was the head coach in his fifth year at Tallahassee and led the team to a 4-6 record. 1958 was the beginning of the longstanding rivalry with the Florida Gators. The Gators won the first meeting by a score of 21–7.

1958 was the first season that the NCAA football allowed teams to go for two points after a touchdown. Extra point kick attempts were still worth one point. Bill Kimber {WR} {New York Giants} was selected in the 1959 NFL draft.

Home games were played at Doak Campbell Stadium

9/13/1958	Florida State	vs		TENNESSEE TECH	22	7	W	
9/20/1958	Florida State	vs		FURMAN (2-7)	42	6	W	
9/26/1958	Florida State	@		Georgia Tech (5-4-1)	3	17	L	
10/4/1958	Florida State	vs		WAKE FOREST (3-7)	27	24	W	
10/11/1958	Florida State	vs		GEORGIA (4-6)	13	28	L	@ Jacksonville
10/18/1958	Florida State	vs		VIRGINIA TECH (5-4-1)	28	0	W	
10/25/1958	Florida State	@		Tennessee (4-6)	10	0	W	
11/1/1958	Florida State	vs		TAMPA	43	0	W	
11/7/1958	Florida State	@		Miami (2-8)	17	6	W	
11/22/1958	Florida State	@	#12	Florida (6-4-1)	7	21	L	
12/13/1958	**Florida State**	**vs**	**#19**	**Oklahoma State (8-3)**	**6**	**15**	**L**	**Bluegrass Bowl**
Coach: Tom Nugent				**Season Record >>**	**218**	**124**	**7-4**	

Schedule Source: Steve's Football Bible LLC

Selected game(s) highlights

TENNESSEE TECH

Vic Prinzi quarterbacked Florida State to a 22-7 decision over Tennessee Tech. Prinzi got FSU's opening touchdown on a 4 yard run. He scored in the second quarter on a 5 yard sweep. The third Seminole touchdown came near the end of the third period on Bobby Renn's 16 yard pass to Tony Romeo. Carroll Wright intercepted three passes, including two in the end zone for Tennessee Tech. FSU had 317 yards of total offense while holding Tech to 135 yards.

FURMAN

Bobby Renn, who ran for 106 yards on his first four carries, ripped Furman open early last night and Florida State sprinted on to 42-6 football success. Renn got the first one on a 50 yard excursion, the third on a 10 yarder. FSU struck for 20 second quarter points and led 28-0 at the half. Four different players scored touchdowns for the Seminoles. Bobby Conrad on a 4 yard sweep, Fred Pickard on a 3 yard plunge, Bill Kimber on a 15 yard pass from Joe Majors and Bud Whitehead on a 20 yard sweep. Renn finished with 130 yards rushing as FSU rolled up 455 yards of total offense while holding Furman to 193 yards.

Georgia Tech

FSU led Georgia Tech for eight minutes and held the Ramblin' Wreck to a 3-3 deadlock for over half the game, but finally stumbled over their own inexperience, 17-3. A near record Grant Field crowd of 40,391 witnessed the fact Tech had a struggle on its hand when Bobby Renn hauled a punt 51 yards to the Jackets' 25 after four minutes of action. That set up a 31 yard field goal by Johnny Sheppard. That stood up until Tech recovered a fumble at the FSU eight, kicked a 22 yard field goal with two minutes left in the quarter. Tech whipped 60 yards in 11 plays to a touchdown the first time it got the ball in the 2nd half. Frank Nix scored from six yards out.

WAKE FOREST

Ahead 21-10 at intermission, Florida State was had to fight from behind for a last quarter touchdown that kayoed Wake Forest, 27-24. The lead changed hands five times after Wake Forest went to the front on a field goal with the game 10 minutes old. Vic Prinzi completed nine of 12 throws for 141 yards, including two TDs. He intercepted two Wake Forest passes, at the FSU 12 yard line and at the FSU 1 yard line. He directed touchdown marches of 86 yards and 75 yards. FSU got 21 of its 27 points in the second period, scoring on Prinzi's 5 yard pass to Bobby Renn, Fred Pickard's 25 yard burst up the middle and Herman Brown's 55 yard runback of an intercepted pass. The winning score was a 21 yard Prinzi pass to Bill Kimber.

GEORGIA

Unable to cash in on some early opportunities, Florida State finally yielded to Georgia 28-13, in the Gator Bowl. Behind 14-0 at the half, FSU cut the score to 14-7. And later behind 21-7 they whacked it to 21-13. Able to connect on only two of 13 passes in the first half, the Tribe hit on 10 of 15 in the final two periods. Both FSU scores came on aerials, the first a 42 yarder from Vic Prinzi to Tony Romeo, the second a 5 yarder from Bobby Renn to Bob Kavanaugh. Tony Romeo caught 5 passes for 103 yards.

VIRGINIA TECH

Florida State chopped out a 28-0 football victory over Virginia Tech in the rain at Doak Campbell Stadium. There were 17 fumbles on the soaked Campbell Stadium turf, eleven by FSU. Each team recovered five opposition bobbles. But the miscues weren't really a factor. None led to any scoring. Tony Romeo made a falling catch of a Vic Prinzi pass for the third touchdown on a 24 yard play, recovered a pair of fumbles, intercepted a pass, and threw key blocks to lead the Noles. Jack Espenship caught an 8 yard TD pass from Prinzi, Bobby Renn ran 72 yards for a touchdown and Joe Majors ran 3 yards for a touchdown for the Noles scoring.

Tennessee

The stunning 10-0 upset was FSU's first victory in 11 tries against Southeastern Conference opposition. All the scoring came during a 3-minute span in the third quarter. FSU drove 89 yards with the opening kickoff, with Fred Pickard getting 51 in one run, to a field goal, which Johnny Sheppard booted from the 16. Seconds later, guard Al Ulmer intercepted a George Wright pass at the Vol 28. After a Vic Prinzi to Tony Romeo for a 27 yard gain, Bobby Renn got the touchdown from the one. The Seminole defense held the Volunteers offense to 111 total yards.

TAMPA

Scoring in every quarter, Florida State's light-footed Seminoles rumbled to a 43-0 homecoming victory over a stumbling Tampa football team. Bobby Renn got a pair of touchdowns that ran his FSU career total to a school-record 99 points. Joe Majors threw four passes, completed two of them - both for touchdowns. FSU got two first quarter scores on Renn's 1 yard run and Majors' 13 yard pass to Bob Fountain, second quarter TDs on Fred Pickard's 21 yard scamper around end and Majors' 37 yard pass to Carl Meyer. After Pickard returned the second-half kickoff 84 yards to the Tampa 16, FSU got its fifth TD on Renn's 11 yard run after taking a screen pass from Vic Prinzi. Pappy Rozman got the last touchdown on a three yard burst with 20 seconds remaining in the game.

Miami

The Seminoles scored in the first quarter when Joe Majors, who had just had one of his own passes stolen, intercepted a throw and raced 42 yards for a touchdown. Johnny Sheppard added the point after and FSU never trailed. Miami came right back to get its only touchdown when Joe Plevel crossed from the one after a 68 yard drive. Miami tried for a 2 points run, failed. FSU upped things to 14-6 early in the second quarter on Vic Prinzi's 8 yard pass to Fred Pickard. This one was paved by a fumble recovery at the 13. Insurance came in the fourth quarter when Johnny Sheppard kicked a field goal from the 22.

Florida

Bobby Renn returned the game-opening kickoff a stunning 78 yards to give the Seminoles a 7-0 lead. The Gators Dave Hudson blocked a punt and returned it 5 yards for a touchdown. Jimmy Dunn scored on runs from 9 yards out and 11 yards out, both on 4th downs, and the Gators had their first win, 21-7, over the Seminoles in the first meeting ever in this rivalry.

1958 BLUEGRASS BOWL

Oklahoma State entered the game ranked #19 in the AP Poll, while Florida State was unranked. Florida State was an independent with a 7–3 regular season record; Oklahoma State was also 7–3 as an independent, having left the Missouri Valley Conference after the 1956 season and not joining the Big Eight Conference until 1960. Florida State, in their final season under head coach Tom Nugent, played in their third bowl game. Oklahoma State, coached by Cliff Speegle, was appearing in its fourth bowl game. The game was played at Cardinal Stadium on the grounds of the Kentucky Exposition Center, just behind Freedom Hall. Kickoff was at 1:30 p.m., with a game time temperature of 20°F, and falling. The playing field was icy and slippery, causing the players to forego cleats and wear tennis shoes instead. The cold weather on top of the general indifference to the contest kept the attendance low; crowd estimates were in the 5,000–10,000 range, and many accounts state that just over 7,000 attended. In the first quarter, Florida State took two drives into Oklahoma State territory but missed 16- and 23 yard field goal attempts. Early in the second quarter, Oklahoma State halfback Duane Wood ran 17 yards for a score, putting the Cowboys up 7–0. Late in the second quarter Oklahoma State again drove deep into Florida State territory but on fourth and 5 Florida State defender Ron Hinson stripped the ball from Oklahoma State's Forrest Campbell just a foot from the goal line. Florida State fumbled twice in the third quarter. Oklahoma State took the second fumble for a 10-play, 39 yard touchdown drive capped by another Duane Wood touchdown run. Wood then caught a pass for a two point conversion to give Oklahoma State a 15–0 lead. Florida State scored a fourth quarter touchdown without a successful conversion, giving Oklahoma State a 15–6 win.

1959 Florida State Seminoles

Perry Moss was the head coach in his first year at Tallahassee and led the team to a 4-6 record. Tom Nugent left to take the Head coaching position at Maryland during the offseason.

Joe Majors {QB}, Fred Pickard {RB} and Al Ulmer {G} were selected as Honorable Mention All-Americans by the Associated Press and United Press International. Pickard led the team in rushing with 481 yards and 5 rushing touchdowns. Majors passed for 1,063 yards and 6 touchdown passes. Pickard led the team in punt returns with a 10.2 average and kickoff returns with a 20.6 average.

Home games were played at Doak Campbell Stadium

9/19/1959	Florida State	vs		WAKE FOREST (6-4)	20	22	L
9/26/1959	Florida State	vs		THE CITADEL (8-2)	47	6	W
10/3/1959	Florida State	vs		MIAMI (6-4)	6	7	L
10/10/1959	Florida State	@		Virginia Tech (6-4)	7	6	W
10/17/1959	Florida State	@		Memphis	6	16	L
10/24/1959	Florida State	vs		RICHMOND (4-5-1)	22	6	W
10/31/1959	Florida State	@	#14	Georgia (10-1)	0	42	L
11/14/1959	Florida State	vs		WILLIAM & MARY (4-6)	0	9	L
11/21/1959	Florida State	@		Florida (5-4-1)	8	18	L
11/28/1959	Florida State	@		Tampa	33	0	W
Coach: Perry Moss				**Season Record >>**	149	132	**4-6**

Schedule Source: Steve's Football Bible LLC

Selected game(s) highlights

WAKE FOREST

Behind 9-0, then ahead 20-9, Florida State fell to Wake Forest, 22-20. Wake's Norman Snead threw for two touchdowns and set up another with a long throw. The winning touchdown, scored by Bobby Robinson from the five after Snead heaved a 34 yard pass to Bobby Allen, came with 1:56 left in the game. FSU's three touchdowns came on two interceptions and a 15 yard pass after a blocked punt. Fred Pickard put the Seminoles in the scoring column with a 30 yard runback of a Snead interception a couple minutes after the 2nd half started. Still down 9-7 after three quarters, FSU went in front on Bud Whitehead's 81 yard run with interception of a Snead pass. Moments later, John Spivey blocked a Wake Forest punt at the 17. Shortly after, Joe Majors passed 15 yards to Jim Daniel for the TD.

THE CITADEL

FSU set a school record for total yardage, netting 514, with 307 rushing and 207 passing in their 47-6 rout of the Bulldogs. Six Seminoles scored touchdowns. Bud Whitehead's 52 yard run following a screen pass from Joe Majors, Roy Bickford's 1 yard run, Fred Pickard's 4 yard run, Majors' 2 yard pass to Whitehead, Ken Cone's 6 yard run, Jack Espenship's 3 yard run and Paul Andrews' 1 yard run. Majors hit four of six passes for 91 yards, Bickford nine of 17 for 116.

MIAMI

Behind 7-6 with 2:52 left in the game after Fred Pickard's 8 yard TD run, FSU faced the big decision. A kick for one point and a tie, or a run or pass for two points and victory? Pickard took a pitchout and ran wide, met guard Jim Crawford, Bob Rosbaugh and Fran Curci hit him, too. He was stopped six inches short.

Virginia Tech

Before a homecoming crowd of 15,000 in Blacksburg, Paul Andrews' runback of an interception set up the Seminoles at Tech's 26. On the opening play of the 4th quarter, Roy Bickford passed 10 yards to Ron Hinson for the TD. Bill Brown kicked what proved to be the decisive point in the Seminoles 7-6 victory. Tech's Leon Tomlin recovered a Hinson fumble at midfield. Tech drove to a score, Don Vaught crashing over on fourth-down from the 1-foot line with 2:15 left in the game. Algar Pugh tried to run for two points. Brown hit him at the two and Tony Romeo reinforced the hit.

Memphis State

Playing with both knees braced by tape, Nickey Buoni passed and ran FSU dizzy in the first 16 minutes, providing a 13-0 lead. Buoni capped an 84 yard drive with a scoring run from the four after the Tigers got their mitts on the ball for the first time. Memphis State grabbed a fumble a bit later and maneuvered 54 yards for a TD. Jack Carter kicked a field goal a minute before halftime, putting the Tigers ahead 16-0. FSU got its touchdown midway in the 4th quarter, Joe Majors scoring from the one.

RICHMOND

Fred Pickard scored FSU's first two touchdowns and totaling, in a dozen runs, 94 of the 131 yards his team netted against a blitzing Spider's defense. The game was closer than the 22-6 final. Ahead 8-0 at the half, FSU nursed an 8-6 margin with a minute left in the third quarter. The Seminoles counted a final touchdown with 40 seconds to go. Bill Brown added a 35 yard field goal and Jim Daniel caught a 5 yard TD pass from Joe Majors.

Georgia

Georgia's most powerful team in years and years gave Florida State it worst football moments in quite some time. The score was 42-0. The Bulldogs racked up 21 points each half as the Homecoming crowd of about 30.000 whooped it up. Georgia's six touchdowns came in succession on Wayne Taylor's 1 yard run, Francis Tarkenton's 4 yard pass to Fred Brown, Jimmy Vicker's catch of a 28 yard pass from Charley Britt, Tarkenton's 9 yard pass to Gordon Kelley, Tommy Lewis' 5 yard run and Dale Williams' 12 yard pass to George Guisler.

WILLIAM & MARY

William and Mary left Doak Campbell Stadium with a 9-0 upset before 16,700 Homecoming fans. The shocking setback, FSU was a two touchdown favorite, came on the heels of the Seminoles' worst beating in history last week at Georgia. W&M scored with a couple of minutes left in the third quarter. Roger Hale scampered 41 yards down the sidelines. Three minutes remained when Dan Barton wrapped it up with a field goal from 21 yards.

Florida

Florida scored the first time it got the ball in the first half, moving 69 yards in 10 plays from the opening kickoff, and the first time it got the ball in the last half, pushing 30 yards in five plays after Bill Hood's pass interception. Jack Westbrook got both, the first from one yard range and the second from the 10. The Gators moved ahead, 18-0, with four minutes left after recovering a fumble at the FSU 40. Don Goodman scored from the two. The Gators outgained FSU 377 yards to 139 yards in their 18-8 victory.

Tampa

Joe Majors completed 20 of 32 passes for 313 yards as Florida State riddled Tampa, 33-0. Majors' 20 completions were a school record for one game. So were his 34 attempts and 313 yardage total. Majors ended the season with 90 completions in 170 attempts for 1,063 yards - all FSU season records. Bud Whitehead caught nine passes to set another school record with a season total of 31. Majors got FSU going late in the first quarter with a short pass to Fred Pickard that was converted into a 63 yard touchdown. Majors whipped a 30 yard strike to Jim Daniel with two seconds left in the half to send FSU to the dressing room with a 13-0 lead. Other TDs came on Pickard's 3 yard run, Whitehead's 3 yard run and Majors' 5 yard sweep. All were set up by passes.

1960 Florida State Seminoles

Florida State was led by first year head football coach Bill Peterson. Peterson had served as Louisiana State's offensive line coach the last five seasons. The Seminoles finished with a 3-6-1 record in Peterson's 1st season.

Bud Whitehead led the team in rushing with 293 yards and receiving with 23 catches and 212 yards. Ed Trancygier led the Seminoles in passing with 539 yards and 6 touchdown passes. Tony Romeo {TE} {Washington} was selected in the 1961 NFL draft.

Home games were played at Doak Campbell Stadium

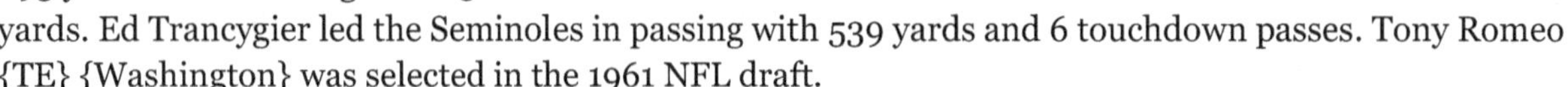

9/17/1960	Florida State	vs		RICHMOND (3-6-1)	28	0	**W**	
9/24/1960	Florida State	@		Florida (9-2)	0	3	**L**	
10/1/1960	Florida State	vs		WAKE FOREST (2-8)	14	6	**W**	
10/8/1960	Florida State	@		The Citadel (8-2-1)	0	0	**T**	
10/15/1960	Florida State	vs		Mississippi Southern	13	15	**L**	**@ Mobile, AL**
10/22/1960	Florida State	vs		WILLIAM & MARY (2-8)	22	0	**W**	
10/29/1960	Florida State	vs		KENTUCKY (5-4-1)	0	23	**L**	
11/4/1960	Florida State	@		Miami (6-4)	7	25	**L**	
11/12/1960	Florida State	vs		HOUSTON (6-4)	6	7	**L**	
11/19/1960	Florida State	@	#9	Auburn (8-2)	21	57	**L**	
Coach: Bill Peterson				**Season Record >>**	111	136	**3-6-1**	

Schedule Source: Steve's Football Bible LLC

Selected game(s) highlights

RICHMOND

Ed Trancygier passed for two touchdowns and ran for a third. Ed Feely got the other TD as the Seminoles cruised to a 28-0 victory. FSU's first TD came 15 seconds before the half on Trancygier's 3 yard pass to Fred Grimes in the end zone. The second came early in the third quarter on Feely's run from the three. #3 was wrought with five minutes to play by Trancygier on a 1 yard sneak. The last was on Trancygier's 36 yard throw to Tony Romeo.

Florida

Billy Cash kicked the first field goal of his career as Florida blunted Florida State's brilliant try, 3-0. It was a 25 yard field goal with 6:31 left in the 2nd quarter and that was all the scoring for the game. The Seminoles drove to the Gator four yard line at the end of the game, but the Gator defense held as time expired. FSU ran for 110 yards, with Ed Trancygier's 39 in six carries leading. The Seminoles hit 11 of 26 passes for 99 yards, had two throws intercepted.

WAKE FOREST

Florida State stunned Wake Forest 14-6 before over 19,000 fans at Doak Campbell Stadium. Florida State moved in front to stay early in the second quarter as Ed Trancygier threw a 17 yard TD pass to end George Tillman and Ken Kestner added an extra point for 7-6. The Seminoles padded their lead on Bud Whitehead's 1 yard run with a couple of minutes left. Wake Forest's Norman Snead hit 13 of 22 throws for 135 yards. The Deacons' lone TD came on a 3 yard pass, Snead to Jerry Ball.

The Citadel

The Citadel played the Seminoles on even terms as 11,200 people hollered their heads off at Hagood-Johnson Stadium as the teams battled to a 0-0 tie. The Citadel got 279 yards, including a stunning 205 on the ground. FSU's attack netted 265, with 165 rushing.

Mississippi Southern

Behind 15-0 at the half, Florida State rallied much, but not enough, as Mississippi Southern pulled out a 15-13 decision. The difference was a 2 point pass that Quarterback Don Fuell fired to End Charles Dedwylder after Southern's second touchdown. Southern picked up an early score after recovering a fumble at FSU's 22. Tommy Morrow tore 20 yards for the TD. Fuell manipulated the Mississippians on a 76 yard scoring march in the second quarter, getting the 6 pointer himself from 1 yard range. Ed Trancygier quarterbacked the Tribe on a 67 yard touchdown drive, scored himself from a yard out. When he passed to Tony Romeo in a bid for two points, officials ruled Romeo caught the ball outside the end zone. Then Ed Feely directed an 80 yard scoring drive for the Seminoles with Paul Andrews getting the TD from a yard out. In the final six minutes, FSU recovered two Southern fumbles, one at the Tribe 44, another at the 50. But the Seminoles couldn't capitalize. Fuell's interception of a pass, with a bit over a minute to play, finished the Seminoles.

WILLIAM & MARY

Florida State struck for two touchdowns in the first 11 minutes, tacked on another after the final gun had sounded and knocked off William & Mary, 22-0. Happy Fick managed the last two touchdowns, running seven yards with a pitchout for one and taking an 18 yard pass from Ed Trancygier for the other. Bud Whitehead scored the first Seminole touchdown on a 3 yard run.

KENTUCKY

Biggest crowd ever to see a Homecoming game at Doak Campbell Stadium. a near capacity 19,200, watched Kentucky forge threat after threat on the way to a 23-0 win over the Seminoles. Kentucky got its first TD in the opening period, with Cal Bird's run from the three climaxing a 76 yard drive. Another TD came in the second quarter on Jerry Eisaman's 37 yard pass to Tom Hutchinson. Clark Mayfield kicked a field goal from the 22 early in the final frame, and Hutchinson iced things with a couple minutes remaining by sprinting seven short yards with an intercepted screen pass. Kentucky rolled up 441 yards of total offense while holding FSU to 187 total yards.

Miami

Behind three points going into the last quarter, Florida State's hard-playing football team was finally put away with a 15 point Hurricane barrage in the 4th quarter. Two fumbles paved 11 points for the Hurricanes. A pass interception gave them seven more. They marched 68 yards for another seven. Charles Yanda stole an Ed Feely pass and ran 51 yards to put Miami in front, 10-0. Feely directed a scoring drive that narrowed things to 10-7, with scoring on a 21 yard run. Edwin Johns ran 5 yards for a touchdown, then the final Miami TD came on Bobby Weaver's 32 yard pass to end Bill Miller, after a fumble recovery at FSU's 39.

HOUSTON

The Cougars, who fumbled away the ball five times in the second quarter, went 52 yards for a 4th quarter touchdown that came on Don Session's 12 yard pass to Ken Bolin. Florida State scored with less than three minutes remaining as Ed Trancygier directed a drive of 87 yards. The TD came on Trancygier's 20 yard pass to George Tillman. The Seminoles elected to go for two points and the lead. Trancygier's pass to Carl Meyer in the end zone was high and the Cougars held on for a 7-6 win.

Auburn

Auburn's powerful football team struck for 26 last quarter points and overwhelmed Florida State, 57-21. Auburn ran up 463 yards of total offense versus FSU's 148. The Tigers threw 23 passes, completed 13 for 212 yards. Bryant Harvard ran for a touchdown and passed for a touchdown and Bobby Hunt ran for one touchdown and passed for two touchdowns to lead the Tigers scoring barrage.

1961 Florida State Seminoles

This was Bill Peterson's second year as head coach, and he led the team to a 4–5–1 record. Keith Kinderman led the team in rushing with 385 yards. Ed Feely was the leading passer with 471 yards and 4 touchdown passes. Jim Daniel and Tom Hillabrand tied for the team lead with 10 pass receptions.

Don Donatelli {C} {St. Louis Cardinals} and Ed Trancygier {QB} {Washington} were selected in the 1962 NFL draft.

Home games were played at Doak Campbell Stadium

9/16/1961	Florida State	vs		GEORGE WASHINGTON (3-6)	15	7	**W**
9/30/1961	Florida State	@	#17	Florida (4-5-1)	3	3	**T**
10/7/1961	Florida State	@	#2	Mississippi (9-2)	0	33	**L**
10/14/1961	Florida State	vs		GEORGIA (3-7)	3	0	**W**
10/21/1961	Florida State	vs		RICHMOND (5-5)	13	7	**W**
10/28/1961	Florida State	@		Virginia Tech (4-5)	7	10	**L**
11/4/1961	Florida State	@		Kentucky (5-5)	0	20	**L**
11/11/1961	Florida State	vs		THE CITADEL (7-3)	44	8	**W**
11/18/1961	Florida State	vs		MISSISSIPPI SOUTHERN	0	12	**L**
11/25/1961	Florida State	@		Houston (5-4-1)	8	28	**L**
Coach: Bill Peterson				**Season Record >>**	93	128	**4-5-1**

Schedule Source: Steve's Football Bible LLC

Selected game(s) highlights

GEORGE WASHINGTON

On the ropes for much of the last half, Florida State settled for a 15-7 decision over George Washington. The Seminoles had looked as though they would kayo the Colonials in the first quarter. They marched 58 yards after the opening kickoff and had a 6-0 lead with less than five minutes gone on a Marion Roberts 2 yard run. Dick Drummond changed things in a hurry with the start of the third quarter. He returned the second half kickoff 82 yards for a touchdown that gave GW a 7-6 lead. FSU wasted little time getting back in front, 9-7, on Doug Messer's field goal from 31 yards. After stopping a GW drive on a fumble recovery inside the FSU end zone, the Seminoles struck for a second touchdown, Eddie Feely scoring from the two on the heels of an 80 yard drive.

Florida

Florida State's upstart football program stunned the Gators on this day with a 3–3 tie. Florida coach Ray Graves likened the result to a "death in the family", Roy Bickford was the star for the Seminoles and was named the game MVP. Bickford blocked a punt to set up the Seminoles' lone FG, intercepted a pass deep in FSU territory to avert a sure UF score, and had another interception on UF's last scoring drive.

Mississippi

Mighty Mississippi, unbeaten at home since 1951, just kept on rolling along, pounding Florida State 33-0. Ole Miss, which led 20-0 at halftime, scored in succession on Louis Guy's 5 yard run that climaxed a 77 yard drive; Billy Ray Adams' 1 yard burst on the heels of a 91 yard drive; Perry Lee Dunn's 15 yard pass to Larry Smith, culminating a 76 yard drive; Doug Elmore's 1 yard sneak following a 38 yard drive and Adams' 1 yard run that ended a 96 yard drive. Florida State was virtually offense-less. Only twice did the Seminoles cross the 50, both times in the last quarter - first with the help of a pass interference penalty, then at game's end. FSU was never any closer than the Ole Miss 38. Ole Miss rang up 520 yards of total offense while holding the Seminoles to 109 yards.

GEORGIA

FSU played host to the Georgia Bulldogs in front of a record crowd of 21,200 fans at Doak Campbell Stadium, the Seminoles turned the tides, escaping with a 3-0 win to snap their losing streak to the neighbor state foe. The Seminoles scored the only points of the game on an opening drive field goal by Doug Messer. The Bulldogs outgained FSU 182 yards to 168 yards but missed a pair of second half field goals and were unable to get onto the scoreboard.

RICHMOND

Florida State football team fought from behind in the last quarter and squeezed out a 13-7 victory over Richmond. It looked like disaster for the Seminoles with Richmond sitting with a 7-6 lead at FSU's 20 early in the fourth period, But Gene McDowell gave new life with a pass interception, and FSU moved 88 yards in 13 quick plays for an Eddie Feely 1 yard touchdown run that was decisive. Keith Kinderman, who scored on a 2 yard TD run that put FSU ahead 6-0 in the first quarter, was the architect of the final drive and this hard earned victory. He accounted for 65 of the 88 yards with eight runs and two pass receptions.

Virginia Tech

A homecoming crowd of 14,000 watched as Virginia Tech's Gobblers parlayed the generous mistakes of Florida State with a freak pass for a 10-7 victory. Tech kicked a field goal for a quick 3-0 lead after claiming an FSU fumble. The Seminoles fought back to a 7-3 halftime lead on Eddie Feely's 19 yard pass to John McConnaughhay as they faked a field-goal attempt. The Gobblers scrambled on a 67 yard drive that culminated when Buddy Weihe grabbed a Warren Price pass that two FSU defenders had deflected from the hands of the intended receiver. It was a 31 yard touchdown. The Seminoles came back big, but in vain as Tech stopped a drive with a fumble recovery at its 14.

Kentucky

Kentucky struck for two quick touchdowns in the last half and whipped Florida State, 20-0. Kentucky, ahead only 7-0 on a Gary Steward 1 yard run, pounded from the second-half kickoff to another TD, sticking pretty much to the ground. Howard Dunneback went over from 9 yards range. Very soon the Wildcats had the game in the bag on Darrell Cox's 84 yard run with an FSU punt.

THE CITADEL

Scoring more points than it had in all of seven previous games this season, Florida State's football team humiliated The Citadel's champions of the Southern Conference, 44-8. Eddie Feely passed for three touchdowns and ran for another as the Seminoles avenged the scoreless tie The Citadel gained last year in Charleston. Feely's 34 yard pass to Jack Forehand, Feely's run from the one, Feely's 32 yard strike to Marion Roberts, Feely's 15 yard throw to Gene Roberts, and Paul Andrews' two straight touchdown runs from the one. Sandwiched in was John Harllee's 30 yard field goal that provided a 23-8 halftime lead. FSU racked up a whopping offensive total of 456 yards, with 285 on the ground. The Seminoles intercepted three passes and recovered two enemy fumbles. Feely hit five of eight passes for 104 yards, added 38 more on 10 runs. Ed Trancygier completed six of 11 throws for 67.

MISSISSIPPI SOUTHERN

Mississippi Southern took Florida State to the woodshed and administered a 12-0 walloping in front of 18,700 homecoming fans at Doak Campbell Stadium. Southern squeezed out a touchdown seconds before halftime. It came on a fake field goal with Billy Coleman, down to hold, rearing up and passing to halfback Jim Havard for a 15 yard touchdown. Don Fuell scored from 1 yard out to complete the scoring on the day. FSU was held to 100 yards of total offense while Southern rang up 346 yards of total offense.

Houston

Two quarterbacks, Don Sessions, and Billy Roland, picked the Tribe to pieces with their passing as Houston won going away 28-8. The Cougars scored 21 points in the second quarter and were in front 28-0, when FSU finally forged a last-period score on Ken Russom's 18 yard run with an interception. A 49 yard drive, climaxed by Larry Broussard's run from the one, brought a first touchdown. Roland passed 13 yards to Milt Perkins for the second. Sessions threw 11 yards to Ben Howe for the third and the fourth was a cheap one that Sessions got from the one after FSU presented the Cougars with a chance from the Seminoles' eight when a punt attempt backfired.

1962 Florida State Seminoles

This was Bill Peterson's third year as head coach, and he led the team to a 4–3–3 record. Gene McDowell was selected as a 3rd team All-American by the Associated Press. Gene Roberts led the team in rushing with 299 yards. Keith Kinderman led the team in receiving with 20 catches for 257 yards. Dave Snyder led the team with 4 pass interceptions. No Seminole players were drafted by the NFL.

Home games were played at Doak Campbell Stadium

9/15/1962	Florida State	**vs**		THE CITADEL (3-7)	49	0	**W**
9/22/1962	Florida State	@		Kentucky (3-5-2)	0	0	**T**
9/29/1962	Florida State	**vs**		FURMAN (4-6)	42	0	**W**
10/5/1962	Florida State	@	#9	Miami (7-4)	6	7	**L**
10/20/1962	Florida State	@		Georgia (3-4-3)	18	0	**W**
10/27/1962	Florida State	**vs**		VIRGINIA TECH (5-5)	20	7	**W**
11/3/1962	Florida State	**vs**		HOUSTON (7-4)	0	7	**L**
11/10/1962	Florida State	@		Georgia Tech (7-3-1)	14	14	**T**
11/17/1962	Florida State	@		FLORIDA (7-4)	7	20	**L**
11/24/1962	Florida State	@		Auburn (6-3-1)	14	14	**T**
Coach: Bill Peterson				**Season Record >>**	170	69	**4-3-3**

Schedule Source: Steve's Football Bible LLC

Selected game(s) highlights

THE CITADEL

Eddie Feely and Steve Tensi made it all look ridiculously easy as they passed Florida State's football team to a 49-0 victory over the Citadel. Tensi threw seven times, completed every one, three for touchdowns. Feely passed 11 times. He completed nine, two for touchdowns. And he ran for another. The Seminoles scored in every quarter. Touchdowns were Feely's 3 yard run from the three, Tensi's 3 yard pass to Keith Kinderman, Marion Robert's 1 yard run, Tensi's 7 yard pass to Doug Messer, Feely's 9 yard strike to Ken Russom, Tensi's 53 yard pass with Don Floyd and Feely's 16 yard pass to Kinderman. The Seminoles totaled offensive yardage of 503, rolled up 206 on the ground, 297 via air on its 16 connections in 19 pass attempts.

Kentucky

Florida State settled for a 0-0 tie with Kentucky. They outran Kentucky, 137 yards to 29, out passed Kentucky, 94 yards to 76 and had more first downs than Kentucky, 13 to six. Both teams misfired on field-goal tries. FSU went up three after penetrating to the 18 in the second quarter. Kentucky tried in the third quarter after going to FSU's 1, then getting rocked back to the 19. Neither attempt was close. Kentucky's move to FSU's 11, primarily on Jerry Woolum's 31 yard pass to Tom Hutchinson, was the deepest the home team ever got. On only two other occasions was Kentucky across midfield, at the 44 and 46.

FURMAN

FSU ran up the biggest one-game yardage total in its history, a staggering 526 yards, with 287 on the ground. That topped the 514 gained against the Citadel in 1959. It was a 7-0 ball game two minutes before halftime and FSU couldn't count this one in the bag until it got a third quarter score for a 20-0 lead. FSU touchdowns, in succession, came like this: Eddie Feely's 22 yard pass to Ken Russom, Steve Tensi's 15 yard throw to Don Floyd, Feely's 9 yard run, Marion Roberts' run from the one, Phil Spooner's 7 yard burst up the middle and Charley Calhoun's 18 yard pass to Red Dawson.

Miami

Florida State fumbled the ball away six times and the Seminoles lost to a possibly inferior Miami team, 7-6. After FSU went ahead, 3-0, the first time it got the ball, on Doug Messer's field goal from 29 yards, Miami's George Mira went to work. Mira ran the first yard of the 72 and Nick Spinelli the other 71. Spinelli took a pass from Mira for 31 yards. Then he raced deep into the end zone for a 39 yard TD reception. FSU cut it to 7-6 with Messer's field goal from 26 yards out in the second quarter. Messer missed another 3 point try, from the 34 yards out, just before half-time. The Seminoles' last three offensive series culminated in fumbles. Four of the five times they had the ball on offense in the last half they fumbled. The other time they punted.

Georgia

Florida State broke Georgia's back with a hard-nosed stand on its one yard line in the first series of plays, then bottled up the Bulldogs offense for an 18-0 victory. Georgia never got closer than FSU's 20 after that initial 75 yard drive to the one. Florida State scored in the second quarter on Doug Messer's field goal from the 27, in the third quarter on Eddie Feely's 6 yard pass to Hank Sytsma, in the fourth quarter on Dave Snyder's 15 yard runback of a pass interception. Feely passed to Gene Roberts for two points after the first TD, and Messer converted with a kick after the second.

VIRGINIA TECH

With Keith Kinderman ripping for a pair of clutch touchdowns, Florida State fought from behind for a 20-7 victory over stubborn Virginia Tech. Although the Gobblers never got closer than the FSU 44, after a fumble recovery and a stunning touchdown in the opening minutes, the Seminoles couldn't breathe with comfort until they scored a third TD in the final minute. Phil Spooner capped a 38 yard drive with a 4 yard touchdown run. Next time the Tribe got the ball they went 80 yards, Kinderman leading the way and scoring from the four. The Seminoles drove 66 yards for their final points, Kinderman going in from 3 yards out.

HOUSTON

The rain came and the bottom fell out for Florida State as a rugged Houston team sprung a 7-0 disappointment on 20,000 Homecoming fans at Doak Campbell Stadium. Bobby Brezina and Frank Brewer led a 59 yard drive that brought the game's only score with 4:36 to play. Brezina scored from a yard out. It was the fourth successive Homecoming shutout for the home team. Houston dominated in the stats department, totaling 339 yards on offense while holding the Seminoles to 149 yards.

Georgia Tech

The scoreboard said it was a 14-14 tie. But the scoreboard was an outrageous liar. Florida State won this football game, just as sure as there's a cow in Georgia. Tech's highly rated, bowl-minded Yellow Jackets had to scramble from behind for a fourth quarter TD to make it 14-14 after FSU twice scored in four furious 3rd quarter minutes. Dave Snyder ran 22 yards up the middle for FSU's first touchdown. Steve Tensi and Fred Biletnikoff collaborated on a 66 yard pass play for the second TD. It was a relatively short throw with Biletnikoff out running Tech defenders. That gave FSU a 14-7 lead with two minutes left in the third period. Tech had grabbed a 7-0 lead in the first five minutes when Mike McNames intercepted an Eddie Feely pass and raced 25 yards for a touchdown. The Yellow Jackets, 14 point favorites going in, managed their last touchdown with 6:28 left on the clock on a McNames 1 yard run.

FLORIDA

Hagood Clark returned punt for 63 yards for a touchdown and the Gators cut down the Seminoles by an emphatic 20-7 score. Clark's big third quarter run brought Florida from behind to a 12-7 lead. FSU was never the same after that. Tom Shannon threw a 15 yard TD pass to Bruce Starling and Florida added a 5 yard touchdown in the 3rd quarter to seal the win.

Auburn

Florida State traveled to the Plains to play Auburn at Cliff Hare Stadium. The Tigers took a 14-0 lead into halftime on a 77 yard Jimmy Sidle touchdown run and a Sidle 9 yard TD pass to Tucker

Frederickson. Sidle rushed for 146 yards on the day. The Seminoles Eddie Feely threw two TD passes in the 2nd half and the game ended in a 14-14 tie.

1963 Florida State Seminoles

This was Bill Peterson's fourth year as head coach, and he led the team to a 4–5–1 record. While an FSU student and before he became famous as lead vocalist for The Doors, Jim Morrison was arrested for public drunkenness, resisting arrest, and disturbing the peace at the September 28 game against TCU.

Dave Snyder led the team in rushing with 500 yards. Fred Biletnikoff led the team in receiving with 24 catches for 358 yards and 4 touchdown receptions. Steve Tensi led the team in passing with 915 yards and 9 touchdown passes. Biletnikoff led the team with 3 interceptions. Bill Dawson {TE} {Los Angeles Rams} was selected in the 1964 NFL draft.

Home games were played at Doak Campbell Stadium

9/20/1963	Florida State	@		Miami (3-7)	24	0	**W**	
9/28/1963	Florida State	**vs**		TCU (4-5-1)	0	13	**L**	
10/12/1963	Florida State	**vs**		WAKE FOREST (1-9)	35	0	**W**	
10/19/1963	Florida State	**vs**		Southern Miss (5-3-1)	0	0	**T**	@ Mobile, AL
10/26/1963	Florida State	**vs**		VIRGINIA TECH (8-2)	23	31	**L**	
11/2/1963	Florida State	**vs**		FURMAN (7-3)	49	6	**W**	
11/9/1963	Florida State	@		Georgia Tech (7-3)	7	15	**L**	
11/16/1963	Florida State	**vs**		NC STATE (8-3)	14	0	**W**	
11/23/1963	Florida State	@	#9	Auburn (9-2)	15	21	**L**	
11/30/1963	Florida State	@		Florida (6-3-1)	0	7	**L**	
Coach: Bill Peterson				**Season Record >>**	167	93	**4-5-1**	

Schedule Source: Steve's Football Bible LLC

Selected game(s) highlights

Miami

In one of the season's biggest shockers, FSU stunned Miami 24–0, in the season opener for both squads. Miami quarterback, George Mira, had been the cover boy for Sports Illustrated's 1963 college football preseason preview. Miami head coach Andy Gustafson, who had been named athletic director in the spring, put off retirement for a year to coach what most pro scouts believed was the best quarterback in all of college football. On this night, however, Steve Tensi and Fred Biletnikoff were the stars and Florida State made its first real appearance on the national stage. Biletnikoff caught two touchdown passes from Tensi and returned an interception 99 yards for a touchdown. This win marked the first of seven straight wins by the Seminoles and the longest winning streak in the series. All the Seminoles wins came on Miami's home turf, the Orange Bowl.

TCU

TCU got a first quarter touchdown on a 46 yard run back of a pass interception by Jim Fauver. The Texans got a third quarter field goal after recovering a fumble on the FSU 46. They added another 3 pointer in the last period, on the heels of an 80 yard drive, and that was enough to beat the Seminoles, 13-0. It rained most of the day and at least half the game as both teams only managed 185 yards of total offense.

WAKE FOREST

Steve Tensi took four warm-up pitches at the start, threw them all wild, then, with his arm finally loose, completed 17 of his next 22 passes in hurling Florida State to a 35-0 shutout of Wake Forest. Tensi threw three passes for touchdowns, 23 yards to Biletnikoff for FSU's first touchdown, nine and 11 yards to Max Wettstein for FSU's last two. In between Marion Roberts ran one yard for a touchdown, and Dave Snyder pounded two yards for another.

Southern Mississippi

Steve Tensi threw 20 passes, completed 5, but Southern intercepted three, and in the end Florida State had to settle with a 0-0 tie. Jim Berry stole two of Tensi's passes. It was also Berry who tackled FSU's Marion Roberts when he appeared headed for a touchdown on a 58 yard runback of the second-half kickoff. On the last play of the game, with the ball on FSU's 17 after an interception of a Tensi pass at the 29, Southern missed a field goal. Earlier FSU had missed two 3 point tries, with the ball on Southern's 14 and 33.

VIRGINIA TECH

Florida State fumbled on the game's first play from scrimmage, and it didn't get much better after that as they fell to Virginia Tech, 31-23. That fumble paved the way for a Tech field goal. Then a high pass from center precipitated a weak punt and set up another Tech touchdown. Tech's second touchdown was set up on a pass interception that gave the Gobblers the ball at FSU's six. A third TD came on a blocked punt, and the fourth was brought about by another deep-down FSU fumble. Those last two came within a 3-minutes span in the fourth quarter and gained a 17-17 tie, after FSU had twice been 10 points behind. Ed Pritchett took the Tribe on a lightning 72 yard drive in a minute and a half, leading to a 44 yard field goal by Les Murdock in the final seconds of the first half, narrowing the score at that stage to 17-10. It was the longest field goal in FSU history. Dave Snyder and Larry Brinkley each had 1 yard touchdown runs. Steve Tensi threw a 10 yard TD pass to Winfred Bailey.

FURMAN

Florida State slammed out 319 yards on the ground and clobbered Furman 49-6. The Seminoles didn't throw a pass until well over half the game had elapsed, when they had a safe 21-0 lead. Larry Brinkley and Dave Snyder spurred the brisk running charge. Snyder carved out 101 yards in eight tries, including a 66 yard scoring run. Brinkley scored three times, on short runs, racked up 83 yards in 16 runs. Steve Tensi went to the air and threw two touchdown strikes, a 43 yard play with Fred Biletnikoff on the receiving end and a 14 yard strike to Marion Roberts. Roberts intercepted two Furman passes.

Georgia Tech

Billy Lothridge picked Florida State to pieces with passes and brought Georgia Tech from behind to a rather difficult 15-7 victory. Lothridge completed 20 of 34 passes for 246 yards and amassed 274 yards of total offense. Five minutes into the game, FSU had a touchdown, covering 68 yards in nine plays, ending with a Steve Tensi 2 yard TD pass to Bill Dawson. Lothridge kicked a 22 yard field goal, then passed 23 yards to Billy Martin for a touchdown followed by Ray Mendhelm 5 yard scoring run.

NC STATE

The scrambling Wolfpack never got out of the hole they dug as the Seminoles won their first Homecoming game since 1958 by 14-0. FSU needed a fumble recovery at the NC State 31 to score its first touchdown. It came in the second quarter, Larry Brinkley scoring from the one after a tricky double reverse with flanker back Fred Biletnikoff away on a 12 yard jaunt, setting things up at the two. Ed Pritchett scored on a quarterback sneak that carried 12 yards to wrap up the scoring for the Noles.

Auburn

Auburn, ranked #9, hosted Florida State at Cliff Hare Stadium before over 28,000 fans on a rain soaked field. The Tigers took a 14-0 lead into halftime and had to withstand a second half Seminole rally to prevail 21-15. Jimmy Sidle scored all three touchdowns for the Tigers and rushed for 132 yards. The Tiger defense held the Seminoles to minus two yards rushing. Ed Pritchett scored from 1 yard out with just over 9 minutes remaining for FSU, but Auburn held on for the win.

Florida

The Gators hosted Florida State at Florida Field. Larry Dupree ran for 131 yards on 31 carries and scored on a 2 yard run to give the Gators all the points they would need in a 7-0 victory over the Seminoles. Florida turned the ball over three times inside Florida State's 5 yard line, blowing scoring opportunities.

1964 Florida State Seminoles

In their fifth season under head coach Bill Peterson, the Seminoles compiled a 9–1–1 record, were ranked #11 in the final UPI Coaches Poll, defeated Oklahoma in the Gator Bowl, and outscored opponents by a total of 263 to 85. After five losses and a tie in the first six games of the Florida–Florida State football rivalry, the Seminoles defeated Florida for the first time. The team's statistical leaders included Steve Tensi with 1,986 passing yards, Phil Spooner with 682 rushing yards, and Fred Biletnikoff with 1,179 receiving yards and 90 points scored (15 touchdowns). Biletnikoff led the country in receiving yards and also with 57 receptions and was a consensus first-team end on the 1964 All-America team. Biletnikoff was drafted by Oakland in the 1965 AFL draft.

FINAL RANK: #11 CP

Home games were played at Doak Campbell Stadium

9/19/1964	Florida State		@		Miami (4-5-1)		14	0	W	
9/26/1964	Florida State		@		Tcu (4-6)		10	0	W	
10/3/1964	Florida State		vs		NEW MEXICO STATE (6-4)		36	0	W	
10/10/1964	Florida State		vs	#5	KENTUCKY (5-5)		48	6	W	
10/17/1964	Florida State	#10	@		Georgia (7-3-1)		17	14	W	
10/24/1964	Florida State	#10	@		Virginia Tech (6-4)		11	20	L	
10/31/1964	Florida State		vs		SOUTHERN MISS (6-3)		34	0	W	
11/7/1964	Florida State		@		Houston (2-6-1)		13	13	T	
11/14/1964	Florida State		vs		NC STATE (5-5)		28	6	W	
11/21/1964	Florida State		vs		FLORIDA (7-3)		16	7	W	
1/2/1965	**Florida State**		**vs**		**Oklahoma (6-4-1)**	**CBS**	**36**	**19**	**W**	**Gator Bowl**
Coach: Bill Peterson					**Season Record >>**		263	85	**9-1-1**	

Schedule Source: Steve's Football Bible LLC

Selected game(s) highlights

Miami

A turnout of 51,605 saw one of the all-time great pass-catching performances in the Orange Bowl. Fred Biletnikoff pulled down a school record of nine passes, two for touchdowns, and led Florida State to an emphatic 14-0 conquest of Miami. Steve Tensi threw both touchdown strikes, one in the first quarter, one in the second and threw for 154 yards. Biletnikoff's touchdown catches were a 15 yarder, the other a 16 yarder. He accounted for 165 yards. FSU outgained Miami, 343 yards to 180, with 226 of the Seminoles' total coming via air.

Tcu

Bill McDowell keyed a vigorous defensive effort that lifted Florida State to a 10-0 victory over Texas Christian. McDowell recovered two fumbles and blocked a field goal attempt. The Seminoles took a 3-0 lead on Les Murdock's 33 yard field goal in the first quarter and nursed it until they finally got a touchdown with 9:38 left in the game. Phil Spooner scored from six yards out, capping a 63 yard drive that followed McDowell's blocking of the field-goal attempt.

NEW MEXICO STATE

The Seminoles rolled to a 36-0 victory over New Mexico State for their 3rd straight shutout of the season. Scoring in every quarter and punting only once, FSU still had its difficulties constructing a 16-0 halftime lead. Tensi passed for the first two touchdowns. Biletnikoff caught one for an eight yard touchdown and Don Floyd grabbed the other, a 37 yard reception. 2nd half touchdowns came on

Spooner's one yard run, Ed Pritchett's one yard run and Green's 7 yard dash. FSU rolled up 468 yards, including 206 via passes on 14 completions in 22 attempts.

KENTUCKY

It was a rout from the start. FSU scored the first two times it got the football, led 21-0 by the end of the first quarter. Steve Tensi took Kentucky apart early with his passes. The crusher was a 53 yard completion with Fred Biletnikoff, bringing a 14-0 lead with the game less than eight minutes old. Tensi threw for three touchdowns, and Biletnikoff was on the receiving end of two. Kentucky, conqueror of Ole Miss and Auburn, had gone into this one ranked #5 in the country. FSU was unranked and unscored upon. FSU's seven touchdowns were scored on Tensi's 2 yard pass to Lee Narramore after a 52 yard drive, Tensi's 53 yarder to Biletnikoff, Phil Spooner's 1 yard run after a fumble recovery at the Kentucky 13, Spooner's 1 yarder that climaxed a 66 yard drive, Tensi's 7 yard pass to Biletnikoff on the heels of a 47 yard drive, Wayne Giardino's 1 yard sweep following a 23 yard drive and Ed Pritchett's run from the three after a 39 yard drive.

Georgia

Fred Biletnikoff and Steve Tensi brought Florida State from behind in the final seven minutes to a 17-14 football victory over Georgia. Ahead 10-0 early in the second quarter, the Seminoles had their backs to the wall from that point on. Georgia marched 79 yards and scored shortly before halftime, narrowing things to 10-7, then went ahead early in the final quarter, on Fred Barber's 7 yard TD dash, after recovering an FSU fumble at the Seminoles' 23. Steve Tensi helped save the day. With 6:21 showing on the clock Tensi passed to Biletnikoff for the winning points on a 20 yard pass play. Biletnikoff hauled in eight catches for 114 yards. Tensi threw 24 times, completed 14 for a 193 yards.

Virginia Tech

Virginia Tech won 20-11 before 22,000 screaming Homecoming fans in Blacksburg. VPI's Bob Schweickert passed 19 yards for one touchdown and ran five yards for two more. Tech's first touchdown and its third touchdown were paved on interceptions of Steve Tensi passes. The Seminoles' touchdown came on a four yard pass from Tensi to Fred Biletnikoff. Biletnikoff pulled in 11 catches for 182 yards. Tensi completed 21 of 39 for 288. Florida State rushed for 133 more yards, with fullback Lee Narramore gaining 82 yards on 20 carries.

SOUTHERN MISSISSIPPI

A rugged Seminole defense rendered Southern almost totally harmless on offense, and the familiar passing work of Steve Tensi and Fred Biletnikoff did the rest as FSU rolled to a 34-0 victory. Biletnikoff caught 10 throws for 170 yards. Tensi tossed for two touchdowns, ran for another. Tensi completed 13 of 17 passes for 165 yards. Biletnikoff grabbed a 42 yarder from Ed Pritchett as the Seminoles went to a trick play on the first play of the game. Later he gathered in a 40 yarder from Pritchett for his eighth touchdown of the season. Florida State scored the first two times it had the football. Tensi's screen pass to halfback Phil Spooner brought the first one, a 17 yard play. And Tensi, on one of his rare carries, got the second himself on a two yard rollout. The third TD was on Larry Green's bright 28 yard dash, bringing a 19-0 halftime lead. Two more came in the third quarter, on Tensi's seven yard pass to Red Dawson and Pritchett's bomb to Biletnikoff.

Houston

Florida State carried a 13-0 lead into the last quarter. A pass interference call against FSU in the end zone precipitated Houston's first touchdown, and an interception paved the other. Bo Burris missed a chance to win it when his extra point attempt hit the upright following the second TD. In the final minute Florida State drove to the seven, but Les Murdock's 24 yards field goal try was wide with 39 seconds left. Murdock's toe gave FSU a 3-0 lead at halftime on a 34 yard field goal. He added another field goal in the third quarter, a 25 yarder. Then the Seminoles drove for their lone touchdown, with Wayne Giardino scoring from the one.

NC STATE

Fred Biletnikoff was ready, and Florida State rolled to an easy, 28-6 football victory over fumbling NC State. Biletnikoff bolstered his All-America stock with touchdown catches of 37 and 11 yards. Frank Pennie recovered two NC State fumbles, and FSU turned each into a touchdown. Phil Spooner slipped in FSU's first touchdown from two yards out on the Seminoles' first offensive drive. Wayne Giardino rammed home another from the one, and it was soon followed by Tensi's 37 yard touchdown strike to Biletnikoff. In the third quarter Florida State pushed things to 28-0 as Tensi tossed 11 yards to Biletnikoff. Biletnikoff finished with seven catches for 100 yards.

FLORIDA

Even though many of the early games in the series were close (and the 1961 contest ended in a 3–3 tie), Florida State had yet to beat their in-state rivals in six attempts. The 1964 game would be the first time that the Gators would journey to Doak Campbell Stadium, and the Seminoles under Coach Bill Peterson were enjoying their best season since joining the ranks of major college football programs. However, the Gators still felt confident that another victory was in the offing, coming out onto the playing field with the boast "Never, FSU, Never!" attached to their helmets. Florida State quarterback Steve Tensi hit Fred Biletnikoff with a first-half touchdown, helping the Seminoles to a 13–0 lead at the half as the Gator offense fumbled four times, including once at the FSU one yard line. Florida, led by quarterback Steve Spurrier, finally scored in the 3rd quarter to cut the lead to 13–7, but were unable to find the endzone again. Les Murdock kicked a 42 yard field goal to secure the win for FSU, 16–7

1965 GATOR BOWL

In front of a capacity crowd of 50,408 fans enjoying 75-degree weather, Florida State University defeated the University of Oklahoma 36-19 in the 20th annual Gator Bowl. The game was watched by the Gator Bowl's biggest crowd and a national television audience. Ronnie Fletcher's 95 yard TD pass to Ben Hart, was an Oklahoma bowl record. Steve Tensi threw 23-of-36 for 303 yards and five touchdowns. Fred Biletnikoff caught four of those passes for touchdowns, along with nine more for a total of 192 yards. Florida State outrushed Oklahoma 217 to 71 and outthrew them 303 to 209 while only punting once in the game.

1965 Florida State Seminoles

In their sixth season under head coach Bill Peterson, the Seminoles compiled a 4-5–1 record. The Seminoles outscored their opponents by a total of 121 to 119. Jack Shinholser {LB} was selected as a 2nd team All-American and Honorable Mention All-American by Associated Press and United Press International. Jim Mankins led the team in rushing with 336 yards. Ed Pritchett led the team in passing with 1,225 yards and 4 touchdown passes. Max Wettstein led in receiving with 24 catches for 365 yards and 3 TD receptions. Shinholser {Washington} and Mankins {RB} {Green Bay} were selected in the 1966 NFL draft.

Home games were played at Doak Campbell Stadium

9/25/1965	Florida State	@		Tcu (6-5)	3	7	L
10/2/1965	Florida State	vs		BAYLOR (5-5)	9	7	W
10/9/1965	Florida State	@		Kentucky (6-4)	24	26	L
10/16/1965	Florida State	vs	#5	GEORGIA (6-4)	10	3	W
10/23/1965	Florida State	@	#2	Alabama (9-1-1)	0	21	L
10/30/1965	Florida State	vs		VIRGINIA TECH (7-3)	7	6	W
11/6/1965	Florida State	vs		WAKE FOREST (3-7)	35	0	W
11/13/1965	Florida State	@		NC State (6-4)	0	3	L
11/20/1965	Florida State	vs		HOUSTON (4-5-1)	16	16	T
11/27/1965	Florida State	@		Florida (7-4)	17	30	L
Coach: Bill Peterson				**Season Record >>**	121	119	**4-5-1**

Schedule Source: Steve's Football Bible LLC

Selected game(s) highlights

TCU

Ahead 3-0 in the third quarter, the Seminoles lost it after TCU's E.A. Gresham intercepted a pass at the FSU 48. Pete Roberts' 23 yard field goal gave FSU a 3-0 lead in the second quarter. Ken Post rammed off the right side for the touchdown as the third quarter ended. Bruce Alford kicked the point for 7-3. Ed Pritchett's Hail Mary pass on the last play was intercepted by TCU at the eight yard line.

BAYLOR

Ed Pritchett hit TK Wetherell with a 59 yard touchdown pass in the closing minutes and it earned the Florida State Seminoles a 9-7 victory over the underdog but previously unbeaten Baylor Bears. Except for its two scoring drives, FSU never seriously threatened. For the game, the Seminoles wound up with just eight first downs as Pritchett completed 10 of 28 passes for 160 yards, and the FSU ground attack added no more than 89 yards.

Kentucky

Ahead 24-20 with 5 1/2 minutes left, Florida State succumbed finally to the passing of Kentucky's Rick Norton 26-24. FSU led 7-0, 7-6, 17-14 and finally 24-20. Two tackle-eligible plays, with Don Davis on the receiving end of Norton throws, helped pave the way for both of Kentucky's last-half touchdowns. It was a 14-14 standoff at intermission. Florida State utilized two big kickoff returns to set a vigorous early pace. The game opening kick was wheeled back 53 yards by FSU's Joe Petko and led eventually to FSU's first touchdown. Quarterback Ed Pritchett scored it from three yards out. After Kentucky fought to a 14-7 lead, FSU worked a nifty on the following kickoff. Bill Moremen and TK Wehterell collaborated on a 102 yard kickoff return touchdown. Bill Moremen took the kick two yards back in the end zone, raced up to the 13, lateraled to TK Wetherell, who steamed the rest of the way. Kentucky's second touchdown was a 39 yard pass from Norton to Bob Winslow. Pete Roberts' 35 yard field goal put FSU ahead 17-14 in the third quarter. After Kentucky drove for an early touchdown in the fourth quarter, FSU retaliated with a drive climaxed by Pritchett's nine yard touchdown pass to Max Wettstein. Kentucky's winning score came with less than three minutes remaining.

GEORGIA

The University of Georgia arrived in Tallahassee ranked fifth in the nation in 1965, but the Seminole defense proved to be simply too much. Florida State held Georgia to just 134 yards but trailed 3-0 entering the fourth quarter. On the first play of the final period, Bill Moremen raced 20 yards for a touchdown and the Seminoles never looked back. The 10-3 victory that day gave Florida State its first win ever over a top 5 opponent.

Alabama

The Crimson Tide shutout the Seminoles 21–0 on homecoming in Tuscaloosa. Alabama took a 13–0 halftime lead after Leslie Kelley scored on a one yard touchdown run in the first and Steve Sloan scored on a two yard touchdown run in the second quarter. After a scoreless third, the Crimson Tide closed the game with a second one yard Kelley touchdown run in the fourth quarter coupled with a Ken Stabler two point conversion that made the final score 21–0.

VIRGINIA TECH

Stymied by two pass interceptions and two lost fumbles in the first half, Florida State scored the first time it got the ball in the third quarter. Bill Moremen sparked and climaxed a 46 yard drive with a scoring run from the two. Tech went 40 yards for its score early in the fourth quarter, with Eddie Bulheller going the final 18 off right tackle on a tricky reverse. The Gobblers' gamble for two points was forced, not planned. Tommy Groom, down to hold the ball, got a high snap, bobbled the ball when he tried to set it up anyhow. He straightened and threw a pass. FSU's Billy Campbell intercepted it in the end zone and the Seminoles held on for a 7-6 victory.

WAKE FOREST

The defense never allowed Wake Forest within smelling distance of the FSU goal. The offense came to life and scored more points in one game than it had all told in five of the six previous ones. Florida State won, going away in the last half, 35-0 and sent 25,600 homecoming fans happy. Ed Pritchett started that last half surge. He set up the first touchdown with a 27 yard run, scored it on an 11 yard sweep, then passed 40 yards to Max Wettstein for the second TD. On his first two series, Kim Hammond took the Seminoles to touchdowns. Phil Spooner and Wayne Giardino each scored from the one. Billy Campbell capped the day with a 70 yard punt return for a touchdown in the last moments.

HOUSTON

Three field-goal attempts in a frantic final 67 seconds all backfired as Florida State and Houston settled for a 16-16 tie. Florida State's Pete Roberts missed from 27 yards range with 1:07 left, from 37 yards with 28 seconds remaining. Houston's Ken Hebert failed on a 38 yard try with six seconds to go. Earlier, on Houston's first turn with the ball in the 2nd half, Hebert kicked a 37 yarder to erase a 16-13 FSU lead. A band-night crowd of 25,135 at Doak Campbell Stadium saw the Seminoles ahead three times, and Houston bouncing back to tie it 6-6, 13-13 and finally 16-16. The Seminoles scored on their opening offensive series with Jim Mankins capping a drive he had led, with a one yard scoring run. Houston's Warren McVea ran 92 yards for a touchdown on the ensuing kickoff. Then, on an early play in the second quarter, Phil Spooner tore loose on an 80 yard scoring run. Houston scored again on Bo Burris' 12 yard pass to Tom Beer. FSU went ahead 16-13 on Roberts' 41 yard field goal with eight seconds remaining in the half.

Florida

Florida traveled to Tallahassee to play the Seminoles. The Gators trailed 17-16 with 1:13 left in the 4th quarter when lightning struck. Steve Spurrier hit Charlie Casey in the end zone to put Florida ahead 23-17. The Seminoles attempt for a comeback went awry when the Gators Alan Trammell intercepted an Ed Pritchett pass and went 46 yards for a touchdown to seal the Gators 30-17 victory. Spurrier threw two touchdown passes to Jack Harper, one for 52 yards and one for 25 yards. Wayne Barfield added a 34 yard field goal. Pritchett threw a 31 yard TD pass to Max Wettstein and a 21 yard TD pass to Jerry Jones for the Noles. Spurrier finished the day 18-28 for 282 yards passing. The Gators ran for 185 yards on the ground. Charlie Casey caught 7 passes for 107 yards.

1966 Florida State Seminoles

In their seventh season under head coach Bill Peterson, the Seminoles compiled a 6-5 record and were invited to play Wyoming in the Sun Bowl. The Seminoles outscored their opponents by a total of 274 to 215. Bill Moremen led the team in rushing with 480 yards. Gary Pajcic led the team in passing with 1590 yards and 8 touchdown passes. Ron Sellers led the team in receiving with 55 catches for 874 yards and had five 100 yards receiving games. Walt Sumner led the team with 4 pass interceptions.

Gary Pajcic was an Associated Press Honorable Mention All-American. Del Williams was a 2nd team All-American on both Associated Press and United Press International teams. Williams {C} {New Orleans} and Larry Kissam {T} {Miami} were selected in the 1967 NFL draft.

Home games were played at Doak Campbell Stadium

9/17/1966	Florida State	vs		HOUSTON (8-2)		13	21	L	
9/24/1966	Florida State	@		Miami (8-2-1)		23	20	W	
10/8/1966	Florida State	vs	#10	FLORIDA (9-2)		19	22	L	
10/15/1966	Florida State	@		Texas Tech (4-6)		42	33	W	
10/22/1966	Florida State	vs		MISSISSIPPI STATE (2-8)		10	0	W	
10/29/1966	Florida State	@		Virginia Tech (8-2-1)		21	23	L	
11/5/1966	Florida State	@		South Carolina (1-9)		32	10	W	
11/12/1966	Florida State	@		Syracuse (8-3)		21	37	L	
11/19/1966	Florida State	vs		WAKE FOREST (3-7)		28	0	W	
11/26/1966	Florida State	vs		MARYLAND (4-6)		45	21	W	
12/24/1966	**Florida State**	**vs**		**Wyoming (10-1)**	**CBS**	**20**	**28**	**L**	**Sun Bowl**
Coach: Bill Peterson				**Season Record >>**		274	215	**6-5**	

Schedule Source: Steve's Football Bible LLC

Selected game(s) highlights

HOUSTON

Defensive end Carl Cunningham led the Houston defense as it shut down the Florida State offense and paved the way for Houston to a 21-13 football victory. Cunningham partially blocked a second quarter attempt for a field goal. On the first play after Cunningham's block, Bo Burris passed to Warren McVea who turned it into an 80 yard touchdown that tied the game 7-7. Led by Kim Hammond, who completed his first eight passes, Florida State scored on the game-opening series, moving 91 yards, with Hammond capping it with an 8 yard scoring toss to Jim Mankins. Houston went ahead 14-7 before halftime following the second of three interceptions by Tom Pociorek. Early in the 2nd half, Houston pushed it to 21-7 when Dick Spratt scored on an 81 yard punt return. FSU narrowed it early in the final quarter on Bill Moremen's 6 yard pass to Chip Glass.

Miami

Florida State headed south to face 15th-ranked Miami. Florida State trailed early but scored 17 second quarter points with spectacular touchdowns from Ron Sellers and T.K. Wetherell. Miami led 20-17 after three quarters, but Gary Pajcic's second touchdown pass of the day — a 27 yard strike to Thurston Taylor — gave the Seminoles the lead for good. The narrow victory would be the third straight for Florida State over the rival Hurricanes.

FLORIDA {Catch or not?}

In an otherwise unremarkable game coming into this eighth annual contest between the burgeoning rivals, this game established the rivalry in full due to the controversy that surrounded its outcome. In a tight contest, the Gators led the Seminoles late in the game, 22–19. FSU had the ball at the

Gators' 45 yard-line with seventeen seconds left in the game.
On first down, little used and previously injured wide
receiver Lane Fenner entered the game in place of FSU's star
receiver Ron Sellers. FSU quarterback Gary Pajcic took the
snap, Fenner got behind UF defenders, and Pajcic lofted a
pass to Fenner in the front corner of the end zone for what
appeared to be a game-winning FSU touchdown. However,
referee Doug Moseley signaled that Fenner did not have
control of the ball before rolling out of bounds and ruled the

pass incomplete. Florida held on for a 22–19 win, but the controversy heated up after the game when
photos that apparently showed Fenner making the catch in the endzone were published in state
newspapers. Debate over whether the play should have been ruled a touchdown continues to this day.

Texas Tech

On 20 successive offensive plays in the first half, Florida State scored four touchdowns, all by Jim
Mankins, and the Seminoles went on to a 42-33 victory over Texas Tech in a frantic football game in
Lubbock. Mankins scored on a 5 yard pass from Gary Pajcic, on a 2 yard run, on a one yard run and on a 9
yard scamper. Ahead by 21-0 at one time, Florida State couldn't put it away, however, until Larry Green
took an early fourth quarter screen pass and sprinted 58 yards to a touchdown for a 35-19 Seminole lead.
The Seminoles pushed it to 42-19 on Kim Hammond's 52 yard throw to Ron Sellers before Tech came
back for two late ones, including a touchdown with one second showing on the clock.

MISSISSIPPI STATE

Mike Blatt led the Seminoles to a 10-0 victory with 2 sacks and a fumble recovery and FSU
recorded its first shutout of the season. In the 2nd quarter, Blatt sacked the Bulldogs QB Don Saget and
recovered the fumble at the State 26 yard line. Seven plays later, Gary Pajcic scored from 1 yard out on
fourth down. Pete Roberts kicked a 25 yard field goal in the early moments of the fourth quarter to ice the
Seminoles' third victory.

Virginia Tech

Virginia Tech sprung a 23-21 upset on Florida State in Blacksburg. Bill Moremen had a career
day, scoring all three Seminole touchdowns. But it was a big goal line stand by Tech after FSU pulled to
within 23-21, that won it in the early moments of the 4th quarter. With the ball perhaps a half yard from
the end zone, Jim Mankins, on fourth down, slammed into the right side. They untangled the pile and
officials declared him short. An interception by Ken Whitley at the Tech 15 blunted FSU's last big bid with
4:31 remaining. FSU threw a school-record number of passes, with Pajcic connecting on 28 of 53 for 312
yards. Ron Sellers caught 13 for 138 yards, to tie Fred Biletnikoff's Gator Bowl record.

South Carolina

With Bill Moremen scoring three touchdowns for the second straight game, Florida State pushed
by South Carolina's error-prone Gamecocks 32-10. Behind 10-6 in the second quarter, ahead just 14-10 at
the half, the Seminoles intercepted five passes, recovered two fumbles in the final two quarters to break
away. Moremen got FSU's first three 6 pointers, two from 1 yard out and another from seven yards. Jim
Mankins also scored from the one. FSU's fifth TD was a 10 yard sweep by Larry Green.

Syracuse

All-American Floyd Little scored three times on runs of exactly 24 yards, leading Syracuse to a
rather easy 37-21 conquest of Florida State before 35,405 at Archbold Stadium. Little rushed for 193 yards
in 25 carries. FSU got on the board just before halftime, moving 47 yards, with Gary Pajcic throwing a 4
yard scoring pass to Thurston Taylor. Syracuse drove from the second half kickoff to another TD, with
Csonka scoring from the one. Alex Gousseff soon kicked a 31 yard field goal to make it 30-7. Kim
Hammond replaced Pajcic and guided FSU to its last two touchdowns, with Larry Green scoring from
eight yards out and Hammond passing to Johnny Hurst on an 8 yard screen for the other.

WAKE FOREST

In front 14-0 before Wake Forest got a first down, Florida State embellished a 28-0 homecoming victory with the longest scoring pass play in its history. Teaming on the 86 yard touchdown in the third quarter were Gary Pajcic and Ron Sellers. The Seminoles drove 71 yards after the opening kickoff, with Bill Moreman scoring from the one. T.K. Wetherell took a punt return by the Deacons and zipped 36 yards to the four, from where Larry Green scored on the next play. FSU picked off three Wake passes, with Walt Sumner, Mike Blatt and Clint Burton bagging one each.

MARYLAND

Florida State routed Maryland 45-21 as quarterback Gary Pajcic broke two school records. Pajcic completed nine of 19 passes for 109 yards. With 39 yards running, he boosted his total offense for the year to 1735, breaking the FSU one-season record Steve Tensi held with 1637. Moving his passing figures for the season to 125 completions in 232 tries, Pajcic also broke Tensi's one-season mark of 121 completions. FSU scored, in sequence, on Frank Loner's 39 yard field goal, Pajcic's 7 yard pass to Thurston Taylor, Larry Green's 2 yard run, Kim Hammond's 20 yard pass to Billy Cox, Jim Mankins' one yard run, Bill Moremen's 6 yard run, and Johnny Hurst's 7 yard burst up the middle.

1966 SUN BOWL

Wyoming junior halfback Jim Kiick rushed for 135 yards on 25 carries, caught four passes for 42 yards, and scored twice (first and third quarters). Florida State quarterback Kim Hammond threw two touchdowns, one to Ron Sellers for 49 yards and four minutes later a 59 yard pass to T.K. Wetherell to give the Seminoles a 14–7 lead at halftime. Cowboy Jerry Marion caught a 39 yard pass from quarterback Rick Egloff to tie the score at fourteen each. Kiick's touchdown of 43 yards reclaimed the lead for Wyoming at 21–14. In the fourth quarter, Egloff added a rushing touchdown to make it 28–14. Hammond and Ron Sellers connected for another touchdown reception to narrow the margin to eight, but the Seminoles failed to score again.

1967 Florida State Seminoles

In their eighth season under head coach Bill Peterson, the Seminoles compiled a 7-2-2 record and were invited to play Penn State in the Gator Bowl. The Seminoles outscored their opponents by a total of 250 to 187.

Ron Sellers {WR} was selected as a Consensus First team All-American. Kim Hammond {QB} was selected as a 2nd team All-American by AP and UPI. Bill Moremen led the team in rushing with 439 yards. Kim Hammond led the team in Passing with 1991 yards and 15 touchdown passes. Hammond had four 300 yard passing games. Ron Sellers led the team in receptions with 70 catches for 1228 yards and 8 touchdown receptions. Sellers had 8 games with 100 or more reception yards. Chuck Eason led the team with 4 pass interceptions. Hammond {Miami}, Lane Fenner {FL} {San Diego}, Thurston Taylor {TE} {Philadelphia}, Bill Moremen {RB} {New York Giants} and Wayne McDuffie {C} {Cleveland} were all selected in the 1968 NFL draft.

FINAL RANK: #15 CP
Home games were played at Doak Campbell Stadium

Date	Team			Opponent					Result	
9/15/1967	Florida State	@		Houston (7-3)		13	33	L	
9/23/1967	Florida State	@	#2	Alabama (8-2-1)		37	37	T	@ Birmingham
9/30/1967	Florida State	vs		NC STATE (9-2)		10	20	L	
10/7/1967	Florida State	@		Texas A&M (7-4)		19	18	W	
10/14/1967	Florida State	vs		SOUTH CAROLINA (5-5)		17	0	W	
10/21/1967	Florida State	vs		TEXAS TECH (6-4)		28	12	W	
10/28/1967	Florida State	vs		MISSISSIPPI STATE (1-9)		24	12	W	
11/4/1967	Florida State	@		Memphis (6-3)		26	7	W	
11/11/1967	Florida State	vs		VIRGINIA TECH (7-3)		38	15	W	
11/25/1967	Florida State	@		Florida (6-4)		21	16	W	
12/30/1967	**Florida State**	**vs**	#10	**Penn State (8-2-1)**	ABC	17	17	T	Gator Bowl
Coach: Bill Peterson				**Season Record >>**		250	187	**7-2-2**	

Schedule Source: Steve's Football Bible LLC

Selected game(s) highlights

Houston

Under a dark, gray man-made dome, the roof fell in on Florida State as the Houston Cougars won the game by a stunning 33-13. Houston had a 33-0 lead before the Seminoles scored. Both Florida State touchdowns came in the final six minutes on 6 yard passes by Kim Hammond, one to Lane Fenner, the other to Thurston Taylor.

Alabama

Alabama played the Florida State Seminoles to a 37–37 tie and ended a 17-game unbeaten and untied streak that stretched back to their 1965 season. The Seminoles opened with a pair of early touchdowns first on an 11 yard Kim Hammond pass to Ron Sellers and next on a 75 yard Walt Sumner punt return for a 14–0 lead. The Crimson Tide then responded with touchdowns on a two yard Ken Stabler run and a 51 yard Stabler pass to Dennis Homan coupled with a successful two point conversion for a 15–14 lead at the end of the first quarter. In the second quarter, Florida State scored first on a 27 yard Grant Guthrie field goal followed by Alabama with an 11 yard Ed Morgan touchdown run. The Seminoles then scored on a 13 yard Hammond touchdown pass to Larry Green for a 24–22 halftime lead. After Florida State scored the only third quarter points in the third quarter on a 38 yard Guthrie field goal, both teams traded fourth quarter points for the 37–37 tie. After Stabler threw a 17 yard touchdown pass to Homan, the Seminoles responded with a 23 yard Guthrie field goal. Then in the final minutes of the game, Alabama scored their final points on a three yard Morgan run only to have Florida State tie the game at 37 with their eight yard touchdown pass to Bill Moremen.

NC STATE

With Gary Pajcic back in at quarterback, FSU fought from a 10-0 halftime deficit to a 10-10 deadlock late in the third quarter. Just after FSU tied it NC State marched 75 yards to three points, Warren kicking a 40 yard field goal. Next time NC State got the ball on an interception by Mike Hilka, the Wolfpack moved 55 yards to a touchdown, with Tony Barchuck scoring from the one and the Wolfpack held on for the 20-10 victory.

Texas A&M

Down 9-0 at halftime, Florida State rose up on a wet field and put down Texas A&M 19-18 on Bill Moremen's 28 yard scoring scramble up the middle with the clock showing 3:14 to go. Moments before, with A&M ahead 18-13, Florida State's last chance appeared to have vanished when Tom Sooy intercepted a pass in the end zone with 4:10 remaining. But John Crowe recovered a Larry Stegent fumble at the Aggies 28 less than a minute later, and Moremen immediately cashed in the turnover opportunity. Mike Blatt intercepted an Ed Hargett pass at the State 38, with 1:10 remaining to seal the win.

SOUTH CAROLINA

Florida State turned up the defense and muscled out a satisfying 17-0 football victory over South Carolina before 33,022 at Doak Campbell Stadium. A 75 yard opening drive, helped by a 45 yard penalty for pass interference on the first play, was climaxed by Bill Moremen's touchdown run from the one. John Crowe picked off two of the five the Seminoles stole during the game. Walt Sumner, Howell Montgomery and T.K. Wetherell intercepted the others. After Sumner's third quarter theft, the Seminoles marched 78 yards to a 24 yard field-goal by Grant Guthrie, bringing a 10-0 lead. A clinching touchdown came with 5:24 left when Bill Gunter led, then climaxed a 59 yard drive with a 9 yard run.

TEXAS TECH

With Ron Sellers catching nine passes and figuring significantly in the scoring of every Florida State touchdown, the Seminoles carved out a 28-12 homecoming football triumph over Texas Tech. Florida State lost four fumbles, and the Red Raiders had 114 penalty yards stepped off against them. Gary Pajcic completed 13 of 20 throws for 177 yards, while Kim Hammond connected on four of seven for 74. Sellers had 147 yards and one TD out of his nine receptions. Overall, the Seminoles stacked up 324 yards of offense, 260 via air against Tech's 278, of which 227 came running. Bill Moremen had two touchdown runs and Bill Gunter had one. Sellers caught an 11 yard TD pass from Pajcic.

MISSISSIPPI STATE

Florida State was on its way to what looked like a rout, but Mississippi State intercepted three third quarter passes, and suddenly a 17-0 deficit was trimmed to 17-12. Kim Hammond came back in at quarterback for a record-breaking finish that lifted the Seminoles to their fourth straight victory, 24-12. Hammond compled 21 of 37, totaling 369 passing yards, breaking the 313 standard set by Joe Majors against Tampa in 1959. Ron Sellers caught seven for 158 yards, including a couple of "bombs." Hammond's TD passes went to Chip Glass (8 yards), Larry Green (32 yards) and Bill Moremen (4 yards).

Memphis

With Kim Hammond at the controls, the Seminoles rolled up 548 yards, with 318 passing. The overall total broke the school record of 526 yards set against Furman in 1952. Hammond completed 24 of 34 passes for 302 yards as the Seminoles won their fifth straight, 26-7. Linebacker Dale McCullers was credited with 15 tackles and two assists. Florida State had the ball for 85 plays, Memphis State for just 38. Grant Guthrie kicked two field goals and Larry Green, Bill Moremen and Kim Hammond all scored on short touchdown runs.

VIRGINIA TECH

Florida State wrapped up a bid to the Gator bowl with a decisive 38-15 thrashing of Virginia Tech. Ron Sellers had another fantastic night, breaking school records, caught three touchdown passes as quarterback Kim Hammond accounted for more than 300 passing yards for the fourth time this season. Four of Hammond's passes were for touchdowns. The Seminoles scoring plays were, Grant Guthrie's school record field goal from 45 yards out, Hammond's 30 yard pass to Billy Cox Hammond's 73 yard pass to Sellers, Al Kincaid's 17 yard pass to Ken Edwards, Bill Moremen's 4 yard pass to Sellers, Hammond's 10 yard pass to Sellers, Edwards' 1 yard run and Hammond's 14 yard pass to Cox. In throwing for four touchdowns, Hammond completed 17 of 30 for 314 yards. Sellers caught eight passes for 229 yards that shot his season total of receptions to a school-record 63.

Florida

The Gators hosted the Seminoles at Florida Field. Florida State was nursing a 14-9 lead in the 4th quarter, Noles quarterback Kim Hammond returned to the game after being knocked out of the game in the 2nd quarter and on the first play back he threw a 38 yard touchdown to Ron Sellers for an insurmountable 21-9 lead. Hammond scored on a 1 yard run and threw a 9 yard TD pass to Bill Moreman to lead the Seminoles to a 21-16 victory over the Gators. Tom Christian scored from 1 yard out and Larry Smith scored from 4 yards out for Florida.

1967 GATOR BOWL

Kim Hammond completed 37-of-53 passes for 362 yards, with four interceptions and one touchdown, while rushing for 28 yards on nine carries. Tom Sherman completed 9-of-17 passes for 69 yards, with two interceptions and two touchdowns, while rushing for 27 yards on six carries, contributing a field goal and two extra points. Florida State scored 17 straight points in the second half, with Grant Guthrie's field goal from 26 yards out contributing to the first tie in a Gator Bowl since 1948. It remains the last tie game in  the Gator Bowl. Florida State had 23 first downs; Penn State had 12. Florida State rushed for only 55 yards while Penn State rushed for 175. Florida State threw for 363 yards; Penn State threw for 69 yards. Both teams turned the ball over four times.

1968 Florida State Seminoles

This was Bill Peterson's ninth year as head coach, and he led the team to an 8–3 record. The Seminoles were invited to the Peach Bowl to play LSU.

Tom Bailey led the team in rushing with 570 yards. Bill Cappleman led the team in passing with 2410 yards and 25 touchdown passes. Ron Sellers led the team in receptions with 86 catches for 1496 yards and 12 touchdown receptions. Walt Sumner and John Crowe tied for the lead with 5 pass interceptions. Sumner led the team in punt returns with a 12.3 average and one touchdown. Sellers had 6 games with more than 100 yards in receptions and Cappleman had three games where he threw for more than 300 yards. **Ron Sellers set a single season record with 1,496 receiving yards.**

Bill Cappleman {QB}, John Crowe {DB}, Jack Fenwick {T}, Dale McCullers {LB} and Ron Sellers {WR} were selected to the 1st team All-South Independent team. Sellers was a Consensus First team All-American. McCullers was selected as First team All-American by Newspapers Enterprise Association. Cappleman and Fenwick were Honorable Mention All-Americans by the Associated Press. Sellers {Boston Patriots}, Chip Glass {TE} {San Diego}, Bill Rhodes {G} {St. Louis Cardinals}, Walt Sumner {DB} {New York Giants} and McCullers {Miami} were selected in the 1969 NFL draft. Sellers was a #1 pick.

FINAL RANK: #14 CP

Home games were played at Doak Campbell Stadium

9/21/1968	Florida State		@		Maryland (2-8)		24	14	**W**	
9/28/1968	Florida State		**vs**	#5	FLORIDA (6-3-1)		3	9	**L**	
10/5/1968	Florida State		**vs**	#17	TEXAS A&M (3-7)		20	14	**W**	
10/19/1968	Florida State		**vs**		MEMPHIS (6-4)		20	10	**W**	
10/26/1968	Florida State	**#20**	@		South Carolina (4-6)		35	28	**W**	
11/2/1968	Florida State	**#18**	**vs**		VIRGINIA TECH (7-4)		22	40	**L**	
11/9/1968	Florida State		@		Mississippi State (0-8-2)		27	14	**W**	
11/16/1968	Florida State		@		NC State (6-4)		48	7	**W**	
11/23/1968	Florida State		**vs**		WAKE FOREST (2-7-1)		42	24	**W**	
11/29/1968	Florida State		**vs**		HOUSTON (6-2-2)		40	20	**W**	@ Jacksonville
12/30/1968	**Florida State**	**#19**	**vs**		**Lsu (8-3)**	**CBS**	**27**	**31**	**L**	**Peach Bowl**
Coach: Bill Peterson					**Season Record >>**		308	211	**8-3**	

Schedule Source: Steve's Football Bible LLC

Selected game(s) highlights

Maryland

The Seminoles didn't wrap this one up until 1:47 remained in the game, when Bill Cappleman culminated an 85 yard drive with a scoring sneak from the one. Bill Gunter rushed 133 yards for the Tribe in 28 runs. Grant Guthrie kicked a 26 yard field goal to give FSU an early 3-0 lead. Gary Pajcic threw two touchdowns, one to John Pittman (6 yards) and one to Ron Sellers (82 yards).

FLORIDA

Florida traveled to Tallahassee to play the Seminoles at Doak Campbell Stadium. Jack Youngblood kicked a 30 yard field goal and Larry Smith scored from 3 yards out as the Gators held on for a 9-3 victory over Florida State. Grant Guthrie kicked a 21 yard field goal for the Noles' only points.

TEXAS A&M

Florida State's comeback kids pulled out a 20-14 decision over Texas A&M in a cliffhanger of a football game. Bill Cappleman went to an assortment of receivers, threw touchdown passes of seven and 14 yards to Jim Tyson and Billy Cox. Grant Guthrie kicked two field goals for the Noles. Not until the last minute could Florida State breathe easy. With A&M at the Seminoles 25, second down, Walt Sumner intercepted one of Edd Hargett's desperation passes. The clock showed just 46 seconds left. **Dale McCullers set a single record with 29 tackles.**

MEMPHIS STATE

Ron Sellers caught seven of the first eight passes Bill Cappleman completed, accounted for both Seminoles' touchdowns on plays of five and 38 yards, and caught 13, as the Seminoles beat Memphis State 20-10. Ahead 3-0 early on Grant Guthrie's 28 yard field goal, the Seminoles fell behind 7-3, then got back up 10-7 on Seller's first TD catch, got tied 10-10, then went ahead for good in the third quarter on Sellers' 38 yard grab. Guthrie wrapped up the scoring with a 30 yard field goal. Sellers had 218 yards in receptions.

South Carolina

Ron Sellers caught 16 passes for 248 yards, both school records, and scored three touchdowns as Florida State finally muzzled South Carolina 35-28 in an incredible, pass happy football game. With Carolina leading 28-21 in the third quarter and standing with a first down at FSU's 25, Steve Gildea intercepted a Tommy Suggs pass and raced 48 yards to Carolina's 33. The Seminoles quickly capitalized for a tying TD. Then, with 50 seconds left in the game, and Carolina in FSU's territory, Gildea intercepted another Suggs pass to kill Carolina's last hopes. The scoring went as follows, Carolina marched from the opening kickoff to a touchdown with Suggs scoring from 5 yards out, (FSU) Sellers caught a 19 yard scoring toss from Cappleman. (FSU) Tom Bailey plunged over from the two after John Pittman ran 24 yards, (SC) Suggs passed to Eddie Bolton for a TD on a 50 yard pass, (FS) Bill Gunter scored on a 42 yard pass from Cappleman, (SC) Suggs tossed a 7 yard touchdown pass to Johnny Gregory, making it a 21-21 halftime tie. (SC) Ben Galloway scored from two yards out, (FSU) Sellers caught a 20 yard scoring pass from Cappleman, (FSU) Sellers grabbed a 16 yard pass from Cappleman, making the score a final 35-28 with 10:15 left in the game.

VIRGINIA TECH

Virginia Tech intercepted six passes and Ken Edwards ran for 197 yards in 17 carries. Making the most of three first-half interceptions, the Gobblers led 31-7 at intermission. FSU pulled within 10-7 on a Bill Cappleman 34 yard TD pass to Jim Tyson. It was all Tech after that as they ripped off 27 straight points to put the game away. Cappleman and Tyson hooked up for a 5 yard touchdown in the 4th quarter, but it was too little, too late for the Noles as VPI left Tallahassee with a 40-22 victory.

Mississippi State

Ahead 17-0 early, Florida State had to hold on late for a 27-14 victory over Mississippi State. Five interceptions by the Seminoles helped their cause. Bill Cappleman threw for all three of the Seminoles' touchdowns. Florida State got six points on field-goal kicks of 27 and 36 yards by Grant Guthrie. Jim Tyson caught a 6 yard pass for FSU's first TD. Tom Bailey got the second on a 14 yard play, and Billy Cox the third on a 32 yard bomb. Cappleman connected on 20 of 30 passes for 285 yards. Ron Sellers grabbed eight throws for 149 yards.

NC State

Florida State, spurred by a hopped-up defense, exploded for a 48-7 triumph over the Wolfpack. The defense was responsible for an early 14-0 lead. Walt Sumner started it. He blocked Gerald Warren's 46 yard try for a field goal, picked up the ball and streaked 58 yards for the first touchdown. Floyd Ratliff pounced on an N.C. State fumble at the Wolfpack 49. With Tom Bailey leading the charge, FSU probed to the 13, where Bill Cappleman hit Phil Abraira with a 13 yard pass for a 14-0 lead. N.C. State soon retaliated, scoring on a 10 yard toss, Jack Klebe to Jimmy Lisk. Florida State scored, in rapid succession, on Bill Gunter's 11 yard run, Cappleman's 1 yard pass to Gunter after Chuck Elliott recovered an N.C. State fumble at the Wolfpack 41, Gunter's 1 yard run after Billy Cox covered a fumbled N.C. State punt at the two, Cappleman's 37 yard bomb to Albraira and Tommy Warren's 18 yard pass to Gary Pajcic.

WAKE FOREST

Florida State came from behind in the third quarter to put down Wake Forest 42-24. Ron Sellers caught 14 passes for 260 yards and five touchdowns and in so doing broke a national record for yards gained on receptions. **Sellers 260 yards and 5 touchdown receptions set records for receiving yards in a game and touchdown receptions in a game.** Bill Cappleman completed 22 of 33 throws for 365 yards. Ahead 14-0, then behind 24-14, Florida State scored 21 points in just over 7 ½ minutes of in the third quarter. A homecoming crowd of 35,108 didn't breathe easy until the Seminoles put the game out of reach with a final TD late in the fourth quarter. The scoring sequence was, (FS) Sellers' 26 yard TD pass from Cappleman, (FS) Sellers' 5 yard TD pass from Cappleman, (WF) Jimmy Johnson's 7 yard TD pass from Freddie Summers, (WF) Gary Winrow's 8 yard TD pass from Summers, (WF) Tom Deacon's 32 yard field goal that gave Wake Forest a 17-14 halftime lead. (WF) Ron Jurewicz' 28 yard TD pass from Summers, (FS) Sellers' 48 yard TD pass from Cappleman, (FS) Bill Gunter's 3 yard TD run, (FS) Sellers' 28 yard TD pass from Cappleman and (FS) Sellers' 30 yard TD pass from Cappleman. Bill Cappleman passed for 365 yards and Ron Sellers caught 14 passes for 260

HOUSTON

Houston was ranked 10th as it met Florida State in Jacksonville for the 1968 regular season finale. The Cougars were 6-1-2 entering the contest but were dominated by the Seminoles from the opening kickoff. FSU racked up over 500 yards of offense and built a 25-0 halftime lead. Bill Cappleman enjoyed the best day ever for a Florida State quarterback, throwing for 351 yards and four touchdowns. Ron Sellers was the recipient of 14 of Cappleman's 25 completions and finished with 214 yards receiving in the win.

1968 PEACH BOWL

Four turnovers by LSU on their first four possessions had been converted by FSU into two first half touchdowns to lead 13–0 at the second quarter. But the Tigers narrowed the lead when Craig Burns returned a short punt 39 yards for a touchdown. Before the half ended, Mark Lumpkin kicked a field goal to make it 13–10 at halftime. The Tigers came alive in the second half, driving 51 yards in eight plays culminated on a Mike Hillman to Bob Hamlett for a touchdown to take the lead 17–13. On their next drive, Hillman threw another touchdown pass, this time to Bill Stober to make their lead 24–13. As the fourth quarter began, the Seminoles drove down the field 72 yards culminated with a Bill Cappleman pass to Ron Sellers touchdown to narrow the lead. On the ensuing kickoff, the Tigers fumbled the ball back to the Seminoles in Tiger territory. A few plays later the Seminoles scored again on another touchdown catch from Sellers to take a 27–24 lead with over six minutes to go. The Tigers went to work, going on a nine play, 61 yard drive (that once had a third and 19 converted) with a Maurice LeBlanc touchdown run. But the 'Noles drove down the field and were in range for a game winner when on 4th down, Barton Frye knocked down a pass intended for Sellers to make it incomplete and seal the game for the Tigers, their 4th straight bowl win.

1969 Florida State Seminoles

This was Bill Peterson's tenth year as head coach, and he led the team to a 6–3–1 record. The Seminoles were not invited to a Bowl game after the season. Tom Bailey led the team in rushing with 630 yards. Bill Cappleman led the team in passing with 2467 yards and 14 touchdown passes. Jim Tyson led the team in receptions with 49 catches for 720 yards. Phil Abraira led the team with 5 pass interceptions and punt returns with a 20.1 average.

Tom Bailey {RB}, Bill Cappleman {QB}, Jim Tyson {WR}, Bill Lohse {LB}, Robert McEachern {DT} and Ron Wallace {DE} were selected to the First team All-South Independent team. Cappleman {Minnesota}, Grant Guthrie {K} {Buffalo}, Jeff Curchin {T} {Chicago} and Abraira {DB} {Chicago} were selected in the 1970 NFL draft.

Home games were played at Doak Campbell Stadium

9/20/1969	Florida State	vs		WICHITA STATE (2-8)	24	0	**W**
9/26/1969	Florida State	@		Miami (4-6)	16	14	**W**
10/4/1969	Florida State	@	#12	Florida (9-1-1)	6	21	**L**
10/18/1969	Florida State	@		Tulsa (1-9)	38	20	**W**
10/25/1969	Florida State	vs		MISSISSIPPI STATE (3-7)	20	17	**W**
11/1/1969	Florida State	vs		SOUTH CAROLINA (7-4)	34	9	**W**
11/8/1969	Florida State	@		Virginia Tech (4-5-1)	10	10	**T**
11/15/1969	Florida State	vs		MEMPHIS (8-2)	26	28	**L**
11/22/1969	Florida State	vs		NC STATE (3-6-1)	33	22	**W**
11/29/1969	Florida State	@	#18	Houston (9-2)	13	41	**L**
Coach: Bill Peterson				**Season Record >>**	220	182	**6-3-1**

Schedule Source: Steve's Football Bible LLC

Selected game(s) highlights

WICHITA STATE

The visiting Shockers fumbled the football an incredible 17 times, with the Seminoles recovering 10 times. Meanwhile, Florida State fumbled 10 times, and Wichita State claimed seven of 'em. The Seminoles won 24-0. The Seminoles scored in the first quarter on Cappleman's 53 yard pass to Tom Bailey and on Grant Guthrie's 40 yard field goal, in the second quarter on Arthur Monroe's 18 yard run, in the last quarter on Cappleman's 9 yard pass to Don Pederson.

Miami

Fourth down and six at the Miami 47 with about five minutes left, Bill Cappleman pitched 10 yards to Ted Zaffran to keep a 90 yard drive going as Florida State squeezed out a 16-14 victory in a football thriller. With 1:59 showing on the clock, Grant Guthrie kicked his third field goal of the night to erase the 14-13 lead Miami had gained with 9:04 remaining. Cappleman 24 of 38 passes for 209 yards. The Seminoles were trailing 7-0 when Guthrie kicked a school record field goal of 53 yards. Soon after he added another 3 pointer, a 27 yarder, to make it 7-6. Then Florida State got its only touchdown, on a 10 yard Cappleman throw to Kent Gaydos, for a 13-7 halftime lead.

Florida

Both Florida and Florida State were 2–0 when the teams met in 1969. The Gators had defeated the number seven ranked University of Houston two weeks prior, and FSU was off to a good start as well. The Gators won this matchup 21–6 on the back of a defensive surge that was unparalleled in Gator history. The Gators defense, led by junior defensive lineman Jack Youngblood and sophomore defensive lineman Robert Harrell, sacked FSU quarterback Bill Cappleman eleven times for 91 yards leaving FSU with a total of negative 18 yards rushing in the game. In addition to the pass rush, the FSU offense fumbled the ball eight times, losing five. Two other Gator Sophomores starred in the game as well, All-American wide out Carlos Alvarez and quarterback John Reaves.

Tulsa

Behind 7-0 early, Florida State put 21 points on the board in the 2nd quarter and coasted to a 38-20 victory over the Golden Hurricane. Bill Cappleman threw scoring passes of 14 yards and 51 yards to Jim Tyson and 73 yards to Don Pederson in the 2nd quarter barrage. After falling behind 7-0, Tom Bailey tied it 7-7 with an 11 yard run on 4th and one. Duane Carrell kicked a 37 yard field goal and Arthur Munroe scored from 7 yards out to finish the scoring for the Seminoles.

MISSISSIPPI STATE

Jim Tyson caught big play passes from Bill Cappleman to keep Florida State alive, but in the end, it was Art Munroe's halfback pass to Mike Gray that lifted the Seminoles to a difficult 20-17 victory over Mississippi State. Tom Bailey ran for 131 yards and scored on a 34 yard run, Art Munroe ran for 101 yards and scored on a 1 yard run to lead the Seminoles offense.

SOUTH CAROLINA

Against the Seminoles in Tallahassee however, the Gamecocks proved to be no match. South Carolina led 3-0 after a quarter, but Florida State scored the game's next 27 points before running away with a 25 point victory. Tom Bailey and Paul Magaliski combined for 224 yards rushing and three total touchdowns. FSU forced four turnovers in the victory including an interception that was returned 27 yards for a touchdown by John Montgomery.

Virginia Tech

Gripped by a frigid, stinging wind that blew at a 20 to 30 miles per hour rate all afternoon long, Florida State receivers dropped a record number of Bill Cappleman's passes as the Seminoles struggled from behind and pulled out a 10-10 tie with Virginia Tech on Grant Guthrie's 51 yard field goal in the final quarter. Guthrie's kick came with 8:18 left in the game. Jim Tyson caught a 9 yard TD pass from Bill Cappleman and Paul Magalski ran for 113 yards for the Seminoles.

MEMPHIS STATE

Florida State ran up a school record 627 yards of offense, and Bill Cappleman passed for a school record 508, but it was all for nothing as Grant Guthrie missed a 36 yard field goal attempt with 21 seconds left and the Seminoles fell to Memphis State 28-26. Trailing 28-20 with 7:42 remaining, the Seminoles rode Cappleman's arm to a touchdown as the clock showed 3:24 to go. On an "Alley Oop" pass into the end zone to Kent Gaydos, he pulled it in for a touchdown. It was a 6 yard touchdown on fourth down. But a 2 point play, a pass to Gaydos, was broken up. Don Pederson caught touchdown passes of 80 yards and 17 yards from Cappleman to give FSU a 17-14 halftime lead. Gaydos caught nine passes for 111 yards. Pederson grabbed four for 119.

NC STATE

Defensive tackle Frank Vohun rumbled 23 yards with a pass interception and defensive back Phil Abraira scampered 92 on a punt return for a pair of touchdowns that keyed Florida State to a 33-22 victory over N.C. State. Ahead 13-3 early, the Wolfpack's Gary Yount ran 24 yards to a TD on an interception of a Bill Cappleman pass, cutting the score to 13-10. Then Vohun, came up with his career highlight 2:26 before intermission. Moments later linebacker Barry Rice set up the Seminoles at the Wolfpack 34 with another interception, and Grant Guthrie's 31 yard field goal brought things to 23-10 just 41 seconds before the half.

Houston

Piling up more yards on a Florida State football team than any opponent ever, Houston rushed to a 41-13 victory as Jim Strong had 200 yards rushing. Strong scored three times, on runs of 16, 37 and 39 yards. The Houston offensive total was 543. Of that 414 came on runs. Still, the Seminoles, behind 20-13 at the half, made a battle of it until the closing quarter when the Cougars cut loose for 21 points. Bill Cappleman threw two touchdown passes, one to Kent Gaydos (6 yards) and one to Mike Gray (37 yards). Gaydos caught 13 passes for 126 yards in the game.

1970 Florida State Seminoles

This was Bill Peterson's eleventh year as head coach, and he led the team to a 7-4 record. The Seminoles were not invited to a Bowl game after the season.

Tom Bailey led the team in rushing with 514 yards. Tommy Warren led the team in passing with 1613 yards and 11 touchdown passes. Rhett Dawson led the team in receptions with 54 catches and 946 yards. David Snell led the special teams with 363 yards in punt returns and 334 yards in kickoff returns. James Thomas led the team in pass interceptions with 6.

Rhett Dawson {WR}, Alan Dees {C}, Robert McEachern {DT}, James Thomas {DB} and Tommy Warren {QB} were selected to the First team All-South Independent team. Tom Bailey {RB} {Philadelphia} was selected in the 1971 NFL draft.

J.T. Thomas was the first African American to play football for the Seminoles. Thomas, an All-America cornerback who later won four Super Bowl rings as part of the Pittsburgh Steelers' vaunted "Steel Curtain" defense, was indeed the first African American to play in a football game at Florida State. In the 1970 opener against Louisville, Thomas blocked what would have been a winning field goal by the Cardinals in the final seconds of FSU's 9-7 victory.

Home games were played at Doak Campbell Stadium

9/12/1970	Florida State	vs	LOUISVILLE (8-3-1)	9	7	W	
9/19/1970	Florida State	@	Georgia Tech (9-3)	13	23	L	
9/26/1970	Florida State	vs	WAKE FOREST (6-5)	19	14	W	
10/10/1970	Florida State	vs	FLORIDA (7-4)	27	38	L	
10/17/1970	Florida State	@	Memphis (6-4)	12	16	L	
10/24/1970	Florida State	@	South Carolina (4-6-1)	21	13	W	
10/30/1970	Florida State	@	Miami (3-8)	27	3	W	
11/7/1970	Florida State	vs	CLEMSON (3-8)	38	13	W	
11/14/1970	Florida State	vs	VIRGINIA TECH (5-6)	34	8	W	
11/21/1970	Florida State	vs	KANSAS STATE (6-5)	33	7	W	
11/26/1970	Florida State	vs	HOUSTON (8-3)	21	53	L	@ Tampa
Coach: Bill Peterson			**Season Record >>**	254	195	**7-4**	

Schedule Source: Steve's Football Bible LLC

Selected game(s) highlights

LOUISVILLE

James Thomas and Dan Whitehurst combined to block a 28 yard field goal attempt with 17 seconds left to preserve the Seminoles 9-7 victory before over 27,000 fans at Doak Campbell Stadium. Frank Fontes kicked a 47 yard field goal and Dave Snell returned a punt 71 yards for a touchdown for the Seminoles points.

Georgia Tech

Mike Wysong ran eight kicks back for 172 yards and that was much the difference in the game as Georgia Tech tripped Florida State 23-13. Wysong provided the Yellow Jackets with superb field position all afternoon, and the Seminole defense got overburdened. Wysong got 120 yards out of six punt returns, 52 more from a pair of kick runbacks. The heat climbed at one point to 98 degrees, Grant Field was one big steam bath for the 50,324 in the stands as well as the players on the field. To combat the humid, exhausting situation Florida State coaches decided to alternate between two full teams on offense. Frank Whigham was in on both of Florida State's touchdown drives, passing five yards to Jim Tyson for the first Seminole score. Whigham completed 10 of 25 passes for 201 yards. Tom Bailey ran 9 yards for a touchdown for the other Seminole score.

WAKE FOREST

The Seminoles got the better of the eventual ACC champion Demon Deacons. Wake Forest led 14-6 at halftime, but the FSU defense blanked the Demon Deacons in the second half. Arthur Monroe's 1 yard touchdown midway through the third quarter put Florida State ahead for good as kicker Frank Fontes finished the day with four field goals.

FLORIDA

The Florida Gators dominated Florida State for the first fifty-three minutes of the 1970 game. FSU quarterbacks Frank Whigham and Tommy Warren failed to move the ball and with seven minutes left in the game the Gators led 38–7. FSU coach Peterson put sophomore Gary Huff into the game, and he quickly completed two long passes, the second a 43 yard touchdown pass. The FSU defense forced John Reaves and the Gator offense into a three and out, and on the next drive Huff used four plays to score a touchdown with 2:30 left in the game. With the score cut to 38–21 FSU tried an onside kick which failed but didn't fail to cause a both bench-clearing brawl. The FSU defense again forced Florida to punt and as time expired, Huff led the Seminoles to another touchdown making the final score 38–27. Gators All-American Jack Youngblood was criticized by the press for doing a "disrespectful rear-end wagging dance" on a wall near the FSU student section. Both teams ended the season 7–4 but neither received a bowl bid. Huff's passing caused FSU to out gain the Gators in the game and it set at the time, a record for most points scored by both teams in the rivalry.

Memphis State

Unable to throw the ball for 59 minutes, Memphis State successfully put the ball in the air in the final 52 seconds and dealt Florida State a painful defeat 16-12. A 3 yard pass, Rick Strawbridge to Tim Boren, with 14 seconds remaining was the winning touchdown. Art Munroe ran 2 yards for a touchdown to give the Seminoles a 6-0 lead. Trailing 7-6, Eddie McMillan returned the kickoff 93 yards for a touchdown to get the lead back for Noles, 12-7. W.D. Weeks kicked a 32 yard field goal for the Tigers and still trailed 12-10 until the game ending dramatics.

South Carolina

Tommy Warren came off the Florida State bench and brought some dynamite with him. Florida State's offense became a little explosive, and the Seminoles beat down South Carolina 21-13 before a Gamecock homecoming crowd of 42,537. The Seminoles trailed 7-0 when Warren replaced Gary Huff at quarterback with 1:44 remaining in the first half. And the clock read 1:12 when Warren passed 21 yards to Rhett Dawson for a touchdown that tied it 7-7. Next time Warren came in, after the Seminoles claimed a fumble just after the third quarter started, he directed another touchdown drive, scoring himself from the four. The Seminoles salted it away on their first series of the fourth quarter, with Warren leading a 65 yard drive climaxed by Tom Bailey's scoring run from 1 yard out.

Miami

Breaking off runs of 38 and 57 yards in an explosive third quarter, Tom Bailey became Florida State's all-time top runner as the Seminoles ran over Miami 27-3. Only 24,168 fans showed up in the Orange Bowl to see the Seminoles beat Miami for the fifth straight time. Frank Fontes kicked two field goals to give the Seminoles a 6-0 lead. The Seminoles then scored on Tommy Warren's 10 yard pass to

Barry Smith after Bailey's 57 yarder set it up, on David Snell's 1 yard run shortly after Rhett Dawson's catch of a Warren pass picked up 43 yards, and on James Thomas' 29 yard runback of an interception.

CLEMSON

Clemson threw more passes (48) and completed more (25) than any football team ever had against Florida State, but the Seminoles' own prolific aerial game was much the difference here Saturday night as they handled the Tigers 38-13. The Seminoles took a 22-6 lead into halftime on two Frank Fontes field goals and a Rhett Dawson 9 yard TD reception from Tom Bailey and a Kent Gaydos 28 yard TD reception from Tommy Warren. Leading 25-13 heading to the 4th quarter, Barry Smith caught two long touchdown passes, 57 yards from Warren and 29 yards from Gary Huff.

VIRGINIA TECH

Florida State's offense ran itself to a state of exhaustion here Saturday afternoon as it struck for 608 yards and the Seminoles' biggest-ever football victory over Virginia Tech, 34-8. David Snell returned a second-half kickoff 96 yards for a touchdown. Frank Fontes kicked field goals of 32 and 39 yards. The Seminoles' first touchdown was a 1 yard pass to James Jarrett, the second on an 8 yarder to Rhett Dawson, the third on Snell's dazzling runback, and the fourth on Paul Magalski's 1 yard run.

KANSAS STATE

Florida State receivers caught 20 passes for 355 yards. Florida State defenders intercepted six Kansas State passes and the Seminoles rolled to a 33-7 victory over the Wildcats. J.T. Thomas intercepted three passes.Tommy Warren threw three touchdown passes, one each to Don Pederson (20 yards), Kent Gaydos (5 yards) and Rhett Dawson (9 yards). Steve Gildea finished the scoring for FSU with a 57 yard interception return for a touchdown.

HOUSTON

Out front 21-12 at halftime, the Seminoles saw their bombs blow up in their face as the Cougars pulled off four interceptions and got just as many touchdowns out of them and put up 41 points in the 2nd half on the way to a 53-21 blowout of the Noles. Tommy Warren threw two touchdowns in the 1st half, one to Rhett Dawson (12 yards) and Barry Smith (65 yards). James Jarrett ran for a 1 yard touchdown for the Noles.

1971 Florida State Seminoles

Larry Jones was the head coach in first season. Jones led the Seminoles to an 8-4 record and an invitation to the Fiesta Bowl to play Arizona State. Steve Sloan was an assistant coach/offensive coordinator, and Bill Parcells coached the linebackers.

Paul Magalski led the team in rushing with 516 yards. Gary Huff led the team in passing with 2736 yards and 23 touchdown passes. Rhett Dawson led the team in receptions with 62 catches for 817 yards. John Lanahan led the team in pass interceptions with 4.

Rhett Dawson {WR}, Frank Fontes {K}, Gary Huff {QB}, Larry Strickland {DT}, Joe Strickler {OT} and James Thomas {DB} were selected to the First team All-South Independent team. Rhett Dawson was selected as a 3rd team All-American by the Associated Press. Gary Huff and James Thomas were Honorable Mention All-Americans by the Associated Press and United Press International. Dawson {Houston Oilers}, Richard Amman {DE} {Dallas} and Kent Gaydos {TE} {Oakland} were selected in the 1972 NFL draft.

FINAL RANK: #19 CP

Home games were played at Doak Campbell Stadium

Date	Team	Rank		OppRank	Opponent	Network				Notes
9/11/1971	Florida State		vs		Southern Miss (6-5)		24	9	W	@ Mobile, AL
9/18/1971	Florida State		@		Miami (4-7)		20	17	W	
9/25/1971	Florida State		vs		KANSAS (4-7)		30	7	W	
10/2/1971	Florida State		@		Virginia Tech (4-7)		17	3	W	
10/9/1971	Florida State		vs		MISSISSIPPI STATE (2-9)		27	9	W	
10/16/1971	Florida State	#19	@		Florida (4-7)		15	17	L	
10/23/1971	Florida State		vs		SOUTH CAROLINA (6-5)		49	18	W	
10/30/1971	Florida State	#19	@		Houston (9-3)		7	14	L	
11/13/1971	Florida State		@		Georgia Tech (6-6)		6	12	L	
11/20/1971	Florida State		vs		TULSA (4-7)		45	10	W	
11/27/1971	Florida State		vs		PITTSBURGH (3-8)		31	13	W	
12/27/1971	**Florida State**		vs	#8	**Arizona State (11-1)**	Mizlou	**38**	**45**	**L**	**Fiesta Bowl**
Coach: Larry Jones					**Season Record >>**		309	174	**8-4**	

Schedule Source: Steve's Football Bible LLC

Selected game(s) highlights

Southern Mississippi

The first game of the Larry Jones era was a successful one as Florida State topped Southern Mississippi in Mobile, Alabama. Arthur Monroe rushed for 147 yards and a touchdown while the Florida State defense was dominant over the final three quarters.

Miami

Eddie McMillan returned the opening kickoff 90 yards for a touchdown, but FSU trailed Miami at halftime 17-7. Florida State stubbornly fought back and won the game 20-17 on a 25 yard Frank Fontes field goal in the final five minutes. The Seminoles went 46 yards and narrowed it to 17-10 on a 20 yard Fontes field goal late in the third quarter. They marched 73 yards for a touchdown soon after, Huff tossing five yards to Rhett Dawson in the end zone. Another big drive of 80 yards brought the winning 3 pointer by Fontes with 4:38 remaining. The Hurricanes outgained Florida State in total offense, 370 to 261.

KANSAS

Three field goals by Frank Fontes and three touchdowns passes by Gary Huff lifted Florida State to an emphatic 30-7 victory over Kansas before 34,784 fans at Doak Campbell Stadium. Barry Smith scored on a school record touchdown pass of 88 yards in the third quarter, not long after he had tallied on a 19 yard Huff pass. Rhett Dawson pulled in eight passes for 65 yards while Barry Smith had 152 yards on his five receptions. Florida State scored the first time it got the football. The first six points came off the toe of Fontes, who kicked field goals from 47 yards and 31 yards, with Huff's TD pass to Kent Gaydos providing a 13-0 lead. It was 16-7 at the half. Fontes added a 42 yard field goal in the 2nd half.

Virginia Tech

Spurred by the furious pass rushing of Charlie Hunt, the defense held down the fort much of the way until Florida State's offense stopped stumbling and started rumbling. The Seminoles slipped by Virginia Tech 17-3 before 30,001 fans in Lane Stadium. The game was tied 0-0 at halftime. The Seminoles struck first on a Rhett Dawson 24 yard TD reception from Gary Huff. Frank Fontes kicked a 35 yard field goal to give the Noles a tenuous 10-3 lead. Huff hit Kent Gaydos for a 63 yard TD pass to seal the game with 6:22 left in the game.

MISSISSIPPI STATE

As the defense played a significant role, making Mississippi State's attack look pathetic, the Seminoles held on for a 27-9 victory here, before a homecoming crowd of over 27,000 at Doak Campbell Stadium. Frank Fontes put the Seminoles out front with a 43 yard field goal in the first quarter, and Glen Ellis tied it 3-3 early in the second on a 40 yarder. Gary Huff threw a 37 yard scoring pass to Barry Smith and Fontes added a 40 yard field goal for 13-3 at halftime. Late in the third quarter, Florida State scored twice, on Shane Gibbs' recovery of an Art Munro fumble after a 26 yard drive following a fumble the Bulldogs lost, and on Huff's 9 yard pass to Mike Glass after a 46 yard drive.

Florida

Florida jumped to a 14-0 halftime lead on a Mike Rich 1 yard TD run and Jimmy Barr 26 yard fumble return for a touchdown. The Seminoles rallied early in the 4th quarter, but the Gators responded with a Richard Franco 42 yard field goal and withstood a late push by the Noles for a 17-15 victory.

SOUTH CAROLINA

#19 for the second straight week, the Seminoles throttled South Carolina 49-18 in front of a crowd of 30,764 at Doak Campbell Stadium. They trailed 10-0 early but rallied in a major way behind the arm of quarterback Gary Huff, who threw for 366 yards and five touchdowns. By halftime, it was 28-10 FSU and the score only got more one-sided from there. The win was FSU's seventh straight over South Carolina.

Houston

Three end-zone interceptions took the sizzle out of Florida State's passing game as Houston won 14-7 in a game stamped with rugged defensive action on both sides. Gary Huff found his target on 17 of 31 passes for 276 yards but the Cougars interceptions were too many to overcome for the Seminoles. Huff's 16 yard pass to Paul Magalski over the middle for a touchdown tied the game at 7-7. The Cougars Robert Newhouse, who ran for 196 yards, got the winning touchdown on a 16 yard sweep in the 2nd quarter. Both teams were scoreless in the 2nd half.

Georgia Tech

Quick and aggressive pass defenders of Georgia Tech gave Florida State's offense its roughest day in years as the Yellow Jackets held on for a 12-6 victory in a hard fought football game. Gary Huff completed just 12 of 41 passes for 171 yards. And the Seminoles netted just 15 more yards on the ground. The only Florida State points came on field goals of 22 and 40 yards by Frank Fontes.

TULSA

Ahead by 14-10 at halftime, Florida State cut loose with a late barrage of touchdowns and throttled Tulsa 45-10. Gary Huff threw just 20 passes and completed 12 for 285 yards, but four were for touchdowns. With Paul Magalski running for 113 yards in 18 carries, the Seminoles got 231 on the ground. The Seminoles totaled 516 yards of offense. Barry Smith started the scoring, catching a 7 yard TD pass from Huff. A 16 yard scoring pass to Kent Gaydos put the Noles in front to stay 14-7. Magalski scored on a 27 yard run in the third quarter. Frank Fontes added a 44 yard field goal. Smith got Florida State's fourth TD on an 8 yard sweep, and it was 31-10 going into the closing quarter. Huff connected with Smith on a 61 yard touchdown pass. Huff threw a 13 yard TD pass to Gaydos to wrap up the scoring.

PITTSBURGH

Gary Huff threw 26 passes, one of which gave Pittsburgh a quick 7-0 lead, then settled down to throw three touchdown passes as Florida State tripped Pittsburgh 31-13. Huff completed 17 of 26 passes for 261 yards. Huff connected with Kent Gaydos on a 52 yard play that tied it 7-7. James Jarrett scored on a 26 yard run, and after a Pitt punt, Huff passed to Gary Parris, who scored on a 23 yard play. With time running out in the half Frank Fontes kicked a 41 yard field goal for a 24-7 lead. A James Thomas interception gave the Seminoles an opportunity in the third quarter, and they stretched their lead to 31-7 on Huff's 7 yard toss to Rhett Dawson.

1971 FIESTA BOWL

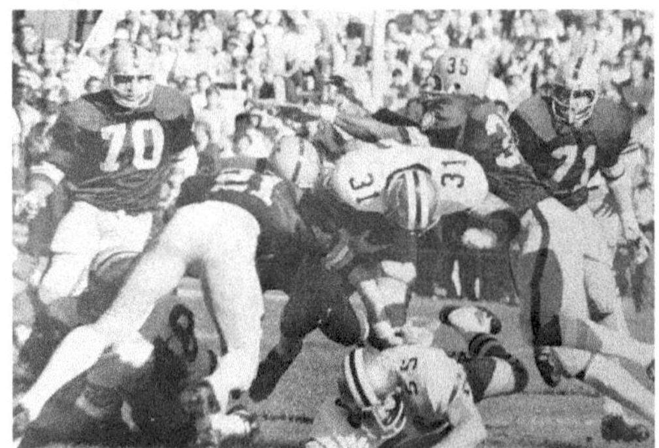

The game kicked off shortly after 1 p.m. MST and was televised by Mizlou. Calvin Demery started the scoring when he caught a touchdown pass from Danny White to give ASU an early lead, but Florida State would tie the game with a Paul Magalski touchdown run and take the lead later in the quarter with a field goal. Woody Green took the lead back for the Sun Devils with his touchdown run in the second quarter, but FSU added a field goal to narrow the lead to one. Later in the quarter, Rhett Dawson caught a pass from Kent Gaydos (normally the wide receiver) for a touchdown to give the Seminoles the lead again, with a successful conversion attempt to make it 21–14. But the Sun Devils tied the game with a Steve Holden touchdown catch from White to make it tied at 21–21. Dawson caught another touchdown, this time from quarterback Gary Huff, to give the Seminoles the lead again, and the Sun Devils went into halftime down 28–21. Arizona State started off small in the second half with an Eckstrand field goal, but later in the quarter Green put the Sun Devils ahead on his second touchdown run. Florida State tied the game with a Frank Fontes field goal in the fourth quarter. Later in the quarter, Florida State punted the ball to Holden, who returned it 58 yards for a touchdown to give Arizona State the lead 38–31. Dawson caught his third touchdown of the day to tie the game at 38. With 4:44 to play after the kickoff, the Sun Devils needed to score to win the game while giving the Noles little time, which they did as Green ran for his third touchdown of the day to give the Arizona State the lead with 34 seconds left. The Seminoles could not muster any more magic as the Sun Devils won their second consecutive bowl game and the first Fiesta Bowl. Woody Green went 101 yards on 24 carries and caught 2 passes for 41 yards for ASU, though FSU's Huff was named Offensive MVP, throwing 25 of 46 yards for 347 yards, throwing two touchdowns and interceptions.

1972 Florida State Seminoles

Larry Jones was the head coach in his second season. Jones led the Seminoles to a 7-4 record. The Seminoles began the season ranked #19 in the AP poll and rose to #13 (#20, #17, #16, #13 in the second through fifth weeks respectively) before falling out completely following their loss to Florida. They entered again at #17 after their victory against Colorado State but dropped out again after the loss at Auburn.

Hodges Mitchell led the team in rushing with 944 yards. Gary Huff led the team in passing with 2893 yards and 25 touchdown passes. Barry Smith led the team in receiving with 69 receptions for 1243 yards and 13 TD receptions. David Snell led the team with 5 pass interceptions. Mitchell had five 100 yard rushing games, Smith had eight 100 yards in receptions games and Huff had three games where he topped 300 yards passing. Phil Arnold {LB}, Gary Huff {QB}, Hodges Mitchell {RB}, Garry Parris {TE}, Barry Smith {WR} and Larry Strickland {LB} were selected to the First team All-South Independent team. Gary Huff, Barry Smith, and James Thomas {DB} were all selected as Consensus First team All-Americans. Larry Strickland was an Honorable Mention All-American by the Associated Press. Smith {Green Bay}, Thomas {Pittsburgh}, Huff {Chicago}, Eddie McMillan {DB} {Los Angeles Rams}, Charlie Hunt {LB} {San Francisco} and Garry Parris {TE} {San Diego} were selected in the 1973 NFL draft. Smith and Thomas were #1 picks.

Home games were played at Doak Campbell Stadium

9/9/1972	Florida State	**#19**	@		Pittsburgh (1-10)	19	7	**W**	
9/16/1972	Florida State	**#20**	@		Miami (5-6)	37	14	**W**	
9/23/1972	Florida State	**#17**	**vs**		VIRGINIA TECH (6-4-1)	27	15	**W**	
9/30/1972	Florida State	**#16**	@		Kansas (4-7)	44	22	**W**	
10/7/1972	Florida State	**#13**	**vs**		FLORIDA (5-5-1)	13	42	**L**	
10/14/1972	Florida State		@		Mississippi State (4-7)	25	21	**W**	**@ Jackson, MS**
10/21/1972	Florida State		**vs**		COLORADO STATE (1-10)	37	0	**W**	
10/28/1972	Florida State	**#17**	@	#12	Auburn (10-1)	14	27	**L**	
11/4/1972	Florida State		**vs**		HOUSTON (6-4-1)	27	31	**L**	
11/11/1972	Florida State		**vs**		TULSA (4-7)	23	21	**W**	
11/18/1972	Florida State		@		South Carolina (4-7)	21	24	**L**	
Coach: Larry Jones					**Season Record >>**	287	224	**7-4**	

Schedule Source: Steve's Football Bible LLC

Selected game(s) highlights

Pittsburgh

The Seminoles traveled to Pitt Stadium to play Pittsburgh. Ahmet Askin kicked two field goals and with help from the defense, the Noles left with a 19-7 victory. James Thomas blocked a Pittsburgh field goal try when the score was 0-0, stopped a Pittsburgh threat at Florida State's 13 with an end zone interception when the score was 0-0 and nailed a Pittsburgh runner for a seven yard loss on a pitchout to blunt the Panthers last real threat when the score was 19-7. Gary Huff threw touchdown passes to Barry Smith (71 yards) and Joe Goldsmith (54 yards) along with his 254 yards for the game.

Miami

The Hurricanes drew first blood, but Miami had no answer for the FSU passing combination of quarterback Gary Huff and receiver Barry Smith. The two hooked up for three touchdowns as Huff finished the day with 329 yards passing in what would eventually be a 23 point rout in favor of the Seminoles.

VIRGINIA TECH

Hodges Mitchell and Joe Goldsmith staked the Seminoles to a 14-0 first quarter lead and the defense intercepted two passes and recovered three fumbles to help beat Virginia Tech 27-15, for the third straight time. Mitchell ran for 138 yards and scored on a 3 yard run. Goldsmith caught a 40 yard TD pass from Mike Caldwell. Barry Smith had a big day, leading the Seminoles with 10 receptions for 146 yards. Gary Huff ran for a touchdown and threw a 6 yard TD pass to Mike Davison to go along with 256 yards passing on the day.

Kansas

Gary Huff passed for three second quarter touchdowns and unbeaten Florida State crushed the Kansas Jayhawks 44-22. Huff threw four touchdown passes, all in the first half, as for the afternoon he connected on 26 of 42 throws for 295 yards. Barry Smith caught two of Huff's TD passes (27 yards and 9 yards), Gary Parris caught a 14 yard TD pass and Ed Davis caught a 3 yard TD pass. Hodges Mitchell and Mike Davison both had touchdown runs in the 2nd half to seal the victory for the Seminoles.

FLORIDA

Florida traveled to Tallahassee to play the Seminoles at Doak Campbell Stadium in front of over 43,000 fans. The Gator defense forced and recovered 6 fumbles and intercepted Noles QB Gary Huff four times. David Bowden threw touchdown passes to Willie Jackson and Hollis Boardman, then Nat Moore scored on touchdown runs of 46 yards and 7 yards and the Gators were on their way to a 42-13 victory over Florida State, who were 14 point favorites going into the game. Chan Gailey added a 4 yard TD pass to Joe Goldsmith for the Gators.

Mississippi State

The Seminoles survived a blistering aerial barrage from Rockey Felker that put two touchdowns on the board in the final 66 seconds and won 25-21. Sandwiched between Felker's touchdown strikes of 21 and 13 yards to Bill Buckley and Tommy Strahan was a 49 yard burst up the middle for a touchdown by Mike Davison. In the first quarter, Gary Huff's 14 yard pass to Barry Smith provided a 7-0 lead. The Bulldogs tied it 7-7 on Melvin Barkum's 7 yard run. Then Huff went to Smith again on a 53 yard scoring strike. Soon after Ahmet Askin boomed a 46 yard field goal and that 17-7 lead stood up until 1:06 was left on the clock. Then all hell broke loose!

Auburn

Down 21-0 before it got to within real striking distance of the Auburn goal line, Florida State staged a game but futile comeback in the 2nd half as it fell 27-14. Auburn's Terry Henley scored the first three touchdowns from short yardage, one yard, four yards and two yards. He picked up 105 yards in 27 carries. Trailing 27-0 in the 4th quarter, Mike Davison ran 9 yards for a touchdown and Mike Allen caught a 17 yard TD pass from Gary Huff.

HOUSTON

Down 10-0 at halftime, and in a hole because of their early mistakes plus Houston's kicking game, the Seminoles were never ahead, were never closer after intermission than in the last half-minute when they got their final touchdown as they fell to Houston, 31-27. Gary Parris caught a 27 yard TD pass from Gary Huff to pull the Noles within 17-7. Fred Miller ran 3 yards for a touchdown and caught a 4 yard TD pass from Huff. Mike Davison ran 1 yard for a touchdown with 24 seconds left, but FSU could get no closer.

TULSA

Gary Huff threw for all three Florida State touchdowns, Mike Davison ran for 155 yards on 23 carries and the Seminoles held on for a 23-21 victory over a stubborn Golden Hurricane team. Mike Allen caught two of Huff's TD passes (30 yards and 11 yards) and Garry Parris caught a 15 yard TD pass. Huff passed for 183 yards on 14 completions in 27 attempts.

South Carolina

Freshmen Bobby Marino kicked a 38 yard field goal with 1:28 left to lift South Carolina to a 24-21 victory. The loss cost the Seminoles a bid to the Peach Bowl. The Gamecocks Neville Files recovered one fumble and intercepted three Gary Huff passes, including one that set the stage for Marino's winning 3 pointer. Gary Huff, hitting on 13 of 28 passes for 186 yards, threw three touchdown passes, all to Barry Smith, who caught five for 104 yards. Hodges Mitchell ran for 118 yards.

1973 Florida State Seminoles

Larry Jones was the head coach in his third season. Jones led the Seminoles to a 0-11 record. The Seminoles were outscored by their opponents, 331-98. The Seminoles were abysmal on offense, never scoring more than 17 points in any game. The offense had only 5 rushing touchdowns and had only 8 passing touchdowns in the season. The defense gave up an average of 30 points a game.

Hodges Mitchell led the team in rushing with 669 yards. Billy Sexton led the team in passing with 754 yards. Mike Shuman led the team in receiving with 21 catches for 380 yards. Buzzy Lewis led the team with 4 pass interceptions. Bert Cooper {DB} {Baltimore Colts} was selected in the 1974 NFL draft.

Home games were played at Doak Campbell Stadium

9/15/1973	Florida State	@		Wake Forest (1-9-1)	7	9	L
9/22/1973	Florida State	vs		KANSAS (7-4-1)	0	28	L
9/29/1973	Florida State	vs	#18	MIAMI (5-6)	10	14	L
10/6/1973	Florida State	@		Baylor (2-9)	14	21	L
10/13/1973	Florida State	vs		MISSISSIPPI STATE (4-5-2)	12	37	L
10/20/1973	Florida State	vs		MEMPHIS (8-3)	10	13	L
10/27/1973	Florida State	@		San Diego State (9-1-1)	17	38	L
11/3/1973	Florida State	@	#18	Houston (11-1)	3	34	L
11/10/1973	Florida State	@		Virginia Tech (2-9)	13	36	L
11/17/1973	Florida State	vs		SOUTH CAROLINA (7-4)	12	52	L
12/1/1973	Florida State	@		Florida (7-5)	0	49	L
Coach: Larry Jones				**Season Record >>**	98	331	**0-11**

Schedule Source: Steve's Football Bible LLC

Selected game(s) highlights

Wake Forest

Chuck Ramsey's 42 yard field goal with three seconds left dealt Florida State its first opening game loss since 1967, losing 9-7 to the Demon Deacons. Hodges Mitchell 5 yard TD run gave FSU a 7-6 lead in the 3rd quarter.

KANSAS

For the first time in 80 games, the Seminoles were shutout by Kansas, 28-0. FSU's offense turned the ball over to the on eight occasions, five interceptions and three fumbles. The Seminoles churned out 17 yards on the ground.

MIAMI

Ahmet Askin kicked a 51 yard field goal and Hodges Mitchell ran 1 yard for a touchdown to give the Seminoles a 10-7 lead going into the 4th quarter. Woody Thompson scored from 4 yards out with 6:24 left in the game to give Miami the 14-10 victory. The Seminoles had an eye-popping 132 yards of total offense compared to the Hurricanes 401 yards.

Baylor

Down 21-7 in the waning minutes of the 4th quarter, FSU rallied for a late touchdown to pull closer to the foe it had trailed all night long but ran out of steam in the last three minutes. Billy Sexton connected on a 57 yard pass to Mike Allen with 6:13 to play and put FSU back in the ball game. Hodges Mitchell ran for 109 yards for the Noles.

MISSISSIPPI STATE

Florida State got 21 first downs, and Florida State threw the football 48 times, but the Seminoles were nothing more than an inept team as they lost 37-12 to Mississippi State, who never before had beaten Florida State. Mike Shuman caught two TD passes from Mark Orlando for the Seminoles only bright spot on the day.

MEMPHIS STATE

Memphis State's defense, keyed by Van Anderson, stacked up Hodges Mitchell one yard shy of the goal line on two consecutive plays late in the third period. The result was a 13-10 Tiger triumph, the sixth straight loss this season, and the first Homecoming loss suffered at Doak Campbell Stadium in 11 years. The Seminoles jumped to a 10-0 lead on Bobby McKinnon's 74 yard TD run and Ahmet Askin's 35 yard field goal. It was all Memphis after that.

San Diego State

San Diego State, with a 38-17 thumping of the Seminoles, amassed 590 yards. Of that, 231 came on the ground, 359 in the air, which was the most FSU has ever given up. Mark Orlando, completing 19 of his 34 throws, accounted for 199 of FSU's 283 passing yards. Hodges Mitchell, with 101 yards in 23 carries, accounted for all except two of FSU's rushing net yardage of 103. Ed Davis caught a 35 yard TD pass from Billy Sexton and Jimmy Everett caught a 9 yard TD pass from Mark Orlando.

Houston

Houston handed out its annual flogging of Florida State in the Astrodome, 34-3. The Houston offense poured it on with 606 yards of total offense while the Seminoles managed 188 yards. The highlight of the game was a D.C. Nobles 83 yard touchdown pass to Brian Willingham that gave Houston a 20-3 lead.

Virginia Tech

The Seminoles traveled to Blacksburg to play a Virginia Tech team that had one win on the season. The Hokies made it two wins after steamrolling the Seminoles, 36-7, in a game that wasn't even close. The Hokies ran through gaping holes in the FSU line, rushing for 346 yards, while holding the Seminoles to 100 yards rushing. Tim McDougal caught a 15 yard TD pass from Mark Orlando and Billy Prescott ran 1 yard for a touchdown for the Noles.

SOUTH CAROLINIA

Suffering its worst loss in 12 seasons, South Carolina ran and passed to 52-12 victory. The Gamecocks rang up 565 yards of total offense and led 31-0 before Florida State decided to put some points on the board. Tom McDougal caught a 5 yard TD pass from Billy Sexton and Ricky Blythe caught a 10 yard pass from Billy Prescott. Both extra point attempts were missed.

Florida

Florida welcomed the Seminoles to Florida Field before over 62,000 fans. Nat Moore ran for two touchdowns, James Richards ran 62 yards for a touchdown, Vince Kendrick ran 1 yard for a touchdown, Don Gaffney threw a 31 yard TD pass to Lee McGriff, Chan Gailey threw a 2 yard TD pass to Glenn Severs and Larry Brinson ran 12 yards for a touchdown as the Gators routed the Seminoles, 49-0.

1974 Florida State Seminoles

Led by head coach Darrell Mudra in his first season, the Seminoles finished the season with a record of 1–10. Mack Brown was a graduate assistant on Mudra's staff. Highlight of the season was the Alabama game, in which the Seminoles took the #3 ranked Crimson Tide down to the wire, only to lose on a field goal with 33 seconds left in the game.

Larry Key led the team in rushing with 602 yards. Ron Coppess led the team in passing with 817 yards. Mike Shuman led the team in receptions with 43 and Joe Goldsmith led the team in receiving yards with 525. Bobby Jackson led the team in punt returns with an 18.2 average and tied for the team lead in pass interceptions with 2, along with Joe Camps who had 2. Bert Cooper {DE} and Mike Shuman {WR} were selected to the First team All-South Independent team. Cooper {New York Jets} was selected in the 1975 NFL draft.

Home games were played at Doak Campbell Stadium

9/14/1974	Florida State	vs	#13	PITTSBURGH (7-4)	6	9	L
9/21/1974	Florida State	vs		COLORADO STATE (4-6-1)	7	14	L
9/28/1974	Florida State	@		Kansas (4-7)	9	40	L
10/5/1974	Florida State	vs		BAYLOR (8-4)	17	21	L
10/12/1974	Florida State	@	#3	Alabama (11-1)	7	8	L
10/19/1974	Florida State	vs	#14	FLORIDA (8-4)	14	24	L
10/26/1974	Florida State	@	#5	Auburn (10-2)	6	38	L
11/2/1974	Florida State	@		Memphis (7-4)	14	42	L
11/8/1974	Florida State	@		Miami (6-5)	21	14	W
11/16/1974	Florida State	vs		VIRGINIA TECH (4-7)	21	56	L
11/23/1974	Florida State	vs	#15	HOUSTON (8-3-1)	8	23	L
Coach: Darrell Mudra				**Season Record >>**	130	289	**1-10**

Schedule Source: Steve's Football Bible LLC

Selected game(s) highlights

PITTSBURGH

Florida State got in front quickly, marching 75 yards to a touchdown from the starting kickoff, Rudy Thomas scoring on a 5 yard pass from Ron Coppess. A Seminole fumble was recovered by Pitt at the FSU 17. On three plays Tony Dorsett went over from the one that tied it 6-6. Pitt went ahead to stay the first time it got the ball in the third quarter, moving 61 yards from the kickoff to a 39 yard field goal by Carson Long. After that, it was a defensive struggle.

COLORADO STATE

Unable to recover from a horrendous beginning Florida State fell 14-7 to Colorado State. The Rams Ron Harris was too much for the Seminoles, who never got untracked on offense, who scored only after it was 14-0. The Seminoles lone touchdown was a Joe Goldsmith 5 yard TD reception from Ron Coppess.

Kansas

In control all the way, an offensively explosive Kansas team tore up Florida State 40-9. Displaying considerable versatility, the Jayhawks ripped away with big play runs and passes. Kansas scored three of the first four times it got the ball for a 21-3 lead by the middle of the second quarter. The Jayhawks led 40-3 when Leon Bright ran 6 yards for a touchdown for the Seminoles. The Noles defense allowed 560 yards, in which 366 yards were on the ground.

BAYLOR

Behind 17-0 at halftime, Baylor came on strong in the late going and handed Florida State its 16th straight defeat 21-17. Baylor drove 61 and 70 yards to touchdowns the first two times it got the ball in the third quarter and went ahead on an 86 yard drive in the fourth quarter. The running of Steve Beaird and the wingback reverses of Philip Kent keyed the charge. Beaird scored all three Baylor touchdowns from down close. Ahmet Askin kicked a 48 yard field goal and Larry Key, and Fred Miller ran for touchdowns to give FSU a halftime lead that they let get away in the 2nd half.

Alabama

Against the Seminoles, the Crimson Tide trailed until the final minute of regulation when Bucky Berrey converted the game-winning field goal for the 8–7 victory. The Seminoles took the opening kickoff and drove 78 yards on nine plays for a 7–0 lead behind a six yard Larry Key touchdown run. Florida State continued to hold their touchdown lead through the third quarter when the Crimson Tide scored their first points on a 44 yard Berrey field goal. With just 1:27 left in the game, Seminoles head coach Darrell Mudra elected to take an intentional safety instead of attempting a punt out of the end zone. He made this decision as Alabama had been close on a couple of previous attempts to block punts during the game and did not want a block to occur in the end zone. Down now 7–5, the Crimson Tide drove into field goal territory and Berrey hit the game winner from 36 yards out with only 0:33 left in the game.

FLORIDA

Florida took a 10-0 lead into halftime on a Jimmy DuBose 31 yard touchdown and a David Posey 21 yard field goal. The Noles cut the lead on a Ron Coppess 3 yard touchdown, but the Gators took over after that. Don Gaffney hit Alan Darby for a 63 yard touchdown pass and Tony Green scored from 12 yards out and the Gators held on for a 24-14 victory.

Auburn

Florida State's defense collapsed quickly in the last half, and Auburn's unbeaten football team raced away to a 38-6 victory. Trailing only 7-6 at halftime, the Seminoles were victims of a 17 point outburst by the Tigers within the first six minutes of the third quarter. Ahmet Askin kicked field goals of 47 yards and 27 yards and that was it for FSU's offensive contribution for the game.

Memphis State

Down 21-0 after the first dozen minutes. Florida State fell 42-14 to Memphis State. The Seminoles rallied to within 21-7 and were knocking at the Memphis 15 with time running out in the first half. Florida State went for a field goal, but the Tigers Steve Cacciola tore through, blocked it, and raced with the ball 78 yards to a touchdown that put the game rather out of reach at 28-7. On the passing of Steve Mathieson, Florida State fought back to within 28-14. Memphis extended the score with two late touchdowns. Larry Key ran 10 yards for a touchdown and Mike Shuman caught a 22 yard TD pass from Mathieson.

Miami

After 20 straight losses, Florida State would earn its only victory of the 1974 season and first under head coach Darrell Mudra. Leon Bright rushed for 105 yards and a score in the rivalry win. Miami made it interesting with two long touchdown passes in the fourth quarter, but a short touchdown run from Jeff Leggett put the game away.

VIRGINIA TECH

Down 14-0 after the first six minutes, Florida State choked on the wishbone offense of Virginia Tech as it fell 56-21 before a homecoming crowd of 27,707 at Doak Campbell Stadium. On the brilliant play of Leon Bright, who scored on a 55 yard pass play and a 100 yard kickoff runback, the Seminoles hung in at halftime 35-21. But Tech scored the first two times it got the football after intermission and put it out of reach. In 71 runs from the wishbone, Tech piled up 410 yards on the ground - most ever against a Florida State team. Bobby Jackson returned a punt 80 yards for a touchdown late in the first half to cut the lead to 35-21.

HOUSTON

Trailing only 7-0 at halftime, Florida State yielded to Houston's formidable running game, 23-8, before over 18,000 fans at Doak Campbell Stadium. Reggie Cherry got 170 yards for the Cougars. The Seminoles avoided the shutout when Jimmy Black threw a 15 yard TD pass to Mike Shuman.

1975 Florida State Seminoles

Led by head coach Darrell Mudra in his second and final season, the Seminoles finished the season with a record of 3–8. FSU showed slight improvement over the previous season and finally got a win against their nemesis, the Houston Cougars, breaking a 7 game losing streak to Houston.

Leon Bright led the team in rushing with 675 yards. Clyde Walker led the team in passing with 1619 yards and 10 touchdown passes. Mike Shuman led the team in receiving with 38 catches and 730 yards. Bobby Jackson led the team in pass interceptions with 5. Leon Bright {RB}, Jeff Gardner {G} and Bobby Jackson {DB} were selected to the First team All-South Independent team. Greg Johnson {DT} {Philadelphia}, Randy Coffield {LB} {Seattle}, Lee Nelson {DB} {St. Louis Cardinals}, Eddie McMillan {DB} {Seattle} and Barry Smith {WR} {Tampa Bay} were selected in the 1976 NFL draft.

Home games were played at Doak Campbell Stadium

9/13/1975	Florida State	@		Texas Tech (6-5)	20	31	L
9/20/1975	Florida State	vs		UTAH STATE (6-5)	17	8	W
9/27/1975	Florida State	vs		IOWA STATE (4-7)	6	10	L
10/4/1975	Florida State	@		Georgia Tech (7-4)	0	30	L
10/11/1975	Florida State	@		Virginia Tech (8-3)	10	13	L
10/18/1975	Florida State	@	#14	Florida (9-3)	8	34	L
10/25/1975	Florida State	vs		AUBURN (3-6-2)	14	17	L
11/1/1975	Florida State	@		Clemson (2-9)	43	7	W
11/8/1975	Florida State	vs		MEMPHIS (7-4)	14	17	L
11/15/1975	Florida State	vs		MIAMI (2-8)	22	24	L
11/22/1975	Florida State	@	#18	Houston (2-8)	33	22	W
Coach: Darrell Mudra				**Season Record >>**	187	213	**3-8**

Schedule Source: Steve's Football Bible LLC

Selected game(s) highlights

Texas Tech

With 9:49 left in the football game, Florida State was very much in it. With 9:39 showing on the clock, the Seminoles were altogether out of it. Scoring two touchdowns within 10 seconds of one another in the fourth quarter, Texas Tech won it 31-20. Bobby Taylor scored from 16 yards out for Tech, then on the ensuing kickoff, Leon Bright fumbled, and Tech recovered and on the next play Rodney Allison ran 21 yards for a touchdown for a 31-14 Red Raider lead. Mike Barnes hauled in 24 yard touchdown pass from Steve Mathieson for FSU's final score.

UTAH STATE

The lone home victory of 1975 saw Florida State get the better of Utah State in a defensive struggle. Leon Bright rushed for 138 yards in the win while quarterback Clyde Walker threw a pair of touchdown passes in the first half, one for 42 yards to Ed Backman and one to Larry Key for 27 yards.

IOWA STATE

Clyde Walker threw to Mike Shumann,for 78 yards and a touchdown that got them a 6-0 lead that stood for a half, then the Seminoles offense was shut down by the Cyclone defense for the rest of the game as Iowa State left Tallahassee with a 10-6 victory. FSU's kicker, Keith Singletary, had an extra point attempt blocked and missed two field goals, one from 24 yards and one from 20 yards.

Georgia Tech

After just three possessions with the football, only 26 plays from scrimmage, the Yellow Jackets had a 20-0 lead on the way to a 30-0 shutout victory over the Seminoles. Steve Raible scored on end around plays, from 17 and 24 yards out and scored on a 42 yard TD reception. Tech, operating without a huddle in the first half, churned out 367 yards running from its wishbone formation.

Virginia Tech

Wayne Latimer's 61 yard field goal, a yard short of the national collegiate record, with eight minutes remaining lifted Virginia Tech to a 13-10 homecoming triumph at Lane Stadium in Blacksburg. The field goal came on the heels of a 36 yard touchdown run by Roscoe Coles that tied it 10-10. Clyde Walker's quarterback sneak from the one, capping a 72 yard drive, Florida State grabbed a 7-3 lead in the second quarter, then stretched it to 10-3 on Keith Singletary's 30 yard field goal in the third period.

Florida

Florida hosted the Seminoles at Florida Field before a crowd of over 64,000. Jimmy Dubose ran for 204 yards and Jimmy Green ran for two touchdowns as the Gators rolled to a 34-8 victory. Jimmy Fisher passed 10 yards to Wes Chandler for a touchdown, Larry Brinson scored from 2 yards out and David Posey added field goals from 51 yards and 50 yards. The Gators offense rolled up 404 yards and the Gators have now won 15 of the 18 meetings in this rivalry.

AUBURN

Auburn traveled to Tallahassee to play the Seminoles at Doak Campbell Stadium. Sedrick McIntyre scored from 1 yard out, Rick Neel returned a kickoff 92 yards for a touchdown and Neil O'Donoghue kicked a 20 yard field goal in the 3rd quarter for the winning points as the Tigers beat FSU 17-14. The Seminoles had a chance to tie the game with under a minute left but Keith Singletary missed a 29 yard field goal attempt.

Clemson

Florida State marched 84, 70 and 80 yards to touchdowns three of the first four times it got the ball. It was 14-0 before the Tigers had managed as many as four plays from scrimmage. And it was 26-7 before Clemson had run as many as 11 plays. Florida State scored in every quarter, including 20 in the first. Amassing 497 yards, with Larry Key's 15 carries getting 105 yards of a 302 total on the ground, the Seminoles extracted six turnovers from the home team as an unbelieving crowd of 33,000 at Memorial Stadium looked on. Florida State's scoring parade went as such: Clyde Walker's 6 yard pass to Shumann, Leon Bright's 2 yard run, Walker's 16 yard pass to Shumann, Key on a 16 yard screen pass from Walker, a 2 yard run by Rudy Thomas, and Mathieson's 1 yard sneak.

MEMPHIS STATE

The kickoff was delayed more than 40 minutes by a power failure that left the whole of the stadium in total darkness. Having twice come from behind, Florida State led 14-10 and had the ball at the Memphis State 40 with 6:24 left when it came to fourth and one. Instead of punting, the Seminoles gambled on making the first down. Clyde Walker was just short of his sneak attempt. The Tigers took over and drove for the winning touchdown in seven plays with Lloyd Patterson scoring from six yards out with 3:04 remaining in the game. The Seminoles scores were on a Rudy Thomas 6 yard run and Ed Beckman's 11 yard TD reception from Walker.

MIAMI

Miami won it 24-22 on a 29 yard field goal by Chris Dennis with 17 seconds remaining. Ahead 14-0 early, then 21-6 with a quarter to play, Miami trailed 22-21 with 4:44 left as Clyde Walker came on at quarterback a Seminoles comeback. Miami had set up its third touchdown by blocking a Florida State punt at the Seminole 35. Miami got itself a last chance by putting pressure on punter Bill Duley, who managed a mere 17 yarder that gave the Hurricanes a chance from the FSU 42 with 2:11 to go. Walker entered the game in the second quarter with the Seminoles behind 14-0. Just before halftime he guided a 56 yard drive, capped by a 1 yard run by Rudy Thomas, cutting the score to 14-6. Early in the third quarter the Seminoles climaxed a 72 yard drive with another Thomas run from the one. The Seminoles got a third touchdown on Larry Key's 31 yard run the play after recovery of a Miami fumble.

Houston

Florida State overcame a 10-0 disadvantage and crushed Houston 33-22 at the Astrodome. Florida State won it despite four lost fumbles and 135 yards in penalties. Trailing 13-10 at intermission, Florida State ran all over the Cougars in the last half. Larry Key carries 22 times for 108 yards and Rudy

Thomas added 78 on 19 carries. Key and Thomas both ran for 2 touchdowns and Keith Singletary kicked two field goals.

1976 Florida State Seminoles

The 1976 season marked the first season for Bobby Bowden as coach. Bowden would go on to coach the Seminoles for 34 seasons until 2009.

Larry Key led the team in rushing with 712 yards and had a season high 97 yard touchdown run. Jimmy Black led the team in passing with 1506 yards and 9 touchdown passes. Ed Beckman led the team in receptions with 37 and Kurt Unglaub led the team in receiving yards with 665 and had a season high 96 yard touchdown reception. Key led the team in punt returns with a 19.3 average. Ed Beckman {TE} and Jon Thames {OT} were selected to the First team All-South Independent team and were both named Honorable Mention All-Americans by the Associated Press. Gary Woolford {DB} {Houston Oilers} and Steve Mathieson {QB} {Detroit} were selected in the 1977 NFL draft.

Home games were played at Doak Campbell Stadium

9/11/1976	Florida State	@		Memphis (7-4)	12	21	L
9/18/1976	Florida State	@		Miami (3-8)	0	47	L
9/25/1976	Florida State	@	#4	Oklahoma (9-2-1)	9	24	L
10/2/1976	Florida State	vs		KANSAS STATE (1-10)	20	10	W
10/9/1976	Florida State	@	#13	Boston College (8-3)	28	9	W
10/16/1976	Florida State	vs	#12	FLORIDA (8-4)	26	33	L
10/23/1976	Florida State	@		Auburn (3-8)	19	31	L
10/30/1976	Florida State	vs		CLEMSON (3-6-2)	12	15	L
11/6/1976	Florida State	vs		SOUTHERN MISS (2-9)	30	27	W
11/13/1976	Florida State	@		North Texas (6-5)	21	20	W
11/20/1976	Florida State	vs		VIRGINIA TECH (6-5)	28	21	W
Coach: Bobby Bowden				**Season Record >>**	205	258	**5-6**

Schedule Source: Steve's Football Bible LLC

Selected game(s) highlights

Memphis State

Early in the game the Seminoles forced a fumble out of Ricky Rivas. FSU recovered and Dave Cappelen kicked a field goal from 20 yards for a 3-0 lead. It held up until a minute and a half before intermission. Helped by penalties, Memphis went ahead 7-3 on a Lloyd Patterson pass of eight yards to fullback Zacky Butler. Memphis dominated the third quarter. The Tigers drove 84 yards to a touchdown that came on Patterson's 12 yard pass to Keith Wright. They got a third one on a 51 yard drive capped by Patterson's scrambling 6 yard run. Florida State narrowed it early in the fourth quarter as Jimmy Black directed a quick 80 yard drive, capped by Larry Key's determined 5 yard run.

Miami

Florida State got blown out 47-0 by Miami. It was the Seminoles' second biggest margin of defeat in history. Miami's I-attack offense gained 453 yards of offense, FSU managed 174, much of it late, only 26 of it running. The Seminoles trailed 31-0 at halftime.

Oklahoma

The Seminoles went ahead, 6-3 on the second time they got the football. They moved 80 yards in a dozen plays, scored on a 5 yard run by Larry Key. Trailing 10-6 late in the first half, Florida State moved inside the Oklahoma 1 yard line. But a fumble following a pitchout was well played by the Sooners ended an opportunity to retake the lead. Oklahoma's Wishbone offense got 513 yards on offense, including 455 running. Horace Ivory scored each of Oklahoma's first two TD's and ran nine times for 112 yards.

KANSAS STATE

Florida State trailed Kansas State 10-0 at the break but drew even in the third quarter. After Dave Cappelen's 41 yard field goal gave FSU its first lead, the Seminoles put the game away on Jimmy Black's second touchdown pass of the day to Kurt Unglaub with 2:46 remaining in the game.

Boston College

Florida State knocked Boston College from the ranks of the nation's unbeaten in one of the season's bigger upsets. The score was 28-9. The Eagles were ranked 13th nationally by The AP poll. Rudy Thomas got the Seminoles on the board first with a 12 yard scoring run. A fumbled pitchout gave Florida State the ball at B.C.'s 15 early in the third quarter, and Jimmy Black scored on an 11 yard keeper. After another BC fumble, Mark Lyles scored a touchdown from the one yard line. Rudy Maloy plucked a fumble out of the air, off the fingertips of Eagle quarterback Ken Smith, and scampered 65 yards to a final Florida State touchdown.

FLORIDA

The Gators traveled to Tallahassee to play the Seminoles before over 42,000 fans at Doak Campbell Stadium. Florida jumped to a 10-0 1st quarter lead on a David Posey 27 yard field goal and a Larry Brinson 15 yard touchdown run. Posey kicked a school record 54 yard field goal in the 2nd quarter, then Jimmy Fisher's 23 yard scoring pass to Wes Chandler, giving Florida a 20-17 halftime lead. Posey added a 47 yard field goal, then Willie Wilder scored on a 5 yard run and the Gators held on for a 33-26 victory. The Gators ran for 264 yards and Jimmy Fisher passed for 139 yards.

Auburn

Florida State traveled to the Plains to play Auburn at Jordan-Hare Stadium before over 58,000 fans. Striking hard in the last half, Auburn's football team gave Florida State a rather harsh 31-19 lesson on Saturday afternoon. Phil Gargis, a rugged scrambler of a quarterback, scored all four of the Tigers' touchdowns on runs of one, 14, one and 82 yards. The Seminoles trailed 14-13 at intermission. The Seminoles pulled to within 21-19 late in the third quarter on Jeff Leggett's sudden scoring run of 53 yards. Gargis ran for 129 yards and Bob Bradley ran for 122 yards as the Tigers ran up an even 400 yards on the ground.

CLEMSON

Clemson traveled to Tallahassee to play Bobby Bowden's Florida State squad at Doak Campbell Stadium. The Tigers trailed 9-0 at halftime and rallied in the 2nd half behind Steve Fuller's 7 yard TD pass to Joey Walter and Fuller scoring from 1 yard out to give Clemson a 15-12 upset of the Seminoles.

SOUTHERN MISSISSIPPI

Rudy Thomas lifted Florida State, on three last quarter touchdowns, to an astonishing 30-27 victory over Southern Mississippi. Trailing 27-10 going into that fourth period, the Seminoles got three touchdowns from Thomas. Thomas scored on runs of 10 yards and 4 yards, then on a 95 yard pass play as quarterback Jimmy Black threw from deep in his end zone.

North Texas

Florida State rose up on the passing arm of Jimmy Black and put down North Texas State 21-20. Snow that fell during the night, then stopped, then started again left Fouts Field covered with the white stuff. No yard line could be seen, only the markers on the concrete walls beyond the sidelines. Snow three to four inches deep covered players' shoe tops. The Seminoles won it with a dramatic drive in the closing minutes. Jeff Leggett capped a 68 yard drive with a run from seven yards out. Coach Bobby Bowden then called for a timeout to get a 2 point play down pat. Florida State made it look easy as Black pitched to Larry Key, who lobbed a pass into Kurt Unglaub's waiting hands in the end zone, shifting the score from 20-19 to 21-20. Black completed 12 of 18 passes for 192 yards. Tops was a 91 yard bomb to Unglaub that provided a 13-7 lead early in the final half.

VIRGINIA TECH

Florida State rallied on the remarkable young arm of Jimmy Jordan for a stirring 28-21 victory over Virginia Tech. Jordan won it with the longest touchdown pass in FSU history, a 96 yarder to Kurt Unglaub with 5:45 to play. Entering the game at the start of the fourth quarter, the Seminoles behind 21-14, Jordan had quickly uncorked a 33 yard scoring pass to Jackie Flowers. Jordan threw only five times, completing four for 163 yards and the two touchdowns. The game also saw the longest scoring run in Florida State's record book, a 97 yarder in the first quarter by Larry Key, who picked up 154 yards rushing. Florida State's other touchdown was also a big play, a 75 yard pass from Jimmy Black to Mike Barnes.

1977 Florida State Seminoles

The 1977 season marked the second season for Bobby Bowden as coach. The Seminoles finished 10-2 on the season and were invited to the Tangerine Bowl to Texas Tech from the Southwest Conference. The Seminoles broke a 9-game losing streak to Florida.

Larry Key led the team with 1117 yards rushing. Wally Woodham and Jimmy Jordan led the team in passing with 1270 yards for Woodham and 1139 yards for Jordan, who led with 10 touchdown passes. Roger Overby led the team in receptions with 38 and Mike Shuman led the team in receiving yards with 701. Key led the team in kickoff returns with a 22.0 average. Ivory Joe Hunter led the team in pass interceptions with 4. **Aaron Carter set a single season record with 181 tackles.**

Wade Johnson {G}, Willie Jones {DE}, Larry Key {RB}, Mike Shuman {WR} and Nat Terry {DB} were selected to the First team All-South Independent team. Johnson, Jones, Key, Ron Simmons {DT} and Terry were named Honorable Mention All-Americans by the Associated Press. Bobby Jackson {DB} {New York Jets}, Louis Richardson {DE} {New York Jets}, Key {Green Bay} and Terry {Pittsburgh} were selected in the 1978 NFL draft.

Home games were played at Doak Campbell Stadium

9/10/1977	Florida State		@		Southern Miss (6-6)		35	6	W
9/17/1977	Florida State		@		Kansas State (1-10)		18	10	W
9/24/1977	Florida State		vs		MIAMI (3-8)		17	23	L
10/1/1977	Florida State		@	#17	Oklahoma State (4-7)		25	17	W
10/8/1977	Florida State		vs		CINCINNATI (5-4-2)		14	0	W
10/22/1977	Florida State		vs		AUBURN (5-6)		24	3	W
10/29/1977	Florida State	#20	vs		NORTH TEXAS (9-2)		35	14	W
11/5/1977	Florida State	#15	@		Virginia Tech (3-7-1)		23	21	W
11/12/1977	Florida State	#16	vs		MEMPHIS (6-5)		30	9	W
11/19/1977	Florida State	#13	@		San Diego State (10-1)		16	41	L
12/3/1977	Florida State	#19	@		Florida (6-4-1)	ABC	37	9	W
12/23/1977	**Florida State**	**#19**	**vs**		**Texas Tech (7-5)**	Mizlou	**40**	**17**	**W**
Coach: Bobby Bowden					**Season Record >>**		314	170	**10-2**

Schedule Source: Steve's Football Bible LLC

Selected game(s) highlights

Southern Mississippi

Florida State settled down in the 2nd half and rolled to a 35-6 victory over a stunned Southern Mississippi. The Seminoles were scoreless until a minute remained in the first half, when Ron Simmons blocked a punt and Scott Warren picked up the ball and ran it 2 yards for a touchdown that put the Noles on top to stay at 7-3. Florida State stretched it out to 14-6 in the third period, then exploded for three fourth quarter touchdowns. Jimmy Jordan threw two touchdown passes, one to Greg Lazzaro (34 yards) and one to Kurt Unglaub (8 yards). Mark Lyles scored from 1 yards out and Greg Ramsey caught a 12 yard TD pass from Wally Woodham.

Kansas State

Larry Key ran for 120 yards and became the first Florida State football player ever to go over the 2,000 mark in career yardage. It was the defense that did it as the Seminoles struggled to an 18-10 victory over Kansas State. The defense held K-State to just seven first downs and 173 total yards. Jimmy Jordan passed nine yards to a wide open Mike Shumann for a touchdown. The Seminoles went for two points, Jordan again hitting Shumann, making it 8-7. In the early going of the last quarter K-State regained the lead, 10-8 on a 19 yard field goal by Kris Thompson. With 6:58 to go in the game the Seminoles capped an 80 yard drive with Dave Cappelen's 27 yard field goal, moving back up 11-10. Then, with 2:27 left, Jordan hit Shumann at the goal line for a 26 yard touchdown.

MIAMI

Down 17-10, Miami ripped off 13 points in the final nine minutes and ended the Seminoles' five-game winning streak 23-17. Behind 10-0 after the 1st quarter, the Seminoles rallied to go ahead 11-10, then 17-10. Kenneth McMillian threw a 3 yard TD pass to Karl Monroe. Chris Dennis tied it 17-17 with 8:46 left. The next series saw a Jordan pass intercepted and Dennis kick the first of two 47 yard field goals for a 20-17 Miami lead as the clock showed 5:02. Then, with 4:11 remaining, Florida State gambled with a fourth-down pass at its 40. The pass was missed. Miami took over, and got another Dennis field goal, for 23-17 with 2:09 left. Miami's fifth interception of the game spoiled FSU's last possession of the football.

Oklahoma State

With Larry Key and Wally Woodham leading the way, Florida State patched up its tattered offense and stuck it to Oklahoma State 25-17. Down 17-3 in the early minutes of the last half, the surprising Seminoles erupted for 22 point in a hurry. Key ran a school-record 32 times, including 14 times in the closing quarter. Key gained 127 yards running, 72 more on three pass receptions, and 60 on his single kickoff return. Woodham took over for starter Jimmy Jordan at quarterback late in the first half, the Seminoles trailing 10-0. With Woodham in, Florida State got points on the board four out of the five times it had the football. He completed nine of his 16 passes for 145 yards. Dave Cappelen kicked 36 and 30 yard field goals, the last one put FSU ahead to stay 18-17 with 6:36 left. Mark Lyles ran 2 yards for a touchdown and Wally Woodham ran 2 yards for a touchdown and threw an 18 yard TD pass to Larry Key.

CINCINNATI

The Seminoles put down a rather pedestrian Cincinnati team 14-0. Wally Woodham threw for 265 yards and two touchdown passes, one to Mike Shuman (15 yards) and one to Roger Overby (36 yards) to lead the Seminoles to victory. The Seminole defense forced six turnovers, 4 interceptions and 2 fumble recoveries.

AUBURN

Auburn traveled to Tallahassee to play #18 ranked Florida State at Doak Campbell Stadium. The Seminoles led 10-3 at halftime as the Tigers had trouble holding on to the ball. Larry Key led the charge in the 2nd half as the Noles held on for a 24-3 victory. Key had 170 yards rushing and ran for two touchdowns.

NORTH TEXAS

With Ron Simmons and Willie Jones putting the spurs to a spectacular clutch defense, Florida State rolled over North Texas State 35-14. Florida State had drove 78 yards to a 7-0 lead on the game's opening series, Wally Woodham scoring from the one. North Texas tied it 7-7 in the second quarter as Mike Jones scored from the one, capping an 85 yard drive. The Seminoles scored two touchdowns within a span of 44 playing seconds without a single offensive play from scrimmage. With 3:08 left in the first half, Bobby Butler blocked a punt that Ivory Joe Hunter picked up and took 19 yards for a touchdown. That made it 14-7. Ken Smith came in at quarterback for the Mean Green and on the first play, an attempted draw, saw a bobbled handoff at the goal line, and Willie Jones claimed the ball in the end zone for an FSU touchdown that brought it to 21-7 at halftime. Simmons sacked the quarterback five times during the game for a total yardage loss of 51.

Virginia Tech

A 29 yard field goal by Dave Cappelen finally beat Virginia Tech 23-21 on a wet, grey homecoming afternoon before 36,500 folks at Lane Stadium in Blacksburg. Just moments before, Tech had drove 77 yards, all on the ground, for a 21-20 lead. A 39 yard pass by Mike Shumann off a reverse set up the winning 3 pointer, with Roger Overby on the receiving end. Cappelen had three field goals for the afternoon, the other two coming from 42 and 26 yards out. Trailing 14-3, Wally Woodham threw a 10 yard

TD pass to Mike Shuman. Woodham sneaked in from the one yard line to give the Noles a 17-14 lead. Cappelen kicked two field goals, the game winner coming with 4:57 remaining in the game.

MEMPHIS STATE

With a stinging defense that threw Memphis State backs for losses at least 15 times, Florida State ground out a 30-9 victory. Nose Guard Fred Igaz sacked Memphis quarterbacks three times. Just before halftime the Noles struck for a 10-0 lead. Dave Cappelen capped an 83 yard drive with a 30 yard field goal. Moments later, Willie Jones tackled a Memphis back and Jimmy Heggins hopped on the fumble at the Tiger 30. Woodham passed 27 yards to Mike Shumann for the touchdown. In the early moments of the fourth quarter, Bowden inserted Jimmy Jordan at quarterback. Jordan promptly directed a 50 yard drive for a touchdown. Mark Lyles scored from the four for a 20-3 lead. With Jordan still in there, the Seminoles got points on their next two series, Cappelen booting a 21 yard field goal and Greg Lazzaro grabbing a 13 yard TD pass, extending it to 30-3.

San Diego State

Unable to cope with the brilliant dropback passing of Joe Davis, error-ridden Florida State fell to San Diego State 41-16. In the first half, a mishandled punt, a fumble, a blocked punt and an interception gave San Diego the football at FSU's 13, 12, 17 and 48. That led to 24 Aztec points. Florida State got a 22 yard field goal from Dave Cappelen late in the first quarter to cut the score to 14-3. Early in the second period Wally Woodham threw a 42 yard TD pass to Mike Shumann to narrow it to 21-10. But later Woodham fumbled at his 12 when blind-sided, and the Aztecs moved to a quick TD to make it 28-10. Trailing 41-10, Jimmy Jordan threw a 19 yard TD pass to Roger Overby for the final points of the game.

Florida

Florida hosted the Seminoles at Florida Field and Bobby Bowden, and his Seminoles broke a 9 game losing streak to Florida with a 37-9 thumping of the Gators. The Seminoles rolled up 578 yards of total offense while holding the Gators to 200 yards of total offense. Berj Yepremian kicked three field goals for all of the Gators points. The Noles quarterbacks, Wally Woodham and Jim Jordan operated the FSU offense with smooth efficiency all game as they combined to pass for 344 yards. The pair was affectionately known as the Seminoles two-headed quarterback, Wally Jim Jordham.

1977 TANGERINE BOWL

Jimmy Jordan threw 18-of-25 for 311 yards and three touchdowns on the way to an MVP effort. Florida State had 22 first downs to Texas Tech's 21 first downs. Tech had 99 rushing yards (on 44 carries) while the Seminoles had 85 (on 37 carries). Florida State threw for 455 passing yards while the Red Raiders threw for 379. The Seminoles had two turnovers, but the Red Raiders turned it over four times. While Florida State had 10 penalties for 130 yards, they managed to convert their opportunities into points, whereas Tech did not do as such, at least until the second half when it was too late. Roger Overby caught two touchdown passes and Larry Key returned a kickoff 93 yards for a touchdown for the Seminoles.

1978 Florida State Seminoles

The 1978 season marked the third season for Bobby Bowden as coach. The Seminoles finished 8-3 on the season and were not invited to a Bowl game.

Holmes Johnson led the team in rushing with 817 yards. Jimmy Jordan and Wally Woodham led the team in passing. Jordan had 1427 yards and 14 touchdown passes. Woodham had 1322 yards and 9 touchdown passes. Jackie Flowers led the team in receiving with 43 catches and 757 yards with 7 touchdowns. Keith Jones led the team in pass interceptions with 4. Jackie Flowers {TD}, Mike Good {G}, Nate Henderson {T}, Willie Jones {DE} and Ron Simmons {NG} were selected to the First team All-South Independent team. Flowers, Good, Jones, Henderson and Simmons were all named Honorable Mention All-Americans by the Associated Press. Jones {Oakland} and Henderson {St. Louis Cardinals} were selected in the 1979 NFL draft.

Home games were played at Doak Campbell Stadium

9/9/1978	Florida State	#17	@		Syracuse (3-8)		28	0	W
9/16/1978	Florida State	#16	vs		OKLAHOMA STATE (3-8)		38	20	W
9/23/1978	Florida State	#13	@		Miami (6-5)	ABC	31	21	W
9/30/1978	Florida State	#10	vs		HOUSTON (9-3)		21	27	L
10/7/1978	Florida State	#18	vs		CINCINNATI (5-6)		26	21	W
10/14/1978	Florida State	#15	@		Mississippi State (6-5)		27	55	L
10/21/1978	Florida State		@	#16	Pittsburgh (8-4)		3	7	L
10/28/1978	Florida State		@		Southern Miss (7-4)		38	16	W
11/11/1978	Florida State		vs		VIRGINIA TECH (4-7)		24	14	W
11/18/1978	Florida State		vs		NAVY (9-3)	ABC	38	6	W
11/25/1978!	Florida State		vs		FLORIDA (4-7)		38	21	W
Coach: Bobby Bowden					**Season Record >>**		312	208	**8-3**

Schedule Source: Steve's Football Bible LLC

Selected game(s) highlights

Syracuse

Florida State's defensive performance led by linebacker Paul Piurowski, end Willie Jones and nose guard Ron Simmons limited the Orangemen to just five first downs. Clinging to a 7-0 lead going into the 4th quarter, Florida State moved to three lightning-like touchdowns in the first eight minutes of 4th quarter. Grady King caught a 4 yard TD pass from Jimmy Jordan, Jackie Flowers caught a 15 TD pass from Wally Woodham and Gator Cherry ran 9 yards for a touchdown as the Seminoles shutout Syracuse, 28-0.

OKLAHOMA STATE

Jimmy Jordan led Florida State to a 38-20 victory over Oklahoma State. Jordan completed 17 of 28 passes for 231 yards and three touchdowns. When Oklahoma State fumbled away the football at its 35, Jordan required just one play, a 35 yard TD pass to Holmes Johnson to get on the board. When the Cowboys fumbled on their next play from scrimmage, with FSU grabbing the ball at the Cowboy 32, Jordan again needed just one play, a 32 yard TD pass to Kurt Unglaub. Johnson later scored on an 8 yard run and caught a 2 yard TD pass from Jordan. Mark Lyles added a 1 yard run to complete the Seminoles scoring.

Miami

The Seminoles came from behind twice and hung on to whip Miami in a strange, error-ridden game 31-21. Ron Simmons blocked a Miami punt, and Mark Macek picked up the bouncing football and rambled 48 yards for a Seminole touchdown. It was the afternoon's biggest play for Florida State. The blocked punt was one of seven turnovers for Miami, which also lost three fumbles and had three passes intercepted. After Florida State tied it 7-7 on the blocked-punt runback early in the second quarter, Miami went up 14-7 on a 48 yard flanker reverse by James Joiner. Florida State drove right back to the tie again, 14-14. Jimmy Jordan passed three yards to Jackie Flowers for the touchdown. Wally Woodham ran for a 1 yard touchdown and passed 22 yards to Mark Lyles for a touchdown to wrap up the scoring for the Noles.

HOUSTON

Behind 27-0 after the first 20 minutes of play, Florida State came within one penalty of registering the most astounding comeback in its history. Houston won the game 27-21 before a crowd of 41,142 in Doak Campbell Stadium. With 2:55 left in the game, Wally Woodham passed 22 yards to Jackie Flowers for an apparent touchdown, but an official's flag had fallen upfield. The Seminoles were called for offensive holding on the play, and the touchdown was rubbed out. Taking over for Jimmy Jordan just after the score became 27-0, Woodham guided Florida State to touchdowns on three of the next four series. Jackie Flowers caught six passes for 165 yards. Woodham finished with 12 completions in 18 attempts for 249 yards. Mark Lyles ran for two touchdowns and Woodham threw a 72 yard TD pass to Flowers.

CINCINNATI

On a fourth down and 22, Jimmy Jordan hit Sam Platt with a pass that he converted into a 54 yard scoring play with 1:29 left, providing a dramatic 26-21 victory over a stubborn Cincinnati team. Wally Woodham ran for a 1 yard touchdown and threw an 18 yard TD pass to Jackie Flowers, who caught 9 passes for 135 yards. Jimmy Jordan threw a 5 yard TD pass to Grady King in addition to the game winner to Platt.

Mississippi State

Busting loose for three touchdowns within a third quarter playing span of 3 minutes and 24 seconds, Mississippi State came from behind and routed Florida State 55-27 in Starkville. Never in the 32 year history of Seminole football had any team run up as many total yards against Florida State, nor had an opponent passed for as many yards. Mississippi State gained 378 yards passing, 596 in total. After falling behind 14-0 at the end of the 1st quarter, the Seminoles put 21 points on the board in the 2nd quarter on Jimmy Jordan's two TD passes to Jackie Flowers (8 yards) and Sam Platt (10 yards). Holmes Johnson added a 1 yard touchdown run. Mississippi State scored the next 41 points. After the game was out of control, Jimmy Jordan threw a 52 yard TD pass to Gator Cherry.

Pittsburgh

Florida State's offense failed to score a touchdown for the first time in 28 games, and the Seminoles lost a football game 7-3 before a homecoming crowd of 55,104 at Pitt Stadium. Dave Cappelan kicked a 26 yard field goal in the 1st quarter and Pitt's Rooster Jones scored on a 14 yard run for all the scoring in the game.

Southern Mississippi

Wally Woodham passed for four touchdowns, Florida State scored in every quarter and thundered to a 38-16 victory before 23,248 homecoming fans in Hattiesburg. Completing 16 of 24 throws for 237 yards, Woodham threw scoring strikes of 23 and 61 yards to Jackie Flowers the two times FSU laid hands on the ball in the last half. He also threw 11 yards to Sam Platt and 1 yard to Grady King for touchdowns. Greg Ramsey scored on a 2 yard run in the 1st quarter to stake the Seminoles to a 7-0 lead.

VIRGINIA TECH

Down 14-3 with seconds remaining in the first half, Florida State rallied behind a suddenly fierce defense and pulled out a 24-14 victory over Virginia Tech. Holmes Johnson, ran for 152 yards on 27 carries for the Seminoles, and scored the touchdown that put the Seminoles in front to stay with 10:20 left in the game. The Seminoles rolled up 470 yards and got 272 on the ground. Mark Lyles ran for two touchdowns to help the Seminole cause.

NAVY

Coming off the bench in the second quarter, Jimmy Jordan threw four touchdown passes and Florida State sank the Navy 38-6. The Seminoles held a tenuous 7-6 lead at halftime. On successive series in the 2nd half, Jordan threw touchdown passes of 4 yards, 36 yards and 51 yards to Sam Platt and then one of 23 yards to Grady King. The Seminoles offense rolled up 453 yards led by Jordan, who threw for 280 yards. Platt caught 6 passes for 145 yards in addition to his 3 TD catches.

FLORIDA

Florida traveled to Tallahassee to play the Seminoles before over 48,000 at Doak Campbell Stadium. Florida State raced to a 21-0 first quarter lead. Gator fumbles led to the first two Noles touchdowns. Florida roared back, tying the game at 21 on David Johnson 1 yard touchdown runs and a John Brantley 12 yard TD pass to Tony Stephens. The Seminoles dominated the second half on the way to a 38-21 victory. **Willie Jones set a single game record with 5 sacks.**

1979 Florida State Seminoles

The team was coached by Bobby Bowden in his fourth season. Bowden was named the All-South Independent Coach of the Year. Florida State finished #6 in the AP poll and #8 in the UPI poll with an 11–1 record. The Seminoles' offense scored 326 points while the defense allowed 160 points. The Seminoles finished the regular season unbeaten for only the second time in program history and played in the Orange Bowl.

Mark Lyles led the team in rushing with 1011 yards and 8 touchdowns. Jimmy Jordan led the team in passing with 1173 yards and threw 13 touchdown passes. Jackie Flowers led the team in receiving with 37 catches for 622 yards and 7 TD receptions. Monk Bonasorte led the team with 8 pass interceptions. Bonassorte {DB}, Bobby Butler {DB}, Jackie Flowers {TE}, Mike Good {G}, Ken Lanier {OT}, Ron Simmons {NG} and Scott Warren {DE} were selected to the First team All-South Independent team. Ron Simmons was selected as a First team All-American. Bonasorte was a 3rd team AP All-American. Bobby Butler {DB}, Jackie Flowers, Mike Good, Jimmy Jordan {QB} and Ken Lanier were named as Honorable Mention All-Americans by the Associated Press and/or The Sporting News. Mark Lyles {RB} {Cincinnati}, Flowers {Dallas}, Walter Carter {DT} {Oakland} and Jordan {New England} were selected in the 1980 NFL draft.

FINAL RANK: #6 AP, #5 CP

Home games were played at Doak Campbell Stadium

9/8/1979	Florida State	#19	vs		SOUTHERN MISS (6-4-1)		17	14	W
9/15/1979	Florida State	#18	vs		ARIZONA STATE (6-6)		31	3	W
9/22/1979	Florida State	#14	vs		MIAMI (5-6)		40	23	W
9/29/1979	Florida State	#12	@		Virginia Tech (5-6)	ABC	17	10	W
10/6/1979	Florida State	#9	@		Louisville (4-6-1)		27	0	W
10/13/1979	Florida State	#9	vs		MISSISSIPPI STATE (3-8)		17	6	W
10/27/1979	Florida State	#7	@		Lsu (7-5)	ABC	24	19	W
11/3/1979	Florida State	#6	@		Cincinnati (2-9)		26	21	W
11/10/1979	Florida State	#7	vs	#19	SOUTH CAROLINA (8-4)		27	7	W
11/17/1979	Florida State	#5	vs		MEMPHIS (5-6)		66	17	W
11/24/1979	Florida State	#5	@		Florida (0-10-1)	ABC	27	16	W
1/1/1980	**Florida State**	#6	vs	#5	**Oklahoma (11-1)**	NBC	7	**24**	L
Coach: Bobby Bowden					**Season Record >>**		326	160	**11-1**

Schedule Source: Steve's Football Bible LLC

Selected game(s) highlights

SOUTHERN MISSISSIPPI

Behind 14-3 with 10 minutes left in the last quarter, Florida State struck for two quick touchdowns and overtook Southern Mississippi 17-14 before 45,467 fans at Doak Campbell Stadium. Jimmy Jordan threw an 8 yard TD pass to Jackie Flowers, then a 65 yard punt return for a touchdown by Gary Henry with 6:28 put the Seminoles in front to stay.

ARIZONA STATE

Florida State romped to an easy 31-3 football victory over Arizona State. It was 24-0 at halftime. Monk Bonasorte helped to provide 10 first half points with two interceptions. Wally Woodham threw 18 yards to Jackie Flowers for a touchdown. Mark Lyles ran 1 yard for a touchdown to give FSU a 14-0 lead. Dave Cappelen kicked a 42 yard field goal and Jimmy Jordan threw his first of two touchdown passes, an 8 yard pass to Grady King. In the 4th quarter he threw 15 yards to Ricky Williams for the final Seminole touchdown.

MIAMI

Miami jumped out to an early lead after the first quarter, but that would pretty much be all they could celebrate during this day in the Capital City. Two Mark Lyles touchdowns in the second quarter helped the Seminoles take a 19-7 lead at the half, while Greg Ramsey would add two rushing scores in the third quarter and the route was on. The Hurricanes scored a touchdown to open the fourth quarter, but Gary Henry's return of a blocked punt cemented the outcome and Florida State was able to celebrate in their own locker room after defeating the Hurricanes at home for the first time, 40-23, pacing the Noles to the first undefeated regular season under Bobby Bowden.

Virginia Tech

It was Virginia Tech's last chance to win. Fourth down and 13 at its 17. As Steve Casey rolled to pass, Seminole linebacker Paul Piurowski was bearing down on him. Casey slipped as he tried to maneuver, and Piurowski was on top of him at the 12 and the Florida State held on for a 17-10 victory. Trailing 7-0 in the 2nd quarter, the Seminoles struck on a Greg Ramsey 16 yard run and Jackie Flowers 18 yard TD pass from Jimmy Jordan. Dave Cappelen added a 20 yard field goal in the 3rd quarter. Wally Woodham and Jimmy Jordan combined for 322 yards passing but threw 4 interceptions.

Louisville

Blocking two punts, holding Louisville to just two first downs until 7:30 was left on the clock, Florida State's defense was again the dominant show as the unbeaten Seminoles won 27-0. FSU did it on two touchdowns, a couple of safeties and a field goal before 27,306 fans at Fairgrounds Stadium. Wally Woodham threw two touchdowns, one to Sam Platt (5 yards) and one to Sam Childers (1 yard). Bobby Butler fell on a blocked punt in the end zone for a touchdown.

MISSISSIPPI STATE

Putting two touchdowns on the scoreboard in the final six minutes of the first half, Florida State held on with its defense in the closing two quarters and claimed a 17-6 victory over Mississippi State. FSU scored on a one yard run by Mike Whiting, and on an 18 yard pass from Jimmy Jordan to Jackie Flowers. Dave Cappelen kicked a 46 yard field goal.

Lsu

Jimmy Jordan gunned three touchdown passes as Florida State muscled past Louisiana State 24-19 before 67,197 in Tiger Stadium. Jordan completed 14 passes for 312 yards. In the 1st half, the Seminoles forced three LSU fumbles and recovered all three. Florida State, in the 2nd half, intercepted two passes. Monk Bonasorte recovered a fumble and intercepted two passes. Florida State totaled 436 yards of offense. Jordan's TD passes went to Sam Platt (3 yards), Jackie Flowers (40 yards) and Hardis Johnson (53 yards).

Cincinnati

The sixth ranked Seminoles squeezed past Cincinnati 26-21 when Mike Whiting crashed into the end zone from eight yards out with 1:38 left to play. The Seminoles trailed 21-7 at the start of the fourth quarter. Ahead 7-0 after their first offensive series, FSU was stunned by a 21 point 2nd quarter onslaught by Cincinnati, a 17 1/2 point underdog. Wally Woodham led the charge in the 4th quarter with touchdown passes to Mark Lyles (7 yards) and Jackie Flowers (5 yards), followed by Whiting's game winner.

SOUTH CAROLINA

A record Doak Campbell Stadium crowd of 49,490 saw the 9-0 Seminoles beat South Carolina 27-7. Wally Woodham completed 15 of 25 passes for 145 yards. Florida State cominated possession, 83 plays to 52, and totaled 381 yards to Carolina's 265. Mark Lyles ran for 132 yards on 25 carries and a 1 yard touchdown run. Dave Capellen kicked four field goals. Jimmy Jordan threw a 7 yard TD pass to Sam Childers.

MEMPHIS STATE

Florida State clobbered Memphis State 66-17 before 48,021 at Doak Campbell Stadium. Memphis State's defense had given up just three touchdown passes. Quarterback Jimmy Jordan threw for that many in the second quarter. Two of those Jordan TD shots came in the last 45 seconds of the half, stretching a 10-3 lead to 24-3. Jordan's touchdown passes were to Jackie Flowers (24 yards), Hardis Johnson (4 yards) and Grady King (5 yards). The defense and special teams got their shots in as well with Paul Piurowski returning an interception 29 yards for a touchdown and Keith Jones returning a blocked punt (by Bobby Butler) 16 yards for a touchdown. Mark Lyles, Ricky Williams, Keith Kennedy and Kelly Burney ran for touchdowns for the Noles.

Florida

Florida hosted Florida State at Florida Field in a regionally televised contest on ABC-TV. A debatable ruling on an interception by FSU's Walter Carter led to a Bill Capece field goal that gave the Seminoles a 20-10 lead in the fourth quarter. The game was tied 10-10 early in the final period. Mark Lyles' two fourth quarter touchdowns, however, would be just what the Seminoles needed as FSU completed a perfect regular season. Lyles rushed for 151 yards while teammate Michael Whiting added 123 yards on the ground. Defensively, Florida State forced six turnovers for their third straight victory over rival Florida. The Noles went on to a 27-16 victory.

1980 ORANGE BOWL

Mike Whiting gave the Seminoles the lead with his touchdown run, but that was their only score of the night. A fumbled field goal snap, three turnovers, over 100 yards of rushing by quarterback J. C. Watts and halfback Billy Sims, and 24 unanswered points by Oklahoma doomed the Seminoles. It all started with a Watts run for a touchdown in the second quarter to tie the game at seven. After the kickoff, the Seminoles turned the ball over on an interception, giving the ball back to Oklahoma. Stanley Wilson then scored a touchdown run to make it 14–7. Mike Keeling added a field goal late in the quarter to give the Sooners a 17–7 lead at halftime. The second half scoring was limited to one Oklahoma touchdown from 22 yards out in the fourth quarter; Watts ran for twelve yards before pitching the ball to Sims, who took it the rest of the way for a 24–7 lead, the final score. The Sooners ran for 411 yards on 59 carries, an average of nearly seven yards per attempt, while having twice as many total yards as the Seminoles.

1980 Florida State Seminoles

The team was coached by Bobby Bowden in his fifth season. Florida State finished #5 in the AP poll and #5 in the UPI poll with a 10–2 record. The Seminoles' offense scored 369 points while the defense allowed 103 points. They were invited to the Orange Bowl for the second straight season where they played Oklahoma again.

Sam Platt led the team in rushing with 983 yards and 6 touchdowns. Rick Stockstill led the team in passing with 1377 yards and 15 touchdown passes. Michael Whiting led the team with 25 receptions while Hardis Johnson led with 419 receiving yards and 9 touchdowns. Keith Jones led the team with 5 pass interceptions.

Monk Bonasorte {DB}, Bobby Butler {DB}, Bill Capece {K}, Greg Futch {G}, Reggie Herring {LB}, Ken Lanier {OT}, Mark Macek {DT}, Paul Piurowski {LB} and Rohn Stark {P} were selected to the First team All-South Independent team. Bobby Butler, Bill Capece, Ron Simmons {NG} and Rohn Stark were selected as First team All-Americans. Bonasorte, Herring and Lanier were selected as 2nd team All-Americans and Futch, Macek and Piurowski were named Honorable Mention All-Americans by the Associated Press. Butler {Atlanta}, Lanier {Denver}, Simmons {Cleveland}, Piurowski {Dallas} and Capece {Houston Oilers} were selected in the 1981 NFL draft. Butler was a #1 pick.

FINAL RANK: #5 AP, #5 CP

Home games were played at Doak Campbell Stadium

Date	Team	Rank		Opp Rank	Opponent	TV			
9/6/1980	Florida State	#13	@		Lsu (7-4)		16	0	W
9/13/1980	Florida State	#10	vs		LOUISVILLE (5-6)		52	0	W
9/20/1980	Florida State	#9	vs		EAST CAROLINA (4-7)		63	7	W
9/27/1980	Florida State	#9	@		Miami (9-3)		9	10	L
10/4/1980	Florida State	#16	@	#3	Nebraska (10-2)		18	14	W
10/11/1980	Florida State	#11	vs	#4	PITTSBURGH (11-1)		36	22	W
10/18/1980	Florida State	#7	vs		BOSTON COLLEGE (7-4)		41	7	W
10/25/1980	Florida State	#6	@		Memphis (2-9)	ABC	24	3	W
11/1/1980	Florida State	#5	vs		TULSA (8-3)		45	2	W
11/8/1980	Florida State	#3	vs		VIRGINIA TECH (8-4)	ABC	31	7	W
12/6/1980	Florida State	#3	vs	#19	FLORIDA (8-4)	ABC	17	13	W
1/1/1981	**Florida State**	#2	vs	#4	**Oklahoma (10-2)**	NBC	**17**	**18**	**L**
Coach: Bobby Bowden					**Season Record >>**		369	103	**10-2**

Schedule Source: Steve's Football Bible LLC

Selected game(s) highlights

Lsu

Bill Capece kicked three field goals and Florida State's defense held Louisiana State without any points as the Seminoles opened their season with a 16-0 victory in Tiger Stadium. Florida State led 6-0 at halftime on field goals of 34 and 35 yards by Capece. The only touchdown of the game came with 2:32 remaining in the third quarter. Sam Platt ran in from four yards out for the score.

LOUISVILLE

Rick Stockstill threw four touchdown passes as the Seminoles routed Louisville 52-0 before the biggest crowd ever (52,623) to see a football game at Doak Campbell Stadium. The Seminoles got the first six of their seven touchdowns on passes, as Kelly Lowrey and Blair Williams followed Stockstill with one apiece. Stockstill threw TD passes to Dennis McKinnon (8 yards), Zeke Mowatt (7 yards), Hardis Johnson

(26 yards) and Phil Williams (19 yards). Johnson and McKinnon caught TD passes from Lowrey and Williams and Ron Hester returned an interception 50 yards for a touchdown.

EAST CAROLINA

With a devastating running game and formidable defense, the Seminoles romped to a 63-7 victory. Sam Platt ran for 130 yards on 29 carries and Mike Whiting 71 yards on 15 carries. Rick Stockstill completed 10 of 11 passes for 132 yards. Ahead 35-7 going into the final quarter, the Seminoles added four more touchdowns and 28 points in the 4th quarter. Michael Whiting, Ken Burnett, and Larry Harris each ran for two touchdowns. FSU rolled up 559 yards of total offense while holding the Pirates to 102 yards of total offense.

Miami

Fumble after fumble after fumble on the quarterback-center exchange stymied the frustrated Seminoles throughout the game as Florida State came tumbling down 10-9 in Miami. Trailing 10-3 late in the 4th quarter, the Seminoles almost pulled it out in the final minutes, driving 55 yards to a touchdown that came on an 11 yard pass from Rick Stockstill to Sam Childers with 39 seconds left. Coach Bobby Bowden made the decision to go for a winning two points, rather than settle for a 10-10 tie. Stockstill's pass in the quest for two hit the helmet of leaping nose guard at the line of scrimmage and never had a chance to reach a Seminole.

Nebraska

Trailing by 4 points as the clock wound down under 15 seconds, Nebraska QB Jeff Quinn was hit only three yards from the end zone, forcing a fumble which was recovered by Florida State. The Seminoles escaped Lincoln with a win. Behind 14-0 by the middle of the second quarter, Florida State fought back. The Seminoles took the lead for good at 15-14, on the third field goal by Bill Capece, with 1:16 left in the third quarter. Capece added a 41 yard field goal with 2:31 left in the game.

PITTSBURGH

Bill Capece kicked five field goals and Florida State fought from behind to a 36-22 victory over previously unbeaten 4th ranked Pittsburgh. Rick Stockstill threw three touchdown passes. Stockstill's TD passes went to Hardis Johnson (23 yards), Sam Childers (4 yards) and Kurt Unglaub (13 yards). Keith Jones, Monk Bonasorte and Bobby Butler intercepted Dan Marino passes to lead the defense.

BOSTON COLLEGE

Bill Capece kicked four field goals, and linebacker Ron Hester twice blocked Boston College punts as Florida State beat Boston College, 41-7, before a homecoming crowd of 52,396 at Doak Campbell Stadium. Hester returned one of his blocked punts 33 yards for a touchdown. Michael Whiting, Rick Stockstill and Kelly Lowery all ran for touchdowns.

Memphis

Sam Platt rushed for 188 yards in 29 carries, breaking the school single-game record, leading the Seminoles to a 24-3 victory. The Seminoles had 464 yards of total offense while holding the Tigers to 183 yards of total offense. Platt and Michael Whiting ran for touchdowns and Rick Stockstill threw an 18 yard TD pass to Hardis Johnson.

TULSA

Florida State routed the Golden Hurricane in a 45-2 victory before 47,683 fans at Doak Campbell Stadium. Florida State outgained Tulsa 444 yards to 160 yards. Michael Whiting ran for two touchdowns, Sam Platt, and Ricky Williams each ran for one. Rick Stockstill passed for two touchdowns, one to Hardis Johnson (17 yards) and Kurt Unglaub (10 yards).

VIRGINIA TECH

Scoring two touchdowns in 51 seconds, Florida State's football team overcame a sluggish start and went on to whip Virginia Tech 31-7 at Doak Campbell Stadium. FSU moved to 8-0 on games televised on ABC under Bobby Bowden. The Seminoles fell behind 7-0, then poured it on, scoring 31 straight points. Rick Stockstill ran for a touchdown and threw two touchdowns to Hardis Johnson. Sam Platt added a 9 yard TD run in the 4th quarter.

FLORIDA

Florida had a 13-3 lead well into the 3rd quarter on a Wayne Peace 53 yard TD pass to Tyrone Young and two Brian Clark field goals, one from 38 yards and the other from 36 yards. The Seminoles stormed back behind quarterback Rick Stockstill, who threw two touchdown passes to Hardis Johnson to lead the Noles to a 17-13 victory.

1981 ORANGE BOWL

After a scoreless first quarter, Ricky Williams put Florida State ahead with his touchdown run, and Oklahoma countered with a long field goal by Mike Keeling; the Seminoles led 7–3 at halftime. To start the second half, Oklahoma drove 78 yards on twelve plays, and halfback David Overstreet scored from four yards out to take a 10–7 lead. A short field goal by Bill Capece tied the game at ten for the last tally of the third quarter. Four minutes into the final quarter, cornerback Bobby Butler recovered a botched punt snap in the end zone to give the Seminoles a 17–10 lead. With 3:19 remaining, Oklahoma's fate lay in the hands of senior quarterback J. C. Watts, who had turned the ball over three times on fumbles. He led the Sooners on a 78 yard drive, culminating with an eleven yard touchdown pass to wide receiver Steve Rhodes with 1:33 remaining. Down by a point, Oklahoma opted for the two point conversion attempt, and Watts completed a pass to tight end Forrest Valora in the end zone for a one point lead. Florida State tried to counter back, but Capece's 62 yard field goal attempt fell short, and the Sooners were victorious

1981 Florida State Seminoles

The team was coached by Bobby Bowden in his sixth season. Florida State finished with a 6-5 record and were not invited to a Bowl game. The Seminoles' offense scored 240 points while the defense allowed 286 points. The Seminoles played a murderers row schedule on the road, as in consecutive weeks, they played at #17 Nebraska, at #7 Ohio State, at Notre Dame, at #3 Pittsburgh and at LSU.

Greg Allen led the team in rushing with 888 yards. Rick Stockstill led the team in passing with 1356 yards and 11 touchdown passes. Michael Whiting led the team in receptions with 29. Phil Williams led the team in receiving yards with 413. Harvey Clayton led the team with 5 pass interceptions.

Jarvis Coursey {DE}, Tim McCormick {C}, Rohn Stark {P} and Barry Voltapetti {OT} were selected to the First team All-South Independent team. Rohn Stark was selected as a First team All-Ameican. Greg Allen {RB}, Garry Futch {G}, McCormick and Voltapetti were named as Honorable Mention All-Americans by the Associated Press. Stark {Baltimore Colts}, Ron Hester {LB}, {Miami} and Mike Whiting {RB} {Dallas} were selected in the 1982 NFL draft.

Home games were played at Doak Campbell Stadium

9/5/1981	Florida State	**#19**	**vs**		LOUISVILLE (5-6)		17	0	**W**
9/12/1981	Florida State	**#18**	**vs**		MEMPHIS (1-10)		10	5	**W**
9/19/1981	Florida State	**#19**	**@**	#17	Nebraska (9-3)		14	34	**L**
10/3/1981	Florida State		**@**	#7	Ohio State (9-3)		36	27	**W**
10/10/1981	Florida State	**#20**	**@**		Notre Dame (5-6)		19	13	**W**
10/17/1981	Florida State	**#11**	**@**	#3	Pittsburgh (11-1)		14	42	**L**
10/24/1981	Florida State	**#17**	**@**		Lsu (3-7-1)		38	14	**W**
10/31/1981	Florida State	**#20**	**vs**		WESTERN CAROLINA (4-7)		56	31	**W**
11/7/1981	Florida State	**#14**	**vs**	#13	MIAMI (9-2)	ABC	19	27	**L**
11/14/1981	Florida State	**#20**	**vs**	#14	SOUTHERN MISS (9-2-1)	ABC	14	58	**L**
11/28/1981	Florida State		**@**		Florida (7-5)		3	35	**L**
Coach: Bobby Bowden					**Season Record >>**		240	286	**6-5**

Schedule Source: Steve's Football Bible LLC

Selected game(s) highlights

LOUISVILLE

Florida State eked out a 17-0 victory over Louisville, but it wasn't easy. Frustrated throughout by a Louisville defense led by tackle Richard Tharpe, the Seminoles staggered and stumbled most of the way. Four times Tharpe got through and sacked quarterback Rick Stockstill. It was 10-0 after the first quarter, as Mike Rendina kicked a 24 yard field goal and Stockstill hit Jessie Hester with an 11 yard scoring pass. With seven minutes left, Billy Allen broke away on a pitchout for a 50 yard scoring run to ice it. Allen ran the ball eight times for 89 yards. Louisville threatened numerous timess only to be denied by the Seminole defense. FSU held the Cardinals to 133 yards of total offense.

MEMPHIS

Florida State's offense managed to get a touchdown and a field goal on the board. Memphis State stayed in it to the end before falling 10-5. Late in the 1st quarter the Seminoles moved on a 77 yard drive for the only touchdown that came on Mike Whiting's 3 yard run in the first moments of the 2nd quarter. That erased a 2-0 deficit, which came when Rick Stockstill was trapped in the end zone by Cedric Wright on FSU's second series of the evening. Early in the 4th quarter Mike Rendina kicked a 46 yard field goal to make it 10-2. A few minutes later Gregg Hauss put through a 27 yarder for 3 points and the final score. Larry Harris intercepted a pass with 4 seconds remaining, did the Seminoles have this one wrapped up.

Nebraska

Nebraska held a close 10-7 lead at halftime, but the momentum quickly turned in favor of the Cornhuskers when WB Irving Fryar scored on an 82 yard punt return, followed up six game clock seconds later when DE Tony Felici's off-the-bench opportunity allowed him to recover a Florida State fumble on the kickoff and return it 13 yards for another touchdown. Nebraska sealed the deal on a 94 yard touchdown run by IB Roger Craig.

Ohio State

The Seminoles knocked #7 Ohio State from the unbeaten ranks 36-27. Rick Stockstill completed 25 of 41 passes for 299 yards and two touchdowns. Stockstill directed two third quarter drives to touchdowns that were the difference. The first covered 88 yards in 11 plays, the second 99 in nine. The Seminoles increased their 23-21 halftime lead because of these drives. No bigger play was Ron Hester's blocked punt that he returned 35 yards for a touchdown in the 2nd quarter. Stockstill's TD passes were to Tony Johnson (13 yards) and Sam Childers (7 yards). Kelly Lowery and Ricky Williams had touchdown runs for the Seminoles.

Notre Dame

Florida State Seminoles, in their first ever visit to Notre Dame Stadium, left with a 19-13 victory. Mike Rendina kicked two field goals and Michael Whiting scored both the Seminoles touchdowns, a 17 yard pass from Rick Stockstill and a 5 yard pass from Stockstill. Ricky Williams ran for 135 yards. Stockstill passed for only 100 yards, but his two TD passes were the difference in the game.

Pittsburgh

#3 ranked Pittsburgh dominated every phase of the game and routed Florida State 42-14 before a crowd of 55,112 at Pitt Stadium. Pitt's Dan Marino threw for 215 yards and touchdowns of 22, 65, and 18 yards. Michael Whiting ran 1 yard for a touchdown and Sam Childers caught a 5 yard TD pass from Blair Williams. Pittsburgh rolled up 503 yards of total offense.

Lsu

Florida State crushed Louisiana State 38-14 before over 74,000 homecoming fans at Tiger Stadium. Offense, defense and special teams all contributed in the rout. Harvey Clayton had an interception and a 48 yard punt return. James Harris had 3 sacks, Warren Hanna blocked a punt and Billy Allen returned a kickoff 97 yards for a touchdown. Greg Allen and Cedric Jones ran for touchdowns. Allen rushed for 202 yards, a new school record. Rick Stockstill passed for two touchdowns, one to Dennis McKinnon (22 yards) and one to Phil Willaims (12 yards).

WESTERN CAROLINA

A homecoming crowd of over 52,000 at Doak Campbell Stadium was treated to an offensive show by both squads. It featured 623 yards of total offense by the Seminoles and 437 yards by Western Carolina. **Greg Allen's 322 yards of rushing on 32 carries was the single game best in college football this season and shattered his own FSU record of 202 yards that was set a week ago at LSU.** Allen had a 5 yard touchdown run and a 95 yard kickoff return for a touchdown. Michael Whiting ran for two touchdowns and Mike Rendina kicked two field goals. Dennis McKinnon, Tony Johnson, and Cedric Jones had touchdowns for the Seminoles.

MIAMI

The Seminole kicking game was missing as they had two field goal attempts and an extra point blocked. The Noles and the Canes were tied 13-13 heading into the 4th quarter. Smokey Roan scored from 6 yards out for a 20-13 Hurricane lead. The Seminoles still had 10:47 left to come back, but two plays later Rick Stockstill's slant pass was tipped and intercepted by Ronnie Tippett. Jim Kelly threw to Speedy Neal and broke two tackles on the way to the end zone for a 27-13 lead with 8:54 left. The Seminoles closed to 27-19 on a Stockstill 7 yard TD pass to Sam Childers.

SOUTHERN MISSISSIPPI

Florida State crashed and burned before 51,819 spectators at Doak Campbell Stadium. Southern Miss did whatever they pleased in a 58-14 rout and moved to 9-0-1 on the season. The Seminoles trailed 51-0 before they finally got on the scoreboard with a Dennis McKinnon 50 yard TD reception from Blair Williams. Tom Wheeler caught a 6 yard TD pass from Williams to close out the scoring for the game.

Florida

Florida took a 13-3 lead into halftime and then poured it on in the 2nd half on the way to a 35-3 victory over the Seminoles. Wayne Peace threw four touchdown passes, including two to Mike Mularkey. Brian Clark added two field goals for the Gators. The Gators dominated the game from the opening drive to the final gun and won for the first time over Florida State since 1976.

1982 Florida State Seminoles

The team was coached by Bobby Bowden in his seventh season. Florida State finished with a 9-3 record and were invited to the Gator Bowl game against West Virginia. The Seminoles' offense scored 410 points while the defense allowed 254 points.

Ricky Williams led the team in rushing with 837 yards. Greg Allen led the team with 20 rushing touchdowns. Kelly Lowery led the team in passing with 1671 yards and 11 touchdown passes. Tony Johnson led the team with 30 pass receptions and Jessie Hester led the team with 541 reception yards. Larry Harris led the team with 6 pass interceptions. Allen led the team in kickoff returns with 515 yards and a 25.8 average. **Allen's 20 rushing touchdowns set a new single season team record.**

Greg Allen {RB}, Alphonso Carreker {DT}, Harvey Clayton {DB}, Tom McCormick (C) and Tommy Young (LB) were selected to the First team All-South Independent team. Allen, Carreker, Clayton, McCormick, Young and Ricky Williams {RB} were named as Honorable Mention All-Americans by the Associated Press. No Seminoles players were selected in the 1983 NFL draft.

FINAL RANK: #13 AP, #10 CP

Home games were played at Doak Campbell Stadium

Date	Team				Opponent					
9/4/1982	Florida State		vs		CINCINNATI (6-5)		38	31	W
9/18/1982	Florida State		vs	#2	PITTSBURGH (9-3)		17	37	L
9/25/1982	Florida State		@		Southern Miss (7-4)		24	17	W
10/2/1982	Florida State		@		Ohio State (9-3)		34	17	W
10/9/1982	Florida State		vs		SOUTHERN ILLINOIS (6-5)		59	8	W
10/16/1982	Florida State	#19	vs		EAST CAROLINA (7-4)		56	17	W
10/30/1982	Florida State	#14	@	#16	Miami (7-4)	CBS	24	7	W
11/6/1982	Florida State	#12	@		South Carolina (4-7)		56	26	W
11/13/1982	Florida State	#9	vs		LOUISVILLE (5-6)	TBS	49	14	W
11/20/1982	Florida State	#7	@	#12	Lsu (8-3-1)		21	55	L
12/4/1982	Florida State		vs		FLORIDA (8-4)		10	13	L
12/30/1982	Florida State		vs	#10	West Virginia (9-3)	ABC	31	12	W
Coach: Bobby Bowden					Season Record >>		419	254	9-3

Schedule Source: Steve's Football Bible LLC

Selected game(s) highlights

CINCINNATI

Trailing 14-0 early in the 1st quarter, the Seminoles came from behind and finally won a thriller over Cincinnati, 38-31. With 1:10 to go, Cincinnati stood at the Seminoles' 19 with a chance to tie or win following a 56 yard runback of an interception by Antonio Gibson of a Blair Williams pass. On first down, Barrett was sacked for a loss of 11 by Allan Campbell. Then he threw three times into the end zone, all incomplete. Greg Allen ran for three touchdowns along with 90 yards on the ground. Ricky Williams ran for 92 yards and a 20 yard touchdown and Tony Johnson caught a 12 yard TD pass from Williams.

PITTSBURGH

The game was tied at halftime, 17-17, then the Panthers steamrolled the Seminoles with 20 second half points on the way to a 37-17 victory over FSU. Pitt blocked a Seminole punt and returned it 5 yards for a touchdown and Dan Marino threw two 2nd half TD passes as the #2 ranked Panthers showed they were worthy of their ranking. Greg Allen and Ricky Williams ran for touchdowns and Philip Hall kicked a 29 yard field goal for the Noles.

Southern Mississippi

With a brilliant passing game led by Kelly Lowrey, Florida State pulled out a 24-17 victory over Southern Mississippi. Lowrey hit 22 of 35 passes for 286 yards and two touchdowns. Southern Miss' Sam Dejarnette ran for a school record 304 yards in 43 carries. Lowrey ran for a touchdown and his touchdown passes were to Zeke Mowatt (3 yards) and Ken Burnett (8 yards). Philip Hall added a 35 yard field goal.

Ohio State

Florida State romped 34-17 before the biggest football crowd in Ohio State football history. The Seminoles trailed 10-7 after the 1st quarter but a Zeke Mowatt 6 yard TD pass from Kelly Lowrey gave FSU the lead they never relinquished. Greg Allen and Ricky Williams ran for touchdowns and Jessie Hester caught a 9 yard TD pass from Blair Williams. Allen rushed for 104 yards while Tony Johnson caught 5 passes for 90 yards. The Seminoles first touchdown was on a halfback option pass where Cedric Jones threw to Lowrey 11 yards for a touchdown.

SOUTHERN ILLINOIS

Florida State broke free in the second quarter and raced on to a 59-8 football victory over Southern Illinois before over 51,000 homecoming fans at Doak Campbell Stadium. The Seminoles were up 31-0 at halftime on a Kelly Lowrey touchdown run and Lowrey threw two TD passes, one to Hassan Jones (28 yards) and Jessie Hester (20 yards). Hester caught a 57 yard pass for a touchdown from Lowrey in the 2nd half. Greg Allen, Cedric Jones, and Tony Smith all ran for touchdowns and Billy Allen caught a 39 yard TD pass from Blair Williams.

EAST CAROLINA

Greg Allen scored four touchdowns and Florida State rolled up a school record 706 yards in a 56-17 rout over East Carolina. The Seminoles led 14-0 after the 1st quarter and 35-0 at the half. Allen scored the game's second touchdown on a 24 yard pass from Blair Williams. He got the Seminoles' third, fourth and sixth TDS on short runs. Kelly Lowrey passed for 237 yards and two touchdowns. Blair Williams passed for 223 yards and two touchdowns. Hassan Jones was on the receiving end of two TD passes.

Miami

With the Seminoles clinging to a 17-7 lead after a Kelly Lowrey 24 yard TD pass to Orson Mobley, Gary Henry intercepted a Mark Richt pass followed by Brian McCrary intercepting a Richt pass, then Greg Allen scoring from the 2 yard line to ice the Seminoles 24-7 victory over the Hurricanes. Philip Hall kicked a 36 yard field goal and Allen scored from 3 yards out as the Noles took a 10-0 lead into halftime.

South Carolina

Florida State shook off turnovers and blew past South Carolina 56-26 before over 62,000 fans at Doak Campbell Stadium. Greg Allen ran for four touchdowns. Kelly Lowrey passed for 269 yards and two touchdowns while Blair Williams passed for 168 yards and one touchdown. Warren Hanna blocked a punt and returned it 28 yards for a touchdown. Lowrey's TD passes were to Tony Johnson (18 yards) and Weegie Thompson (48 yards). Williams threw an 83 yard strike to Dennis McKinnon.

LOUISVILLE

Greg Allen ran for 173 yards and four touchdowns and Ricky Williams chipped in with 140 yards on 10 carries as Florida State routed Louisville 49-14. Gary Henry returned a blocked punt 42 yards for a touchdown. Kelly Lowrey ran 2 yards for a touchdown and Tony Smith ran 4 yards for a touchdown.

Lsu

LSU turned the evening into a rout, defeating the Seminoles 55-21. The Tigers scored first early in the first quarter, and although FSU tied it at 7-7 and 14-14, LSU led the rest of the way. Kelly Lowrey passed for 172 yards, ran for a touchdown, and threw a 34 yard TD pass to Tony Smith. Blair Williams passed for 135 yards and threw a 20 yard TD pass to Jessie Hester.

FLORIDA

The Seminoles jumped out to a 10-0 lead in the first half before the Gators woke up and started their comeback. Jim Gainey kicked a 23 yard field goal and Bob Hewko scored from 10 yards out on fourth down to draw the Gators into a 10-10 tie. Gainey kicked the game winning field from 22 yards with 3:32 remaining and the Gator defense held on for a 13-10 victory.

1982 GATOR BOWL

Billy Allen scored on a 95 yard kickoff return and Greg Allen  scored twice as Florida State overpowered 10th ranked West Virginia 31-12 in the Gator Bowl. The Seminoles, a slight favorite, turned the game into a rout on Blair Williams' 27 yard scoring pass to Dennis McKinnon with only 15 seconds left in the first half and on Greg Allen's two third quarter scores, a 29 yard run and 1 yard dive over the Mountaineer line. Greg Allen finished with 138 yards on 15 carries. The Mountaineers had a field goal and punt blocked and squandered several scoring opportunities, including one when Willie Drewrey raced 82 yards to the FSU 6 on the longest punt return in Gator Bowl history. Williams passed for 202 yards.

1983 Florida State Seminoles

The team was coached by Bobby Bowden in his eighth season. Florida State finished with a 7-5 record and were invited to the Peach Bowl game to play North Carolina. The Seminoles' offense scored 381 points while the defense allowed 312 points.

Greg Allen led the team in rushing with 1167 yards and scored 13 touchdowns. Kelly Lowrey led the team in passing with 1720 yards and 12 touchdown passes. Jessie Hester and Weegie Thompson led the team in receptions with 31 and Hester led with 576 receiving yards. Brian McCrary led the team with 5 pass interceptions.

Greg Allen {RB}, Alphonso Carreker {DT} and Tom McCormick {C} were selected to the First team All-South Independent team. Greg Allen was selected as a Consensus First team All-American. Carreker and McCormick were named Honorable Memtion All-Americans by the Associated Press. Carreker {Green Bay} and Weegie Thompson {WR} {Pittsburgh} were selected in the 1984 NFL draft. Carreker was a #1 pick.

Home games were played at Doak Campbell Stadium

9/3/1983	Florida State	**#7**	vs		EAST CAROLINA (8-3)		47	46	**W**
9/10/1983	Florida State	**#12**	@	#13	Lsu (4-7)	ABC	40	35	**W**
9/17/1983	Florida State	**#9**	@		Tulane (4-7)		28	34	**L**
10/1/1983	Florida State	**#17**	@	#10	Auburn (11-1)		24	27	**L**
10/8/1983	Florida State		@		Pittsburgh (8-3-1)		16	17	**L**
10/15/1983	Florida State		vs		CINCINNATI (4-6-1)		43	17	**W**
10/20/1983	Florida State		vs		LOUISVILLE (3-8)		51	7	**W**
10/29/1983	Florida State		@		Arizona State (6-4-1)		29	26	**W**
11/5/1983	Florida State		vs		SOUTH CAROLINA (5-6)		45	30	**W**
11/12/1983	Florida State		vs	#6	MIAMI (11-1)		16	17	**L**
12/3/1983	Florida State		@	#12	Florida (9-2-1)	CBS	14	53	**L**
12/30/1983	**Florida State**		**vs**		**North Carolina (8-4)**	**CBS**	**28**	**3**	**W**
Coach: Bobby Bowden					**Season Record >>**		381	312	**7-5**

Schedule Source: Steve's Football Bible LLC

Selected game(s) highlights

EAST CAROLINA

With the Seminoles trailing 46-41 and six minutes left, Eric Riley intercepted a pass, tipped by teammate Pat Milligan, to give the Seminoles a shot from the Pirates 21 yard line. FSU scored the winning touchdown moments later on Kelly Lowrey's 5 yard pass to Tom Wheeler. Riley ended East Carolina's last hope when he recovered a fumble following a 39 yard run by Kevin Ingram to FSU's 31. Lowrey completed 28 of 35 passes for 322 yards and three touchdowns. Greg Allen ran 33 times for 154 yards and three touchdowns. Wheeler caught a 5 yard TD pass from Lowrey in the 1st quarter and Hassan Jones caught an 8 yard TD pass from Lowrey. Weegie Thompson caught 8 passes for 103 yards. The Seminoles special teams were absent as they allowed a punt return and kickoff return for touchdowns.

Lsu

Florida State surprised LSU 40-35, in a game that wasn't as close as the final score. Kelly Lowrey ran for three touchdowns and passed for two more. Greg Allen ran for 201 yards on 22 carries and scored on a 28 yard run. Behind 14-0 early, the Seminoles rallied to go ahead 33-14 before LSU came back in the final minutes against Seminole reserves. Lowrey's touchdown passes were to Hassan Jones (16 yards) and Jessie Hester {20 yards}.

Tulane

Tulane won 34-28 before 35,463 Superdome fans. The Seminoles fell behind early 14-0 after one Tulane player ran 99 yards with an intercepted pass and another raced 76 yards to score on a punt return. Florida State rallied to tie 14-14, then went ahead 21-14 in the last seconds of that first half, But that was all. Tulane was back up 31-21. After it became 34-28, the Seminoles had one turn with the football and couldn't complete a pass. Greg Allen ran for 115 yards and two touchdowns. Kelly Lowrey passed for 241 yards and ran for one touchdown and passed 55 yards to Jessie Hester for a touchdown.

Auburn

Auburn, ranked #10, hosted Florida State at Jordan-Hare Stadium before a sellout crowd of over 75,000 fans. Randy Campbell threw a 15 yard touchdown pass to Lionel James with just over 2 minutes remaining, to lift the Tigers to a 27-24 victory over the Seminoles. Gregg Carr intercepted a pass with 50 seconds left in the game to seal the win. Campbell threw for 152 yards and three touchdown passes. Bo Jackson ran for 123 yards and Al Del Greco kicked two field goals.

Pittsburgh

The Seminoles went down to yet another close defeat, their third in a row, 17-16. Philip Hall missing an extra point following the Seminoles' first touchdown was the difference. Pitt dominated in possession 37:26 of playing time to 22:34, and ran 25 more plays, 83 to 58. Kelly Lowrey threw two touchdown passes, one to Tom Wheeler for 1 yard and a 16 yard strike to Weegie Thompson. Hall kicked a 25 yard field goal with 8:34 left in the game, but the Seminoles never got the ball back.

CINCINNATI

Before 55,102 fans, the third-largest crowd in Doak Campbell Stadium history, the Seminoles put a whipping on Cincinnati, 43-17. Greg Allen ran for 125 yards on 21 carries and one touchdown, and Roosevelt Snipes got 121 yards on 17 carries and one touchdown. Kelly Lowrey completed 11 of his 19 passes for 164 yards. Lowrey ran for one touchdown and threw a 16 yard TD to Weegie Thompson. Bob Davis threw a 29 yard TD pass to Jessie Hester.

LOUISVILLE

Rolling up 545 yards of offense, 336 of it on the ground, the Seminoles lost no fumbles and had no passes intercepted as Florida State stormed past Louisville 51-7. Greg Allen ran for 145 yards and three touchdowns. Roosevelt Snipes chipped in with 109 yards and one touchdown. Billy Allen added a 2 yard touchdown and Jessie Hester caught a 45 yard TD pass from Kelly Lowrey. Bob Davis threw a 7 yard TD pass to Pete Panton in the 3rd quarter to make the score 38-0.

Arizona State

Bob Davis shot Arizona State down with six seconds left on a 10 yard TD pass to Jessie Hester. Davis, replacing the injured Kelly Lowrey, directed two scoring drives in the 4th quarter to lead the Seminoles to a 29-26 victory. Davis threw a 38 yard TD pass to Roosevelt Snipes to give the Noles a 22-19 lead. Earlier, Snipes scored on a 12 yard TD run to give FSU a 14-10 lead. Davis threw for 140 yards after coming into the game.

SOUTH CAROLINA

Florida State struck for four touchdowns in rapid 2nd half succession and came from behind to knock off South Carolina 45-30 Saturday night. It was 17-17 at halftime and after falling behind 24-17, the Seminoles rattled off 28 straight points to put the game away. Ken Roe blocked a punt, and it was recovered in the end zone by Eric Riley for a touchdown. Roosevelt Snipes ran for 106 yards and two touchdowns. Bob Davis threw two touchdowns, including a 36 yarder to Weegie Thompson.

MIAMI

Jeff Davis kicked a 19 yard field goal on the game's last play to lift Miami to a 17-16 victory. The Hurricanes drove 47 yards on 7 plays in the last 2:12 of the game to set up the winning kick. Behind 7-0 early, the Seminoles rallied to lead 16-7 in the 3rd quarter. David Ponder blocked a punt out of the end zone for the Noles' first 2 points. Greg Allen ran 3 yards for a touchdown and Bob Davis ran 1 yard for a touchdown for the lead late in the 3rd quarter.

Florida

Florida inflicted the worst loss in ten years in the rivalry with the Seminoles, routing them 53-14. Five different Gators scored touchdowns and Bobby Raymond kicked a school record six field goals. Wayne Peace completed 14 of 20 passes for 190 yards and then let his running backs do the rest. The Noles committed six turnovers and were outgained by the Gators, 509 yards to 257 yards.

1983 PEACH BOWL

Making his first collegiate start ever, quarterback Eric Thomas connected on a pair of first quarter touchdown passes to Weegie Thompson as Florida State defeated North Carolina 28–3, in the 16th annual Peach Bowl Classic. Thomas, who played sparingly throughout the year after missing of 1982 with a shoulder injury, led FSU to a 14–0 lead on its first two possessions. Taking over on the FSU 38, Thomas directed a nine-play 62 yard march that ended on a 15 yard pass to Thompson in the left corner of the end zone for the score. Philip Hall added the extra point and FSU led 7–0. On the next possession, Thomas displayed some veteran composure, eluding a strong North Carolina blitz to hit Thompson on an 18 yard to cap a 54 yard, five play drive. Florida State's much maligned defense shut out the Tar Heels for the entire half; while Pete Panton set up a one yard touchdown run by Rosie Snipes by recovering a fumbled punt return on the North Carolina 16 midway through the second quarter as the Seminoles took a 21–0 lead into the locker room. After holding North Carolina to 30 net yards in the third quarter, FSU's defense allowed North Carolina its only points of the game early in the fourth quarter on a 36 yard Brooks Barwick field goal. North Carolina drove down to the FSU 12 on its next possession, but the Seminole defense forced four straight incomplete passes to take over on downs. Thomas and company took over, running all but 31 seconds off the game clock as Thomas capped and 88 yard drive with a 1 yard touchdown run and the Seminoles had their biggest winning margin ever in a bowl game. Thomas completed seven of 13 passes for 99 yards and added 41 yards rushing to lead the Seminoles offensively as he earned MVP honors for the game All-American Greg Allen paced a 265 yard rushing attack with 97 yards on 17 carries. Alphonso Carreker earned defensive MVP honors for the Seminoles. Carreker, who had six tackles broke up a pass and sacked NC quarterback Scott Stankavage once, spearheaded a defensive effort that allowed Carolina just 32 yards rushing in the game.

1984 Florida State Seminoles

The team was coached by Bobby Bowden in his ninth season. Florida State finished with a 7-3-2 record and were invited to the Florida Citrus Bowl game to play Georgia. The Seminoles' offense scored 406 points while the defense allowed 254 points.

Greg Allen led the team in rushing with 971 yards and 8 touchdowns. Eric Thomas led the team in passing with 1218 yards and 14 touchdown passes. Jessie Hester led the team in receiving with 42 catches for 832 yards and 9 touchdowns. Eric Williams led the team with 4 pass interceptions. Roosevelt Snipes led the team in kickoff returns with a 23.4 average.

Greg Allen {RB}, Louis Berry {P}, Jamie Dukes {G}, Jessie Hester {WR}, Derek Schmidt {K} and Henry Taylor {LB} were selected to the First team All-South Independent team. Greg Allen was a Consensus First team All-American. Louis Berry, Jamie Dukes, Jessie Hester, Derek Schmidt, and Henry Taylor were named Honorable Mention All-Americans by the Associated Press. Hester {Los Angeles Raiders}, Allen {Cleveland}, Bill Allen {RB} {New Orleans}, Eric Riley {DB} {Denver} and Roosevelt Snipes {RB} {San Francisco} were selected in the 1985 NFL draft. Hester was a #1 pick.

FINAL RANK: #17 AP, #19 CP

Home games were played at Doak Campbell Stadium

9/1/1984	Florida State	#20	vs		EAST CAROLINA (2-9)		48	17	W
9/15/1984	Florida State	#18	@		Kansas (5-6)		42	16	W
9/22/1984	Florida State	#15	@	#4	Miami (8-5)	CBS	38	3	W
9/29/1984	Florida State	#9	vs		TEMPLE (6-5)		44	27	W
10/6/1984	Florida State	#6	@		Memphis (5-5-1)		17	17	T
10/13/1984	Florida State	#9	vs	#16	AUBURN (9-4)		41	42	L
10/20/1984	Florida State	#15	vs		TULANE (3-8)		27	6	W
11/3/1984	Florida State	#14	@		Arizona State (5-6)		52	44	W
11/10/1984	Florida State	#11	@	#5	South Carolina (10-2)	ABC	26	38	L
11/17/1984	Florida State	#17	vs		TENNESSEE-CHATT		37	0	W
12/1/1984	Florida State	#12	vs	#3	FLORIDA (9-1-1)	ABC	17	27	L
12/22/1984	**Florida State**	**#15**	**vs**		**Georgia (7-4-1)**	**NBC**	**17**	**17**	
Coach: Bobby Bowden					**Season Record >>**		**406**	**254**	**7-3-2**

Schedule Source: Steve's Football Bible LLC

Selected game(s) highlights

EAST CAROLINA

Florida State cruised to a stunning 48-17 victory over East Carolina. Eric Thomas completed 12 of 19 passes for 177 yards and two touchdowns. Greg Allen ran 17 times for 113 yards and one touchdown. The Seminoles led 31-3 at halftime on a Roosevelt Snipes 5 yard run, Darrin Holoman 13 yard run, Hassan Jones 17 yard TD pass from Thomas and a Jessie Hester 31 yard TD pass from Thomas. Greg Allen added a 3 yard TD run and Holoman ran 9 yards for a touchdown.

Kansas

Greg Allen ran 16 times for 133 yards and two touchdowns leading the Seminoles to a 42-16 victory over the Jayhawks. After falling behind 3-0, the Jones boys took over. Hassan Jones caught 15 yard TD pass from Eric Thomas and Cletis Jones ran 40 yards for a touchdown and added a 1 yard score to put the Noles up 31-10. The Special teams got involved when Joe Wessel blocked a punt and Bruce Heggie picked it up and ran 7 yards for a touchdown.

Miami

Running for 284 yards, Florida State rolled up 478 yards on the way to a blowout victory over the Hurricanes, 38-3. The Seminoles sacked Bernie Kosar 6 times and sacked his replacement, Vinny Testaverde, 2 times. Derek Schmidt kicked three field goals. Jessie Hester caught five passes for 116 yards and got 102 yards on reverse runs and ran 77 yards for a touchdown. Roosevelt Snipes ran for two touchdowns. Hassan Jones caught a 25 yard TD pass from Eric Thomas.

TEMPLE

Joe Wessel blocked two kicks leading to a 14-0 lead. Greg Allen ran 43 yards for a touchdown after the first block and Eric Riley returned the second block 40 yards for a touchdown. Eric Thomas threw three touchdown passes, two to Jessie Hester (39 yards and 11 yards) and one to Hassan Jones (10 yards) as the Seminoles cruised to a 44-27 victory over the Owls.

Memphis

On the game's last play, Derek Schmidt kicked a 42 yard field goal that brought Florida State from behind to a 17-17 tie with Memphis State at the Liberty Bowl. Greg Allen ran for 143 yards and had a 10 yard touchdown run. Hassan Jones caught an 11 yard TD pass from Eric Thomas.

AUBURN

Auburn, ranked #16, traveled to Tallahassee to play #9 ranked Florida State at Doak Campbell Stadium before a record crowd of 58,671 fans. In a mid-season thriller, Brent Fullwood scored from 3 yards out with 48 seconds left in the game to give the Tigers a 42-41 victory. Ed Graham recovered Fullwood's fumble on a kickoff return and took it the remaining 60 yards for an Auburn touchdown. Collis Campbell had a 69 yard TD run for the Tigers.

TULANE

Tied 6-6 at halftime, the Seminoles blocked back-to-back punts for touchdowns that silenced Tulane 27-6. Len Chavers blocked the first punt and Joe Wessel picked it up at the 10 to score. Jesse Solomon blocked the next one, then fell on the ball in the end zone for a TD that gave FSU a 20-6 lead. Greg Allen rushed for 111 yards and scored on a 42 yard touchdown run.

Arizona State

Behind 17-0, Florida State rallied behind a superb kicking game and the quarterback work of Kirk Coker to triumph 52-44. Coker came in with the Seminoles trailing 20-10 shortly before halftime. In his first four series, Coker led the team to four touchdowns as he completed eight of his first 10 passes for 203 yards. Greg Allen scored on an 81 yard run and gained 223 yards on 23 carries. Allen scored on a pitchout from the one to cut the score to 20-17 with just seven seconds left in the half. The Special Teams were big in the game as Lenny Chavers blocked a punt and Joe Wessel picked it up and ran it in 8 yards for a touchdown. Wessel blocked a punt himself and ran that one in too, on a 34 yard play. Arizona State quarterback Jeff Van Raaphorst completed 38 of 59 passes for 532 yards and four touchdowns. Jessie Hester caught a 28 yard TD pass from Coker and then added another on a 69 yard TD pass from Coker.

South Carolina

The unbeaten Gamecocks took the Seminoles to the woodshed, winning 38-26. In Columbia, they called it the single most important football game in South Carolina history. The Seminoles ran into a buzz saw as the Gamecocks "Fire-Ants" defense pressured the quarterback and shut down the running game. South Carolina led 17-7 at halftime and 31-7 at the end of the 3rd quarter. Roosevelt Snipes ran 3 yards to give the Noles a 7-0 lead and it didn't last long. Jessie Hester and Pat Carter caught touchdown passes in the 2nd half after Carolina had built up a 38-7 lead.

TENNESSEE-CHATTANOOGA

Florida State's football team won 37-0 as the Seminoles ran the ball 64 plays out of 82 plays total. Roosevelt Snipes and Cletis Jones gained more than 100 yards, and Cedric Jones almost made it. On 22 carries, Snipes got 151 yards and two touchdowns, Cletis 111 yards in 14 carries and Cedric 86 yards in just seven carries. It was 10-0 after a quarter as the Seminoles scored on Derek Schmidt's 31 yard field goal and a 6 yard run by Snipes. In the second quarter, 10 more points came on a 43 yard Schmidt field goal and a 3 yard Snipes run. The score jumped to 27-0 on a Coker pass of 47 yards to Jessie Hester. For the night, Coker hit 10 of 17 passes for 164 yards and Hester caught seven for 117.

FLORIDA

Florida traveled to Tallahassee to play the #12 ranked Seminoles at Doak Campbell Stadium in a thunderstorm. The Gators Big-3 backs combined to rush for 259 yards and Kerwin Bell threw two touchdown passes, a 33 yarder to Lorenzo Neal and a 5 yarder to John L. Williams. Lorenzo Hampton added an 8 yard TD run while Bobby Raymond kicked two field goals in the Gators 27-17 victory.

1984 CITRUS BOWL

Georgia jumped to 14-0 halftime lead on Lars Tate touchdown runs of 4 yards and 2 yards. Florida State rallied with a Derek Schmidt 32 yard field goal and a Tony Smith 1 yard run to pull the Seminoles within 14-9. Kevin Butler kicked a 36 yard field goal to give the Bulldogs a 17-10 lead with 12:10 remaining in the 4th quarter. The Seminoles Lenny Chavers blocked a punt and Joe Wessel returned it 14 yards for a touchdown. Darrin Holoman ran in the 2 point conversion to tie the game, 17-17 with 3:58 left in the game. Georgia made one last drive and tried a desperation 70 yard field goal by Butler, but it fell short as time expired.

1985 Florida State Seminoles

The team was coached by Bobby Bowden in his tenth season. Florida State finished with a 9-3 record and were invited to the Gator Bowl game to play Oklahoma State. The Seminoles' offense scored 402 points while the defense allowed 258 points.

Tony Smith led the team in rushing with 678 yards. Chip Ferguson led the team in passing with 990 yards and 11 touchdown passes. Hassan Jones led the team in receiving with 34 catches for 738 yards. Eric Williams led the team in pass interceptions with 4. Deion Sanders led the team in punt returns with an 8.5 average and 1 touchdown.

Louis Berry {P}, Jamie Dukes {G}, John Ionata {T}, Hassan Jones {WR}, Paul McGowan {LB}, Derek Schnidt {K} and Isaac Williams {DT} were selected to the First team All-South Independent team. Jamie Dukes was selected as Consensus First team All-American. Louis Berry, Victor Floyd {RB}, John Ionata, Hassan Jones, Martin Mayhew {CB}, Paul McGowan, Gerald Nichols {DT}, Derek Schmidt, Pat Tomberlin {T} and Isaac Williams were all named as Honorable Mention All-Americans by the Associated Press. Jones {Minnesota}, Ionata {Dallas}, Cletis Jones {RB} {New England}, Garth Jax {LB} {Dallas}, Jesse Solomon {LB} {Minnesota} and Williams {Indianapolis} were selected in the 1986 NFL draft.

FINAL RANK: #15 AP, #13 CP

Home games were played at Doak Campbell Stadium

Date	Team	Rank		Opp Rank	Opponent	TV			Result
8/31/1985	Florida State	#19	@		Tulane (1-10)	TBS	38	12	W
9/7/1985	Florida State	#17	@	#10	Nebraska (9-3)	ABC	17	13	W
9/21/1985	Florida State	#6	vs		MEMPHIS (2-7-2)	TBS	19	10	W
9/28/1985	Florida State	#4	vs		KANSAS (6-6)		24	20	W
10/12/1985	Florida State	#4	@	#12	Auburn (8-4)	TBS	27	59	L
10/19/1985	Florida State	#13	vs		TULSA (6-5)		76	14	W
10/26/1985	Florida State	#11	@		North Carolina (5-6)		20	10	W
11/2/1985	Florida State	#10	vs	#11	MIAMI (10-2)	ABC	27	35	L
11/9/1985	Florida State	#16	vs		SOUTH CAROLINA (5-6)	ESPN	56	14	W
11/16/1985	Florida State	#15	vs		WESTERN CAROLINA		50	10	W
11/30/1985	Florida State	#12	@	#6	Florida (9-1-1)		14	38	L
12/30/1985	**Florida State**	**#18**	**vs**	**#19**	**Oklahoma State (8-4)**	**ABC**	**34**	**23**	**W**
Coach: Bobby Bowden					**Season Record >>**		**402**	**258**	**9-3**

Schedule Source: Steve's Football Bible LLC

Selected game(s) highlights

Tulane

Danny McManus passed for two touchdowns and ran for two more as Florida State opened the season with a 38-12 victory over the Green Wave. McManus was 15 for 19 for 191 yards. Cletis Jones ran 14 yards for a touchdown. Phillip Bryant (15 yards) and Darrin Holoman {22 yards} were on the receiving end of McManus' touchdown passes.

Nebraska

The Seminoles grilled mighty Nebraska 17-13 On the hottest day for football the state of Nebraska ever had experienced. It was 93 degrees before the kickoff, 96 at halftime, and the heat on the field's artificial turf was measured at more than 130 degrees. Florida State led 17-13 at halftime on a Darrin Holoman 15 yard TD pass from Danny McManus, a Derek Schmidt 20 yard field goal and Cletis Jones 2 yard run. Both teams were unable to score in the 2nd half.

MEMPHIS

Behind 10-0 early, Florida State's defense put the stops to Memphis State and rallied for a 19-10 victory. Derek Schmidt kicked four field goals and Kirk Coker threw a 13 yard pass to Darrin Holloman for a touchdown. The FSU defense held the Tigers to 208 yards of total offense.

KANSAS

Down by 10 going into the final quarter, Florida State rallied behind Chip Ferguson for two quick touchdowns and slipped past Kansas 24-20. Phillip Bryant caught two TD passes, one a 68 yarder to pull the Seminoles within 20-17. Martin Mayhew's interception set up Victor Floyd's 6 yard TD run to put the Seminoles ahead with 10:19 remaining in the game.

Auburn

Auburn, ranked #12, hosted #4 ranked Florida State in an early season Southern showdown at Jordan-Hare Stadium before over 75,000 fans. The Tigers led 31-27 with just under 7 minutes left in the game, then exploded for 28 points in five minutes to cruise to a 59-27 victory over the Seminoles. Kevin Porter returned an interception 33 yards for a touchdown, Ron Stallworth returned an interception 22 yards for a touchdown and Demetrius Threatt ran 8 yards for a touchdown after an FSU fumble that blew the game open. Bo Jackson had touchdown runs of 53 yards and 35 yards.

TULSA

Florida State stormed to a record-breaking 76-14 victory over the Golden Hurricane. Deion Sanders finished it off with a 100 yard runback of an interception. Paul McGown returned an interception 31 yards for a touchdown and five other Seminoles scored touchdowns, including Tony Smith, Hassan Jones and Phillip Bryant, who all scored twice each. Eric Thomas passed for two touchdowns and Chip Ferguson threw three touchdowns. Tony Smith ran for 147 yards.

North Carolina

North Carolina was ahead 10-0 going into the 2nd half, but the Seminoles overcame six turnovers, three in the first quarter, five in the first half to pull out a 20-10 victory at Kenan Stadium. Derek Schmidt kicked two field goals and Hassan Jones caught a 10 yard TD pass from Chip Ferguson to give the Noles a tenuous 13-10 lead. Martin Mayhew sealed the deal with a 62 yard interception for a touchdown with 3 seconds left in the game.

MIAMI

Ahead 24-14 at halftime, Florida State got outscored by Miami 21-3 in the 2nd half, including 14-0 in the 4th quarter, and fell 35-27. Despite being sacked seven times by the Seminole defense, Vinny Testaverde completed 23 of 41 passes for four touchdowns and 339 yards. Chip Ferguson threw two touchdown passes, one to Hassan Jones (8 yards) and one to Pat Carter (26 yards). John Hadley blocked a 2nd quarter Miami punt and Brian Davis fell on it in the end zone for a touchdown. Derek Schmidt kicked two field goals for the Seminoles.

SOUTH CAROLINA

Victor Floyd ran for 212 yards on just 15 carries, as the Seminoles blew out South Carolina 56-14. Pounding out 409 yards running of its 542 total, Keith Ross had 163 yards on 23 carries. Five different Seminoles scored as FSU raced to a 35-0 halftime lead. Chip Ferguson threw for three touchdowns and ran for one. Victor Floyd and Keith Ross each had two touchdown runs, Floyd for 14 yards and 61 yards. Ross TD runs were for 53 yards and 5 yards.

WESTERN CAROLINA

A crowd of 52,778 at Doak Campbell Stadium, watched as Bobby Bowden won his 10th straight Homecoming game. Ahead 19-0 at halftime, the Seminoles cruised to a 50-10 victory over the Catamounts. Derek Schmidt kicked three field goals. Tony Smith ran for 114 yards and one touchdown. Keith Ross ran for 103 yards and two touchdowns. Chuck Wells and Victor Floyd each scored touchdowns and Hassan Jones caught a 10 yard TD pass from Chip Ferguson.

Florida

Florida hosted the Seminoles at Florida Field. The Gators were ranked #6 and the Seminoles were ranked #12. Kerwin Bell led the Gator offense completing 14 of 22 passes for 343 yards and 3 touchdown passes on the way to a 38-14 rout of the Noles. Neal Anderson ran for 6 yard and 3 yard touchdown runs while Ricky Nattiel caught TD passes of 75 yards and 14 yards. Frankie Neal contributed with an 82 yard TD reception as the Gators rang up 478 yards of total offense.

1985 GATOR BOWL

Freshman quarterback Chip Ferguson threw for 338 yards and a pair of touchdowns, and Tony Smith added 201 yards rushing as Florida State defeated Oklahoma State, 34–23, in the 41st annual Gator Bowl. FSU, which entered the game without its top three receivers, tricked Oklahoma State's defense by throwing on 15 of its first 20 plays. Derek Schmidt field goals of 23 and 39 yards, and a 39 yard touchdown catch by Herb Gainer sandwiched in between, gave FSU a 13–0 halftime lead. Oklahoma State got on the scoreboard following the intermission when a 63 yard drive ended in a 33 yard field goal by Brad Dennis. Ferguson, who was named Florida State's MVP, went back to the air, taking the Seminoles 73 yards on the next series before handing it off to senior fullback Cletis Jones for a three yard touchdown run. An interception by Deion Sanders gave the ball back to FSU, and Ferguson used just five plays before hitting Gainer with a 19 yard touchdown pass. That made the score 27–3, Florida State. Oklahoma State didn't give up with Cowboy quarterback Ronnie William passing 29 yards to All-America tailback Thurman Thomas for an Oklahoma State touchdown. Following a Ferguson fumble, Williams handed it off to Thomas, who threw back to the quarterback for a 12 yard touchdown that closed the score to 27–17. Early in the fourth quarter, Ferguson scored from one yard out to give the Seminoles a 17 point cushion. The Cowboys added a late touchdown on a 31–yard pass from Williams to Hart Lee Dykes. Sophomore wide receiver Randy White, who had never caught a pass at FSU, grabbed four passes for 87 yards in the first half while Gainer, who had caught just five during the regular season, hauled in seven for 148 yards and two touchdown. Smith's 201 rushing yards came on 24 carries. The Seminole defense held Thomas in check the entire game, limiting him to 97 yards on 26 attempts. Florida State finished the season with a 9–3 record.

1986 Florida State Seminoles

The team was coached by Bobby Bowden in his eleventh season. Florida State finished with a 7-4-1 record and were invited to the All-American Bowl game to play Indiana. The Seminoles' offense scored 393 points while the defense allowed 218 points.

Victor Floyd led the team in rushing with 654 yards. Danny McManus led the team in passing with 872 yards. Herb Gainer led the team in receiving with 27 catches for 441 yards and 5 touchdowns. Deion Sanders led the team with 4 pass interceptions.

Louis Berry {P}, Pat Carter {TE}, Paul McGowan {LB}, Gerald Nichols {DT}, Deion Sanders {DB} and Pat Tomberlin {T} were selected to the First team All-South Independent team. Deion Sanders was selected as a Consensus All-American. Louis Berry, Pat Carter, Fred Jones {LB}, Paul McGowan, Gerald Nichols, Derek Schnidt {K} and Pat Tomberlin were named Honorable Mention All-Americans by the Associated Press. Nichols {New York Jets} was selected in the 1987 NFL draft.

FINAL RANK: #20 CP

Home games were played at Doak Campbell Stadium

Date	Team	Rank		Opp #	Opponent	TV			
8/30/1986	Florida State	**#11**	vs		TOLEDO (7-4)		24	0	W
9/6/1986	Florida State	**#11**	@	#8	Nebraska (10-2)	ABC	17	34	L
9/20/1986	Florida State	**#15**	vs		NORTH CAROLINA (7-4-1)	TBS	10	10	**T**
9/27/1986	Florida State	**#20**	@	#5	Michigan (11-2)	TBS	18	20	L
10/11/1986	Florida State		vs		TULANE (4-7)		54	21	W
10/18/1986	Florida State		vs		WICHITA STATE (3-8)		59	3	W
10/25/1986	Florida State		@		Louisville (3-8)		54	18	W
11/1/1986	Florida State	**#20**	@	#1	Miami (11-1)	CBS	23	41	L
11/8/1986	Florida State		@		South Carolina (3-6-2)		45	28	W
11/15/1986	Florida State		vs		SOUTHERN MISS (6-5)		49	13	W
11/29/1986	Florida State		vs		FLORIDA (6-5)		13	17	L
12/31/1986	**Florida State**		vs		**Indiana (6-6)**	TBS	27	13	W
Coach: Bobby Bowden					**Season Record >>**		393	218	7-4-1

Schedule Source: Steve's Football Bible LLC

Selected game(s) highlights

Nebraska

This was the first ever night game at Memorial Stadium. Nebraska's loss to FSU in Lincoln the previous year was avenged when the Cornhuskers came back from a halftime deficit, outscoring FSU 24-3 and holding the Seminoles to -2 yards in the second half. Victor Floyd caught a 30 yard TD pass from Chip Ferguson and Sammie Smith ran 57 yards for a touchdown before the Cornhusker defense put the clamps on the Seminole offense.

NORTH CAROLINA

Derek Schmidt missed a 37 yard field goal with 8 seconds left in the game and the Seminoles had to settle for a 10-10 tie with the Tar Heels. After Felton Hayes blocked a Tar Heel punt out of the end zone for a safety, Ronald Lewis caught a 28 yard TD pass from Peter Tom Willis, then Willis threw to Herb Gainer for the 2 point conversion to tie the game at 10-10.

Michigan

Michigan defeated Florida State, 20–18, before a homecoming crowd of 105,507 at Michigan Stadium. It was the first game ever played between Michigan and Florida State football programs. Michigan out-gained Florida State by 332 yards to 285 yards. For the Wolverines, Jim Harbaugh completed nine of 16 passes for 122 yards, and Jamie Morris rushed for 99 yards on 19 carries.

For the Seminoles, Chip Ferguson completed six of 19 passes for 73 yards, and Sammie Smith rushed for 75 yards on 13 carries. Michigan's defense recovered a fumble and intercepted three passes, including three by Ivan Hicks.

TULANE

All three phases of the game were working for the Seminoles as they scored on offense, defense and special teams on the way to a 54-21 victory over the Green Wave. Felton Hayes returned an interception 20 yards for a touchdown. John Parks blocked a Tulane punt through the end zone for a safety. Keith Ross returned the free kick/punt 70 yards for a touchdown. Five different Seminoles ran for touchdowns.

WICHITA STATE

Rolling to a 38-0 halftime lead, Florida State cruised on to a 59-3 victory over the Shockers. Danny McManus threw for 201 yards and three touchdowns. Ronald Lewis caught two touchdown passes. David Palmer ran for two touchdowns and four different Seminoles added touchdowns as the Seminoles rang up 493 yards of total offense.

Louisville

The Seminoles recovered from a 7-0 deficit and raced past Louisville 54-18. Danny McManus misfired on his first pass attempt of the evening, then connected on eight straight, including three for touchdowns, to lead the Seminoles to a 37-18 halftime advantage. FSU quickly extended it to 44-18 five plays into the second half on a 9 yard McManus run. Victor Floyd ran for 118 yards and a touchdown. Herb Gainer caught two touchdown passes from Danny McManus. Darrin Holloman, Dayne Williams and Dexter Carter scored for the Seminoles as well.

Miami

Ahead 17-14 with 7:49 left in the first half, the Seminoles lost their quarterback and the game to #1 Miami 41-23. With Danny McManus sidelined due to a thumb injury, Florida State struggled on, leading 20-14 at the half, hanging on to a 23-21 lead going into the final quarter. Miami then went on a 20 point eruption in the 4th quarter as Testaverde finished the day with three TDs passing, and two running, completing 21 of 35 throws for 315 yards. Derek Schmidt kicked three field goals and Dexter Carter returned a kickoff 105 yards for a touchdown, which was the highlight of the day for the Seminoles.

South Carolina

Down 15 points in the second quarter, the Seminoles exploded for 29 third quarter points and won 45-28. Chip Ferguson completed 15 of 22 passes for 228 yards and threw a 24 yard TD pass to Victor Floyd. Floyd and Dayne Williams led the 3rd quarter charge with both running for two touchdowns each. Derek Schmidt kicked three field goals for the Noles.

SOUTHERN MISS

Danny McManus led the Seminoles to a 28-0 halftime lead. Much of the rest was mop-up work, including Sammie Smith on a 62 yard run for the last touchdown of the day as the Seminoles routed Southern Miss 49-13. Dedrick Dodge and Eric Williams both returned interceptions for touchdowns. Dayne Williams, Victor Floyd and Keith Ross each ran for touchdowns. Tom O'Malley caught a 14 yard pass from Chip Ferguson.

FLORIDA

Florida traveled to Tallahassee to play the Seminoles at Doak Campbell Stadium in front of over 61,000 fans. The teams were 10-10 at halftime and the Noles had a 13-10 lead late in the 4th quarter. Kerwin Bell threw an 18 yard TD pass to Ricky Nattiel with 3:50 left in the game and the Gators held on for a 17-13 victory.

1986 ALL-AMERICAN BOWL

Tailback Sammie Smith had his best game to date as a Seminole, rushing for 205 yards and two touchdowns, as the FSU scored a 27-13 win over Indiana in the 10th annual All-American Bowl. Although FSU was outgained in total yards and time of possession, Indiana seemed to be its own worst enemy, missing four scoring opportunities inside the FSU 31 yard line. The Hoosiers gained 383 yards to the

Seminoles' 342 and held on to the ball almost 15 more minutes than FSU. The Hoosiers scored first in the game. After driving 60 yards in 13 plays, Pete Stoyanovich kicked a 35 yard field goal to give his team the 3-0 lead. FSU then opened its running game and found that its weapon for the evening would be Smith, a redshirt freshman. He ran for 28 yards on four carries and caught a pass for 7 more as the Seminoles moved down the field. Capping the drive, Sammie took it in from the 4 yard line. Hoosier linebacker Van Waiters blocked the PAT attempt. FSU took a 6-3 lead. Following a missed 47 yard field goal attempt by Stoyanovich, FSU scored on a 9 yard run by Smith. The Seminoles would carry that 13-3 lead into intermission after another Indiana drive stalled with a missed field goal. The Hoosiers had moved to the FSU 5 yard line but following a penalty and a Terry Warren sack of IU quarterback Dave Kramme, Stoyanovich missed from 41 yards. Florida State made it 20-3 on the first possession of the second half when Smith ran three times for 20 yards and the Holloman brothers, Darrin, and Tanner, did the rest. The drive was sparked by a 36 yard reverse by Darrin, while senior fullback Tanner collected 15 yards, including the 8 yard TD. IU came right back on a long drive of its own, but Stoyanovich missed a third time, this time from 49 yards out. The Hoosier defense continued to hold the Seminoles and late in the third period, Indiana tried to get back into the game. First, Tony Buford pulled in a 20 yard pass from Kramme at the FSU 37. Freshman running back Anthony Thompson then gained 17 tough yards on five carries to push the Hoosiers to the FSU 4. Fullback Andre Powell closed the gap to 20-10 with a two yard plunge at the 1:19 mark of the quarter. Following a Danny McManus interception in the opening minutes of the fourth quarter, Indiana drove 56 yards on 7 plays and a Stoyanovich 30 yard field goal closed the score to 20-13. But FSU put its fans' worries aside, marching right back behind a handful of carries by Smith that netted 44 yards, and scoring on a 10 yard run by Tanner Holloman. For his performance, Smith was awarded the MVP trophy, and the Seminoles finished the season with a 7-4-1 record. Indiana finished the season with a 6-6 record.

1987 Florida State Seminoles

The team was coached by Bobby Bowden. The Seminoles finished with an 11-1 record and finished #2 in the Polls. They finished the season with a 31-28 win in the Fiesta Bowl over #5 ranked Nebraska. Pat Carter, Paul McGowan and Deion Sanders were selected as first team All-Americans. McGowan won the Butkus Award. Pat Carter {TE} {Detroit}, Paul McGowan {LB} {Minnesota}, Martin Mayhew {DB} {Buffalo} and Danny McManus {QB} {Kansas City} were selected in the 1988 NFL Draft.

FINAL RANK: #2 AP, #2 CP

Home games were played at Doak Campbell Stadium

Date	Team	Rank		Opp Rank	Opponent	TV			Result
9/5/1987	Florida State	#8	vs		TEXAS TECH (6-4-1)		40	16	W
9/12/1987	Florida State	#8	@		East Carolina (5-6)		44	3	W
9/19/1987	Florida State	#7	vs		MEMPHIS (5-5-1)		41	24	W
9/26/1987	Florida State	#6	@		Michigan State (9-2-1)		31	3	W
10/3/1987	Florida State	#4	vs	#3	MIAMI (12-0)	CBS	25	26	L
10/10/1987	Florida State	#6	@		Southern Miss (6-5)		61	10	W
10/17/1987	Florida State	#4	vs		LOUISVILLE (3-7-1)		32	9	W
10/31/1987	Florida State	#4	vs		TULANE (6-6)		73	14	W
11/7/1987	Florida State	#4	@	#6	Auburn (9-1-2)	CBS	34	6	W
11/14/1987	Florida State	#4	vs		FURMAN		41	10	W
11/28/1987	Florida State	#3	@		Florida (6-6)	CBS	28	14	W
1/1/1988	**Florida State**	#3	vs	#5	**Nebraska (10-2)**	NBC	**31**	**28**	**W**
Coach: Bobby Bowden					**Season Record >>**		**481**	**163**	**11-1**

Schedule Source: Steve's Football Bible LLC

Selected game(s) highlights

TEXAS TECH

The Seminoles opened the season ranked #8 and hosted **Texas Tech**. Florida State beat the Red Raiders 40-16, behind Danny McManus' 275 yards passing. Herb Gainer caught 6 passes for 128 yards.

East Carolina

Still ranked #8, Florida State traveled to Greenville to play **East Carolina**. Sammie Smith ran for 244 yards. The defense was dominating, holding the Pirates to 222 yards, and left with a 44-3 victory.

MEMPHIS STATE

Now ranked #7, the Seminoles hosted **Memphis State**. FSU jumped to a 21-0 first quarter lead and held on for a 41-24 win. Dexter Carter led the way with 311 all-purpose yards (135 rush, 63 receiving, 113 return), and three touchdowns. Danny McManus had 247 yards passing.

Michigan State

Ranked #6, FSU traveled to East Lansing to play the eventual Big Ten Champs, **Michigan State**. Ronald Lewis scored on a 56 yard run and an 8 yard pass from Danny McManus to lead the Seminoles to a 31-3 win. The defense held the Spartans to 215 yards.

MIAMI

This is the game that is widely accepted as elevating the rivalry to a national level. The Seminoles held a 10-3 halftime lead and returned a block punt for a touchdown in the third quarter, extending their lead to 16-3, but senior kicker Derek Schmidt missed the extra point attempt in what was perhaps a sign of things to come. The Hurricanes scored just before the start of the fourth quarter, and sophomore quarterback Steve Walsh connected with wide receiver Brian Blades to convert the 2 point try, trimming FSU's lead to 19-11 heading into the final 15 minutes. Miami scored again early in the fourth quarter and again converted on a 2 point try to tie the game. The Seminoles were driving when senior quarterback Danny McManus fumbled the snap and Hurricanes cornerback Bennie Blades recovered the football. Walsh and company capitalized on FSU's miscue, finding junior wide receiver Michael Irvin in the end zone to take a 26-19 lead. When McManus connected with sophomore wide receiver Ronald Lewis on 18 yard touchdown with 42 seconds left in the game, FSU head coach Bobby Bowden was faced with a choice: attempt the extra point and settle for a 26-26 tie (the NCAA didn't institute overtime until 1996) or go for the win. Bowden initially sent out Schmidt to kick the extra point, but he was persuaded by his team to let the offense try to win it. Miami safety Bubba McDowell broke up McManus' underthrown pass intended for tight end Pat Carter in the end zone, handing the Seminoles their only loss of the season.

Southern Mississippi

The Noles' fell to #6 in the polls as they traveled to Hattiesburg to play **Southern Miss**. FSU spoiled the Golden Eagles homecoming game with a 61-10 blowout victory. Bill Ragans returned a blocked punt 32 yards for a touchdown. Sammie Smith ran for 142 yards and a touchdown and Derek Schmidt added three field goals.

LOUISVILLE

Back up to #4 in the polls, FSU hosted **Louisville**. Victor Floyd ran for 124 yards and one TD; Sammie Smith ran for 119 yards and one TD, and the Seminoles cruised to a 32-9 win.

TULANE

Still ranked #4, FSU hosted **Tulane** in their homecoming game before 53,210 at Doak Campbell Stadium. Sammie Smith rushed for 111 yards and three touchdowns. Dayne Williams scored two touchdowns and Deion Sanders returned a blocked punt 49 yards for a touchdown in the Seminoles 73-14 victory over the Green Wave.

Auburn

In one of the most anticipated games of the season, the #4 ranked Florida State Seminoles came to Jordan-Hare to face #6 Auburn before a packed stadium of over 85,000 fans. The Seminoles dominated, giving the Tigers their first loss of the season, 34-6. The Seminoles jumped to a 27-3 halftime lead and never looked back. Herb Gainer caught two TD passes from Danny McManus for the Noles.

FURMAN

Still ranked #4, FSU hosted **Furman** at "The Doak". Sammie Smith ran for 176 yards and two touchdowns. The Seminoles defense held the Paladins to 70 yards passing on the way to a 41-10 victory.

Florida

Florida entertained the Seminoles at Florida Field before over 74,000 fans. The Gators jumped to a 14-3 lead midway in the 2nd quarter on two Emmitt Smith touchdown runs. The Seminoles Dan Schmidt kept FSU in the game with 4 field goals and then put the game away in the 2nd half on two Dayne Williams 1 yard TD runs for a 28-14 victory. The win broke a 6 game losing streak to the Gators.

1988 FIESTA BOWL

Florida State, ranked #3, got on the board in the second quarter when quarterback Danny McManus threw a 10 yard touchdown pass to Herb Gainer. With under five minutes left in the first half, running back Dayne Williams scored from four yards out to tie the game at fourteen. With 44 seconds left in the half, McManus connected with Gainer on a 25 yard touchdown pass, marking their second hook-up of the game, and the Seminoles took a 21–14 advantage into halftime. Just over three minutes into the third quarter, #5 Nebraska quarterback Steve Taylor notched the equalizer, rumbling in from two yards out to tie the game at 21. Florida State settled for a field goal for a 24–21 lead. With forty seconds left in the quarter, running back Tyreese Knox scored on a four yard run, giving Nebraska a 28–24 lead. In the fourth quarter, Nebraska got the ball back on its 26 yard line. Following a methodical drive, they managed to move all the way to the FSU two yard line for a first and goal. Knox took the handoff, looking for a sure touchdown, when a defender forced a fumble at the goal line, recovered by Florida State. Ten plays later, Florida State had advanced to the Nebraska 15 and McManus threw a touchdown pass to Ronald Lewis for the clinching 31–28 score.

1988 Florida State Seminoles

The team was coached by Bobby Bowden. The Seminoles finished with an 11-1 record and ranked #3 in both polls. They played in the Sugar Bowl and beat SEC Champion Auburn, 13-7. Deion Sanders was selected as a first team All-American. Sanders won the Jim Thorpe award. Sanders {Atlanta}, Sammie Smith {RB} {Miami}, Pat Tomberlin {G} {Indianapolis}, Marion Butts {RB} {San Diego}, Victor Floyd {RB} {San Diego} and Stan Shiver {DB} {Green Bay} were selected in the 1989 NFL Draft. Sanders (Atlanta) and Sammie Smith (RB) (Miami) were #1 picks.

FINAL RANK: #3 AP, #3 CP

Home games were played at Doak Campbell Stadium

Date	Team	Rank		Opp Rank	Opponent	TV			Result
9/3/1988	Florida State	#1	@	#6	Miami (11-1)	CBS	0	31	L
9/10/1988	Florida State	#10	vs		SOUTHERN MISS (10-2)		49	13	W
9/17/1988	Florida State	#10	@	#3	Clemson (10-2)	CBS	24	21	W
9/24/1988	Florida State	#9	vs		MICHIGAN STATE (6-5-1)	ESPN	30	7	W
10/1/1988	Florida State	#6	@		Tulane (5-6)		48	28	W
10/8/1988	Florida State	#6	vs		GEORGIA SOUTHERN		28	10	W
10/15/1988	Florida State	#5	vs		EAST CAROLINA (3-8)		45	21	W
10/22/1988	Florida State	#5	vs		LOUISIANA TECH (4-7)		66	3	W
11/5/1988	Florida State	#5	@	#15	South Carolina (8-4)	ESPN	59	0	W
11/12/1988	Florida State	#5	vs		VIRGINIA TECH (3-8)		41	14	W
11/26/1988	Florida State	#5	vs		FLORIDA (7-5)	ESPN	52	17	W
1/2/1989	**Florida State**	#4	vs	#7	**Auburn (10-2)**	ABC	13	7	W
Coach: Bobby Bowden					**Season Record >>**		455	172	11-1

Schedule Source: Steve's Football Bible LLC

Selected game(s) highlights

Miami

Florida State opened the season ranked #1 and made the trip to the Orange Bowl to face #6 **Miami**. The Hurricanes rolled, shutting out the Seminoles 31-0. The Hurricanes outgained FSU 450 yards to 242 yards. The Canes defense picked off five passes.

SOUTHERN MISSISSIPPI

The Seminoles fell to #10 in the polls and hosted **Southern Miss** at Doak Campbell Stadium. Deion Sanders returned an interception 39 yards for a touchdown in the game's first 20 seconds. Lawrence Dawsey caught two touchdown passes from Chip Ferguson, including a 93 yarder. Chip Ferguson passed for 239 yards and three TD Passes. Casey Weldon passed for two TD passes as the Seminoles cruised to a 49-13 victory.

Clemson {Puntrooskie}

Florida State traveled to "Death Valley" for the second time ever. The #10 Seminoles, tied 21-21 at #3 Clemson, lined up in punt formation at their own 21. As the punt team faked a bad snap and moved right, upback Dayne Williams put the ball between his legs. LeRoy Butler took it and sprinted left 78 yards to the Tigers 1. Florida State won, 24-21 on Richie Andrews 19 yard field goal and the "Puntrooskie" became instant legend.

MICHIGAN STATE

Now ranked #9, FSU hosted **Michigan State** to "The Doak". Leroy Butler returned an interception 26 yards for a touchdown and Chip Ferguson passed for 215 yards and one TD pass. The Seminoles prevailed 30-7 over the Spartans.

Tulane

Ranked #6, Florida State traveled to New Orleans to play **Tulane**. Sammie Smith ran for 212 yards and two touchdowns. Tracy Sanders returned an interception 34 yards for a touchdown and the Seminoles cruised in a 48-28 win over the Green Wave. Terry Anthony caught two TD passes from Chip Ferguson.

GEORGIA SOUTHERN

Still ranked #6, FSU entertained **Georgia Southern** for homecoming. In a lackluster effort, the Seminoles won 28-10. Chip Ferguson passed for 247 yards and two TD passes. Ronald Lewis caught 7 passes for 140 yards and a TD reception.

EAST CAROLINA

Moving up to #5 in the polls, FSU hosted **East Carolina**. Freshman Chris Parker ran for 158 yards and two touchdowns. Chip Ferguson passed for 150 yards and two TD passes in the Seminoles 45-21 victory.

LOUISIANA TECH

Still #5 in the polls, FSU hosted **Louisiana Tech** at "The Doak". Fourteen plays into the game, the Seminoles led 28-0. The Noles special teams blocked two punts out of the end zone in the 1st quarter. Deion Sanders returned an interception 30 yards for a touchdown. Chirs Parker ran for 125 yards and one touchdown. Terry Anthony caught 6 passes for 106 yards and two TD receptions. Bruce LaSane caught two TD passes to wrap up the scoring for the Noles, making it a 66-3 final.

South Carolina

Florida State, ranked #5, traveled to Brice-Williams Stadium to play #15 **South Carolina**. Anthony Moss returned a blocked punt 8 yards for a touchdown and Lawrence Dawsey caught two TD passes. Bruce LaSane caught 6 passes for 114 yards and Peter Tom Willis passed for 271 yards and four TD passes. The Seminoles rolled in a 59-0 rout of the Gamecocks.

VIRGINIA TECH

Still ranked #5, FSU hosted **Virginia Tech**. Dexter Carter rushed for 119 yards and Sammie Smith rushed for 87 yards. Chip Ferguson and Peter Tom Willis combined for 275 passing yards and two TD passes. The Seminoles rolled to a 41-14 victory over the Hokies.

FLORIDA

Florida traveled to Doak Campbell Stadium to play the Seminoles in front of over 62,000 fans. Florida State scored early and often as they raced to 45-10 lead after 3 quarters. The teams exchanged touchdowns in the 4th quarter and the Noles had a 52-17 rout of their rivals. Chip Ferguson threw for three touchdowns and Odell Haggins returned an interception 11 yards for a touchdown to highlight some of the big play{ers} for Florida State.

1989 SUGAR BOWL

#4 **Florida State** played well on its first offensive possession and running back Dayne Williams capped an 84 yard drive with a two yard touchdown run. That would mark the only touchdown Florida State would score in the game. #7 Auburn quarterback Reggie Slack's first pass of the game was intercepted by strong safety Stan Shiver at the Auburn 44 yard line. Florida State's four-play drive ended with a 25 yard Bill Mason field goal to put the score at 10–0 Florida State. At the end of the first quarter, Florida State defensive back Dedrick Dodge intercepted a Reggie Slack pass at the Auburn 38 yard line and the succeeding drive Mason's second field goal of the game, a 31 yarder, more than three minutes into the second quarter, which was FSU's last score of the game. With 4:09 left in the first half, Reggie Slack threw a 20 yard touchdown pass to Walter Reeves, on a play action pass, making it Florida State 13–7, and neither team scored again. The game was filled with several mistakes from Florida State. Running back Sammie Smith score on a 69 yard touchdown run was wiped out by a holding penalty. Despite the penalty, he would still finish the game with a game high 115 yards rushing. Florida State had first and goal at the Auburn 4 yard line but came up empty after a fake field goal missed. These errors nearly cost Florida State the game. With 3:30 left in the game, Auburn drove from its own 4 yard line to Florida State's 22 yard line. With five seconds left, after a defensive pass interference penalty went uncalled that would have put the Tigers at the one yard line with first and goal to go, Reggie Slack's pass was intercepted in the end zone by Deion Sanders, sealing Florida State's win.

1989 Florida State Seminoles

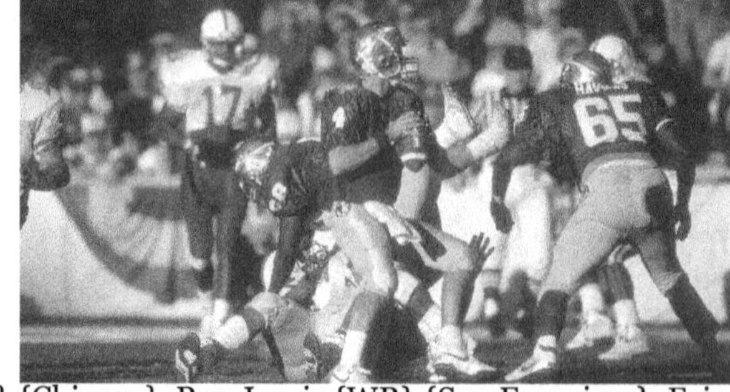

The team was coached by Bobby Bowden. After losing the first two games of the season, the Seminoles ripped off 10 straight wins to finish 10-2 on the season, ending with a dominating 41-17 win over Nebraska in the Fiesta Bowl.

Leroy Butler was selected as a first team All-American. Dexter Carter {RB} {San Francisco}, LeRoy Butler {DB} {Green Bay}, Peter Tom Willis {QB} {Chicago}, Ron Lewis {WR} {San Francisco}, Eric Hayes {DT} {Seattle}, Odell Haggins {DT} {San Francisco} and Terry Anthony {WR} {Tampa Bay} were selected in the 1990 NFL Draft. Dexter Carter was a #1 pick.

FINAL RANK: #3 AP, #2 CP

Home games were played at Doak Campbell Stadium

Date	Team	Rank		Opp Rank	Opponent	TV			
9/2/1989	Florida State	#6	vs		SOUTHERN MISS (5-6)	TBS	26	30	L
9/9/1989	Florida State	#16	vs	#10	CLEMSON (10-2)	ESPN	23	34	L
9/16/1989	Florida State		@	#21	Lsu (4-7)	ESPN	31	21	W
9/23/1989	Florida State		vs		TULANE (4-8)		59	9	W
10/7/1989	Florida State	#22	@	#17	Syracuse (8-4)		41	10	W
10/14/1989	Florida State	#19	@		Virginia Tech (6-4-1)		41	7	W
10/21/1989	Florida State	#14	vs	#11	AUBURN (10-2)	ESPN	22	14	W
10/28/1989	Florida State	#9	vs	#2	MIAMI (11-1)	ESPN	24	10	W
11/4/1989	Florida State	#6	vs		SOUTH CAROLINA (6-4-1)		35	10	W
11/18/1989	Florida State	#5	vs		MEMPHIS (2-9)		57	20	W
12/2/1989	Florida State	#6	@		Florida (7-5)	ESPN	24	17	W
1/1/1990	**Florida State**	#5	vs	#6	**Nebraska (10-2)**	NBC	**41**	**17**	**W**
Coach: Bobby Bowden					**Season Record >>**		424	199	10-2

Schedule Source: Steve's Football Bible LLC

Selected game(s) highlights

SOUTHERN MISSISSIPPI

Florida State opened the season ranked #6 and played **Southern Mississippi** in Jacksonville. Brett Favre hit Anthony Harris for a 2 yard scoring pass to give the Golden Eagles an upset 30-26 victory over the Seminoles. Dexter Carter ran for 118 yards and two touchdowns. Peter Tom Willis passed for 269 yards and one touchdown pass. Bill Mason added two field goals.

CLEMSON

The #10 Auburn Tigers traveled to Doak Campbell Stadium to play #16 Florida State. Terry Allen scored on a pair of one yard runs on Clemson's first possessions of the first and second periods. Clemson linebacker Wayne Simmons came through with a 73 yard interception return for touchdown in the second quarter, the second longest interception return in Clemson history by a linebacker. Terry Allen went 73 yards for a score just 1:16 before halftime to give Clemson a 28-7 lead. Chris Gardocki put the game out of reach with a pair of field goals in the fourth quarter. Gardocki hit a 29 yarder and a 26 yarder in the first 5:51 of the last quarter. Clemson controlled the clock much of the second half behind the ball handling expertise and passing proficiency of quarterback Chris Morocco. Morocco hit 8-9 passes for the evening for 134 yards, leading the Tigers to a 34-23 upset victory.

Lsu

Unranked Florida State traveled to Baton Rouge to play #21 **LSU**. Trailing 21-17 early in the 4th quarter, the Seminoles rallied behind Peter Tom Willis' 7 yard TD run and Edgar Bennett's 7 yard TD run. Terry Anthony caught 7 passes for 101 yards and Peter Tom Willis passed for 301 yards and a TD pass to Anthony.

Syracuse

Now ranked #22, Florida State traveled to #17 **Syracuse**. Coach Bowden stated, "The Defense wrote the checks and the Offense cashed them in". Terrell Buckley returned a blocked punt 69 yards for a touchdown and Leroy Butler returned an interception 87 yards for a touchdown, to blow the game open in a 41-10 Seminole victory. Peter Tom Willis passed for 213 yards and a touchdown.

AUBURN

A 16 point second quarter doomed the visiting #11 Tigers as #14 **Florida State** was able to build a 22-3 lead going into the second half. The Seminoles were held off the scoreboard the rest of the night, but Auburn was only able to muster two scores and 265 yards as they fell 22-14 in Tallahassee.

MIAMI

Florida State beat Miami 24–10 as Miami was missing their starting QB and was forced to play freshman Gino Toretta. However, Miami's defense was the strength of the team having given up an average of only eight points a game in the six games Miami played before facing FSU, so Toretta was not the reason FSU's offense scored 24 points on their defense. Miami went on to win the National Championship upon Craig Erickson's return. FSU did not compete for it, as they suffered two losses at the beginning of the season to a Brett Favre led Southern Miss and Clemson.

SOUTH CAROLINA

Moving up to #6 in the polls, FSU hosted **South Carolina** at "The Doak". Before a homecoming crowd, the Seminoles cruised to a 35-10 win over the Gamecocks. Peter Tom Willis passed for 362 yards and three TD passes. Terry Anthony caught two TD passes. Ronald Lewis rushed for 116 yards.

MEMPHIS STATE

Now ranked #5, FSU hosted **Memphis** in Tallahassee. The Seminoles bolted to a 51-13 halftime lead. Peter Tom Willis passed for 482 yards and six TD passes. Bruce LaSane caught six passes for 111 yards and a touchdown. Ronald Lewis caught two TD passes. The Noles cruised to a 57-20 victory. **Willis' six touchdown passes set a new single game record for FSU.**

Florida

Florida hosted the Seminoles at Ben Hill-Griffin Stadium before over 75,000 fans. Peter Tom Willis completed 20 of 32 passes for 319 yards and three touchdown passes to lead Florida State to a 24-17 victory over the Gators. Stacey Simmons scored on a 3 yard run and Emmitt Smith scored from 2 yards out to lead the Gator offense.

1990 FIESTA BOWL

Less than four minutes into the game, #6 **Nebraska** quarterback Gerry Gdowski threw a 9 yard touchdown pass to Morgan Gregory for the only score of the first quarter. #5 Florida State got on the scoreboard with a 14 yard touchdown pass from quarterback Peter Tom Willis to wide receiver Terry Anthony, tying the game at seven early in the second quarter. Chris Drennan responded with a 39 yard field goal to put Nebraska ahead 10–7 with over twelve minutes left in the half. Willis connected with wide receiver Reggie Johnson for a 5 yard touchdown pass and a 14–10 Seminole lead. He later connected with Dexter Carter for a 10 yard touchdown pass with 24 seconds left in the half, as the Seminoles took a 21–10 lead into the locker room. With six minutes left in the third quarter, Paul Moore scored for Florida State on a 1 yard touchdown run, but the extra point attempt was blocked, and the score was 27–

10. With 3:37 left in the quarter, Willis threw his fourth touchdown pass of the game, an 8 yard strike to Johnson, widening the gap to 34–10. With two seconds left in the quarter, Willis threw a 24 yard touchdown pass to Terry Anthony for a 41–10 lead. In the second and third quarters, Florida State outscored Nebraska 41–3. Nebraska scored the only points of the fourth quarter on a touchdown run by quarterback Mickey Joseph with 1:16 remaining. It was the Huskers' worst defeat in a bowl game in 23 years.

1990 Florida State Seminoles

The team was coached by Bobby Bowden. The Seminoles played Penn State in the Blockbuster Bowl and won 24-17. Lawrence Dawsey was selected a first team All-American. Reggie Johnson {TE} {Denver}, Lawrence Dawsey {WR} {Tampa Bay}, Anthony Moss {LB} {New York Giants}, Richie Andrews {PK} {Detroit} and Hayward Haynes {G} {New Orleans} were selected in the 1991 NFL Draft.

FINAL RANK: #4 AP, #4 CP
Home games were played at Doak Campbell Stadium

9/8/1990	Florida State	#3	vs		EAST CAROLINA (5-6)			45	24	W
9/15/1990	Florida State	#3	vs		GEORGIA SOUTHERN			48	6	W
9/22/1990	Florida State	#2	@		Tulane (4-7)			31	13	W
9/29/1990	Florida State	#2	vs		VIRGINIA TECH (6-5)			39	28	W
10/6/1990	Florida State	#2	@	#9	Miami (10-2)	CBS		22	31	L
10/20/1990	Florida State	#7	@	#5	Auburn (8-3-1)	ESPN		17	20	L
10/27/1990	Florida State	#12	vs		LSU (5-6)	TBS		42	3	W
11/3/1990	Florida State	#12	@		South Carolina (6-5)			41	10	W
11/10/1990	Florida State	#12	vs		CINCINNATI (1-10)			70	21	W
11/17/1990	Florida State	#9	vs		MEMPHIS (4-6-1)			35	3	W
12/1/1990	Florida State	#8	vs	#6	FLORIDA (9-2)	ESPN		45	30	W
12/28/1990	**Florida State**	**#6**	**vs**	**#7**	**Penn State (9-3)**			**24**	**17**	**W**
Coach: Bobby Bowden					**Season Record >>**			**459**	**206**	**10-2**

Schedule Source: Steve's Football Bible LLC

Selected game(s) highlights

EAST CAROLINA

Florida State opened the season ranked #3 and hosted **East Carolina**. Brad Johnson passed for 187 yards and three touchdowns. He also scored on a 1 yard run. Terrell Buckley returned a punt 63 yards for a touchdown and Edgar Bennett added a 4 yard TD reception and a 10 yard run for a touchdown. The Seminoles went on to win 45-24.

GEORGIA SOUTHERN

The #3 ranked Seminoles hosted **Georgia Southern** next. Amp Lee scored two rushing TD's and Terrell Buckley returned a punt 67 yards for a touchdown. The Noles defense held the Eagles offense to 161 yards. Shannon Baker caught two touchdown passes.

Tualne

Now ranked #2, FSU traveled to New Orleans to play **Tulane**. The Seminoles scored the first 24 points of the game and held on for a 31-13 win vs the Green Wave. Brad Johnson and Casey Weldon combined for 280 yards passing and two TD passes.

VIRGINIA TECH

Still ranked #2, FSU welcomed **Virginia Tech** to Tallahassee. The Hokies jumped out to a 21-3 first half lead before the Seminoles came roaring back. Behind Brad Johnson's 254 passing yards and two touchdown passes, FSU still trailed 28-25 in the 3rd quarter. Then the defense and special teams took over. Terrell Buckley returned an interception 53 yards for a touchdown and Errol McKorvey returned a fumble 77 yards for a touchdown to propel the Seminoles to a 39-28 vicotry.

Miami

Ranked #2, the Seminoles traveled to the Orange Bowl in Miami to play #9 ranked **Miami** Hurricanes. FSU fell behind 24-0 in the first half, rallied to cut the lead to 24-16, but the Hurricanes finished strong and went on to a 31-22 victory. Lawrence Dawsey caught 13 passes for 160 yards and one TD reception. Brad Johnson passed for 251 yards. The defense gave up 334 rushing yards.

Auburn

Auburn, ranked #5, hosted #7 ranked Florida State in another Southern showdown at Jordan-Hare Stadium. The Tigers rallied from a 10 point halftime deficit to defeat the Seminoles 20-17. Jim Von Wihl kicked a 39 yard field goal with 2 seconds remaining for the winning margin after the Tigers stopped the Seminoles on a gambling fourth-and-five play with just over a minute remaining. Tony Richardson and Stacey Danley ran for touchdowns for the Tigers.

LSU

Dropping to #12 in the polls, FSU hosted the **LSU** Tigers. Amp Lee rushed for three touchdowns and Casey Weldon passed for 229 yards and one TD pass. The defense held LSU to 207 total yards and forced five turnovers in a dominating 42-3 victory.

South Carolina

Still ranked #12, FSU traveled to Columbia to play **South Carolina**. Amp Lee rushed for 94 yards and scored three touchdowns. Sean Jackson rushed for 119 yards. The Seminoles rushed for 344 yards total in a dominating win vs the Gamecocks, 41-10.

CINCINNATI

Still ranked #12, FSU hosted the **Cincinnati** Bearcats next for homecoming. The Seminoles jumped to a 28-0 1st quarter lead on the way to a 70-21 victory. Lawrence Dawsey caught 7 passes for 141 yards and two TD receptions. Amp Lee and Paul Moore ran for two touchdowns and Terrell Buckley returned an interception 83 yards for a touchdown. Casey Weldon passed for 217 yards and 2 TD passes.

MEMPHIS STATE

Now ranked #9, FSU hosted **Memphis** at The Citrus Bowl in Orlando. Lawrence Dawsey caught eight passes for 133 yards and two TD receptions and added 67 yards on 3 carries. Casey Weldon passed for 252 yards and three TD passes. The defense held the Tigers to 223 total yards.

FLORIDA

In a game dubbed the "Seminole Bowl" due to Florida being ineligible for postseason action, #6 Florida traveled to Tallahassee to play #8 **Florida State**. The Seminoles jumped to a 24-10 halftime lead and led by 22 points in the 2nd half. The Gators closed the gap but ended up on the short end of a 45-30 loss. Shane Matthews completed 29 of 48 passes for 351 yards and two TD passes. TE Kirk Kirkpatrick caught eight passes for 72 yards and a TD pass.

1990 BLOCKBUSTER BOWL

On their first drive, the #6 Seminoles scored on a Richie Andrews 41 yard field goal. #7 **Penn State** could not respond, Florida State benefited off a 39 yard punt return that culminated with an Amp Lee touchdown. Tony Sacca threw a touchdown to David Daniels to put the Nittany Lions on the board with 1:13 remaining in the first quarter. Amp Lee ran for his second touchdown of the game early into the second quarter, giving the Seminoles a ten point lead, which they retained up until the third quarter. In that quarter, Craig Fayak narrowed the lead on a 32 yard field goal. In response, Casey Weldon scored on a touchdown run to make the score 24–10. Penn State narrowed the lead to seven on a Terry Smith touchdown catch from Tom Bill. The Nittany Lions had one final chance to tie the game after getting into the Seminoles' red zone. With three minutes remaining, Seminole John Davis intercepted a pass near the end zone, as the Seminoles soon ran the clock out, winning the first annual Blockbuster Bowl. Amp Lee was named MVP of the game after rushing for 86 yards on 21 attempts for two touchdowns, while also catching 5 passes for 32 yards. Florida State dominated the possession of the game, having it for 33:47, opposed to Penn State's 26:13.

1991 Florida State Seminoles

The team was coached by Bobby Bowden. This was Florida State's final season as an independent; it joined the Atlantic Coast Conference the following season. Florida State finished the season ranked #4 in both polls. They started the season ranked at the top of the polls, but were dropped in the rankings after Wide Right I. The Seminoles offense scored 449 points while the defense allowed 188 points. After the completion of the regular season, they competed in the Cotton Bowl Classic. **Terrell Buckley set a single season record with 12 interceptions.**

Quarterback Casey Weldon was runner-up for the Heisman Trophy. Weldon won the Johnny Unitas Golden Arm Award. Terrell Buckley won the Jim Thorpe Award and the Jack Tatum Award. Marvin Jones (LB), Casey Weldon (QB) and Terrell Buckley (CB) were selected first team All-Americans. Buckley {DB} {Green Bay}, Amp Lee {RB} {San Francisco}, Howard Dinkins {LB} {Atlanta}, Casey Weldon {QB} {Philadelphia}, Edgar Bennett {RB} {Green Bay} and Brad Johnson {QB} {Minnesota} were drafted in the 1993 NFL Draft. Jones (New York Jets) was a #1 pick.

FINAL RANK: #4 AP, #4 CP

Home games were played at Doak Campbell Stadium

8/29/1991	Florida State	#1	vs	#19	Byu (8-3-2)	CBS	44	28	W
9/7/1991	Florida State	#1	vs		TULANE (1-10)		38	11	W
9/14/1991	Florida State	#1	vs		WESTERN MICHIGAN (6-5)		58	0	W
9/28/1991	Florida State	#1	@	#3	Michigan (10-2)	ABC	51	31	W
10/5/1991	Florida State	#1	vs	#10	SYRACUSE (10-2)	ABC	46	14	W
10/12/1991	Florida State	#1	vs		VIRGINIA TECH (5-6)	JPS	33	20	W
10/19/1991	Florida State	#1	vs		MIDDLE TENNESSEE		39	10	W
10/26/1991	Florida State	#1	@		Lsu (5-6)	ESPN	27	16	W
11/2/1991	Florida State	#1	@		Louisville (2-9)		40	15	W
11/9/1991	Florida State	#1	vs		SOUTH CAROLINA (3-6-2)	JPS	38	10	W
11/16/1991	Florida State	#1	vs	#2	MIAMI (12-0)	ABC	16	17	L
11/30/1991	Florida State	#3	@	#5	Florida (10-2)	ABC	9	14	L
1/1/1992	**Florida State**	**#5**	vs	**#9**	**Texas A&M (10-2)**	**CBS**	**10**	**2**	**W**
Coach: Bobby Bowden					**Season Record >>**		**449**	**188**	**11-2**

Schedule Source: Steve's Football Bible LLC

Selected game(s) highlights

Byu

Florida State opened the season ranked #1 vs #19 **BYU** in the Pigskin Classic at Anaheim. Edgar Bennett scored three touchdowns and rushed for 98 yards. Casey Weldon passed 262 yards and one TD pass. The Seminoles outgained BYU 543 yards to 262. Dan Footman tackled Ty Detmer in the end zone for a Safety as FSU whipped the Cougars, 44-28.

TULANE

Ranked #1, FSU hosted **Tulane** in Tallahassee. Warren Hart caught three TD passes and Amp Lee rushed for 112 yards. Lonnie Johnson caught 6 passes for 154 yards and Casey Weldon passed for 249 yards and three TD passes.

WESTERN MICHIGAN

Still ranked #1, FSU hosted **Western Michigan** to Doak Campbell Stadium. Eight different Seminoles scored touchdowns in a 58-0 blowout of the Broncos. The defense forced four turnovers and held Western Michigan to 142 yards.

Michigan

Still ranked #1, FSU traveled to Ann Arbor for a showdown with the #3 ranked **Michigan** Wolverines. Top-ranked FSU humbled Michigan 51-31 before a Michigan Stadium crowd of 106,145. Terrell Buckley started the scoring with a 40 yard interception return for a touchdown and Toddrick McIntosh ended the scoring with a 49 yards interception return for a touchdown. Amp Lee rushed for 122 yards and two touchdowns. Casey Weldon passed for 268 yards and threw 3 TD passes. The Seminole defense forced five turnovers.

SYRACUSE

Ranked #1, FSU hosted the #10 **Syracuse** Orangemen. A crowd of 61,231 watched the Seminoles roll over the Orangemen 46-14. Shannon Baker caught five passes for 139 yards and a TD reception. Amp Lee rushed for 106 yards and Edgar Bennett ran for two touchdowns. Casey Weldon passed for 347 yards and threw 3 TD passes. Toddrick McIntosh tackled Marvin Graves in the end zone for a safety and the defense held Syracuse to 185 yards.

VIRGINIA TECH

Ranked #1 FSU welcomed **Virginia Tech** to the Citrus Bowl in Orlando. Terrell Buckley scored again with a 71 yards interception return for a touchdown. Kevin Knox caught four passes for 132 yards and a touchdown. Amp Lee rushed for 106 yards and a touchdown.

MIDDLE TENNESSEE

Playing its third straight home game, #1 Florida State hosted **Middle Tennessee** for homecoming. The offense led the way again as Shannon Baker caught six passes for 100 yards and two TD receptions. Casey Weldon passed for 294 yards and two TD passes. Dan Mowery added three field goals.

Lsu

The #1 ranked Seminoles traveled to Baton Rouge to play **LSU**. They trailed the Tigers 16-7 at halftime. Behind Amp Lee's 106 yards rushing and three touchdowns, FSU rallied for a 27-16 victory. The Seminoles held LSU to 27 yards rushing.

Louisville

Next up was a trip to **Louisville** to play the Cardinals. Still ranked #1, FSU extended its winning streak to 15 with a 40-15 victory. Brad Johnson passed for 190 yards and a touchdown. Gerry Thomas kicked four field goals. Chris Cowart finished the scoring with a 10 yards interception return for a touchdown. The defense held the Cardinals to 35 yards rushing.

SOUTH CAROLINA

The #1 ranked Seminoles hosted **South Carolina** next. Terrell Buckley intercepted his 9th pass of the season. Amp Lee scored two touchdowns and Casey Weldon passed for 184 yards and 3 TD passes. The defense held the Gamecocks to 92 yards rushing in a 38-10 victory.

MIAMI {Wide Right I}

The Seminoles came into this game as the number one team in the nation, while the Hurricanes were the number two team. It marked only the second time in the AP poll's existence that the top two teams came from the same state. The Seminoles had an impressive 10-0 record and had the third ranked scoring offense in the country with 41 points per game. Miami, in the meantime, was also undefeated at 8-0. Miami came into the game only allowing 58 points all season. Miami won the toss and scored on their first possession to take a 7-0 lead. FSU returned the favor and took the lead scoring 16 straight points to take the lead early in the fourth quarter, 16-7. Miami quickly responded with a field goal of their own to cut the FSU lead to six, 16-10. The Hurricanes got the ball back and Miami fullback, Larry Jones snuck in for a one yard touchdown with 3:01 left to play. FSU was able to march down the field and thanks to a pass interference call, FSU had the ball on Miami's 18 yard line with just 29 seconds to play. With a possibility of a bad snap, FSU decided to try for the 34 yard field goal even though it was only third down. Gerry Thomas came onto the field for the game winning field goal, but it sailed wide right, giving Miami the thrilling victory, 17-16.

Florida

The #5 Gators scored touchdowns on a first quarter run by tailback Errict Rhett, and a 72 yard bomb from Shane Matthews to wide receiver Harrison Houston in the third quarter, and held on to win vs #3 **Florida State**. Gators defensive ends Darren Mickell and Harvey Thomas kept Seminoles quarterback Casey Weldon off balance and on the run in the second half, and, in the fourth quarter, Gators safeties Will White and Del Speer combined to break up a fourth-down pass to the end zone by Weldon with two minutes remaining, thus saving the victory for Florida.

1992 COTTON BOWL

Rain turned out to be the enemy for the **Texas A&M** Aggies, who could only muster a safety after Quentin Coryatt sacked Casey Weldon five minutes into the game. But the Seminoles responded eight minutes later with a Weldon touchdown run that had been set up by an fumble recovery by Clifton Abraham. The game was marred by missed opportunities and 13 turnovers, which tied a bowl record. With 2:40 to go, Gerry Thomas would seal A&M's fate with a 27 yard field goal, making the final score 10-2. This was the first Cotton Bowl Classic to have a team's only score be a safety since the 1981 Cotton Bowl Classic. Sean Jackson rushed for 119 yards on 27 carries for the Seminoles and Chris Crooms had two interceptions for A&M, and both were named MVP.

1992 Florida State Seminoles

The team was coached by Bobby Bowden. Florida State finished #2 in the AP and Coaches polls with an 11–1 record. Bobby Bowden won the Walter Camp coach of the year award. The season was FSU's first in the Atlantic Coast Conference and saw them win the league championship with an undefeated record in conference play. The Seminoles offense scored 446 points while the defense allowed 186 points.

Linebacker Marvin Jones finished in fourth place in the Heisman voting while quarterback Charlie Ward finished sixth. Ward was voted the ACC Player of the Year. Marvin Jones won the Lombardi Award, the Butkus Award, and the Jack Lambert Trophy. Tamarick Vanover and Jones were selected as a first team All-American. Jones {LB} {New York Jets}, Carl Simpson {DT} {Chicago}, Dan Footman {DE} {Cleveland}, Reggie Freeman {LB} {New Orleans}, Sterling Palmer {DE} {Washington} and Shannon Baker {WR} {Atlanta} were drafted in the 1993 NFL Draft. Jones (New York Jets) was a #1 pick.

FINAL RANK: #2 AP, #2 CP

Home games were played at Doak Campbell Stadium

9/5/1992	Florida State	#4	vs		DUKE (2-9)		48	21	W
9/12/1992	Florida State	#5	@	#15	Clemson (5-6)	ESPN	24	20	W
9/19/1992	Florida State	#3	@	#16	NC State (9-3-1)	JPS	34	13	W
9/26/1992	Florida State	#3	vs		WAKE FOREST (8-4)		35	7	W
10/3/1992	Florida State	#3	@	#2	Miami (11-1)	ABC	16	19	L
10/10/1992	Florida State	#8	vs		NORTH CAROLINA	JPS	36	13	W
10/17/1992	Florida State	#6	@	#16	Georgia Tech (5-6)	ESPN	29	24	W
10/31/1992	Florida State	#6	@	#23	Virginia (7-4)	ABC	13	3	W
11/7/1992	Florida State	#6	vs		MARYLAND (3-8)	JPS	69	21	W
11/14/1992	Florida State	#5	vs		TULANE (2-9)		70	7	W
11/28/1992	Florida State	#3	vs	#6	FLORIDA (9-4)	ABC	45	24	W
1/1/1993	**Florida State**	#3	vs	#11	Nebraska (9-3)	NBC	27	14	W
Coach: Bobby Bowden					Season Record >>		446	186	11-1

Schedule Source: Steve's Football Bible LLC

Selected game(s) highlights

DUKE

Florida State opened the season ranked #4 and hosted **Duke**. Leon Fowler opened the scoring with a 94 yard interception return for a touchdown. Kez McCorvey caught 3 TD passes from Charlie Ward. Ward passed for 269 yards and threw four TD passes in a 48-21 victory over the Blue Devils.

Clemson

FSU dropped to #5 in the polls as they went to "Death Valley" to play #15 **Clemson**. Kevin Knox caught a 9 yard pass for a touchdown with just over 2 minutes left to rally the Seminoles to a 24-20 victory over the Tigers. John Davis intercepted a pass to seal the win. Charlie Ward passed for 258 yards and threw two TD passes. Ward threw 4 interceptions for the second straight game.

NC State

Moving up to #3 in the polls, the Seminoles traveled to Raleigh to play **NC State**. Corey Sawyer intercepted three passes to lead the defense in a 34-13 win over the Wolfpack. Shannon Baker caught two TD passes and Tamarick Vanover caught five passes for 105 yards. Charlie Ward passed for 275 yards and threw 3 TD passes.

WAKE FOREST

Still ranked #3, FSU hosted **Wake Forest** in Tallahassee. Tamarick Vanover caught 8 passes for 94 yards and one TD reception. Vanover returned a kickoff 96 yards for a touchdown. Sean Jackson added an 88-yard touchdown run. Charlie Ward passed for 240 yards and the Seminoles won easily, 35-7 over the Demon Deacons.

Miami {Wide Right II}

The Hurricanes, the 1991 National Champions, were rolling with a 20-game win streak and a #2 ranking. FSU, on the other hand, came into the game undefeated with a #3 ranking. FSU jumped out to a quick lead as Tamarick Vanover returned the opening kick of 94 yards for a touchdown. Miami came back and scored 10 unanswered points to take a 10-7 lead. FSU would add a field goal to tie the score at ten heading into halftime. The second half became a defensive battle as FSU would score the next six points with two field goals to take a 16-10 lead with just nine minutes remaining in the game. Miami responded on the very next possession as Gino Torreta found Lamar Thomas for a 33 yard touchdown pass to put Miami in the lead at 17-16. Both defenses held tight, but when Miami punted to the Seminoles Corey Sawyer, he attempted an illegal forward pass while in the end zone, resulting in a safety for Miami, now giving them a 19-16 lead. The FSU defense held strong again, forcing Miami to punt the ball to FSU with just 1:35 left to play. Seminoles stand out quarterback Charlie Ward conducted a 59 yard drive to take the ball to Miami's 22 yard line with just seconds to spare. In came the Seminoles kicker Dan Mowrey to try and tie the game with a 39 yard field goal, but the kick went wide right for the second straight year against the Hurricanes.

NORTH CAROLINA

Dropping to #8 after the Miami loss, FSU hosted **North Carolina**. In a somewhat lackluster effort, the Seminoles controlled the clock and defeated the Tar Heels, 36-13. Corey Sawyer returned a punt 74 yards for a touchdown and the Seminole defense held the Tar Heels to 223 yards on offense.

Georgia Tech

Now ranked #6, FSU traveled to historic Grant Field to play #16 **Georgia Tech**. The Noles rallied with 22 fourth quarter points to defeat the Rambling' Wreck 29-24. Kez McCorvey caught a 17 yard pass from Charlie Ward with 1:48 left in the game. Reggie Freeman tackled Tech QB Shawn Davis in the end zone for a safety to seal the victory. William Floyd scored two touchdowns for the Seminoles.

Virginia

Still ranked #6, the Tribe traveled to Charlottesville to play **Virginia**. Charlie Ward threw for a touchdown and passed for a touchdown. Tiger McMillon rushed for 138 yards. The Seminole defense held the Cavaliers to 195 yards of offense.

MARYLAND

Ranked #6, the Tribe welcomed **Maryland** to "The Doak" for homecoming. Charlie Ward passed for 395 yards and four TD passes. Ward added 111 yards on the ground and rushed for a touchdown. Clyde Allen rushed for 103 yards and two touchdowns. Tamarick Vanover caught 7 passes for 107 yards. The Seminoles cruised to a 69-21 victory over the Terrapins.

TULANE

Now ranked #5, Florida State hosted **Tulane**. The Seminoles jumped to 35-0 1st quarter lead on the way to a 70-7 blowout of the Green Wave. Clifton Abraham returned a blocked punt 18 yards for a touchdown and returned an interception 32 yards for a touchdown. Shannon Baker returned a kickoff 90 yards for a touchdown. Charlie Ward threw four TD passes. William Floyd ran for two touchdowns. The defense held Tulane to 186 yards on offense.

FLORIDA

The #6 Gators traveled to Tallahassee to play rival #3 **Florida State** for the "Governors Cup". The Seminoles dominated, jumping out to a 38-17 halftime lead. FSU quarterback Charlie Ward threw for 331 yards. The Gators were held to 40 yards rushing. The teams exchanged touchdowns in the 2nd half and the Seminoles won 45-24.

1993 ORANGE BOWL

The #3 ranked Florida State played #11 ranked **Nebraska** Cornhuskers in the 59th Orange Bowl. In the first quarter, FSU quarterback Charlie Ward found wide receiver Tamarick Vanover for a 25 yard touchdown pass and a 7-0 Seminole lead. FSU's placekicker Dan Mowerey nailed a 41 yard field goal in the second quarter to give Florida State a 10-0 lead. Florida State's Charlie Ward threw a second touchdown pass to give Florida State a 17-0 second quarter lead. Dan Mowerey added 1 24 yard field goal with 2:34 left in the half to give FSU a 20-0 lead. Tommie Frazier threw a 41 yard touchdown pass to wide receiver Corey Dixon with just over a minute in the half to make the halftime score 20-7 FSU. Late in the third quarter, Florida State's Sean Jackson took a handoff, and rushed 11 yards for a touchdown giving FSU a 27-7 lead. Tommie Frazier threw a 1 yard touchdown pass to Gerald Armstrong in the fourth quarter to make the margin 27-14, but the Cornhuskers would get no closer. Florida State held on for a 27-14 win.

1993 Florida State Seminoles {National Champions}

The team was coached by Bobby Bowden and played their home games at Doak Campbell Stadium. Bowden was voted the ACC Coach of the Year. The season gave the Seminoles their first national title as well as their first Heisman winner in quarterback Charlie Ward. Ward also won the Johnny Unitas Award, Walter Camp Award, Maxwell Award and the Davey O'Brien Award and was voted the ACC Player of the Year. FSU beat its first five opponents by an average score of 46–3, during which linebacker Derrick Brooks outscored all five opponents combined.

Brooks was voted the ACC Defensive Player of the Year. The Seminoles were involved in two #1 vs #2 matchups. Ward, Derrick Brooks (LB) and Corey Sawyer (CB) were selected as first team All-Americans. William Floyd {FB} {San Francisco}, Lonnie Johnson {TE} {Buffalo}, Sawyer {Cincinnati}, Sean Jackson {RB} {Houston Oilers}, Kevin Knox {WR} {Buffalo} and Toddrick McIntosh {DT} {Dallas} were selected in the 1994 NFL Draft. William Floyd (RB) (San Francisco) was a #1 pick.

NATIONAL CHAMPIONS					FINAL RANK: #1 AP, #1 CP				
Home games were played at Doak Campbell Stadium									
8/28/1993	Florida State	#1	vs		KANSAS (5-7)	ABC	42	0	W
9/4/1993	Florida State	#1	@		Duke (3-8)		45	7	W
9/11/1993	Florida State	#1	vs	#17	CLEMSON (9-3)	JPS	57	0	W
9/18/1993	Florida State	#1	@	#13	North Carolina (10-3)	ESPN	33	7	W
10/2/1993	Florida State	#1	vs		GEORGIA TECH (5-6)	ABC	51	0	W
10/9/1993	Florida State	#1	vs	#3	MIAMI (9-3)	ABC	28	10	W
10/16/1993	Florida State	#1	vs	#15	VIRGINIA (7-5)	ESPN	40	14	W
10/30/1993	Florida State	#1	vs		WAKE FOREST (2-9)		54	0	W
11/6/1993	Florida State	#1	@		Maryland (2-9)	JPS	49	20	W
11/13/1993	Florida State	#1	@	#2	Notre Dame (11-1)	NBC	24	31	L
11/20/1993	Florida State	#2	vs		NC STATE (7-5)	ESPN	62	3	W
11/27/1993	Florida State	#1	@	#7	Florida (11-2)	ABC	33	21	W
1/1/1994	Florida State	#1	vs	#2	Nebraska (11-1)	NBC	18	16	W
Coach: Bobby Bowden					Season Record >>		536	129	12-1

Schedule Source: Steve's Football Bible LLC

Selected game(s) highlights

KANSAS

Florida State opened the season ranked #1 and met **Kansas** in the Kickoff Classic in East Rutherford, NJ. The Seminoles defense dominated, holding Kansas to 240 yards, in a 42-0 victory over the Jayhawks. Clifton Abraham fell on a blocked punt in the end zone for a touchdown. Sean Jackson ran for 2 touchdowns. Charlie Ward passed for 194 yards and Kez McCorvey caught 5 passes for 107 yards.

Duke

Ranked #1, the Tribe traveled to Durham to play **Duke**. The defense was dominant again, holding the Blue Devils to 147 yards of offense. Derrick Brooks returned an interception 32 yards for a touchdown. Sean Jackson rushed for 107 yards and a touchdown. Charlie Ward passed for 272 yards and two TD passes. The Seminoles cruised to a 45-7 victory.

CLEMSON

The #1 ranked Seminoles hosted #17 **Clemson** at "The Doak". Florida State demolished the Tigers, 57-0, in a dominating offensive performance. Clifton Abraham fell on a blocked punt in the end zone for a touchdown. Derrick Brooks added an 83 yard fumble return for a touchdown. Charlie Ward passed for 317 yards and threw four TD passes. Lonnie Johnson caught two TD passes.

North Carolina

Still ranked #1, the Seminoles traveled to Chapel Hill to play **North Carolina**. After falling behind 7-0, the Tribe scored 33 unanswered points for a 33-7 victory over the Tar Heels. Derrick Brooks returned an interception 49 yards for a touchdown. Charlie Ward passed for 303 yards and two TD passes. Scott Bentley added two field goals.

GEORGIA TECH

Ranked #1, the Seminoles hosted **Georgia Tech**. Florida State rolled up 582 yards of offense and the defense held the Ramblin' Wreck to 110 yards of offense in a 51-0 victory. Warrick Dunn scored three touchdowns. Charlie Ward passed for 222 yards and threw 4 TD passes.

MIAMI

Sean Jackson ran 69 yards on just the third offensive play for Florida State and the Noles had the lead. After Miami tied it up with their own rushing touchdown, the Seminoles against went with the big play as Charlie Ward found Matt Frier for the 72 yard strike and FSU football didn't look back the rest of the game. Ward added a two yard run right before the half and the Seminoles had their biggest lead in the series in quite some time. Both teams would go scoreless in the third quarter, with Miami kicking a field goal early in the fourth and be driving for something late in the quarter when Devin Bush stepped in front of a Frank Costa pass and went 40 yards for a touchdown. The Seminoles held the Miami offense to just 320 yards on the day and their lowest point total since the two teams played during the 1989 season.

VIRGINIA

Florida State, ranked #1, welcomed #15 **Virginia** to Tallahassee. The Seminoles rolled to a 30-0 halftime lead on the way to a 40-14 win over the Cavaliers. Tamarick Vanover caught 6 passes for 129 yards and a touchdown. Charlie Ward passed for 322 yards and three TD passes. Scott Bentley added two field goals.

WAKE FOREST

The #1 ranked Seminoles hosted **Wake Forest** next. The Tribe dominated the Demon Deacons, cruising to a 54-0 win. Warrick Dunn ran for 162 yards and a touchdown. Sean Jackson ran for 116 yards. Charlie Ward and Jon Stark combined for 233 yards passing. Clifton Abraham returned an interception 29 yards for a touchdown.

Maryland

The Seminoles traveled to College Park to play **Maryland**. Still ranked #1, FSU rolled to a 49-20 victory. Danny Kanell, playing for an injured Charlie Ward, passed for 341 yards and five TD passes. Kez McCorvey caught 10 passes for 122 yards and a touchdown. Kevin Knox caught 5 passes for 89 yards and two TD passes. Sean Jackson ran for 95 yards and two touchdowns.

Notre Dame {#1 vs #2}

In the most anticipated game of the season, which was dubbed a "Game of the Century", #1 Florida State traveled to South Bend to play #2 **Notre Dame**. Charlie Ward's final pass was knocked down at the goal line by Shawn Wooden as time expired, giving second ranked Notre Dame a thrilling 31-24 victory before 59,075 fans at Notre Dame Stadium. Notre Dame outplayed Florida State the entire game to the tune of a 31-17 lead in the fourth quarter. The offense had hung its shoulders around their junior back Lee Becton who had yet another 100+ yard afternoon. With 1:39 left, Ward drove Florida State down the field and hit Kez McCorvey on 4th-and-20 for a touchdown. The pass bounced off of Notre Dame safety Brian McGee and into McCorvey's hands. Notre Dame then went three-and-out on their next possession, giving Florida State one last shot. In just three plays, Ward led Florida State to the Notre Dame 14 with three seconds to play. On the last play of the game, Ward rolled out and had his final pass attempt batted down, giving the Irish a 31–24 victory.

NC STATE

Florida State returned home, ranked #2, to host **NC State**. The Seminoles led 34-3 at halftime on the way to a 62-3 win over the Wolfpack. Charlie Ward passed for 278 yards and threw four TD passes. Matt Frier caught 8 passes for 91 yards and a touchdown and Kevin Knox caught 7 passes for 91 yards and two TD reception.

Florida

The Seminoles came into The Swamp with a 10−1 record and aspirations of playing for a national championship. Florida State's lone defeat in 1993 was two weeks earlier at the hands of the Notre Dame Fighting Irish, 31−24, in South Bend. The Gators entered the contest 9−1, with a loss at Auburn, but had already clinched the SEC Eastern Division. The 'Noles took an early 13−0 lead in front of what was a state record 85,507 fans at Florida Field. FSU would never relinquish that lead. The Gators finally answered just before halftime when freshman Quarterback Danny Wuerffel hit his receiver Willie Jackson for an 11 yard touchdown pass to cut the Florida State lead to 13−7. Florida State got back to work on their first drive of the second half. Heisman Trophy winning quarterback Charlie Ward completed 5 of 7 passes for 62 yards, including a 7 yard touchdown strike to Kez McCorvey, giving the Seminoles a 20−7 lead. From this point, FSU appeared to have the upper hand as they took an impressive 27−7 lead entering the final quarter. Florida answered with another touchdown pass to Willie Jackson, this time from Terry Dean. FSU stormed right back and just when it appeared the 'Noles would seal the victory, fullback William Floyd coughed up the football and the Florida defense recovered at its own 9 yard line, giving the Gators and its crowd new life. After converting several fourth downs, Florida, behind Quarterback Terry Dean, drove all the way to the FSU 31. Florida would cut the lead to 27−21 when Dean hit his receiver Jack Jackson for a remarkable, juggling, 31 yard touchdown pass which electrified the record crowd at The Swamp. With the crowd roaring louder than it had all day, Ward led the Seminoles back onto the field with just under 6 minutes left in the game. The Seminoles faced third down at their own 21 yard-line. Unfazed, Charlie Ward hit freshman Warrick Dunn up the sideline for a 79 yard game-clinching touchdown run and a 33−21 FSU win.

1994 ORANGE BOWL

In the second #1 vs #2 matchup of the season, Florida State (#1) met Nebraska (#2) in Miami for the National Championship. Florida State's Scott Bentley provided the first points of the contest, after he kicked a 33 yard field goal to open a 3−0 lead. Nebraska quarterback Tommie Frazier got the Huskers back on track, after he fired an errant pass that was tipped into the hands of wide receiver Reggie Baul. The touchdown gave Nebraska a 7−3 lead. With only 29 seconds left in the first half, Bentley drilled a 25 yard field goal to bring the Seminoles to 7−6, which was the halftime score. Florida State's running back William Floyd gave the Seminoles a 12−7 lead when he scored on a 1 yard touchdown run. Later in the third, a Scott Bentley field goal increased the lead to eight. Nebraska running back Lawrence Phillips scored on a 12 yard touchdown run. The Huskers attempted a two point conversion which would have tied the game, but failed, and trailed 15−13. The Huskers held the Seminoles and took over the ball late, driving to the FSU 10 yard line before stalling. Byron Bennett kicked a 27 yard field goal with just 1:16 remaining on the clock to give the Huskers a slim 16−15 lead. FSU took over with excellent field position at their own 35 yard line. FSU's Heisman trophy winning quarterback Charlie Ward drove the Seminoles all the way to the Nebraska 3 yard line. The Huskers held and forced Bentley to kick his fourth field goal of the night, which was good, and FSU led 18−16 with just 21 seconds remaining. Florida State players and coaches went wild on the sidelines, and were penalized for excessive celebration, costing them 15 yards on the ensuing kickoff. As a result, the Huskers were able to get a decent return and began their final possession at their own 43 yard line.

As time ran down, Frazier hit tight end Trumane Bell for a 29 yard gain to the FSU 28 yard line. The clock ticked down to 0:00, setting off more chaos on the FSU sideline, complete with the compulsory Gatorade bath given to FSU coach Bobby Bowden. However, referee John Soffey ruled that Bell was down with one second left on the clock, and ordered the field cleared, allowing Nebraska placekicker Byron Bennett an opportunity to kick the game-winning field goal. But the 45 yard kick sailed wide left, preserving the 18–16 win for the Seminoles.

1994 Florida State Seminoles {ACC Champions}

The team was coached by Bobby Bowden. Bowden was awarded the Home Depot Coach of the Year Award. Derrick Brooks won the Jack Lambert Trophy. Derrick Alexander was voted the ACC Defensive Player of the Year.

Clifton Abraham (CB), Derrick Alexander (DE), Derrick Brooks (LB), Kez McCorvey (WR) and Clay Shiver (C) were selected as first team All-Americans.

Alexander {Minnesota}, Devin Bush {DB} {Atlanta}, Brooks {Tampa Bay}, Corey Fuller {DB} {Minnesota}, Zach Crockett {RB} {Indianapolis}, Tamarick Vanover {WR} {Kansas City}, Chris Cowart {LB} {San Diego}, Abraham {Tampa Bay}, McCorvey {Detroit} and 'Omar Ellison {WR} {San Diego} were selected in the 1995 NFL Draft. Alexander (Minnesota), Brooks (Tampa Bay) and Devon Bush (DB) (Atlanta) were #1 picks.

ACC CHAMPIONS				FINAL RANK: #4 AP, #5 CP				
Home games were played at Doak Campbell Stadium								
9/3/1994	Florida State	#4	vs		VIRGINIA (9-3)	ABC	41	17	W
9/10/1994	Florida State	#4	@		Maryland (4-7)	JPS	52	20	W
9/17/1994	Florida State	#3	@		Wake Forest (3-8)		56	14	W
9/24/1994	Florida State	#3	vs	#13	NORTH CAROLINA	ESPN	31	18	W
10/8/1994	Florida State	#3	@	#13	Miami (10-2)	ESPN	20	34	L
10/22/1994	Florida State	#10	vs		CLEMSON (5-6)	JPS	17	0	W
10/29/1994	Florida State	#9	vs	#16	DUKE (8-4)	ABC	59	20	W
11/5/1994	Florida State	#8	@		Georgia Tech (1-10)	JPS	41	10	W
11/12/1994	Florida State	#8	vs		NOTRE DAME (6-5-1)	ABC	23	16	W
11/19/1994	Florida State	#8	@	#25	NC State (9-3)	ESPN	34	3	W
11/26/1994	Florida State	#7	vs	#4	FLORIDA (10-2-1)	ABC	31	31	T
1/2/1995	Florida State	#7	vs	#5	Florida (10-2-1)	ABC	23	17	W
Coach: Bobby Bowden					Season Record >>		428	200	10-1-1

Schedule Source: Steve's Football Bible LLC

Selected game(s) highlights

VIRGINIA

Florida State opened the season ranked #4 and hosted **Virginia**. The Noles started off fast and rolled to a 41-17 victory over the Cavaliers. Kez McCorvey caught 11 passes for 107 yards and two TD receptions. Danny Kanell passed for 330 yards and threw four TD passes.

Maryland

Ranked #4, the Seminoles traveled to College Park to play **Maryland**. After falling behind 13-3, the Tribe got things rolling. Zak Crockett rushed for 123 yards and two touchdowns. Warrick Dunn rushed for 104 yards and one touchdown. Wayne Messam caught 4 passes for 122 yards and Danny Kanell passed for 427 yards and one TD pass. Florida State prevailed 52-20.

Wake Forest

Now ranked #3, FSU traveled to Winston-Salem to play **Wake Forest**. The Seminoles quickly dispatched the Demon Deacons, winning 56-14. Clifton Abraham fell on a blocked punt in the end zone for a touchdown. Andre Cooper caught 5 passes for 105 yards and a TD reception. Danny Kanell passed for 189 yards and a TD pass. Jon Stark passed for 147 yards and threw two TD passes.

NORTH CAROLINA

FSU returned home ranked #3 to play #13 **North Carolina**. Despite a late rally by the Tar Heels, the Tribe held on for a 31-18 victory. Warrick Dunn led the way with 121 yards rushing and Danny Kanell passed for 233 yards and three TD passes. Kez McCorvey caught 5 passes for 83 yards and a TD reception.

Miami

Still ranked #3, the Seminoles traveled to the Orange Bowl to play rival #13 ranked **Miami**. Florida State turned over the ball 7 times, leading to a 34-20 Hurricane win. Zak Crockett scored twice but Danny Kanell passed for only 153 yards and threw 3 interceptions, one which was returned for a Miami touchdown.

CLEMSON

Falling to #10 in the polls, Florida State held **Clemson** to under 150 yards of total offense and allowed the visiting Tigers just 3 of 18 third down conversions en route to a 17-0 victory in front of a Doak Campbell homecoming crowd of 75,902. Warrick Dunn ran for 133 yards and scored two touchdowns.

DUKE

Now ranked #9, the Seminoles hosted #16 **Duke**. Danny Kanell sparked a 32 point second quarter and Kez McCorvey had a career day as Florida State posted a 59-20 victory over the undefeated Blue Devils. McCorvey caught 10 passes for 207 yards. 'Omar Ellison caught 5 passes for 122 yards and two TD receptions. Danny Kanell passed for 394 yards and three TD passes. The Tribe defense held Duke to 225 yards of offense.

Georgia Tech

Ranked #8, the Seminoles traveled to historic Grant Field to play **Georgia Tech**. The defense held the Ramblin' Wreck to 5 yards rushing in a 41-10 rout. Danny Kanell passed for 154 yards and two TD passes to Melvin Pearsall. Warrick Dunn rushed 13 times for 174 yards and one touchdown.

NOTRE DAME

Still ranked #8, Florida State met **Notre Dame** at The Citrus Bowl in Orlando before 72,868 fans. The defense held the Fighting Irish to 83 yards passing. Dan Mowery kicked three field goals. Rock Preston rushed for 165 yards and a touchdown and Warrick Dunn rushed for 163 yards and a touchdown. Danny Kanell passes for 185 yards.

FLORIDA {The Choke at Doak}

Both teams entered the game with identical 9–1 records. Florida, ranked fourth, and Florida State, the defending national champions, ranked seventh. Florida, under head coach Steve Spurrier, jumped out to an early lead. In the fourth quarter, Florida held a 31–3 lead over Bobby Bowden's Florida State squad. In the greatest fourth quarter comeback of the series, the Seminoles rallied and scored four unanswered touchdowns. With 1:45 left in the game, a 4 yard touchdown run by Rock Preston made the game 31–30. Coach Bowden had to make a decision—he chose to kick the extra  point to tie rather than attempt a 2 point conversion to win the game, resulting in a final score of 31–31. Florida State scored 28 unanswered points in the final fifteen minutes to cap off the biggest fourth quarter comeback of the series. Both teams were selected to the Sugar Bowl for a rematch and the first bowl game between the two teams.

1995 SUGAR BOWL

The 61st Sugar Bowl game was a rematch between the #5 Florida Gators and the #7 Florida State Seminoles. Judd Davis and Dan Mowrey traded field goals in the first quarter before Fred Taylor fumbled the ball, recovered by the Seminoles, which set up a crucial score. Warrick Dunn (who had 182 all-purpose yards) threw a 73 yard touchdown pass to O'mar Ellison that gave the Seminoles a 10-3 lead early in the second quarter as FSU added a McCorvey touchdown catch from Danny Kanell later in the quarter to make it 17-3. But Danny Wuerffel retaliated with an 82 yard touchdown pass to Ike Hilliard to make it 17-

10. Mowrey kicked a field goal before halftime to give the Seminoles a 20-10 lead at halftime. He later kicked his fourth field goal of the day in the third quarter to make it 23-10. But in the fourth quarter, Wuerffel would not be deterred, driving the Gators on an 80 yard drive that took 17 plays, culminating in a Wuerffel touchdown run with 3:47 left to play. Florida was given a chance at their own 19 with 2:27 remaining after a Seminole punt, but Derrick Brooks intercepted Wuerffel's pass as the Seminoles held on to win their first Sugar Bowl since 1989.

1995 Florida State Seminoles {ACC Co-Champions}

The team was coached by Bobby Bowden. This was the first year of the "Jefferson-Eppes" Trophy which went to the winner of the Florida State-Virginia game. It was named for former President of the United States and founder of the University of Virginia, Thomas Jefferson, and Jefferson's grandson Francis W. Eppes, a two-time mayor of Tallahassee and founder of the West Florida Seminary (now Florida State University). **Andre Copper set a single season record with 15 touchdown receptions.**

Danny Kanell was voted the ACC Player of the Year. Clay Shiver (C) was selected as a first team All-American. Shiver {Dallas}, Danny Kanell {QB} {New York Giants}, Phillip Riley {WR} {Philadelphia} and Orpheus Roye {DE} {Pittsburgh} were selected in the 1996 NFL Draft.

ACC CO-CHAMPIONS				FINAL RANK: #4 AP, #5 CP				
Home games were played at Doak Campbell Stadium								
9/2/1995	Florida State	#1	vs		DUKE (3-8)	ABC	70	26	W
9/9/1995	Florida State	#1	@		Clemson (8-4)	ABC	45	26	W
9/16/1995	Florida State	#1	vs		NC STATE (3-8)	JPS	77	17	W
9/23/1995	Florida State	#1	vs		CENTRAL FLORIDA		46	14	W
10/7/1995	Florida State	#1	vs		MIAMI (8-3)	ESPN	41	17	W
10/14/1995	Florida State	#1	vs		WAKE FOREST (1-10)		72	13	W
10/21/1995	Florida State	#1	vs		GEORGIA TECH (6-5)	ABC	42	10	W
11/2/1995	Florida State	#2	@	#24	Virginia (9-4)	ESPN	28	33	L
11/11/1995	Florida State	#6	@		North Carolina (7-5)	JPS	28	12	W
11/18/1995	Florida State	#6	vs		MARYLAND (6-5)	JPS	59	17	W
11/25/1995	Florida State	#6	@	#3	Florida (12-1)	ABC	24	35	L
1/1/1996	**Florida State**	#8	vs	#6	Notre Dame (9-3)	CBS	31	26	W
Coach: Bobby Bowden					Season Record >>		563	246	10-2

Schedule Source: Steve's Football Bible LLC

Selected game(s) highlights

Clemson

Warrick Dunn rushed for 180 yards in 12 carries, with 2 touchdowns, as the #1-ranked Seminoles overwhelmed Clemson, 45-26, before 80,000 at Memorial Stadium. The Seminoles dominated the game as Clemson never got closer than 11 points once FSU got rolling. Pooh Bear Williams ran for two touchdowns. Danny Kanell passed for 170 yards and threw two TD passes.

NC STATE

Still ranked #1, FSU played their first game at "The Doak" and played **NC State.** The Tribe rolled up 745 yards of offense and scored a school record 11 touchdowns. Warrick Dunn ran for 101 yards and scored three touchdowns. Dee Feaster had two rushing touchdowns. E.G. Green caught 5 passes for 122 yards and two TD receptions. Andre Cooper caught 8 passes for 114 yards and two TD receptions. Danny Kanell passed for 310 yards and threw 5 TD passes.

CENTRAL FLORIDA

Ranked #1, FSU hosted **Central Florida**. Pooh Bear Williams scored three touchdowns to lead the way for the Tribe in a 46-14 win vs Golden Knights. Warrick Dunn ran for 100 yards and one touchdown. E.G. Green caught two TD passes. Danny Kanell passed for 232 yards.

MIAMI

The #1 ranked Seminoles hosted rival **Miami** next. Florida State avenged rival Miami's recent success with a 41-17 rout in front of a record Doak Campbell Stadium crowd of 80,350. Warrick Dunn led the way with a career high 184 yards on 20 carries, setting the FSU record with his fifth straight game with over 100 yards. Danny Kanell completed 17 of 27 passes for 170 yards and three touchdowns. Andre Cooper caught 2 TD receptions and the Tribe defense held the Hurricanes to 223 yards of offense.

GEORGIA TECH

Home again, the #1 ranked Seminoles hosted **Georgia Tech**. Danny Kanell completed 41 of 51 passes for 302 yards and four touchdowns to lead Florida State to a win over Georgia Tech 42-10. His 41 completions broke his own FSU single game record of 40 set against Florida last year. E.G. Green caught 9 passes for 83 yards and two TD receptions. Andre Cooper had 10 catches for 103 yards.

Virginia

The #2 Seminoles traveled to Charlottesville to play #24 **Virginia**. Warrick Dunn came just inches away from the goal line on the final play and Virginia fans, which had seen their team lose two games on the final play already in 1995, stormed the field to celebrate a historic 33-28 win over the Seminoles. FSU sent a direct snap to Dunn who stumbled through the line and came up inches short. Danny Kanell passed for 454 yards and threw 3 TD passes. E.G. Green caught 7 passes for 169 yards and Andre Cooper caught 6 passes for 116 yards. Dunn scored two touchdowns for the Tribe.

North Carolina

Falling to #6 in the polls, the Seminoles traveled to Chapel Hill to play **North Carolina**. Mario Edwards returned a blocked punt 24 yards for a touchdown to start the scoring for the Tribe. Warrick Dunn ran for 143 yards and two touchdowns. Danny Kanell passed for 172 yards and threw one TD pass. Andre Cooper caught a TD pass and the Seminoles left with a 28-12 victory.

MARYLAND

Still ranked #6, the Seminoles hosted **Maryland**. The Tribe made quick work of the Terrapins, rolling to a 59-17 victory. Andre Cooper caught 12 passes for 182 yards and two TD receptions. E.G. Green caught 6 passes for 166 yards and a TD reception. Warrick Dunn and Pooh Bear Williams both ran for two touchdowns. Danny Kanell passed for 346 yards and two TD passes.

Florida

#6 **Florida State** Seminoles were beaten 35–24. Danny Wuerffel threw for 453 yards and four touchdowns as Florida held off a second half rally by Florida State and erased the memories of the "Choke at Doak" from the previous season. A 42 yard pass to Ike Hilliard, who evaded multiple defenders on the run after the catch, made it 21–6. The Gators intercepted the Noles three times in the last quarter. Florida tied the all-time school record for consecutive wins with 11.

1996 ORANGE BOWL

The 62nd Orange Bowl featured the #8 Florida State Seminoles and the #6 **Notre Dame** Fighting Irish. This would be the last Orange Bowl played in the Orange Bowl Stadium. Danny Kanell threw two fourth quarter touchdown passes to lead Florida State to a 31-26 come from behind win over Notre Dame.

Notre Dame opened the scoring in the first quarter with a perfect 39 yard scoring strike from Tom Krug to Derrick Mayes. FSU tied the score when Andre Cooper collected a 15 yard scoring pass from Kanell with 6:08 left in the quarter. Trailing 10-7 after a Notre Dame field goal, Kanell found Cooper in the endzone from 10 yards out to give the Seminoles a 14-10 lead at halftime. Mayes regained the lead for the Irish in the third quarter on an acrobatic tip and catch in the endzone over FSU defender Samari Rolle. Trailing 26-14, the Seminoles came on strong with 17 points over the final few minutes of the game. Kanell used just five plays to cover 73 yards and his touchdown pass to E.G. Green with 9:47 left revived the FSU offense. The Tribe defense held Notre Dame without a first down on its next possession and a 30 yard punt return by Dee Feaster set the Seminoles up at the Notre Dame 30. Six plays later Kanell hit Cooper with a TD and then found him for a two point conversion to give the Seminoles the lead. FSU's defense forced the Irish into a fumble and a safety on their last two possessions to preserve the win. Kanell completed 20 of 32 passes for 290 yards and four touchdowns, while Warrick Dunn rushed for 151 yards on 22 carries.

1996 Florida State Seminoles {ACC Champions}

The team was coached by Bobby Bowden. Florida State completed just their third undefeated regular season, and for the second straight season, running back Warrick Dunn was a Heisman Trophy finalist. The Seminoles beat arch-rival Florida in the season finale but lost in a rematch vs the Gators in the Sugar Bowl and were denied a National Championship. Peter Boulware was voted the ACC Defensive Player of the Year. **Peter Boulware set a single season record with 19 sacks.**

Warrick Dunn (RB), Peter Boulware (DE) and Reinard Wilson (DE) were selected as first team All-Americans. Dunn (Tampa Bay), Boulware (Baltimore), Wilson (Cincinnati), Walter Jones {RB} {Tampa Bay}, Henri Crockett {LB} {Atlanta}, Vernon Crawford {LB} {New England} and Byron Capers {DB} {Philadelphia} were selected in the 1997 NFL Draft. and Walter Jones (OT) (Seattle) were #1 picks.

ACC CHAMPIONS					FINAL RANK: #3 AP, #3 CP				
Home games were played at Doak Campbell Stadium									
9/7/1996	Florida State	#3	vs		DUKE (0-11)	ABC	44	7	W
9/19/1996	Florida State	#3	@		NC State (3-8)	ESPN	51	17	W
9/28/1996	Florida State	#2	vs	#11	NORTH CAROLINA (10-2)	ABC	13	0	W
10/5/1996	Florida State	#2	vs		CLEMSON (7-5)	ESPN	34	3	W
10/12/1996	Florida State	#3	@	#6	Miami (9-3)	CBS	34	16	W
10/26/1996	Florida State	#3	vs	#14	VIRGINIA (7-5)	ABC	31	24	W
11/2/1996	Florida State	#3	@		Georgia Tech (5-6)	ESPN	49	3	W
11/9/1996	Florida State	#3	vs		WAKE FOREST (3-8)	JPS	44	7	W
11/16/1996	Florida State	#3	vs	#25	SOUTHERN MISS (8-3)	ESPN	54	14	W
11/23/1996	Florida State	#3	vs		MARYLAND (5-6)	ABC	48	10	W
11/30/1996	Florida State	#2	vs	#1	FLORIDA (12-1)	ABC	24	21	W
1/2/1997	**Florida State**	**#1**	**vs**	**#3**	**Florida (12-1)**	**ABC**	**20**	**52**	**L**
Coach: Bobby Bowden					**Season Record >>**		**446**	**174**	**11-1**

Schedule Source: Steve's Football Bible LLC

Selected game(s) highlights

DUKE

Florida State opened the season ranked #3 and hosted the **Duke** Blue Devils. The Seminole defense forced four turnovers, sacked Duke's quarterbacks four times, set up five FSU scores and limited the Blue Devils to 91 yards of total offense. Scott Bentley kick three field goals and the Noles cruised to a 44-7 victory. Dee Feaster returned a punt 59 yards for a touchdown.

NC State

Florida State, ranked #3, scored three touchdowns within a seven minute span of the first half and cruised to a 51-17 victory over **NC State** in Raleigh in front of 45,700. Warrick Dunn and quarterback Thad Busby ignited the Seminole attack, which churned out 527 yards of total offense. Dunn tied Greg Allen's career record with the 16th 100 yard rushing game of his career. Dunn finished the night with 108 yards and a touchdown. Busby completed 17 of 26 passes for 251 yards and two touchdowns. The FSU defense held the Wolfpack to just 71 yards rushing and 196 total yards. The Seminoles recorded eight quarterback sacks, led by Peter Boulware with two. Byron Capers fell on a blocked punt in the end zone for a touchdown and Shevin Smith returned an interception 61 yards for a touchdown.

NORTH CAROLINA

Florida State climbed to #2 in the polls and once again used its defense and great special teams play to shutout #11 ranked **North Carolina** 13-0 before 80,120 in a steady rain in Tallahassee. The Seminole defense limited the Tar Heels to just 187 yards. The defense forced three turnovers while its special teams blocked two punts and a field goal attempt. Peter Boulware and Greg Spires combined for five sacks. The offense could muster just 213 yards.

CLEMSON

Clemson traveled to Tallahassee to play the #2 ranked Seminoles at Doak Campbell Stadium. Thad Busby passed for 304 yards and four touchdowns -- two to Ernie Green -- as Florida State defeated Clemson 34-3. The Seminoles started slowly, but then Busby got going. In the first half, Busby connected on pass plays covering 37, 60 and 23 yards for touchdowns and also completed passes that covered 50 and 42 yards to keep drives going. Matt Padgett put Clemson on the scoreboard 10 seconds into the second period with a 29 yard field goal. It was Clemson's first points in 10 quarters at Florida State. Clemson's Raymond Priester was held to 27 yards on 18 carries.

Miami

The #3 ranked Florida State ended a 12 year drought against #6 **Miami** in the Orange Bowl as Warrick Dunn rushed for 163 yards and a touchdown to lead the Seminoles to a 34-16 win over the Hurricanes. An Orange Bowl crowd of 75,913 witnessed the Seminole defense put together another big play afternoon as the Tribe forced three turnovers and sacked Miami quarterback Ryan Clement eight times. Seminole defensive end Reinard Wilson had four sacks to become FSU's all-time leader with 29. Shevin Smith returned a fumble 54 yards for a touchdown. Scott Bentley added two field goals.

VIRGINIA

The #3 ranked Florida State's Thad Busby threw for 316 yards and Warrick Dunn rushed for 131 in leading the Seminoles to a 31-24 Homecoming win over #13 **Virginia** in Doak Campbell Stadium. The Cavs went into the locker room with a 17-14 lead at the half. Florida State took control of the game with three unanswered scores in the second half and then held off a late UVA charge. Andre Cooper recorded his first 100 yard receiving game of the season with seven receptions for 102 yards.

Georgia Tech

The Seminoles, ranked #3, traveled to historic Grant Field to play **Georgia Tech**. Florida State used big plays by its offense, defense and special teams to fuel a 28 point second quarter and an eventual 49-3 win over the Ramblin' Wreck. Thad Busby threw three interceptions on the night, all to Brian Wilkins, and finished with 148 yards passing. Lamont Green returned an interception 56 yards for a touchdown and Shevin Smith fell on a blocked punt in the end zone for a touchdown. Warrick Dunn ran for 121 yards and a touchdown.

WAKE FOREST

Still ranked #3, the Seminoles played **Wake Forest** at the Citrus Bowl in Orlando. The Noles started redshirt freshman Dan Kendra at quarterback, and he responded by throwing for 281 yards and three touchdowns in leading FSU to a 44-7 victory. The Seminole defense continued to smother opposing offenses allowing Wake Forest just 186 yards of total offense, including just 60 on the ground. Warrick Dunn ran for two touchdowns and E.G. Green caught 6 passes for 126 yards and a touchdown. Scott Bentley added 3 field goals.

SOUTHERN MISSISSIPPI

The Seminoles returned to Tallahassee ranked #3. Warrick Dunn was brilliant in accounting for 204 yards of total offense and three touchdowns to lead Florida State to a 54-14 win over #25 **Southern Mississippi**. Thad Busby passed for 302 yards and two TD passes. Laveranues Coles caught two TD passes and the defense held the Golden Eagles to 95 yards of offense.

MARYLAND

The #3 ranked Seminoles hosted **Maryland** at Pro Player Stadium in Miami. The defense held the Terrapins to minus 8 yards rushing, and the Tribe dominated in a 48-10 victory. Warrick Dunn ran for 109 yards and two touchdowns. Thad Busby passed for 156 yards and two TD passes and Dan Kendra passed for 141 yards and a TD pass.

FLORIDA {#1 vs #2}

The #1–ranked and undefeated Gators came into Tallahassee favored against the second-ranked Seminoles. The 'Noles got off to a quick start when Peter Boulware blocked the Gators first punt of the game, resulting in a touchdown. Florida's eventual Heisman Trophy winner quarterback Danny Wuerffel threw three interceptions in the first half, and FSU had a 17–0 lead after one quarter of play. Wuerffel got on track after that, throwing for three touchdowns. The last one (to WR Reidel Anthony) cut the Florida State lead to three points with just over a minute left to play. The ensuing onside kick went out of bounds, however, and the Seminoles held on for the 24–21 upset win. The stars of the game were FSU running back Warrick Dunn, who rushed for 185 yards; Wuerffel, who threw for 362 yards; and the FSU defense, which sacked Wuerffel six times and knocked him to the turf on many other occasions. That Seminole pass rush became a source of controversy after the game when Gators' coach Steve Spurrier claimed that FSU players had deliberately tried to injure his star quarterback with late hits and "cheap shots". The Seminoles had been flagged for roughing the passer twice during the game

1997 SUGAR BOWL

In the 63rd edition of the Sugar Bowl, #1 ranked Florida State met #3 ranked **Florida** in a rematch of their regular season finale. Florida defeated Florida State in convincing fashion, with a final score of 52–20, and with the victory earned it's first-ever consensus national championship. After a halftime score of 24–17 in favor of Florida, Florida State closed to 24–20 with a third quarter field goal. Florida then outscore Florida State 28–0 for the remainder of the game, for a 52–20 final. Gator quarterback Danny Wuerffel threw three touchdown passes to Ike Hilliard in the game, and ran for another score. Wuerffel became the second Heisman Trophy winner in four years to win a national championship, following Charlie Ward of the 1993 Florida State team. Thad Busby passed for 271 yards and a touchdown pass. The Gator defense held the Tribe to 42 yards rushing.

1997 Florida State Seminoles {ACC Champions}

The team was coached by Bobby Bowden. Bowden was voted the ACC Coach of the Year. Once again, the Seminoles won their first 10 games of the season only to be upset by Florida in the season finale. They were invited to the Sugar Bowl where they beat Ohio State. Andre Wadsworth was voted the ACC Player of the Year and ACC Defensive Player of the Year. Thad Busby was voted ACC Offensive Player of the Year.

Sam Cowart (LB), Andre Wadsworth (DE) and Kevin Long (C) were selected first team All-Americans. Wadsworth {Arizona}, Tra Thomas {T} {Philadelphia}, Cowart {LB} {Buffalo}, Samari Rolle {CB} {Tennessee}, E.G. Green {WR} {Indianapolis}, Greg Spires {DE} {New England}, Julian Pittman {DT} {New Orleans}, Shevin Smith {S} {Tampa Bay} and Kevin Long {C} {Tennessee} were selected in the 1998 NFL Draft. Wadsworth {Arizona} and Tra Thomas {Philadelphia} were #1 picks.

ACC CHAMPIONS				FINAL RANK: #3 AP, #3 CP				
Home games were played at Doak Campbell Stadium								
9/6/1997	Florida State	#5	@	#21	Usc (6-5)	ABC	14	7	W
9/13/1997	Florida State	#6	vs		MARYLAND (2-9)	ABC	50	7	W
9/20/1997	Florida State	#5	@	#15	Clemson (7-5)	ABC	35	28	W
10/4/1997	Florida State	#4	vs		MIAMI (5-6)	ABC	47	0	W
10/11/1997	Florida State	#4	@		Duke (2-9)		51	27	W
10/18/1997	Florida State	#3	vs	#25	GEORGIA TECH (7-5)	ABC	38	0	W
10/25/1997	Florida State	#3	@		Virginia (7-4)	ESPN	47	21	W
11/1/1997	Florida State	#3	vs		NC STATE (6-5)	ABC	48	35	W
11/8/1997	Florida State	#2	@	#5	North Carolina (11-1)	ESPN	20	3	W
11/15/1997	Florida State	#1	vs		WAKE FOREST (5-6)	JPS	58	7	W
11/22/1997	Florida State	#1	@	#10	Florida (10-2)	CBS	29	32	L
1/1/1998	Florida State	#4	vs	#10	Ohio State (10-3)	ABC	31	14	W
Coach: Bobby Bowden					Season Record >>		468	181	11-1

Schedule Source: Steve's Football Bible LLC

Selected game(s) highlights

Usc

Florida State opened the season ranked #5 and traveled to Los Angeles to play the #21 ranked **USC** Trojans. In a defensive struggle, the Seminoles scored a 4th quarter touchdown to win 14-7. The Noles defense held USC to 184 yards of offense. Thad Busby passed for 276 yards and threw 2 interceptions. Dan Kendra and Dee Foster scored for the Tribe.

MARYLAND

Ranked #6, FSU hosted **Maryland**. Thad Busby threw for over 300 yards and FSU's defense allowed Maryland just 105 total yards as the Seminoles routed the Terrapins, 50-7. E.G. Green caught 6 passes for 118 yards and two TD receptions. Peter Warrick caught two TD passes from Dan Kendra.

Clemson

Peter Warrick accounted for three long touchdowns, including the first punt return score at Memorial Stadium since 1988. Warrick's #4 ranked Seminoles squeezed past Clemson 35-28. Nealon Greene, connected for a 17 yard touchdown pass with Brian Wofford and made a 2 point conversion to cut Florida State's lead to 28-25, Warrick zipped down the right sidelines for an 80 yard touchdown catch to restore the double-digit lead. Warrick finished with eight catches for 249 yards, while quarterback Thad Busby had a career-high 332 yards. The Tigers Raymond Priester was held to 77 yards rushing.

MIAMI

Florida State ripped Miami 47-0 for the Hurricanes worst lost since 1927. The Seminoles crushed Miami with 422 yards while limiting Mami to 131 yards of offense and -33 yards rushing. To this day it is still the largest margin of victory between the two teams.

Duke

The #4 ranked Seminoles traveled to Durham and left with a closer than expected 51-27 win over the **Duke** Blue Devils. Sam Cowart returned a fumble 24 yards for a touchdown and Derrick Gibson returned a blocked punt 1 yard for a touchdown. Peter Warrick caught 5 passes for 134 yards and a touchdown while Thad Busby passed for 250 yards.

GEORGIA TECH

Moving up to #3 in the polls, FSU hosted **Georgia Tech**. The Noles defense tossed a shutout and held the Ramblin' Wreck to 144 total yards in a 38-0 victory. E.G. Green caught 6 passes for 166 yards and a touchdown. Thad Busby passed for 399 yards and three TD passes.

Virginia

Still ranked #3, the Seminoles traveled to Charlottesville to play **Virginia**. Travis Minor got his first start and rushed for 157 yards and scored three touchdowns, including one for 87 yards. E.G. Green caught 5 passes for 151 yards and a touchdown. Thad Busby passed for 291 yards and threw three TD passes.

NC STATE

Holding at #3 in the polls, FSU hosted **NC State** for homecoming. Travis Minor and E.G. Green led the way, both scoring three touchdowns in a 48-35 win. Minor rushed for 64 yards and Green caught 8 passes for 184 yards. Thad Busby passed for a career high 463 yards and 5 TD passes.

North Carolina

Now ranked #2, Florida State traveled to Chapel Hill to play #5 ranked **North Carolina** in what was billed as the biggest game in ACC history. With an ESPN audience watching in, as well as a Kenan Stadium record 62,000, the Seminoles dismantled the Tar Heels with nine quarterback sacks and a 20-3 win that assured FSU of a share of its sixth straight conference crown. The Noles defense held the Tar Heels to minus 28 yards rushing and 73 yards total offense. Travis Minor rushed for 128 yards. Thad Busby passed for 159 yards and two TD passes and Sebastian Janikowski added two field goals.

WAKE FOREST

Now ranked #1, FSU hosted **Wake Forest**. The Seminoles scored 28 first quarter points, including a Tony Bryant 19 yard interception return for a touchdown. The defense held the Demon Deacons to minus 1 yard rushing on the way to a 58-7 victory. Thad Busby passed for 390 yards and four TD passes. E.G. Green caught 7 passes for 120 yards and two TD receptions and Melvin Pearsall caught 4 passes for 114 yards and a touchdown. Sebastian Janikowski kicked three field goals.

Florida

Florida State entered the game ranked #1 and a double-digit favorite over #10 Florida. After a pregame fight, the Gators drove the ball 83 yards for a touchdown on the opening series. Spurrier implemented a two quarterback system with Doug Johnson and senior walk-on Noah Brindise, and rotated the two nearly every play. Florida State led 17–6 early in the second quarter after Seminoles quarterback Thad Busby found tight end Melvin Pearsall for a five yard touchdown. The Gators fought back, however, as wide receiver Travis McGriff caught a touchdown from Johnson, and running back Fred Taylor scored from the 4 yard line to put Florida ahead 18–17 at halftime. In the second half, kicker Sebastian Janikowski boomed his second of three field goals to put Florida State back on top, but Taylor responded with a 61 yard touchdown run to retake the lead, 25–20. Seminoles running back Travis Minor scored on an 18 yard touchdown run, to give Florida State a 26–25 lead. The first twelve minutes of the fourth quarter were scoreless, but the Seminoles drove inside the Gators' 5 yard line until the Gators defense, led by Jevon Kearse and Mike Peterson, stopped the 'Noles on three consecutive running plays and the Seminoles settled for another Janikowski field goal after which Janikowski performed a mock Gator Chomp in celebration. On first down from the Gators' own 20 yard line, Johnson hit receiver Jacquez Green for a 62 yard pass play. Fred Taylor completed the drive with his fourth rushing touchdown of the night, and Florida took the lead after the three-play drive for good, 32–29. Florida State's final comeback attempt ended when senior Florida linebacker Dwayne Thomas intercepted a third-down pass from Busby, sealing the victory for the Gators, and costing Florida State a chance to play for the national championship.

1998 SUGAR BOWL

The 64th edition to the Sugar Bowl featured the #10 **Ohio State** Buckeyes (10-2), and the #4 Florida State Seminoles (10-1). Ohio State scored the first points of the contest with a 40 yard field goal from kicker Dan Stultz, giving the Buckeyes an early 3–0 lead. Later in the first quarter, quarterback Thad Busby threw a 27 yard touchdown pass to wide receiver E. G. Green, giving the Seminoles a 7–3 lead. In the second quarter, Busby scored on a 9 yard touchdown run increasing the Seminole lead to 14–3.

William McCray also scored for the Seminoles, pounding it in from one yard out, to increase Florida State's lead to 21–3 at halftime. Stultz kicked his second field goal of the game, cutting the margin to 21–6. Ohio State later got a safety on Florida State pulling them within 21–8. Early in the fourth quarter, Sebastian Janikowski kicked a 35 yard field goal, increasing Florida State's lead to 24–8. Quarterback Joe Germaine threw a 50 yard touchdown pass to John Lumpkin. The ensuing two point conversion failed, and the score was 24–14. Florida State capped the scoring with a one yard touchdown run from McCray, making the final margin 31–14.

1998 Florida State Seminoles {ACC Champions}

The team was coached by Bobby Bowden and played their home games at Doak Campbell Stadium. The Seminoles were the runner up in the first BCS Championship game at the Fiesta Bowl against the Tennessee Volunteers. For the third consecutive season, they finished ranked #3 in the polls. **Sebastian Janikowski set a single season record for field goals made with 27.**

Sebastian Janikowski (K), Corey Simon (DT), Peter Warrick (WR) and Jason Whitaker (OG) were selected as first team All-Americans. Janikowski won the Lou Groza Award. Tony Bryant {DE} {Oakland}, Larry Smith {DT} {Jacksonville}, Dexter Jackson {S} {Tampa Bay} and Lamarr Glenn {FB} {Tampa Bay} were selected in the 1999 NFL Draft.

ACC CHAMPIONS				FINAL RANK: #3 AP, #3 CP				
Home games were played at Doak Campbell Stadium								
8/31/1998	Florida State	#2	vs	#14	Texas A&M (11-3)	ABC	23	14	W
9/12/1998	Florida State	#2	@		NC State (7-5)	ABC	7	24	L
9/19/1998	Florida State	#11	vs		DUKE (4-7)		62	13	W
9/26/1998	Florida State	#10	vs	#18	USC (8-5)	ABC	30	10	W
10/3/1998	Florida State	#9	@		Maryland (3-8)		24	10	W
10/10/1998	Florida State	#8	@		Miami (9-3)	CBS	26	14	W
10/17/1998	Florida State	#6	vs		CLEMSON (3-8)	espn2	48	0	W
10/24/1998	Florida State	#5	@	#23	Georgia Tech (10-2)	ESPN	34	7	W
10/31/1998	Florida State	#5	vs		NORTH CAROLINA	ESPN	39	13	W
11/7/1998	Florida State	#6	vs	#12	VIRGINIA (9-3)	ABC	45	14	W
11/14/1998	Florida State	#5	@		Wake Forest (3-8)	espn2	24	7	W
11/21/1998	Florida State	#5	vs	#4	FLORIDA (10-2)	ABC	23	12	W
1/4/1999	Florida State	#2	vs	#1	Tennessee (13-0)	ABC	16	23	L
Coach: Bobby Bowden					Season Record >>		401	161	11-2

Schedule Source: Steve's Football Bible LLC

Selected game(s) highlights

Texas A&M

Florida State opened the season ranked #2 and faced #14 **Texas A&M** in the Kickoff Classic in East Rutherford, NJ. Travis Minor rushed for 134 yards and a touchdown and Chris Weinke passed for 207 yards and a TD pass. The defense held the Aggies to 133 yards total offense in a 23-14 win. Sebastian Janikowski kicked three field goals.

NC State

Ranked #2, the Seminoles traveled to Raleigh to play **NC State**. Chris Weinke hit wide receiver Peter Warrick with a 74 yard touchdown pass on FSU's first play from scrimmage, but that would be the only score for the Noles as the Wolfpack pulled off the upset, 24-7. Weinke threw six interceptions and completed just nine passes. Warrick caught 4 passes for 130 yards.

DUKE

The Seminoles dropped to #11 in the polls as they hosted **Duke** in Tallahassee. Chris Weinke passed for 241 yards and three TD passes. Laveranues Coles returned a kickoff 97 yards for a touchdown.

Peter Warrick caught two TD passes. Travis Minor scored two touchdowns and Jeff Chaney rushed for two touchdowns. The defense held the Blue Devils to 194 yards of offense.

USC

Ranked #10, the Seminoles hosted #18 **USC**. The defense held the Trojans to 23 passing yards in a 30-10 victory. Chris Weinke passed for 228 yards and a TD pass. Sebastian Janikowski kicked three field goals.

Maryland

Ranked #9, FSU traveled to College Park to play **Maryland**. Chris Weinke completed 16 of 32 passes for 261 yards and one touchdown. Sebastian Janikowski tied an FSU record with five field goals as the Seminoles defeated Maryland 24-10. Jeff Chaney rushed for a career high 133 yards on 30 carries.

Miami

Now ranked #8, the Seminoles traveled to **Miami** to play the Hurricanes in a nationally televised game of CBS. Peter Warrick caught seven passes for 190 yards and a touchdown and Chris Weinke completed 17 of 32 passes for 316 yards and two touchdowns in a convincing 26-14 victory. For the second straight game, the Noles defense recorded a safety. Marvin Minnis caught a TD pass.

CLEMSON

Ranked #6, FSU hosted **Clemson** at Doak Campbell Stadium. The Tribe put together their most impressive team performance with a 48-0 home shutout of Clemson, outgaining the Tigers 455 to 129 in total yardage. Chris Weinke passed for 302 yards and four TD passes. The defense held Clemson to five first downs.

Georgia Tech

Ranked #5, the Seminoles traveled to historic Grant Field to play **Georgia Tech**. Peter Warrick scored three touchdowns and FSU's defense dominated after Georgia Tech's first drive as Florida State won a pivotal ACC game 34-7 in Atlanta. Warrick caught six passes for 82 yards. Chris Weinke passed for 208 yards and two TD passes.

NORTH CAROLINA

Still ranked #5, FSU hosted **North Carolina** at "The Doak". Quarterback Chris Weinke passed for a career high 338 yards and two TD passes as he led the Seminoles to a 39-13 victory over the Tar Heels. Sebastian Janikowski kicked four field goals. Peter Warrick caught three passes for 125 yards and one TD reception. Laveranues Coles caught 5 passes for 120 yards and one TD reception.

VIRGINIA

Ranked #6, FSU hosted #12 **Virginia**. Chris Weinke left the game late in the second quarter after a jarring sack herniated a disc which knocked him out for the season. FSU's lead was only 21-14 at the half, but the defense held Virginia scoreless and the `Noles outscored the Cavs 24-0 in the second half on the way to a 45-14 victory. Backup Marcus Outzen came in and passed for 67 yards. Weinke passed for a touchdown and ran for one before leaving the game. Travis Minor rushed for 130 yards and one touchdown and Peter Warrick caught 5 passes for 123 yards and a TD reception.

Wake Forest

Ranked #5, FSU traveled to Winston-Salem to play **Wake Forest**. The defense held the Demon Deacons to 179 yards of offense. Marcus Outzen passed for 164 yards and ran for one touchdown. Travis Minor ran for 102 yards and two touchdowns. **Mario Edwards set a single game record with 4 interceptions for the Seminoles.**

FLORIDA

This 1998 battle between the in state rivals started before the whistle even blew. A pre-game fight caused Florida's starting senior safety, Tony George, and a couple walk-on FSU players who were not dressed, to be ejected from the game. In the midst of the fight, it is rumored that Florida quarterback Doug Johnson attempted to hit FSU coach Bobby Bowden with a football. Johnson later apologized to Bowden for almost hitting him but said that he had thrown the ball into a group of FSU players during the scuffle with no particular target. Florida State's defense came in the ballgame rated #1 in the nation, Florida's defense was rated #1 in the SEC, so the game was set to be a defensive battle. Florida struck first with a 50 yard Doug Johnson touchdown pass, but Seminoles Peter Warrick and Travis Minor put the Seminoles in scoring position twice and Placekicker Sebastian Janikowski kicked two field goals to make the game 7–6. After a Florida punt the Seminoles were at their own 5 yard-line and Florida forced a safety. And then Doug Johnson drove Florida deep into Florida State territory after the safety kick, but Florida State's defense stiffened and forced Florida to settle for three points. At halftime, the game was 12–6, Florida. In the second half, Florida State's defense held Florida scoreless. Florida State's first touchdown of the game came when quarterback Marcus Outzen threw a pass that was deflected by a Gator defender right to Peter Warrick, who ran it in for the score. Later in the game, Peter Warrick threw a touchdown to Ron Dugans on a trick play. The game ended 23–12, with Florida State the winner.

1999 FIESTA BOWL

In the 28th Fiesta Bowl, #1 **Tennessee** from the SEC, played #2 Florida State from the ACC. Played at Sun Devil Stadium in Tempe, AZ, it was the first BCS National Championship game.

After a scoreless first quarter, Tennessee's QB Tee Martin fired a 4 yard touchdown pass to FB Shawn Bryson for the Vols to open an early 7–0 lead. Bryson's TD came after the Vols took a Jeff Hall field goal off the board due to a roughing-the-kicker penalty. Shortly thereafter, Florida State had the ball near midfield. Seminoles QB Marcus Outzen threw an interception to Vol CB Dwayne Goodrich who was covering WR Peter Warrick, and it was returned 54 yards for a touchdown; thus, Tennessee opened a 14–0 lead. The two scores both occurred in the first 25 seconds of the second quarter. Goodrich's interception changed the complexion of the game and forced Florida State to play from behind. Florida State did get on the board later in the second quarter with a 1 yard run by FB William McCray, but Sebastian Janikowski missed an extra point off the crossbar, so the score stood at 14–6. At the end of the half, Janikowski drilled a 34 yard field goal, and the lead was cut to 14–9.

After the scoreless third quarter, the Vols got back on the scoreboard again. Tee Martin fired a 79 yard touchdown pass to Peerless Price, and the Vols claimed a 20–9 lead after a missed extra point by K Jeff Hall. Later, Tennessee added a 23 yard field goal by Hall, and the lead extended to 23–9. But Florida State was not conceding the outcome yet. Seminole quarterback Marcus Outzen scrambled for a 7 yard touchdown, capping a Florida State drive, and the lead was cut to 23–16. With less than 2 minutes to go in the game, Tennessee RB Travis Henry fumbled and turned the ball over to Florida State. However, Florida State was intercepted by CB Steve Johnson, and the Vols ended with a victory.

1999 Florida State Seminoles {National Champions}

Winning the Atlantic Coast Conference (ACC) Championship and winning the 2000 Sugar Bowl BCS National Championship game, the team was coached by Bobby Bowden and played their home games at Doak Campbell Stadium. The team entered the season with high expectations after losing to Tennessee in the inaugural BCS Championship game. FSU entered the 1999 pre-season ranked #1 in all national pre-season polls. The Seminoles finished the 1999 season with a perfect 12-0 record and was the first in NCAA history to go "wire-to-wire" being ranked continuously as the nation's #1 team from the preseason through the bowl season. This marked the 13th consecutive season that the Seminoles will have finished in the Top 5 rankings of both the AP and coaches poll.

Sebastian Janikowski (K), Corey Simon (DT), Peter Warrick (WR) and Jason Whitaker (OG) were selected first team All-Americans. Warrick won the Paul Warfield Award and Janikowski won the Lou Groza Award. Warrick {Cincinnati}, Simon {Philadelphia}, Janikowski {Oakland}, Ron Dugans {WR} {Cincinnati}, Lavernanues Coles {WR} {New York Jets}, Jerry Johnson {DT} {Denver} and Mario Edwards {CB} {Dallas} were selected in the 2000 NFL Draft. Warrick (Cincinnati), Simon (Philadelphia) and Janikowski (Oakland) were all #1 picks.

NATIONAL CHAMPIONS				FINAL RANK: #1 AP, #1 CP				
Home games were played at Doak Campbell Stadium								
8/28/1999	Florida State	#1	vs		LOUISIANA TECH (8-3)	espn2	41	7	W
9/11/1999	Florida State	#1	vs	#10	**GEORGIA TECH (8-4)**	ABC	41	35	W
9/18/1999	Florida State	#1	vs	#20	**NC STATE (6-6)**	ABC	42	11	W
9/25/1999	Florida State	#1	@		**North Carolina (3-8)**	ABC	42	10	W
10/2/1999	Florida State	#1	vs		**DUKE (3-8)**	JPS	51	23	W
10/9/1999	Florida State	#1	vs	#19	MIAMI (9-4)	ABC	31	21	W
10/16/1999	Florida State	#1	vs		**WAKE FOREST (7-5)**		33	10	W
10/23/1999	Florida State	#1	@		**Clemson (6-6)**	ESPN	17	14	W
10/30/1999	Florida State	#1	@		Virginia (7-5)	ESPN	35	10	W
11/13/1999	Florida State	#1	vs		**MARYLAND (5-6)**	ABC	49	10	W
11/20/1999	Florida State	#1	@	#4	Florida (9-4)	CBS	30	23	W
1/4/2000	**Florida State**	#1	vs	#2	Virginia Tech (11-1)	ABC	46	29	W
Coach: Bobby Bowden					**Season Record >>**		458	203	12-0

Schedule Source: Steve's Football Bible LLC

Selected game(s) highlights

LOUISIANA TECH

Florida State opened the season ranked #1 and hosted **Louisiana Tech**. The Seminoles cruised to a 41-7 victory over the Bulldogs. Peter Warrick caught 9 passes for 121 yards and ran for a touchdown. Anquan Boldin caught two TD passes. Theon Rackley returned an interception 10 yards for a touchdown.

GEORGIA TECH

Ranked #1 for the rest of the season, FSU hosted #10 **Georgia Tech** in Tallahassee. In a wild, back and forth game, the Seminoles outlasted the Ramblin' Wreck, 41-35. Tech's Joe Hamilton completed 22 of 25 passes for 387 yards and four TD passes. Chris Weinke passed for 262 yards and three TD passes. Peter Warrick caught 8 passes for 142 yards and two TD receptions. Travis Minor rushed for 122 yards and a touchdown.

NC STATE

Florida State hosted #20 **NC State** at "The Doak". The Noles defense scored two touchdowns and the offense did enough as they beat the Wolfpack 42-11. Jamal Reynolds fell on a fumble in the end zone for a touchdown and Abdual Howard returned an interception 47 yards for a touchdown. Chris Weinke passed for 229 yards. Sebastian Janikowski kicked five field goals.

North Carolina

The Seminoles traveled to Chapel Hill to play **North Carolina**. The Tribe jumped out to a 28-0 first quarter lead on the way to a 42-10 win over the Tar Heels. Sean Key returned an interception 25 yards for a touchdown and Pater Warrick returned a punt 75 yards for a touchdown. Warrick caught 4 passes for 103 yards. Travis Minor ran for two touchdowns and Chris Weinke passed for 272 yards and one TD pass.

DUKE

Florida State hosted **Duke** at Jacksonville next. The Seminoles rolled to a 44-0 halftime lead on the way to a 51-23 victory over the Blue Devils. Chris Weinke passed for 290 yards and five TD passes. Peter Warrick caught three TD passes and passed for one. Ron Dugans caught 5 passes for 141 yards and one TD reception.

MIAMI

The Seminoles hosted rival #19 **Miami** next. Chris Weinke connected with 11 different receivers for 332 yards and two touchdowns as Florida State overcame a sloppy first half for a 31-21 victory over Miami for the fifth straight season. Travis Minor rushed for 146 yards and one touchdown.

WAKE FOREST

Florida State hosted **Wake Forest** in Tallahassee. Sebastian Janikowski kicked four field goals and Chris Weinke passed for 354 yards and two TD passes leading the Seminoles to a 33-10 victory over the Demon Deacons. Atrews Bell caught two TD passes.

Clemson

Clemson missed a 41 yard field goal with two minutes left and went scoreless in the second half of a 17-14 loss to the Seminoles before a record 86,200 fans at Death Valley. This was the first father-son coaching matchup in major-college football. It was Bobby Bowden, who had to face son Tommy and all the trick plays the kid learned from dad. Clemson led 14-3 at halftime. Florida State tied the score with its last drive of the third quarter. Behind 14-12, Florida State went for two points and was called for delay of game. Backed up to the 8 by the penalty, Weinke lofted the ball over the middle to fullback Dan Kendra to tie the score. Sebastian Janikowski's 39 yard field goal with 5:30 left in the game was the first time the Seminoles led in the game.

Virginia

Florida State traveled to Charlottesville to play **Virginia**. Trailing 10-7 at halftime, the Seminoles scored 28 unanswered points on the way to a 35-10 victory over the Cavaliers. Chris Weinke threw three first half interceptions but finished with 297 yards passing and three TD passes. Marvin Minnis caught two TD passes.

MARYLAND

Florida State hosted **Maryland** at "The Doak". Chris Weinke threw six touchdown passes - three to Peter Warrick - as the Seminoles clobbered Maryland 49-10, reaching 10 victories for the 13th straight season. Weinke passes for 304 yards and Warrick caught 9 passes for 134 yards. The defense held the Terrapins to 221 yards. **Weinke's 6 touchdown passes tied a single game record for FSU.**

Florida

Despite both teams being among the tops nationally in offense, the first half was pretty quiet according to standards. Warrick got things started with a touchdown run from four yards out. Both teams would exchange field goals twice in the half and Florida State held on to a seven point lead heading into the locker room. While Chris Weinke and the offense was held to near season lows for a half, the Florida passing attack of alternating quarterbacks Doug Johnson and Jesse Palmer was held in check for much of the first half as well. In the second half, the Gators took the lead after a field goal and interception return for a score – and the Seminoles started to seem a little worried that their national title hopes could be dashed. Less than three minutes later, FSU football tied the game with a field goal and took the lead when Jeff Chaney punched it in. Weinke found Snoop Minnis in the fourth quarter for a score – set up by a long catch from Warrick – and the Seminoles survived a late touchdown and Hail Mary attempt from their rivals to leave the way they entered....undefeated.

2000 SUGAR BOWL

In the 66th edition of the Sugar Bowl, An estimated total of 79,280 people attended the game in person, while approximately 18.4 million US viewers watched the game on ABC television.

Florida State scored first and took advantage of a blocked punt for a touchdown, giving the Seminoles a 14–0 lead in the first quarter. **Virginia Tech** answered with a touchdown drive of its own before the end of the quarter, but Florida State scored two quick touchdowns to begin the second quarter. Virginia Tech scored a touchdown before halftime, but halfway through the game, Florida State held a 28–14 lead. In the third quarter, Virginia Tech's offense gave the Hokies a lead with a field goal and two touchdowns. Tech failed to convert two two point conversions but held a 29–28 lead at the end of the third quarter. Florida State answered in the fourth quarter, however, taking a 36–29 lead with a touchdown and successful two point conversion early in the quarter. From this point, the Seminoles did not relinquish the lead, extending it to 46–29 with another touchdown and a field goal. For his performance in the game, Florida State wide receiver Peter Warrick was named the game's most valuable player.

2000 Florida State Seminoles {ACC Champions}

The team was coached by Bobby Bowden. The Seminoles reached the title game for the third straight year, only to lose to Oklahoma in the Orange Bowl. Chris Weinke led the nation in passing with 4,167 yards and won the Heisman Trophy, awarded to college football's best player, as well as the Davey O'Brien Award, Sammy Baugh Trophy and the Johnny Unitas Award. Weinke was voted the ACC Player of the Year. Jamal Reynolds won the Lombardi Trophy. **Weinke set a new single season record for passing yards with 4,167.** Tay Cody {CB}, Marvin Minnis {WR}, Jamal Reynolds {DE}, Tarlos Thomas {OT} and Chris Weinke {QB} were all selected first team All-Americans. Reynolds {Green Bay}, Derrick Gibson {DB} {Oakland}, Tommy Polley {LB} {St. Louis Rams}, Cody {San Diego}, Minnis {Kansas City}, Brian Allen {LB} {St. Louis Rams}, Travis Minor {RB} {Miami}, Weinke {Carolina} and Char-ron Dorsey {T} {Dallas} were selected in the 2001 NFL Draft. Reynolds {Green Bay} and Gibson {Oakland} were #1 picks.

ACC CHAMPIONS				FINAL RANK: #3 AP, #3 CP				
Home games were played at Doak Campbell Stadium								
8/26/2000	Florida State	#2	vs		BYU (6-6)	ABC	29	3	W
9/9/2000	Florida State	#2	@		**Georgia Tech (9-3)**	ABC	26	21	W
9/16/2000	Florida State	#2	vs		**NORTH CAROLINA**	ABC	63	14	W
9/23/2000	Florida State	#2	vs		LOUISVILLE (9-3)	espn2	31	0	W
9/28/2000	Florida State	#2	@		**Maryland (5-6)**	ESPN	59	7	W
10/7/2000	Florida State	#1	@	#7	Miami (11-1)	CBS	24	27	L
10/14/2000	Florida State	#7	vs		**DUKE (0-11)**		63	14	W
10/21/2000	Florida State	#7	vs		**VIRGINIA (6-6)**	ABC	37	3	W
10/28/2000	Florida State	#6	@	#20	**NC State (8-4)**	ESPN	58	14	W
11/4/2000	Florida State	#4	vs	#10	**CLEMSON (9-3)**	ESPN	54	7	W
11/11/2000	Florida State	#3	@		**Wake Forest (2-9)**		35	6	W
11/18/2000	Florida State	#3	vs	#4	FLORIDA (10-3)	ABC	30	7	W
1/3/2001	**Florida State**	#2	vs	#1	Oklahoma (13-0)	ABC	2	13	L
Coach: Bobby Bowden					**Season Record >>**		511	136	11-2

Schedule Source: Steve's Football Bible LLC

Selected game(s) highlights

BYU

Florida State opened the season ranked #2 and played **BYU** in the Pigskin Classic in Jacksonville. The Seminole defense held the Cougars to minus 2 yards rushing. Chris Weinke passed for 318 yards and two TD passes. Marvin Minnis caught 9 passes for 137 yards and Atrews Bell scored 2 touchdowns.

Georgia Tech

The #2 Seminoles traveled to historic Grant Field to play **Georgia Tech**. The Ramblin' Wreck kept it close, but Florida State prevailed 26-21, behind Chris Weinke's 443 passing yards and two TD passes. Anquan Boldin caught 3 passes for 100 yards.

NORTH CAROLINA

Ranked #2, Florida State hosted **North Carolina** in Tallahassee. Eight different players scored as the Seminoles routed the Tar Heels, 63-14. Chris Hope returned a fumble 12 yards for a touchdown. Marvin Minnis caught 5 passes for 132 yards and two TD receptions. Atrews Bell caught 3 passes for 96 yards and two TD receptions. Travis Minor rushed for 112 yards and Chris Weinke passed for 262 yards and four TD passes.

LOUISVILLE

The #2 ranked Seminoles hosted **Louisville** in Tallahassee next. The Tribe's defense held the Cardinals to 3 yards rushing and Tommy Polley returned an interception 4 yards for a touchdown in a 31-0 shutout victory. Travis Minor rushed for 120 yards and a touchdown. Chris Weinke passed for 221 yards and a TD pass. Weinke also ran for a touchdown but threw 3 interceptions.

Maryland

Still ranked #2, FSU traveled to College Park to play **Maryland**. The Tribe cruised to its 17th straight victory, routing the Terrapins, 59-7. William McCray ran for two touchdowns and Atrews Bell caught 2 TD passes. Robert Morgan caught 3 passes for 100 yards and Chris Weinke passed for 234 yards and three TD passes. Marcus Outzen passed for 119 yards and one TD pass.

Miami {Wide Right III}

The Hurricanes came into this game 3-1, while the Seminoles, who were carrying a 17 game winning streak into the game, were 4-0 for the season. Miami quickly jumped the gun on FSU and led at halftime 17-0. Florida State, led by Chris Weinke's 496 yards passing, got FSU within seven, 17-10. Miami would end the third quarter with a 20-10 lead on Todd Sievers 37 yard field goal. The problem was Miami could not stop Weinke as he threw two unanswered touchdown passes giving the Seminoles a 24-20 lead late in the fourth quarter. Miami quarterback, Ken Dorsey, quickly came back throwing a touchdown to Tight End Jeremy Shockey with just 46 seconds left in the game, to give Miami a 27-24 lead. Fortunately for FSU, Weinke was able to get the Seminoles into field goal range with just seconds remaining. Seminole freshman Matt Munyon came out to attempt the 49 yard field goal, but for the third time in the rivalry, the kick went wide right. Miami wins 27-24.

DUKE

Now ranked #7, the Tribe hosted **Duke** in Tallahassee. The Seminoles took out their frustration on the winless Blue Devils. **Chris Weinke threw for a school record 536 yards** and five touchdowns as Florida State bounced back from last week's loss at Miami with a 63-14 victory over Duke. Rufus Bell was one of eight players to score touchdowns. Bell returned an interception 28 yards for a touchdown. Jeff Chaney caught 8 passes for 99 yards. Robert Morgan caught 4 passes for 98 yards and one TD reception. Atrews Bell caught two TD passes. **Weinke also set a single game record with 527 total yards of offense.**

VIRGINIA

Still ranked #7, FSU hosted **Virginia**. The Seminoles extended the nation's longest home field unbeaten streak to 50 games, including 33 straight wins, with a 37-3 victory over the Cavaliers. Marvin Minnis caught two touchdown passes and William McCray scored twice on short runs and freshman Chance Gwaltney added three field goals. Chris Weinke passed for 274 yards and two TD passes and Marcus Outzen passed for 152 yards.

NC State

Ranked #6, Florida State traveled to Raleigh to play #20 **NC State**. The Seminoles built a 27-0 halftime lead on the way to a 58-14 win over the Wolfpack. Tay Cody returned an interception 52 yards for a touchdown. Travis Minor rushed for 129 yards and two touchdowns. Chris Weinke passed for 185 yards and one TD pass. The Tribe scored on 5 rushing touchdowns.

CLEMSON

Now ranked #4, the Seminoles hosted #10 **Clemson**. Chris Weinke threw for 521 yards and Florida State rolled to a 54-7 victory, turning Bowden Bowl II into a complete embarrassment for Clemson and Coach Tommy Bowden. The Seminoles improved to 37-0 in Atlantic Coast Conference games at home and clinched the ACC title for the ninth straight time. The Seminoles finished with 771 yards, the most ever allowed by Clemson. Brett Cimorelli kicked four field goals. Marvin Minnis caught a 98 yard TD pass from Chris Weinke. Randy Golightly and Jeff Chaney each scored two touchdowns. Minnis, Atrews Bell and Javon Walker all finished with over 100 yards receiving.

Wake Forest

Moving up to #3 in the polls, Florida State traveled to Winston-Salem to play **Wake Forest**. Chris Weinke threw for 324 yards and five touchdowns, three to Marvin Minnis, to lead Florida State to a 35-6 win over the Demon Deacons. Marvin Minnis had 122 yards in receptions and Anquan Boldin caught two TD passes.

FLORIDA

With FSU football ranked #3 and Florida #4 in the BCS standings at the time the winner of the game was likely going to jump another in-state rival Miami and be in a position to play for the national title. Quarterback Chris Weinke, who had been suffering from the flu and was still a game time decision for this showdown, played like a man possessed in his final home game with the Seminoles. Weinke started the scoring when he hit Atrews Bell on the team's opening drive – and responded after Florida tied the game by leading them down the field and finding Snoop Minnis to retake the lead, a lead the Seminoles would not relinquish for the remainder of the night. Florida State would extend their lead in the third quarter when William McCray plowed in from one yard out and cement the outcome when Weinke and Minnis connected for a 51 yard touchdown that sent the then record crowd inside Doak Campbell Stadium into a frenzy that night. The Seminoles' defense would do their part by coming up with three interceptions – including two from Tay Cody – while holding the Gators to just 37 yards on the ground to seal a third straight victory over the orange and blue. The blowout win was enough to send FSU football to their third straight national title game

2001 ORANGE BOWL

In the 67th edition of the Orange Bowl which also was the BCS National Championship game, #1 **Oklahoma** entered with a perfect 12-0 record, but was still a 10 point underdog to #2 Florida State.

A smothering defense shut down Florida State and Josh Heupel generated enough offense to give Oklahoma a startling 13-2 victory in the Orange Bowl and its first national title in 15 years. Chris Weinke passed for 274 yards and had two interceptions and a fumble. He did not throw a touchdown pass for the first time this season. Atrews Bell was the lone bright spot for FSU, catching 7 passes for 137 yards. The Sooner defense held the Tribe to 27 yards rushing. The best scoring chance for the Noles in the 1st half was a 30 yard field goal attempt by Brett Cimorelli, which of course, went wide right.

2001 Florida State Seminoles

The team was coached by Bobby Bowden in his 26th season. The Seminoles finished with an 8-4 record and played Virginia Tech in the Gator Bowl.

Darnell Dockett {DT}, Chris Hope {FS}, Bradley Jennings {LB} and Brett Williams {OT} were selected as First team All-ACC. Williams was awarded the Jacobs Blocking Trophy.

Javon Walker {WR} {Green Bay} and Chris Hope {FS} {Pittsburgh} were selected in the 2002 NFL draft.

FINAL RANK: #15 AP, #15 CP

Home games were played at Doak Campbell Stadium

9/1/2001	Florida State	**#6**	@		**Duke (0-11)**		55	13	**W**
9/8/2001	Florida State	**#6**	vs		ALABAMA-BIRMINGHAM	espn2	29	7	**W**
9/22/2001	Florida State	**#6**	@		**North Carolina (8-5)**	ABC	9	41	**L**
9/29/2001	Florida State	**#18**	vs		**WAKE FOREST (6-5)**		48	24	**W**
10/13/2001	Florida State	**#16**	vs	#2	MIAMI (12-0)	ABC	27	49	**L**
10/20/2001	Florida State	**#21**	@		**Virginia (5-7)**	ESPN	43	7	**W**
10/27/2001	Florida State	**#19**	vs	#10	**MARYLAND (10-2)**	ABC	52	31	**W**
11/3/2001	Florida State	**#14**	@	#24	**Clemson (7-5)**	ABC	41	27	**W**
11/10/2001	Florida State	**#10**	vs		**NC STATE (7-5)**	ABC	28	34	**L**
11/17/2001	Florida State	**#20**	@	#3	Florida (10-2)	CBS	13	37	**L**
12/1/2001	Florida State		vs		**GEORGIA TECH (8-5)**	ESPN	28	17	**W**
1/1/2002	**Florida State**	**#24**	vs	#15	**Virginia Tech (8-4)**	**NBC**	**30**	**17**	**W**
Coach: Bobby Bowden					**Season Record >>**		403	304	**8-4**

Schedule Source: Steve's Football Bible LLC

Selected game(s) highlights

Duke

Chris Rix threw two touchdown passes and the #6 Seminoles blocked two punts for scores to beat Duke 55-13. The Seminoles spotted the Blue Devils an early touchdown, then clamped down on defense and made a pair of special team plays in the second quarter that turned the game around. Jerome Carter blocked a punt and returned it 12 yards for a touchdown. Kyler Hall blocked another punt and Gennaro Jackson recovered in the end zone for a touchdown to give the Noles a 38-6 lead. Nick Maddox scored two touchdowns and William McCray, Craphonso Thorpe, and Greg Jones each scored one.

North Carolina

Florida State took a major hit in its bid to return to a fourth straight national title game, turning the ball over five times in the second half in a 41-9 loss to North Carolina. The Tar Heels, a 17 point underdog, used a 34 point second half to stun the #6 Seminoles. Darian Durant threw a pair of touchdown passes for the Tar Heels and Jeff Reed had two field goals as North Carolina took command in the third period.

WAKE FOREST

Chris Rix threw for 345 yards and three touchdowns as the 18th-ranked Seminoles raced to an early 42-7 lead on the way to a 48-24 victory over the Demon Deacons. Nick Maddox and Greg Jones each ran for two touchdowns, and Rix teamed with Talman Gardner, Javon Walker and B.J. Ward on scoring passes.

MIAMI

Miami came into the Florida State game with a chip on their shoulder. The previous year Florida State got the nod over the Hurricanes for the National Championship, although Miami beat FSU head to head. The problem was they were playing in Doak Cambell stadium, a place where the Seminoles hadn't lost in 54 prior games. Miami started the first quarter scoring two touchdowns to take a 14-0 lead. In the second, Miami scored first to bring the score to 21-0, FSU came back scoring two touchdowns to make in 21-13 at half time. At half time Miami came out firing, scoring the first 14 points to go up 35-13. FSU returned the favor cutting the lead to 35-20, but Miami reeled off two more touchdowns to take the lead to 49-20 heading into the fourth. FSU scored one more touchdown to make it a final score of 49-27, ending the 54 home field winning streak FSU had.

Virginia

The #21 Seminoles overcame a shaky first half and beat Virginia 43-7. Xavier Beitia kicked three field goals and five different Seminoles scored touchdowns as FSU rolled up 533 yards of total offense. Greg Jones ran for 107 yards. Abdual Howard returned an interception 80 yards for a touchdown in the 3rd quarter to put the Seminoles up 26-7.

MARYLAND

Chris Rix threw five touchdown passes as the Seminoles ended Maryland's hopes of a perfect season, 52-31, before 82,565 at Doak Campbell Stadium. Rix completed 15 of 24 passes for 350 yards. Down 14-0 six minutes before halftime, Florida State used four straight completions for 58 yards by Rix to score. The payoff came on a 16 yarder to flanker Talman Gardner, who would catch two more touchdown passes. Thirteen seconds later, the Seminoles tied the game on linebacker Michael Boulware's 23 yard interception return for a touchdown. On the Seminoles' next chance, Rix hit flanker Craphonso Thorpe for 51 yards and then found Gardner for a 9 yard touchdown and a 21-14 lead. Three of Rix's touchdown passes came in the second half, in which the Seminoles outscored Maryland, 31-14.

Clemson

Despite an impressive performance from the offense, Clemson could not overcome an early Florida State lead and a consistent passing attack that led to a 41-27 Seminole victory. Chris Rix threw for 369 yards and four touchdowns. Javon Walker and Talman Gardner both recorded over 100 yards receiving and caught all four of Rix's touchdown passes.

NC STATE

The Wolfpack upset FSU again behind a 17-0 second quarter. The Noles had the ball, down 34-28 with 2 minutes left but failed to capitalize. It was Florida State's first-ever ACC loss at home. Chris Rix passed for 302 yards and threw 3 touchdowns and ran for one, but it wasn't enough. Talman Gardner was on the receiving end of two of those TD passes and Javon Walker hauled in a 63 yarder for a touchdown.

Florida

Ranked #4, Florida finished the regular season in the annual "Governors' Cup" game, hosting **Florida State** at "The Swamp". Rex Grossman passed for two touchdowns and ran for one as the Gators swamped the Seminoles, 37-13. The Seminoles points came on two Xavier Beitia field goals and a P.K. Sam 5 yard touchdown pass from Chris Rix.

GEORGIA TECH

Chris Rix threw two touchdown passes and ran for another as Florida State ended its first two-game losing streak since 1991, beating Georgia Tech 28-17. Greg Jones rushed for 101 yards to help Florida State rally from a 10-7 halftime deficit. Florida State scored 21 straight points, building a 28-10 lead on William McCray's 2 yard TD run with 11:18 left in the game.

2001 GATOR BOWL

The game's early going seemed promising for the defense-minded Hokies. In the first quarter, Tech held Florida State scoreless despite only managing a single field goal on offense. In the second quarter, however, Florida State began to find gaps in the Hokie defense and scored 10 points. At halftime, Florida State held a 10–3 lead. In the third quarter, Tech struck back. The Hokies scored 14 points in the quarter, while Florida State managed just a field goal. The Hokies' All-American tailback Lee Suggs had suffered a season-ending injury in the first game of the season, but freshman Kevin Jones had carried the offense for the season and continued to perform well in the post-season Gator Bowl game. With a 5 yard run from Jones and a 55 yard pass from Grant Noel to André Davis, Tech took a 17–13 lead going into the fourth quarter. But the lead quickly evaporated on a 77 yard catch and run from Chris Rix to Javon Walker. Florida State added ten more points after the long touchdown pass, and the Seminoles went on to win the game, 30–17.

2002 Florida State Seminoles {ACC Champions}

The team was coached by Bobby Bowden in his 27th season. They finished the season 9–5 (7–1 ACC) to finish in 1st place in the ACC. They were invited to the Sugar Bowl, where they lost to Georgia 26–13. During the season, Bobby Bowden passed Bear Bryant on the all-time coaching wins list.

Montrae Holland {G}, Alonzo Jackson {DE} and Brett Williams {T} were selected as First team All-ACC. Williams was selected as a Consensus First team All-American. Anquan Boldin {WR} {Arizona}, Jackson {Pittsburgh}, Holland {New Orleans}, Williams {Kansas City}, Todd Williams {G} {Tennessee} and Talman Gradner {WR} {New Orleans} were selected in the 2003 NFL draft.

ACC CHAMPIONS				FINAL RANK: #21 AP, #23 CP				
Home games were played at Doak Campbell Stadium								
8/24/2002	Florida State	#3	vs		Iowa State (7-7)	FSN	38	31	W
8/31/2002	Florida State	#5	vs		VIRGINIA (9-5)	ABC	40	19	W
9/14/2002	Florida State	#5	@		Maryland (11-3)	ESPN	37	10	W
9/21/2002	Florida State	#5	vs		DUKE (2-10)		48	17	W
9/26/2002	Florida State	#4	@		Louisville (7-6)	ESPN	20	26	L
10/3/2002	Florida State	#1	vs		CLEMSON (7-6)	ESPN	48	31	W
10/12/2002	Florida State	#9	@	#1	Miami (12-1)	ABC	27	28	L
10/26/2002	Florida State	#11	vs	#6	NOTRE DAME (10-3)	ABC	24	34	L
11/2/2002	Florida State	#18	@		Wake Forest (7-6)	espn2	34	21	W
11/9/2002	Florida State	#17	@		Georgia Tech (7-6)	ABC	21	13	W
11/16/2002	Florida State	#15	vs		NORTH CAROLINA	ABC	40	14	W
11/23/2002	Florida State	#14	@		NC State (11-3)	ABC	7	17	L
11/30/2002	Florida State	#23	vs	#15	FLORIDA (8-5)	ABC	31	14	W
1/1/2003	Florida State	#16	vs	#4	Georgia (13-1)	ABC	13	26	L
Coach: Bobby Bowden					Season Record >>		428	301	9-5

Schedule Source: Steve's Football Bible LLC

Selected game(s) highlights

Iowa State

Kendyll Pope and Jerel Hudson stopped Iowa State's Seneca Wallace at the goal line on the final play Saturday night, giving #4 ranked Florida State a wild 38-31 victory and moving Bowden past Bear Bryant on the career victory list with 324. Chris Rix threw two TD passes and engineered two other first-half scoring drives. The Seminoles raced to a 24-0 lead with the help of an Alonzo Jackson 48 yard interception return for a touchdown and Anquan Bolding's 2 yard TD reception from Rix. Greg Jones 9 yard TD run made it 31-7, then the Seminoles had to withstand a furious Cyclone rally. Boldin's 31 yard TD reception from Rix pushed the lead to 38-24 but the Cyclones Wallace threw a 39 yard strike to Jamaul Montgomery to cut the lead to 38-31 with 5:26 left and set the stage for a dramatic finish.

VIRGINIA

Greg Jones ran for a career-high 173 yards Saturday as the fifth-ranked Seminoles racked up 397 yards rushing in a 40-19 victory. The Seminoles jumped to a 33-0 lead after 3 quarters on touchdown runs by Chris Rix, Torrance Washington, and Jones' two TD runs. Willie Reid added a 5 yard TD run in the 4th quarter.

Maryland

Chris Rix threw two touchdowns passes and ran for another score as the fifth-ranked Seminoles took a 30 point halftime lead and rolled past Maryland 37-10. Turning three turnovers into touchdowns, Florida State went up 30-0 at halftime and cruised the rest of the way. Xavier Beitia kicked three field goals and four different Seminoles scored touchdowns. Rix threw for 227 yards, Greg Jones rushed for 106 yards and a touchdown, while Anquan Boldin caught 5 passes for 91 yards and a touchdown. Talman Gardner had 109 yards in receptions (4) for the Seminoles.

DUKE

Chris Rix threw two touchdown passes during Florida State's 21 point burst in the second quarter, helping the fifth-ranked Seminoles break open a tight game on the way to a 48-17 victory. Florida State ignored its running game to work on its passing attack, throwing for 404 of its 510 yards. The Seminoles led 45-3 at one point. Three Florida State quarterbacks (Rix, McPherson, and Walker) combined to throw to 10 different receivers for 404 yards and four touchdowns. Leon Washington fell on a Duke fumble in the end zone for an FSU touchdown. Anquan Boldin led the receiving corps with 7 receptions for 110 yards and a touchdown.

Louisville

Henry Miller ran 25 yards for a touchdown in overtime as Louisville upset #4 Florida State, 26-20, in a game played in a steady rain. Louisville's Anthony Floyd intercepted a pass by quarterback Chris Rix on the first play of Florida State's possession in overtime. Miller then broke through the line on the Cardinals' opening play, shook off a tackler at the 15 yard line and ran into the end zone. Florida State is the highest-ranked team that Louisville has ever beaten. Louisville pushed the game into overtime after Dave Ragone connected on a 1 yard touchdown pass to Damien Dorsey with 11 minutes 37 seconds to go in the fourth quarter, tying the score at 20-20. After the teams traded field goals in the first quarter, Florida State went up, 10-3, when Rix, who completed 14 of 32 passes for 172 yards, threw a 23 yard touchdown pass to Talman Gardner. Nathan Smith pulled the Cardinals to within 10-6 with a 26 yard field goal with 4:30 left in the first half, but Florida State increased its lead to 13-7 when Xavier Beitia hit a 20 yard field goal on the last play of the first half. Louisville tied the score on Joshua Tinch's 30 yard touchdown reception with 4:50 remaining in the third quarter. Florida State answered two minutes later on Gardner's second touchdown catch of the game.

CLEMSON

The Seminoles showed little confidence in their passing game and benched sophomore quarterback Chris Rix for most of the second quarter, capitalizing on four Clemson turnovers and a punishing ground game for the 48-31 victory. Greg Jones ran for three touchdowns, breaking eight tackles on the final one, and set up a fourth with a long run that helped the Seminoles take a 28-24 halftime lead. He finished with 165 yards on 22 carries. Trailing 17-14, Leon Washington returned the ensuing kickoff 97 yards for a touchdown. Chris Rix ran for one touchdown and threw a 5 yard TD pass to Talman Gardner.

Miami {Wide Left}

The Miami Hurricanes came into this contest on a 28 game winning streak and sat at 5-0 for the season, while the Seminoles were 5-1. The contest started good for Miami as running back Willis McGahee scored from four yards out giving Miami a 7-0 lead. The lead wouldn't last as the Seminoles score the next 17 straight points to take a 17-7 lead. Miami quickly scored before the half, cutting the Seminole lead to three at 17-14. FSU scored the only points, a field goal, in the third quarter to give the Seminoles a 20-14 lead heading into the fourth quarter. FSU scored first in the fourth quarter giving the Seminoles a larger lead at 27-14. Miami quickly came back and scored two touchdowns in the fourth quarter to take a 28-27 lead. The Seminoles kicker, Xavier Beitia had a chance to win the game as time expired, but the 43 yard field goal sailed left this time, giving the Hurricanes the victory, 28-27.

NOTRE DAME

Carlyle Holiday threw for 185 yards and two touchdowns as #6 Notre Dame beat #11 Florida State 34-24 to remain unbeaten. Chris Rix was 13-of-32 passing for 207 yards with two interceptions and a fumble for the Seminoles. The game was tied 10-10 at halftime, but the Fighting Irish exploded for 24 straight points to put the game away. Adrian McPherson threw two 4th quarter touchdowns, one to Anquan Boldin (5 yards) and one to Nick Maddox (29 yards), but the Seminoles could get no closer.

Wake Forest

Adrian McPherson threw for 278 yards and two touchdowns in his first start and Nick Maddox rushed for a career-high 122 yards rushing as the 18th-ranked Seminoles rallied for a 34-21 victory over Wake Forest. The Seminoles trailed 14-0 after the 1st quarter and 21-17 at halftime. Nick Maddox ran for two touchdowns and Xavier Beitia kicked a 28 field goal in the 2nd half and the Seminole defense shutout the Demon Deacons to hold on for the win.

Georgia Tech

Stanford Samuels had two interceptions, including a game saving pick in the end zone with 20 seconds left, as the 17th-ranked Seminoles held off Georgia Tech 21-13. Adrian McPherson threw two touchdown passes, including a 72 yarder to Craphonso Thorpe, and Nick Maddox tied his career high with 122 yards, but Samuels' interceptions proved to be the difference. He returned his other one 82 yards for a tying touchdown in the first quarter. Anquan Boldin caught a 32 yard TD pass from McPherson in the 3rd quarter and the Seminole defense shut down the Ramblin' Wreck, setting up Samuels late game heroics.

NORTH CAROLINA

Adrian McPherson threw four touchdown passes as the 15th ranked Seminoles defeated North Carolina 40-14. McPherson threw three scoring passes to Anquan Boldin, two in the second quarter as Florida State took a 17-0 halftime lead. Boldin caught five passes for 104 yards. Xavier Beitia kicked two field goals and Talman Gardner and Craphonso Thorpe each caught TD passes.

NC State

T.A. McLendon rushed for 114 yards and one touchdown and North Carolina State's defense held #14 Florida State to 162 total yards for a 17-7 victory. Florida State's offensive output was the lowest in Bobby Bowden's 325 games with the Seminoles. The Seminoles only points were on a Michael Boulware 84 yard fumble return for a touchdown.

FLORIDA

Chris Rix ran for 83 yards and threw two touchdowns to Anquan Boldin to help the #23 Seminoles earn their biggest win of the year, 31-14 over #15 Florida. Freshman tailback Leon Washington ran for 134 yards. Linebacker Kendyll Pope returned an interception for a touchdown. Grossman flipped a pass to tight end Aaron Walker. Walker tipped it into the hands of Pope, whose 13 yard interception return gave the Seminoles a 24-6 lead. Grossman, who finished with 303 yards, led the Gators on an 84 yard touchdown drive to cut the deficit to 10.

2003 SUGAR BOWL

The 69th edition to the Sugar Bowl featured the Georgia Bulldogs, and the Florida State Seminoles. Georgia came into the game 12–1 and ranked 3rd in the BCS, whereas Florida State came into the game 9–4 and ranked 14th in the BCS. Kicker Billy Bennett kicked a 23 yard field goal with 10 minutes left in the opening quarter to account for the quarter's only points. In the second quarter, FSU quarterback Fabian Walker threw a 5 yard slant pass to Anquan Boldin as FSU took a 7–3 lead. Florida State was driving again in the second quarter before cornerback Bruce Thornton stepped in front of a Walker pass and raced 73 yards to the opposite end zone, to give Georgia a 10–7 lead. Quarterback D.J. Shockley threw a 37 yard touchdown pass to Terrence Edwards before halftime to give the Bulldogs a 17–7 half time lead. Billy Bennett accounted for two more Georgia field goals in the third quarter, as Georgia posted a 23–7 lead. On the final play of the third quarter, wide receiver Anquan Boldin (who had replaced quarterback Fabian Walker) threw a 40 yard touchdown pass to Craphonso Thorpe. The ensuing two point conversion failed, and the lead was 23–13. Billy Bennett kicked another field goal in the fourth quarter, as Georgia held off Florida State. Georgia's running back Musa Smith won the MVP award.

2003 Florida State Seminoles {ACC Champions}

The team was coached by Bobby Bowden in his 28th season. They finished the season 10-3 (7–1 ACC) to finish in 1st place in the ACC. They were invited to the Orange Bowl, where they lost to Miami 16-14 in a rematch of the regular season game.

Alex Barron {T}, Michael Boulware {LB}, Darnell Dockett {DT}, Stanford Samuels {CB} and Craphonso Thorpe {WR} were selected as First team All-ACC. Dockett was named the ACC defensive player of the Year. Alex Barron was selected as a Consensus First team All-American. Boulware {Seattle}, Greg Jones {RB}, Dockett {Arizona}, Kendall Pope {LB} {Indianapolis} and P.K. Sam {WR} {New England} were selected in the 2004 NFL draft.

ACC CHAMPIONS					**FINAL RANK: #11 AP, #10 CP**				
Home games were played at Doak Campbell Stadium									
8/30/2003	Florida State	#13	@		North Carolina (2-10)	ABC	37	0	W
9/6/2003	Florida State	#11	vs	#2	MARYLAND (10-3)	espn2	35	10	W
9/13/2003	Florida State	#10	vs		GEORGIA TECH (7-6)	ABC	14	13	W
9/20/2003	Florida State	#10	vs		COLORADO (5-7)	ABC	47	7	W
9/27/2003	Florida State	#6	@		Duke (4-8)		56	7	W
10/11/2003	Florida State	#5	vs		MIAMI (11-2)	ABC	14	22	L
10/18/2003	Florida State	#7	@		Virginia (8-5)	ESPN	19	14	W
10/25/2003	Florida State	#6	vs		WAKE FOREST (5-7)	ABC	48	24	W
11/1/2003	Florida State	#5	@		Notre Dame (5-7)	NBC	37	0	W
11/8/2003	Florida State	#3	@		Clemson (9-4)	espn2	10	26	L
11/15/2003	Florida State	#13	vs		NC STATE (8-5)	ABC	50	44	W
11/29/2003	Florida State	#9	@	#11	Florida (8-5)	CBS	38	34	W
1/1/2004	**Florida State**	#9	vs	#10	Miami (11-2)	ABC	14	16	L
Coach: Bobby Bowden					Season Record >>		419	217	10-3

Schedule Source: Steve's Football Bible LLC

Selected game(s) highlights

North Carolina

Chris Rix ran for a pair of short touchdowns and threw for another score as the 13th-ranked Seminoles built a 27 point halftime lead and cruised to a season opening 37-0 victory over North Carolina. The Florida State offense rolled up 301 yards and 18 first downs in the opening 30 minutes. Rix completed 11 of his first 12 passes with a pair of 1 yard scoring runs in the opening half and a 7 yard TD pass late in the third quarter. Greg Jones scored on a 5 yard run to open the scoring. Less than two minutes later, a 43 yard pass by Rix set up his first short keeper. Lorenzo Booker raced 21 yards for his first career TD and a 21-0 lead. Rix then capped a 79 yard drive 1:08 before halftime with a 1 yard sneak.

MARYLAND

Greg Jones ran for two touchdowns and Chris Rix passed for two more #11 Florida State wiped out an early 10 point deficit and defeated Maryland 35-10. Jones broke free for a 44 yard touchdown run with 11:29 left in the first half to give the Seminoles a 14-10 lead. Jones scored his second touchdown on a 1 yard run to culminate a 99 yard drive that gave the Seminoles a 21-10 lead with 5:38 left in the half. P.K. Sam caught a 34 yard touchdown pass that gave Florida State a 28-10 lead in the final seconds of the third quarter. Willie Reid's 2 yard TD run completed the scoring.

GEORGIA TECH

The Seminoles scored two touchdowns in the final 7:09 for a 14-13 victory over Georgia Tech. Chris Rix shook off two interceptions to run for one touchdown and pass for another. Georgia Tech's P.J. Daniels ran 47 yards for touchdown and Dan Burnett kicked two field goals as the Yellow Jackets built a 13-0 lead midway through the fourth quarter. Rix scored on a 3 yard run with 7:09 left to pull to within 13-7. Rix's 5 yard touchdown pass to P.K. Sam, and Xavier Beitia's extra point put Florida State ahead with 2:57 left. Florida State allowed Georgia Tech only 69 yards offense and three first downs in the second half.

COLORADO

Chris Rix and Craphonso Thorpe combined on two long scoring plays in the 10th ranked Seminoles' 47-7 victory over outmanned Colorado. Rix passed for a career-high 394 yards in three quarters, completing 30 of 39 attempts. Backup Fabian Walker added 64 yards as the Seminoles totaled 458 yards passing. Thorpe scored on passes of 56 and 37 yards and finished with 205 yards on eight catches. P.K. Sam chipped in with a career high 10 passes for 119 more yards as the Seminoles rolled up 551 yards offense compared to Colorado's 275. Chauncey Davis' 31 yard blocked punt return for a touchdown gave Florida State a 40-7 lead.

Duke

Chris Rix threw two touchdown passes and A.J. Nicholson and Antonio Cromartie added defensive touchdowns as #6 Florida State beat Duke 56-7. B.J. Ward blocked two field goals for the Seminoles. The Seminoles got rushing touchdowns from three players, B.J. Dean (6 yards), Greg Jones (2 yards) and Willie Reid (1 yard). Florida State scored touchdowns on its first three drives and took a 28-7 halftime lead. A.J. Nicholson scooped up Mike Schneider's fumble at the Blue Devils 23, fumbled it on the way to the end zone, but picked it up in stride and scored. He was credited with a 3 yard TD return for a 35-7 lead. Antonio Cromartie added a 71 yard interception return for a touchdown late in the fourth quarter.

MIAMI

Jarrett Payton caught a 14 yard touchdown pass and ran for a career-high 97 yards, and #2 Miami forced five turnovers in a 22-14 win Saturday over #5 Florida State. Sean Taylor intercepted two passes, returning one 50 yards for a score, and Miami built a 22-0 lead. Jon Peattie kicked three field goals, Kellen Winslow caught seven passes for 106 yards and the defense held Florida State to 61 yards rushing. Miami's Brock Berlin threw three interceptions, including one that set up Willie Reid's 18 yard touchdown catch in the third quarter to make it 22-7. FSU's Chris Davis had a 17 yard touchdown catch on the last play of the game.

Virginia

Chris Rix threw a 79 yard touchdown pass to Craphonso Thorpe and Xavier Beitia kicked four field goals Saturday night as #7 Florida State gave Bowden his 338th career coaching victory, 19-14 over Virginia. Florida State won with defense, holding the Cavaliers to minus 5 rushing yards on just nine attempts as Virginia tried to win on the arm of Matt Schaub. He was 39-for-53 for 326 yards and two touchdowns

WAKE FOREST

Sixth-ranked Florida State kept its national title hopes alive with a 48-24 victory over Wake Forest. Bobby Bowden became major college football's winningest coach with his 339th career victory. Chris Rix matched Bowden's victory total by passing for 339 yards and a pair of scores and ran for one touchdown. Rix threw a pair of touchdown passes to Craphonso Thorpe on plays covering 25 yards and 10 yards, the first giving the Seminoles a 27-14 halftime lead. Leon Washington returned a punt 65 yards for a touchdown.

Notre Dame

Chris Rix passed for 327 yards and three touchdowns to lead the Seminoles to a 37-0 victory over Notre Dame in South Bend. Craphonso Thorpe had seven catches for 217 yards, including TD catches of

35 and 38 yards. Rix completed 17 of 31 passes with three interceptions. Xavier Beitia kicked three field goals for the Seminoles. P.K. Same caught a 6 yard TD pass from Rix and Leroy Smith returned an interception 90 yards for a touchdown.

Clemson

Charlie Whitehurst threw for one touchdown and ran for another as Clemson snapped an 11-game losing streak to the Seminoles. Charlie Whitehurst made the game's biggest plays. A 17 yard pass to Kevin Youngblood led to Hunt's second field goal from 35 yards out and a 6-0 Clemson lead. With 2:50 to go in the half, Whitehurst led a 65 yard touchdown drive -- 51 on a pass to Youngblood. Whitehurst finished it off himself with a 1 yard scoring run with 15 seconds left that made it 13-0. Whitehurst lofted a pass to a wide-open Derrick Hamilton for a 58 yard touchdown that gave Clemson a 23-3 lead late in the third quarter. Whitehurst finished with 272 yards passing.

NC STATE

Leon Washington's 12 yard touchdown run gave #13 Florida State a 50-44 double overtime victory over North Carolina State. NC State's Philip Rivers completed 28 of 38 passes for 422 yards and four touchdowns and ran for another score. North Carolina State gambled and lost in the second overtime. Instead of trying a field goal, the Wolfpack went on fourth and 1 at the Florida State 16 and Rivers' pass for Jerricho Cotchery was broken up by Allen Augustin at the 5. Then Washington reeled off successive runs of 13 and 12 yards to give the Seminoles the win in their first home overtime game. Washington finished with 121 yards on 17 carries. Florida State took a 44-37 lead in the first overtime on 4 yard TD throw by Chris Rix to Craphonso Thorpe, but North Carolina State countered on a 7 yard scoring throw from Rivers to Tramaine Hall. Regulation play ended when North Carolina State's Derek Morris blocked a 32 yard field goal try by Florida State's Xavier Beitia with only 2 seconds left.

Florida {Swindle at the Swamp}

Florida State was ranked #9 and Florida #11 coming into the 2003 contest in Gainesville. It turned out to be a close and high-scoring affair, but it is most remembered for several controversial referee calls by the ACC officiating crew and was christened the "Swindle in the Swamp" by several national and Florida sportswriters for the questionable calls on multiple fumble/no-fumble plays that went against Florida. Florida nevertheless held a slim 34–31 lead late in the fourth quarter when Seminoles quarterback Chris Rix hit wide receiver PK Sam for a 52 yard touchdown pass with under a minute to go, giving Florida State a 38–34 lead. Before the winning score, Rix had completed a first down pass on a fourth-and-14 play deep in Seminoles territory to keep the drive alive. The Seminoles went on to hold off the Gators, 38–34. After the game, a fight broke out on the field between the Florida and Florida State players after some Seminole players celebrated the win by jumping on the "F" logo in the center of Florida Field.

2004 ORANGE BOWL {Wide Right IV}

This game was the first and only rematch to date between the state rivals. The Seminoles had already lost to Miami 22-14 earlier in the season in a rain-soaked game that is perhaps best remembered for the crushing hit that senior cornerback Stanford Samuels laid on Roscoe Parrish, sending the sophomore wide receiver to a Tallahassee hospital with internal bleeding. Both teams fell short of their national championship aspirations, instead settling for conference crowns (Florida State won the Atlantic Coast Conference and Miami won the Big East Conference) and a New Year's Day date in the Orange Bowl. Like several other memorable games between the teams, the outcome was decided by a kicker. Florida State jumped out to a 14-3 lead early in the second quarter on a 7 yard touchdown pass from junior quarterback Chris Rix to sophomore tight end Matt Henshaw, but it would be the last time the Seminoles scored. Miami reeled off the final 13 points of the game. Freshman running back Tyrone Moss crossed the goal line on a 3 yard score with 5:34 to go in the second quarter for Miami's only touchdown of the game, and kicker Jon Peattie, who led all freshmen nationally in scoring, booted a 44 yard field goal just before halftime. Peattie's third field goal of the game was a 51 yard kick that gave the Hurricanes a 16-14 lead in the third quarter. FSU had a chance to retake the lead, but kicker Xavier Beitia missed a 39 yard field-goal attempt with 5:30 to play. The kick sailed, where else, wide right. Although the Seminoles got another possession, the game was dubbed "Wide Right IV."

2004 Florida State Seminoles

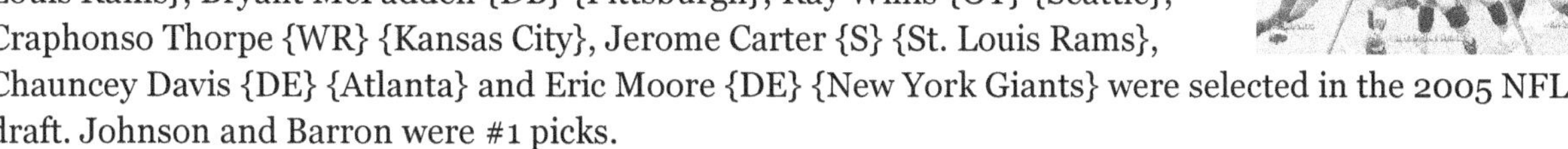

The team was coached by Bobby Bowden in his 29th season. They finished the season 9-3 (6-2 ACC). They were invited to the Gator Bowl, where they played and beat West Virginia, 30-13.

Alex Barron {OT}, Antonio Cromartie {EB} and Travis Johnson {DT} were selected to the First team All-ACC team. Barron and Johnson were Consensus First team All-Americans. Johnson {Houston Texans}, Barron {St. Louis Rams}, Bryant McFadden {DB} {Pittsburgh}, Ray Willis {OT} {Seattle}, Craphonso Thorpe {WR} {Kansas City}, Jerome Carter {S} {St. Louis Rams}, Chauncey Davis {DE} {Atlanta} and Eric Moore {DE} {New York Giants} were selected in the 2005 NFL draft. Johnson and Barron were #1 picks.

FINAL RANK: #13 AP, #14 CP

Home games were played at Doak Campbell Stadium

Date	Team	Rank		Opp Rank	Opponent	TV			
9/10/2004	Florida State	#4	@	#5	**Miami (9-3)**	ABC	10	16	**L**
9/18/2004	Florida State	#8	vs		ALABAMA-BIRMINGHAM	espn2	34	7	**W**
9/25/2004	Florida State	#8	vs		**CLEMSON (6-5)**	ABC	41	22	**W**
10/2/2004	Florida State	#9	vs		**NORTH CAROLINA (6-6)**	espn2	38	16	**W**
10/9/2004	Florida State	#8	@		Syracuse (6-6)	espn2	17	13	**W**
10/16/2004	Florida State	#7	vs	#6	**VIRGINIA (8-4)**	ESPN	36	3	**W**
10/23/2004	Florida State	#5	@		**Wake Forest (4-7)**	ABC	20	17	**W**
10/30/2004	Florida State	#5	@		**Maryland (5-6)**	ABC	17	20	**L**
11/6/2004	Florida State	#13	vs		**DUKE (2-9)**		29	7	**W**
11/11/2004	Florida State	#11	@		**NC State (5-6)**	ESPN	17	10	**W**
11/20/2004	Florida State	#10	vs		FLORIDA (7-5)	ESPN	13	20	**L**
1/1/2005	**Florida State**	#16	vs		**West Virginia (8-4)**	**CBS**	**30**	**18**	**W**
Coach: Bobby Bowden					**Season Record >>**		**302**	**169**	**9-3**

Schedule Source: Steve's Football Bible LLC

Selected game(s) highlights

Miami

The Seminoles opened the 2004 season the same way they ended the previous season -- with a loss to Miami. The inaugural Atlantic Coast Conference game for Miami, originally scheduled to be played on Labor Day, was postponed four days because of Hurricane Frances. Florida State had a 10-0 lead against the Hurricanes in the fourth quarter when Miami kicker Jon Peattie, who missed two earlier kicks, notched an 18 yard field goal for Miami's first points of the game. The Seminoles failed to score an offensive touchdown. Their lone touchdown came when Miami wide receiver Roscoe Parrish fumbled the football that was recovered by sophomore cornerback Antonio Cromartie and returned 61 yards for a touchdown in the second quarter. Senior kicker Xavier Beitia, who had been the goat in previous losses to Miami, didn't miss any kicks this time, but a 34 yard field goal attempt was blocked with 3:58 to play. The kick would have sealed a victory for the Seminoles. Instead, Miami got the ball back with a chance to tie the game. Senior quarterback Brock Berlin connected with junior wide receiver Sinorice Moss for a 30 yard touchdown with 30 seconds left to tie the game. Senior quarterback Chris Rix, a four-year starter for the Seminoles, threw two interceptions and fumbled twice, including on FSU's first possession in overtime. The Hurricanes recovered and scored two plays later on an 18 yard touchdown run by junior running back Frank Gore. Rix became the only FSU quarterback to finish with a 0-5 record against Miami. The Seminoles, playing Miami for the third time in less than 11 months, lost their sixth straight against the Hurricanes

ALABAMA-BIRMINGHAM

Leon Washington ran for 104 yards and a touchdown and Florida State sacked Darrell Hackney eight times to rebound 34-7 victory over the Blazers. B.J. Dean, James Coleman and Chris Rix scored on 1 yard runs and Xavier Beitia kicked two field goals for Florida State. Florida State had 489 yards of total offense and didn't punt until late in the fourth quarter. In addition to getting to Hackney for 54 yards in losses, the Florida State defense limited UAB to 144 total yards and a minus-24 yards rushing.

CLEMSON

Wyatt Sexton threw for 162 yards and a touchdown after replacing an injured Chris Rix, and #8 Florida State forced five turnovers in a 41-22 victory over Clemson. Sexton completed 17 of 26 passes with a 47 yard scoring pass to Chauncey Stovall. Justin Miller matched a school record with two kickoff return touchdowns, one for 97 yards and one 86 yards, for Clemson. Miller set an ACC record with 282 yards on six returns. The Seminoles' defense intercepted Charlie Whitehurst three times and forced two fumbles. The defense scored one touchdown (Leroy Smith 41 yard interception return) and set up another (Charles Howard fumble recovery) just 18 seconds apart in the second quarter. Five different players scored touchdowns for the Seminoles and Xavier Beitia kicked field goals of 29 and 38 yards.

NORTH CAROLINA

Wyatt Sexton threw three touchdown passes as #9 Florida State defeated North Carolina 38-16. Florida State built a 24-6 lead early in the third quarter but didn't put the game out of reach until Sexton's 15 yard TD pass to Chauncey Stovall completed the scoring with 6:53 left. Stovall also caught a 5 yard scoring pass in the final minute of the first half. Leon Washington ran for 153 yards on just 10 carries and ran 18 yards for the first touchdown of the game. Lorenzo Booker added 84 yards, including a 12 yard scoring run in the second quarter. Sexton teamed with Craphanso Thorpe on an 11 yard touchdown in the third quarter.

Syracuse

Leon Washington rushed for a career high 164 yards and scored on runs of 21 and 45 yards in the second half, and #8 Florida State survived a major scare, rallying past Syracuse 17-13. Xavier Beitia kicked a 28 yard field to even the score at 3-3.

VIRGINIA

Wyatt Sexton's passing took care of the offense as the #7 Seminoles rolled to a 36-3 victory over previously undefeated #6 Virginia and picked up their first win over a higher ranked team for the first time since the 1998 season. Lorenzo Booker rushed for a career high 123 yards and two touchdown runs, while Florida State's defense limited Virginia to 20 yards rushing. Sexton completed 20 of 26 passes for 275 yards and a touchdown. Virginia's only points came on a 23 yard field goal by Connor Hughes as time expired in the first half. Ernie Sims broke free from his left side and blocked Sean Johnson's punt into the end zone midway through the first quarter for a safety and a 2-0 Florida State lead. Leon Washington scored on a 5 yard run and finished with 68 yards rushing while Xavier Beitia kicked two field goals

Wake Forest

Xavier Beitia kicked a 22 yard field goal with 1:03 to play to help #5 Florida State pull off a surprisingly close 20-17 victory over Wake Forest. Seminoles quarterback Wyatt Sexton helped Wake Forest build a 14-3 lead before halftime with an interception and a fumble, and both turnovers were returned for touchdowns. Ryan Plackemeir's 41 yard field goal that tied the game at 17 with 4:32 to play. Florida State then needed a 46 yard run by Lorenzo Booker on third-and-10 and a 14 yard pass from Sexton to Dominic Robinson on third-and-6 to set up the game-winning field goal.

Maryland

Joel Statham threw for 333 yards and ran for a score, and the Terrapins held on to beat the fifth-ranked Seminoles 20-17. Florida State had a perfect 14-0 record against Maryland. The Seminoles fell behind 20-10 before turning to Chris Rix at the start of the fourth quarter. On his second series, Rix moved FSU to the 35 before a 52 yard field goal try by Xavier Beitia hit the left crossbar. On his next drive, Rix threw his first touchdown pass of the season, a 16 yarder to Chauncey Stovall with 7:43 remaining that made it 20-17. After a Maryland punt, Rix got the Seminoles in position for another field goal attempt by Beitia, who was wide left on 45 yard field goal try with 4:45 left. Rix got one final chance two minutes later, but his fourth-down pass from the FSU 27 soared over the head of Lome Sam with 1:38 to go.

DUKE

Wyatt Sexton led three long scoring drives in the second half, and Gary Cismesia tied a school record with five field goals in his college debut to lead 13th ranked Florida State past Duke 29-7. Sexton completed 11 of 15 passes for 220 yards and a touchdown while taking the Seminoles on drives of 93, 80 and 70 yards to break open a tight game with 20 straight points. Chris Davis and Lamar Lewis scored touchdowns for the Seminoles.

NC State

Lorenzo Booker and James Coleman each ran for third-quarter touchdowns, helping #11 Florida State rally past North Carolina State 17-10 in a game that featured 22 punts, four turnovers and less than 250 yards of combined offense. The lone touchdown for the Wolfpack came on Darrell Blackman's 87 yard punt return in the second quarter that gave them a 10-0 lead. Gary Cismesia kicked a 44 yard field goal for the Seminoles.

FLORIDA

Chris Leak threw a touchdown, Ciatrick Fason ran for a score, and Florida upset #10 ranked Florida State 20-13 to win in Tallahassee for the first time since 1986. Fason's 8 yard touchdown run with 4:59 remaining put the Gators ahead for good. Chris Rix came off the bench and threw a touchdown 27 yard pass to Chauncey Stovall with 8:30 left to play that cut the lead to 13-10. Rix drove the Seminoles to the 18 yard line in the waning seconds, but his last pass was intercepted by Jarvis Harris with 8 seconds to play.

2005 GATOR BOWL

Chris Rix sparked #17 Florida State with two long second half touchdown drives Saturday, beating West Virginia 30-18 in the Gator Bowl. Rix fumbled three times and threw two interceptions, one of which led to a touchdown, but Coach Bowden stuck with him. Rix completed five straight passes during a 90 yard drive late in the third quarter, capped by his 14 yard TD pass to Craphonso Thorpe. Rix led an 80 yard scoring drive in the fourth, capped by James Coleman's 1 yard run. Rix finished 16-of-31 for 157 yards. Leon Washington carried Florida State much of the day, finishing with 195 yards rushing and a 69 yard touchdown run to give the Noles a 7-0 lead. Xavier Beitia kicked three field goals for the Seminoles.

2005 Florida State Seminoles {ACC Champions}

The team was coached by Bobby Bowden in his 30th season. The Seminoles won their division and competed in the ACC title game, defeating Virginia Tech in the inaugural championship game. Florida State finished the season ranked number 23 in both the final AP and Coaches college football polls. Florida State's trip to the Orange Bowl marked the 24th consecutive post season bowl game under Bobby Bowden.

Broderick Bunkley {DT} was named a 1st team All-American by cnnsi.com, Football Writers Association and College & Pro Football Weekly. Kamerion Wimbley {DE} was selected to College & Pro Football Weekly as a 1st Team All-American. A.J. Nicholson {LB}, was selected to cnnsi.com as an All-American - Honorable Mention and Willie Reid {WR} was selected to the College Football News as an All-American Honorable Mention. Ernie Sims {LB} {Detroit}, Wimbley {Cleveland}, Bunkley {Philadelphia}, Antonio Cromartie {San Diego}, Reid {Pittsburgh}, Leon Washington {RB} {New York Jets}, Pat Watkins {S} {Dallas} and Nicholson {Cincinnati} were selected in the 2006 NFL draft. Sims, Wimbley, Bunkley and Cromartie were all #1 picks.

ACC CHAMPIONS				FINAL RANK: #23 AP, #23 CP					
Home games were played at Doak Campbell Stadium									
9/5/2005	Florida State	#14	vs	#9	MIAMI (9-3)	ABC	10	7	W
9/10/2005	Florida State	#11	vs		THE CITADEL	ESPNU	62	10	W
9/17/2005	Florida State	#8	@	#17	Boston College (9-3)	ESPN	28	17	W
10/1/2005	Florida State	#6	vs		SYRACUSE (1-10)	ABC	38	14	W
10/8/2005	Florida State	#4	vs		WAKE FOREST (4-7)	JPS	41	24	W
10/15/2005	Florida State	#4	@		Virginia (7-5)	ESPN	21	26	L
10/22/2005	Florida State	#11	@		Duke (1-10)	ESPNU	55	24	W
10/29/2005	Florida State	#10	vs		MARYLAND (5-6)	ABC	35	27	W
11/5/2005	Florida State	#9	vs		NC STATE (7-5)	ABC	15	20	L
11/12/2005	Florida State	#17	@		Clemson (8-4)	ESPN	14	35	L
11/26/2005	Florida State	#23	@	#19	Florida (9-3)	CBS	7	34	L
12/3/2005	Florida State	#22	vs	#5	Virginia Tech (11-2)	ABC	27	22	W
1/3/2006	Florida State	#23	vs	#3	Penn State (11-1)	ABC	23	26	L
Coach: Bobby Bowden					Season Record >>		376	286	8-5

Schedule Source: Steve's Football Bible LLC

Selected game(s) highlights

MIAMI

The Seminoles found some good fortune against their rivals when the Hurricanes botched a short, potential game-tying field goal in the closing minutes of Florida State's 10-7 victory. Jon Peattie lined up for a 28 yarder after a 19 play, 81 yard drive by Miami stalled with about 2:30 left. But holder Brian Monroe dropped a low snap that bounced off his hands and rolled back into the pile, never giving Peattie a chance to try the kick. Florida State overcame its own inept offense (170 total yards) with a defense that registered nine sacks and some solid special teams plays. The Seminoles grabbed a 10-0 lead in the first quarter, with help from the first interception thrown by Kyle Wright. From the Miami 29, the Seminoles drove to the 1 yard line where James Coleman ran for a touchdown. Gary Cismesia kicked a 37 yard field goal.

THE CITADEL

Drew Weatherford bounced back from after struggling in his first collegiate start to throw for 342 yards and two touchdowns as No. 11 Florida State beat Division I-AA The Citadel 62-10. Weatherford completed 26 of 37 passes for 342 yards and two touchdown passes. Trailing 10-3 with just over a minute left in the half, Florida State scored 45 straight points, including five third-quarter touchdowns, to lead 48-10 after three quarters. Greg Carr caught two touchdown passes and six other Seminoles scored touchdowns.

Boston College

A.J. Nicholson intercepted two passes, scoring on a 19 yard return on the first play of the game, and Greg Carr caught two touchdowns to help eighth ranked Florida State beat #17 Boston College 28-17. Nicholson's interceptions sparked the Seminoles to a 14-0 lead in the first five minutes before BC scored 17 unanswered points to take the lead. Drew Weatherford hit Greg Carr on a 6 yard slant across the middle of the end zone with 10:13 left in the fourth quarter, then Darius McClure blocked a punt deep in BC territory and Lorenzo Booker scored from 4 yards out to make it 28-17. BC drove to the Florida State 2 in the final three minutes but couldn't score in seven tries.

SYRACUSE

Drew Weatherford passed for 234 yards and three touchdowns, including a 71 yard swing pass to Lorenzo Booker, and #6 Florida State defeated Syracuse 38-14. Weatherford also scored a touchdown as the Seminoles rolled up a 24-0 lead. Florida State sacked Syracuse quarterback Perry Patterson seven times. Weatherford completed 17 of 26 passes, throwing touchdown passes covering 43 yards to Willie Reid and 15 yards to Chris Davis. Xavier Lee passed for 162 yards, including a 75 yard completion to freshman Kenny O'Neal that set up the Seminoles final touchdown, an 11 yard run by Lamar Lewis.

WAKE FOREST

Greg Carr caught a 63 yard pass to set up the first of three fourth-quarter scores, helping #4 Florida State beat pesky Wake Forest 41-24. Leon Washington ran for 87 yards and another 92 yards on four catches, including a 61 yard TD reception from Drew Weatherford. Carr caught a 28 yard touchdown pass from Weatherford in the first quarter. Weatherford threw for 351 yards and three touchdowns and ran for another as the offense rolled up 585 yards.

Virginia

Marques Hagans threw for a career best 306 yards and two touchdowns and Connor Hughes kicked four field goals for the Cavaliers topped the Seminoles 26-21 and beat a top 5 team for only the second time in their history. Lorenzo Booker scored on a 58 touchdown run and Chris Davis caught a 22 yard TD pass from Drew Weatherford. Gary Cismesia kicked a 22 and 32 yard field goal. Weatherford finished 35-for-59 for 377 yards.

Duke

Drew Weatherford threw two touchdown passes and backup Xavier Lee added two of his own to help #11 Florida State bounce back from its first loss of the season with a 55-24 victory over Duke. Greg Carr caught three TDs and third-string tailback Antone Smith ran for two scores for the Seminoles. Gary kicked field goals from 30 yards and 49 yards.

MARYLAND

Drew Weatherford and James Coleman scored fourth-quarter touchdowns to lead #10 Florida State to a 35-27 come-from-behind victory over Maryland. Weatherford's 15 yard run with 8:52 left gave the Seminoles a 28-27 lead and they scored three minutes later on Coleman's 1 yard run. Coleman's score was set up by Ernie Sims' interception. Maryland's final bid for a tie ended with 52 seconds left when Joel Statham was sacked by A.J. Nicholson at the Florida State 40. Leon Washington scored on a 3 yard run on Florida State's first offensive series and Willie Reid added a 61 yard punt return TD to give the Seminoles a 14-0 lead in the opening minute of the second quarter. But Maryland countered with three touchdowns in a span of nine minutes to take a 21-14 halftime lead.

NC STATE

Andre Brown ran for 179 yards and a touchdown and North Carolina State intercepted Drew Weatherford three times to upset #9 Florida State 20-15 for its third victory in five years over the Seminoles. Florida State's offense managed only 43 yards rushing. The Seminoles scored its lone touchdown midway through the second quarter when Chris Davis went 33 yards with a slant pass from Weatherford for a 10-7 lead. The Seminoles' only other points came on field goals of 25 and 48 yards by Gary Cismesia, and a safety.

Clemson

Charlie Whitehurst threw for 269 yards and three touchdowns to lead the Tigers over the #17 Seminoles 35-14. Whitehurst went 21-of-32 and Chansi Stuckey had 11 catches for 156 yards and two TDs for Clemson. The Seminoles gained just 226 yards. A blocked punt recovered for a touchdown and two field goals helped Florida State tie it at 14 at the half, but the Tigers defense took over in the third quarter.

Florida

Chris Leak threw two touchdown passes, the defense created four turnovers and the #19 Gators overwhelmed 23rd ranked Florida State 34-7 at The Swamp. Leak capped a 71 yard drive with an 8 yard TD pass to Chad Jackson on the first play of the second quarter. Jackson finished with nine catches for 97 yards. Leak finished 19-of-28 for 211 yards. Trailing 34-0, Florida State scored on a De'Cody Fagg 6 yard TD pass from Drew Weatherford

2005 ACC CHAMPIONSHIP

Willie Reid returned a punt 83 yards for a touchdown, the defense continually harassed Marcus Vick and Florida State upset #5 Virginia Tech 27-22 in the inaugural Atlantic Coast Conference title game. Reid finished with 210 all-purpose yards and was the game's most valuable player. The Seminole defense sacked Vick six times. After intercepting Vick, Drew Weatherford completed consecutive passes to Fred Rouse and De'Cody Fagg, then Leon Washington sprinted up the middle for a 14 yard score. Gary Cismesia kicked two field goals for the Noles.

2006 ORANGE BOWL

The 72nd edition to the Orange Bowl featured the Penn State Nittany Lions and the Florida State Seminoles. This game was known for being the eighth, and ultimately final meeting, between the two coaches, Joe Paterno of Penn State and Bobby Bowden of Florida State. The three-overtime game took over four hours. It is regarded as one of the more entertaining Orange Bowls due to the high excitement level and some key missed kicks. Trailing 7-0 after the 1st quarter, Willie Reid returned a punt 87 yards for a touchdown. Drew Weatherford threw a 57 yard TD pass to Lorenzo Booker for a 13-7 Noles lead.  The Nittany Lions took a 14-13 halftime lead on a 24 yard Michael Robinson TD pass to Ethan Kilmer. Penn State notched a safety to take a 16-13 lead, but Gary Cismesia kicked a 48 yard field goal to tie the game at 16-16. Florida State started on offense to begin the first overtime. Kicker Gary Cismesia's 44 yard attempt went wide right. Penn State conservatively rushed three times and attempted a 38 yard field goal on their first overtime drive. However, kicker Kevin Kelly's try pushed wide left. In the second overtime, both team scored on 1 yard touchdown runs tying the game at 23–23. In the third overtime, Florida State's kicking woes continued. Cismesia's 38 yard attempt hit the right upright. On 2nd and 9 on the 12 yard line, Kelly hit a 29 yard field goal to give Joe Paterno and the Nittany Lions the win over Bobby Bowden and the Seminoles.

2006 Florida State Seminoles

The team was coached by Bobby Bowden in his 31st season. The Seminoles finished with an overall record of 7–6, which was head coach Bobby Bowden's worst record since going 5–6 in 1976, his first year as Florida State's head coach. The Seminoles were picked by the ACC media as the preseason favorite to win the ACC's Atlantic Division.

Buster Davis {LB} was selected the All-ACC first team and was Selected as an All-American by the American Football Coaches Association. Lawrence Timmons {LB} {Pittsburgh}, Davis {Arizona}, Lorenzo Booker {RB} {Miami}, Mario Henderson {OL} {Oakland} and Chris Davis {WR} {Tennessee} were selected in the 2007 NFL draft. Timmons was a #1 pick.

Home games were played at Doak Campbell Stadium

9/4/2006	Florida State	**#10**	@	#11	**Miami (7-6)**	ESPN	13	10	W
9/9/2006	Florida State	**#9**	vs		TROY (8-5)		24	17	W
9/16/2006	Florida State	**#10**	vs		**CLEMSON (8-5)**	ESPN	20	27	L
9/23/2006	Florida State	**#17**	vs		**RICE** (7-6)	ESPNU	55	7	W
10/5/2006	Florida State	**#16**	@		**NC State (3-9)**	ESPN	20	24	L
10/14/2006	Florida State		@		**Duke (0-12)**		51	24	W
10/21/2006	Florida State		vs	#21	**BOSTON COLLEGE (10-3)**	ABC	19	24	L
10/28/2006	Florida State		@		**Maryland (9-4)**	espn2	24	27	L
11/4/2006	Florida State		vs		**VIRGINIA (5-7)**		33	0	W
11/11/2006	Florida State		vs	#19	**WAKE FOREST (11-3)**	ABC	0	30	L
11/18/2006	Florida State		vs		WESTERN MICHIGAN (8-5)		28	20	W
11/25/2006	Florida State		vs	#4	FLORIDA (13-1)	ABC	14	21	L
12/27/2006	**Florida State**		**vs**		**Ucla (7-6)**	**ESPN**	**44**	**27**	**W**
Coach: Bobby Bowden					**Season Record >>**		**345**	**258**	**7-6**

Schedule Source: Steve's Football Bible LLC

Selected game(s) highlights

Miami

The final game in the Orange Bowl between the rivals is likely memorable for Florida State fans and forgettable for Miami fans. The Seminoles trailed Miami 10-3 at halftime but held Miami scoreless in the second half. Florida State scored the tying touchdown on a 1 yard run by junior fullback Joe Surratt in the fourth quarter and took the lead with a 33 yard field goal by sophomore kicker Gary Cismesia with 8:06 left to play. The Seminoles preserved the win when cornerback Michael Ray Garvin intercepted Miami quarterback Kyle Wright with 29 seconds remaining. The Hurricanes managed only 17 second-half yards, and their 2 rushing yards on 26 carries was the second-lowest total in school history. That was better than FSU, which finished with 1 yard on one less carry. Nevertheless, FSU fans walked out of the Orange Bowl victorious against the Hurricanes one last time, winning in Miami for the first time since 1998.

TROY

Buster Davis' interception set up a 4 yard touchdown run by Joe Surratt with 1:56 left, and #9 Florida State rallied late to escape with a 24-17 victory over Troy. Davis intercepted Omar Haugabook's third down pass at the Troy 29 moments after Florida State had tied the game at 17-17. Drew Weatherford threw a 5 yard tying TD pass to Chris Davis. Weatherford passed for 336 yards, also connected on a 17 yard scoring pass with Greg Carr.

CLEMSON

Dubbed "Bowden Bowl VIII," Tommy Bowden's Clemson Tigers traveled to Doak Campbell Stadium for a pivotal ACC match-up with his father's Seminole team. Clemson had lost to ACC foe Boston College in overtime the week before and was looking to reinsert themselves into the ACC Championship picture. Again, the Florida State offense struggled. The only points scored by the 'Noles in the first half of the game were scored by cornerback Tony Carter, who returned a blocked extra point for 2 points and a blocked field goal for a touchdown. With the game tied 20–20 late in the fourth quarter, Clemson switched to a no-huddle offense and running back James Davis gashed the unprepared Seminole defense for 47 yards, setting up a Clemson score with eight seconds left on the clock. Backup Seminole quarterback Xavier Lee entered the game and attempted a Hail Mary pass, but the ball was batted to the ground and Clemson left Tallahassee with a 27–20 win. It was the first time Clemson had won at Doak Campbell Stadium since 1989 and the third time Tommy Bowden had beaten his father since becoming Clemson's head coach in 1999.

RICE

Antone Smith ran for 137 yards and two touchdowns and Lorenzo Booker added 115 yards and a score as #18 Florida State beat winless Rice 55-7. The Seminoles led 26-7 at halftime on Drew Weatherford's 18 yard touchdown pass to Greg Carr, who also caught a 57 yard TD pass in the fourth quarter from Xavier Lee. Florida State scored earlier in the half on short runs by Joe Surratt and Smith and a pair of field goals by Gary Cismesia, including a 53 yarder. Florida State ran for 287 of its 500 total yards

NC State

FSU attempted to use more motion on offense and seemed determined to establish a running game, despite mixed results from running backs Lorenzo Booker and Antone Smith. After the Seminole defense stopped the Wolf Pack from scoring one yard away from the end zone, 'Nole quarterback Drew Weatherford led the offense on a 14-play, 99 yard scoring drive to give FSU a 20–10 lead in the third quarter. It was not enough, as NC State quarterback Daniel Evans led his team to two scores late in the game to put the Wolf Pack up 24–20.

Duke

The 'Noles struck first early when linebacker Lawrence Timmons returned a Duke fumble 37 yards for a touchdown. After beginning the game with six straight incompletions, QB Drew Weatherford had his most solid performance of the season, going 16/18 for the remainder of time he was in the game. Weatherford threw four touchdown passes (three to WR Greg Carr) and had no interceptions. Backup QB Xavier Lee entered the game in the second quarter but struggled, throwing three picks. For the second time in the 2006 season, the Seminoles blocked an opponent's extra point attempt and returned it for two points.

BOSTON COLLEGE

Tribble's 36 yard interception return for a touchdown capped a 21 point 2nd quarter and the 22nd ranked Eagles held off Florida State 24-19. Florida State had taken a 10-7 lead with 1:49 left in the half when Carr caught a 22 yard touchdown pass from Drew Weatherford. Weatherford, whose 1 yard TD early in the fourth quarter pulled Florida State to within 24-17, completed 32 of 48 passes for 326 yards and two interceptions. Chris Davis had 10 catches for 100 yards.

Maryland

Xavier Lee for the injured Drew Weatherford, Florida State was unable to break out of its funk, losing its second straight game and fourth out of five. Lee completed 22 of 36 passes for 286 yards and 2 touchdowns. Receiver Chris Davis caught 8 passes for 132 yards and 1 touchdown. But it wasn't enough against a determined Maryland Terrapins squad. Trailing 27–24, the Seminoles had an opportunity to tie the game up in the final minute, but a 46 yard field goal attempt by kicker Gary Cismesia was blocked by Maryland, sealing the win for Maryland.

VIRGINIA

Tony Carter returned an interception 35 yards for a touchdown 74 seconds into the game, and Florida State was on its way to snapping a two game skid with a 33-0 victory over Virginia. Eli Charles blocked a punt to set up Lorenzo Booker's 1 yard TD run. Gary Cismesia's 44 yard field goal with 2:21 left in the second quarter gave the Seminoles a 17-0 lead at halftime. Florida State boosted its lead to 26-0 five minutes into the third quarter. Buster Davis sacked Sewell in the end zone for a safety and the Seminoles needed just four plays on the ensuing possession to get into the end zone on Xavier Lee's 37 yard pass to Chris Davis.

WAKE FOREST

Quarterbacks Xavier Lee and Drew Weatherford combined for 4 costly interceptions as Wake Forest beat Florida State for the first time in ACC play. The 30–0 loss was the worst in years for the Seminoles and was also the first time Bobby Bowden had been shut out in Tallahassee since he became the head coach of Florida State 31 years earlier.

WESTERN MICHIGAN

Florida State beat Western Michigan 28–20, allowing Florida State to become bowl eligible for the 25th consecutive season. The Homecoming game was watched by about 70,000 fans in Doak Campbell Stadium. Sophomore quarterback Drew Weatherford started but was relieved in the second quarter by Xavier Lee, who threw two touchdown passes to WR Greg Carr. RB Antone Smith started for the first time in his college career but was lost for the remainder of the season when he dislocated his elbow on the Seminoles' first offensive series. Lorenzo Booker, who was originally going to be used as a slot receiver in the game, reclaimed the rushing duties from that point on. Florida State LB Lawrence Timmons broke open a close game in the third quarter when he scored on a 22 yard interception return. Western Michigan pulled to within eight points late in the fourth quarter and twice converted on 4th-and-10 during their last drive of the game. However, Broncos QB Ryan Cubit's pass into the end zone on 4th-and-29 as time expired was incomplete, and the Seminoles preserved the victory.

FLORIDA

To beat the struggling **Florida State** Seminoles, Chris Leak threw for 283 yards and two touchdowns, Percy Harvin ran for a score and the #4 ranked Gators won 21–14 to stay in the national title hunt. Florida (11–1) won its third straight against Florida State. Florida took a 14–0 lead in the first half, but Florida State came back to tie the game at 14–14 at the beginning of the fourth quarter. Florida scored the final touchdown of the game a few minutes later to pull out the victory.

2006 EMERALD BOWL

Florida State scored first following a 25 yard touchdown run by Lorenzo Booker, making it 7–0 FSU. UCLA responded just 34 seconds later after quarterback Patrick Cowan threw a 78 yard touchdown pass to wide receiver Brandon Breazell to tie the game at 7–7. With 20 seconds left in the first quarter, Justin Medlock kicked a 46 yard field goal to put the Bruins up 10–7. With 12:20 left in the half, Gary Cismesia kicked a 39 yard field goal to tie the game at 10. With 8:40 left in the half, Cowan found wide 
receiver Junior Taylor for a 7 yard touchdown pass, to put UCLA up 17–10. With 2:34 in the half, Medlock nailed a 19 yard field goal, increasing UCLA's lead to 20–10. Florida State answered with a 21 yard field goal from Gary Cismesia before halftime, making it 20-13 UCLA. In the third quarter, Cismesia kicked a 36 yard field goal, pulling FSU to within 20–16. With 8:58 left in the quarter, Lawrence Timmons recovered a blocked punt, and returned it 25 yards for a touchdown, giving FSU a 23–20 lead. Chane Moline later scored on an 8 yard touchdown run, as UCLA reclaimed the lead at 27–23. In the fourth quarter, Drew Weatherford threw a 30 yard touchdown pass to wide receiver Greg Carr, and Florida State took a 30–27 lead with 9:46 left in the game. Lorenzo Booker added a 3 yard touchdown run with 6:17, to increase the lead to 37–27. With 5:04 left in the game, Florida State sealed the deal with an 86 yard interception return by cornerback Tony Carter, making the final score 44–27, FSU.

2007 Florida State Seminoles

The team was coached by Bobby Bowden in his 32nd season. Florida State entered the 2007 season coming off a 2006 season that ended with an overall record of 7–6, which was head coach Bobby Bowden's worst since having a losing record in 1976, matching that mark in 2007. **Gary Cismesia tied a single season record for field goals made with 27.**

Geno Hayes {LB} was selected to the All-ACC first team. Andre Fluellen {DT} {Detroit}, Leroy Guion {DT} {Minnesota} and Geno Hayes {Tampa Bay} were selected in the 2008 NFL draft.

Home games were played at Doak Campbell Stadium

9/3/2007	Florida State	**#21**	@		**Clemson (9-4)**	ESPN	18	24	L
9/8/2007	Florida State		vs		ALABAMA-BIRMINGHAM	ESPNU	34	24	W
9/15/2007	Florida State		@		Colorado (6-7)	ESPN	16	6	W
9/29/2007	Florida State		vs	#24	ALABAMA (7-6)	CBS	21	14	W
10/6/2007	Florida State		vs		**NC STATE (5-7)**	ABC	27	10	W
10/11/2007	Florida State	**#21**	@		**Wake Forest (9-4)**	ESPN	21	24	L
10/20/2007	Florida State		vs		**MIAMI (5-7)**	ABC	29	37	L
10/27/2007	Florida State		vs		**DUKE (1-11)**	ESPNU	25	6	W
11/3/2007	Florida State		@	#2	**Boston College (11-3)**	ABC	27	17	W
11/10/2007	Florida State		@	#11	**Virginia Tech (11-3)**	ABC	21	40	L
11/17/2007	Florida State		vs		**MARYLAND (6-7)**		24	16	W
11/24/2007	Florida State		@	#14	Florida (9-4)	CBS	12	45	L
12/31/2007	**Florida State**		vs		**Kentucky (8-5)**	**ESPN**	**28**	**35**	L
Coach: Bobby Bowden					**Season Record >>**		303	298	7-6

Schedule Source: Steve's Football Bible LLC

Selected game(s) highlights

Clemson

Florida State's terrible first half on both sides of the ball lead to a 24–3 deficit. The Seminoles adjusted at halftime and swung the momentum in their direction holding Clemson to just 46 yards in the 2nd half. FSU had 196 2nd half yards led by Running Back, Antone Smith. Drew Weatherford and the Seminole offense couldn't shake the Clemson pressure in the second-to-last drive of the game, getting to the Clemson 30 yard line, but falling short of the end zone.

Colorado

The game was mostly a defensive struggle. Late in the 1st quarter, Antone Smith broke away for a 36 yard touchdown run. For the rest of the game, Florida State's offense could not score, even when, at one point, their starting field position was at the Colorado 15 yard line. Instead, they had to settle for three field goals by Gary Cismesia. With 3:40 remaining in the game, Colorado scored a touchdown on a 4th-and-10 play from the Florida State 11 yard line. However, the 2 point conversion attempt failed, and the Seminoles recovered the ensuing onside kick to preserve the victory.

ALABAMA

The game got off to another very slow start. It was another first half full of defense. In the 2nd quarter, an ineffective Drew Weatherford was pulled for Xavier Lee. After a halftime score of 0–0, Lee led a strong drive to put FSU up 7–0. After a forced fumble by Everette Brown, a toss sweep to Antone Smith put FSU up 14–0. Alabama's offense took advantage of FSU's prevent defense to score a TD to make it 14–7. Lee then hit Decody Fagg on a 75 yard pass to put FSU up 21–7. Alabama scored late to make it 21–14, but FSU recovered the onside kick, and held on for a 21–14 win.

NC STATE

Xavier Lee, making his first start of the season at quarterback, ran 2 yards for the Seminoles' first touchdown 2:11 into the game, three plays after a 58 yard pass to Greg Carr on the game's first play. Although N.C. State led 10–7 in the first quarter, it was again plagued by four turnovers—boosting its number to 21 in coach Tom O'Brien's first year at the school. Michael Ray Garvin returned an interception 43 yards for a touchdown to spark Florida State's scoring. Garvin gave Florida State a 17–10 lead early in the third quarter with his first interception of the season. The game was delayed late in the third quarter for 49 minutes because of a lightning threat. Greg Carr caught a 40 yard touchdown pass early in the fourth quarter to give the Seminoles a 24–10 lead. Daniel Evans was intercepted three times Saturday— once at the end of the half that killed a Wolfpack drive that had reached Florida State's 26.

Wake Forest

Wake Forest's defense in the first half allowed two big plays that set up the Seminoles' two scoring drives, then shut them down after halftime. Wake Forest moved 80 yards in nine plays late in the third quarter to force a 14–14 tie – a drive that started when Alphonso Smith intercepted Lee in the end zone. Skinner capped the drive with a nifty play in which he faked a handoff to Adams, deked like he would roll right and instead reversed field and flipped to the wide-open tailback for a 6 yard score. The Demon Deacons forced five second-half punts, intercepted two passes and allowed 105 total yards after the break – with a good chunk coming after Swank's late kick. Florida State's rushing offense never could get going, finishing with 47 yards on 24 carries. Riley Skinner's 35 yard touchdown pass to Kenneth Moore in the fourth quarter led the Demon Deacons past Florida State 24–21. Skinner led the Demon Deacons 82 yards in nine plays, converting three third downs during their game-winning drive. The biggest came when Skinner sidestepped a pass rush, stepped forward in the pocket and found Moore, who had a step on cornerback Jamie Robinson at the goal line, for the easy score that put Wake Forest up 21–14 with 6:41 remaining. Florida State gave the ball right back to Wake Forest on the first play of its ensuing drive, when Chip Vaughn intercepted Xavier Lee's deep pass at the 26. The Demon Deacons milked the clock and set up Sam Swank's 48 yard field goal with 1:40 to play that made it a 10 point game. Lee scored on a 17 yard run with 17 seconds left to draw the Seminoles within three, but Wake Forest recovered an onside kick to seal it.

MIAMI

Florida State and Miami both entered this game unranked for the first time since 1977. The teams exchanged turnovers (nine total, five by FSU) and scores, keeping things close for most of the game. With 5:29 left in the fourth quarter, the Hurricanes, trailing 29–24, appeared to have lost their best chance to win when Kirby Freeman was stopped for no gain on a fourth-and-1 at the Florida State 1. But Freeman, who replaced injured Kyle Wright in the first half, drove Miami 83 yards in under two minutes to take the lead 30–29 on a 13 yard pass to Dedrick Epps with 1:15 left. FSU quarterback Xavier Lee, who was intercepted twice, then fumbled after being hit by Miami's Teraz McCray, and Colin McCarthy ran it in for the clincher.

DUKE

Florida State led 9–0 at halftime on three field goals by Gary Cismesia. After going more than five quarters without an offensive touchdown, the Seminoles made it to the end zone six minutes into the third quarter when Parker raced 9 yards with a short sideline pass from Drew Weatherford, giving Florida State a 16–0 lead. Parker scored his second TD late in the third quarter on a 14 yard run to make the score 22–0. After Cismesia kicked his fourth field goal, Duke avoided a shutout when Thaddeus Lewis lofted a 3 yard pass to a wide-open Brandon King in the right front corner of the end zone with 8:07 left. Florida State rolled up a season-high 534 yards and 30 first downs while holding Duke to 222 yards and 9 first downs. The Blue Devils managed only 49 yards and two first downs in the first half. Patrick Robinson had an interception for the fourth straight game.

Boston College

The game began in a frigid and soaking downpour, with wind gusts forecast at up to 50 mph as the remnants of Hurricane Noel proceeded up the East Coast. The rain had stopped by the end of the first quarter, but the winds battered the U.S. flag and played havoc with a couple of second quarter field goal attempts. Drew Weatherford completed 29-of-45 passes for 354 yards for Florida State (6–3, 3–3), hitting Preston Parker nine times for 93 yards and a touchdown and De'Cody Fagg on six catches for 111 yards and a TD. Matt Ryan finished 25-for-53 for two touchdowns and 415 yards—his fourth career 400 yard game, tying Doug Flutie for the most in school history, but his interceptions were costly. Ryan was picked off once in the first quarter inside the Seminoles 10 by Patrick Robinson, making this his fifth consecutive game recovering an interception. Ryan also threw an interception early in the third that allowed Florida State to move into position for a 40 yard field goal that made it 10–0. Ryan led BC on a four-play, 70 yard drive over 63 seconds, hitting Ryan Purvis for 26 yards to the Florida State 30, and then Brandon Robinson for the touchdown. The teams traded field goals, then Weatherford hit Fagg on a 42 yard touchdown pass to give the Seminoles a 20–10 lead. Ryan hit Rich Gunnell on a 42 yard pass to the Florida State 6 with 7:24 left. Two plays later, including a penalty that moved the ball to the 3, Ryan hit a wide-open Purvis in the middle of the end zone to make it 20–17. BC forced a punt and got the ball back at its own 7 with 3:30 left and a chance to take the lead. Ryan moved the Eagles out to the 33 before Hayes ripped the ball free from Purvis on a pass across the middle. Geno Hayes returned Matt Ryan's third interception for a 38 yard touchdown with 1:10 to play to help Florida State beat second-ranked Boston College 27–17, ending the Eagles' run at an unbeaten season.

Virginia Tech

The Hokies blew a 14 point halftime lead and trailed 21-20 entering the final quarter, but Taylor drove them to his go ahead 3 yard scoring run, and three late Seminoles turnovers made a close game turn lopsided as the Hokies beat Florida State, 40-21. Trailing 20-9, Dekoda Watson returned an interception 40 yards for a touchdown and then Christian Ponder threw an 8 yard TD pass to De' Cody Fagg to put the Noles up 21-20. The Hokies with responded with 19 straight points to put the game on ice.

MARYLAND

Florida State got 133 yards rushing and a touchdown from Preston Parker in a 24-16 victory against Maryland. Parker scored on an 18 yard TD run to give the Noles a 14-3 lead. Florida State took a 21-3 lead 44 seconds into the second quarter when Weatherford and De'Cody Fagg hooked up on a 10 yard touchdown pass. Gary Cismesia added a 30 yard field goal in the 4th quarter.

Florida

Senior day in the Swamp saw the #9 Gators start strong, scoring four touchdowns and a field goal on their first five possessions en route to a 45–12 victory over the in-state rival **Florida State** Seminoles. The Gator offense compiled 541 total yards to the Seminoles' 287 and were often able to finish drives with touchdowns while Florida State was forced to settle for field goals. With his 262 passing yards and 89 rushing, Tebow set a new school record for most yards of total offense in a season with 3,970.

2007 MUSIC CITY BOWL

In the first quarter, Kentucky scored first on a 14 yard André Woodson touchdown pass to tight end Jacob Tamme. Florida State quarterback Drew Weatherford then scored on a 6 yard touchdown run. Kentucky built a 14–7 lead in the second quarter on a 13 yard touchdown pass from Woodson to Steve Johnson. Kentucky's defense then held Florida State to a turnover on downs inside the Kentucky five yard line, but immediately after that Florida State tied the game before halftime when Tony Carter intercepted a Woodson pass and  returned it 24 yards for a touchdown. Kentucky struck first in the third quarter when Woodson threw a 2 yard touchdown pass to Rafael Little. A 4 yard touchdown run by Tony Dixon boosted Kentucky's third quarter lead to 28–14. Florida State scored first in the fourth quarter with a 1 yard Weatherford touchdown run to make it 28–21. Woodson's 38 yard touchdown pass to Steve Johnson extended the Kentucky lead to 35–21. The game's final score was a 7 yard touchdown pass from Weatherford to Greg Carr to bring about the final tally: Kentucky 35, Florida State 28. The game appeared iced when Kentucky linebacker Micah Johnson intercepted a Weatherford pass with less than one minute remaining, but in attempting to return the interception Johnson fumbled the ball away and Florida State recovered. Florida State threw a pass into the end zone at the end of regulation, but Kentucky defenders batted it down to seal the win. The attendance of 68,661 set a record for the Music City Bowl. In Kentucky's 35–28 victory, 2006 game MVP André Woodson repeated as the 2007 MVP after throwing four touchdown passes. Florida State's Antone Smith gained a career-high 156 rushing yards; Kentucky's Rafael Little rushed for 152 yards and caught one touchdown pass, but he also fumbled twice.

2008 Florida State Seminoles

The team was coached by Bobby Bowden in his 33rd season. It was Florida State's 17th season as a member of the Atlantic Coast Conference (ACC). The Seminoles were without as many as 12 scholarship players for the first three games of the season because of suspensions carrying over from the previous season for violating team rules, although it has not been disclosed how many of those were involved with an academic cheating scandal at the school. Junior wide receiver Preston Parker was suspended for the first two games of the season, after pleading guilty to two misdemeanor charges.

Everette Brown {DE}, Graham Gano {K} and Rodney Hudson {G} were selected to the All-ACC first team. Graham Gano was selected a First team All-American by CBS Sports, Rivals.com and Scout. Michael Ray Garvin {DB} was selected as a First team All-American by The Sporting News. Everette Brown {Carolina} was selected in the 2009 NFL draft.

FINAL RANK: #21 AP, #23 CP

Home games were played at Doak Campbell Stadium

9/6/2008	Florida State		vs		WESTERN CAROLINA		69	0	W
9/13/2008	Florida State		vs		TENNESSEE-CHATT	ESPNU	46	7	W
9/20/2008	Florida State	#25	vs	#18	**WAKE FOREST (8-5)**	espn2	3	12	L
9/27/2008	Florida State		vs		COLORADO (5-7)	ABC	39	21	W
10/4/2008	Florida State		@		**Miami (7-6)**	ABC	41	39	W
10/16/2008	Florida State		@		**NC State (6-7)**	ESPN	26	17	W
10/25/2008	Florida State	#23	vs		**VIRGINIA TECH (10-4)**	ABC	30	20	W
11/1/2008	Florida State	#16	@		**Georgia Tech (9-4)**	ABC	28	31	L
11/8/2008	Florida State	#24	vs		**CLEMSON (7-6)**	ABC	41	27	W
11/15/2008	Florida State	#19	vs		**BOSTON COLLEGE (9-5)**	ABC	17	27	L
11/22/2008	Florida State		@	#23	**Maryland (8-5)**	ESPN	37	3	W
11/29/2008	Florida State	#24	vs	#4	FLORIDA (13-1)	ABC	15	45	L
12/27/2008	**Florida State**		vs		**Wisconsin (7-6)**	**ESPN**	42	13	W
Coach: Bobby Bowden					**Season Record >>**		434	262	9-4

Schedule Source: Steve's Football Bible LLC

Selected game(s) highlights

WESTERN CAROLINA

The start of the game was delayed almost an hour and a half due to lightning in the area, and then almost another hour during the 1st quarter. The first player to touch the ball for FSU, to start the 2008 season, was Tony Carter who promptly returned a punt 68 yards for a touchdown and the game's first score. Sophomore Christian Ponder started his first game at quarterback. Ponder completed 11 of 17 passes for 196 yards and 3 touchdowns. At the start of the second drive in the second half (when FSU was up 35–0), sophomore D'Vontrey Richardson came into the game. Richardson went 5 for 6 through the air with one touchdown and had two rushing touchdowns, one for over 50 yards. With several players serving suspensions due to the school wide "academic scandal", the Seminoles had 28 freshman play in the game.

TENNESSEE-CHATTANOOGA

Christian Ponder threw for 183 yards and three first-half touchdowns before being relieved by D'vontrey Richardson in the 3rd quarter. Richardson threw for 117 yards with one touchdown. Richardson also had a 55 yard rushing touchdown, the longest scoring run for a quarterback in the school's history. Corey Surrency led Florida State in receiving with 87 yards and two touchdowns on just three receptions. Florida State's defense allowed their first score of the season after a 62 yard passing touchdown thrown by Chattanooga quarterback Tony Pastore. This was also the first score by Chattanooga against Florida State all-time, dating back to 1984.

WAKE FOREST

Sam Swank kicked four field goals and No. 18 Wake Forest forced seven Florida State turnovers in running its winning streak over the 24th-ranked Seminoles to three games with a 12-3. Swank made field goals from 48, 29, 49 and 31 yards. Florida State's only points also came on a 37 yard field goal by Graham Gano. Christian Ponder played most of the first half at quarterback for Florida State while D'Vontrey Richardson took over for most of the second half, but neither was effective. Ponder was intercepted three times and Richardson twice.

COLORADO

Antone Smith ran for 154 yards and three touchdowns Saturday as Florida State defeated previously unbeaten Colorado 39-21. Florida State scored three times in the final 2:29 of the first half to take a 19-7 lead. Smith, who carried 25 times, went 60 yards for a touchdown with 2:29 left in the half to give the Seminoles a 14-7 lead. Dekoda Watson blocked Matt DiLallo's punt out of the end zone for a safety and Graham Gano finished off the half with a 36 yard field goal. He added field goals of 52 and 44 yards in the second half. Florida State relied on its running game for 259 yards while quarterback Christian Ponder completed just 10 of 22 passes for 119 yards and one interception. Michael Ray Garvin returned a 94 yard kickoff for a touchdown to give the Seminoles a 32-14 lead.

Miami

Antone Smith rushed for a career-best four touchdowns, including a game-clinching 20 yarder with 3:57 remaining, and Florida State wasted most of an early 24-point lead before hanging on to beat Miami 41-39. Christian Ponder ran for 144 yards, becoming the first Florida State quarterback since Charlie Ward in 1992 to run for triple-figures, and Tony Carter made two interceptions for the Seminoles. Travis Benjamin had an 18 yard touchdown run on an end-around, caught a 51 yard TD pass from running back Graig Cooper, and finished with 274 all-purpose yards for Miami. The Hurricanes trailed 24-3 at the half and 31-10 in the third quarter, then closed to within 34-32 with 8 minutes remaining. Two botched snaps on Florida State punts led to Miami points and Sean Spence ran an interception in for a touchdown. Smith sealed the win with a third-down 20 yard run for a touchdown. Smith's other scoring runs were for 2, 19 and 5 yards, part of Florida State's 281 yard rushing day as a team. Ponder completed 14 of 31 passes for 159 yards for Florida State, including a 15 yard score to Greg Carr

NC State

Christian Ponder threw the go ahead touchdown pass, and Graham Gano kicked two of his four field goals in the final 4 ½ minutes to help Florida State beat North Carolina State 26-17. Antone Smith ran for 89 yards and a touchdown for Florida State, which scored the last 13 points of the game. Ponder was 23-of-35 for 254 yards, including the go ahead 17 yard touchdown to Bert Reed after Russell Wilson's 67 yard scoring pass to Owen Spencer had put N.C. State up 17-13. The Seminoles finished with 392 yards and held the ball for more than 38 minutes.

VIRGINIA TECH

Two fingertip grabs by Greg Carr on long pass plays set up a pair of third quarter Florida State touchdowns as the 25th ranked Seminoles rallied from an early 10 point deficit to defeat Virginia Tech 30-20. Taiwan Easterling's leaping catch just in front of the goal post on a high throw from Ponder gave Florida State its first lead, 17-13, and Marcus Sims scored from the 1 to hike the advantage to 24-13 after Carr's second grab put the ball on the Virginia Tech 1 yard line. Graham Gano added three field goals.

Georgia Tech

Christian Ponder threw for a touchdown and ran for another, Antone Smith ran for two scores, and the 22nd ranked Seminoles defeated Clemson 41-27. Clemson started fast with C.J. Spiller going 44 yards on a short pass from Cullen Harper to finish off a quick 80 yard opening drive. The Tigers went ahead 10-0 five minutes later Mark Buchholz's 41 yard field goal. Defensive end Neefy Moffett scored on an 18 yard interception of a pass by Harper to get the Seminoles a 10-10 tie, after Graham Gano made a 52 yard field goal. Ponder's 1 yard TD run put Florida State the lead for keeps at 20-17 with 1:25 left in the half and he hit Corey Surrency on a 14 yard touchdown pass on the opening drive of the second half as the Seminoles stretched their advantage to 27-17. Smith scored his 12th and 13th rushing touchdowns of the season on runs of 1 and 41 yards in the fourth quarter around Spiller's 2 yard TD that got Clemson to within a touchdown with 2:20 left.

CLEMSON

Christian Ponder threw for a touchdown and ran for another, Antone Smith ran for two scores, and the 22nd ranked Seminoles defeated Clemson 41-27. Florida State overcame an early 10-0 deficit to lead 20-17 at halftime after both teams converted turnovers into touchdowns. Clemson started fast with C.J. Spiller going 44 yards on a short pass from Cullen Harper to finish off a quick 80 yard opening drive. The Tigers went ahead 10-0 five minutes later Mark Buchholz's 41 yard field goal. Defensive end Neefy Moffett scored on an 18 yard interception of an ill-advised throw by Harper to get the Seminoles a 10-10 tie. After Gano put Florida State up 13-10 with his 17th consecutive made field goal, this from 37 yards, Clemson took its last lead at 17-13 on Harper's 8 yard touchdown pass to Michael Palmer. Ponder's 1 yard TD run put Florida State the lead for keeps at 20-17 with 1:25 left in the half and he hit Corey Surrency on a 14 yard touchdown pass on the opening drive of the second half as the Seminoles stretched their advantage to 27-17.

BOSTON COLLEGE

Montel Harris ran for 121 yards and a touchdown, and Marcellus Bowman went 87 yards with an interception for another score to help Boston College knock off the 19th ranked Seminoles 27-17, a day after five Florida State players were suspended for fighting. The Eagles picked off Florida State quarterback Christian Ponder three times and held the Seminoles to just 73 yards rushing. Boston College jumped to a 14-0 lead and never trailed. Preston Parker's 29 yard touchdown pass to Greg Carr was set up by punter Graham Gano's 24 yard run on a fake and got Florida State within a touchdown in the first minute of the final quarter.

Maryland

Everette Brown had 3 ½ sacks and forced a fumble, part of an overwhelming performance by the Florida State defense in a 37-3 rout of the 25th ranked Terrapins. Florida State turned two turnovers into touchdowns in taking a 21-0 halftime lead. Christian Ponder went 19-for-24 for 143 yards and led the Seminoles with 81 yards rushing. The Seminoles had six sacks, two interceptions and forced two fumbles. Derek Nicholson scooped up a fumble and ran 22 yards for a touchdown and a 14-0 lead.

FLORIDA

Tim Tebow threw three touchdown passes, ran for 80 yards and another score, and the #2 Gators thumped #23 **Florida State** 45-15 in sloppy conditions Saturday. It was the most points Florida has ever scored at Doak Campbell Stadium. The win set up a 1-2 showdown with Alabama in next week's Southeastern Conference title game. Florida scored on five of its first seven possessions, held the Seminoles (8-4) without a touchdown for the first 2½ quarters. Tebow finished 12-of-21 passing for 185 yards and the Gators ran for 317 yards.

2008 CHAMPS SPORTS BOWL

Derek Nicholson and Dekoda Watson returned fumbles for touchdowns, Christian Ponder threw two TD passes and the Seminoles got a game MVP performance from punter Graham Gano, as the Seminoles routed the Badgers, 42-13. Nicholson had two fumble recoveries, including one he returned 75 yards for a first-quarter score. P.J. Hill ran for 140 yards on 15 carries for the Badgers, but quarterback Dustin Sherer completed only four of nine for 55 yards through the first three quarters. His fumble early in the fourth quarter was returned 51 yards for a score by Watson to put FSU up 35-6. Antone Smith scored on a 6 yard run off right tackle to put the Seminoles up 21-6 in the third quarter.

2009 Florida State Seminoles

The team was coached by Bobby Bowden in his 34th season. It was Florida State's 18th season as a member of the Atlantic Coast Conference (ACC). Head coach Bobby Bowden retired at the end of the 2009 season after 34 seasons at the helm for Florida State and 33 consecutive winning seasons. Bowden was named National Coach of the Year six times (1979, 1980, 1991, 1992, 1996 and 1999), and a national award presented by The Fellowship of Christian Athletes bears his name. He led Florida State to national championships in 1993 and again in 1999, the latter being the first team in the history of the Associated Press poll to go wire-to-wire ranked #1.

Rodney Hudson {G} was selected to the All-ACC first team and received the Jacobs Blocking Trophy. Hudson was selected as a First team All-American by cnnsi.com and the Football Writers Association. Patrick Robinson {CB} {New Orleans}, Myron Rolle {S} {Tennessee} and Dekoda Watson {LB} {Tampa Bay} were selected in the 2010 NFL draft.

Home games were played at Doak Campbell Stadium

9/7/2009	Florida State	**#18**	vs		**MIAMI (9-4)**	ESPN	34	38	L
9/12/2009	Florida State		vs		JACKSONVILLE STATE		19	9	W
9/19/2009	Florida State		@	#9	Byu (11-2)		54	28	W
9/26/2009	Florida State	**#18**	vs		SOUTH FLORIDA (8-5)	ESPNU	7	17	L
10/3/2009	Florida State		@		**Boston College (8-5)**	ABC	21	28	L
10/10/2009	Florida State		vs	#23	**GEORGIA TECH (11-3)**	espn2	44	49	L
10/22/2009	Florida State		@		**North Carolina (8-5)**	ESPN	30	27	W
10/31/2009	Florida State		vs		**NC STATE (5-7)**		45	42	W
11/7/2009	Florida State		@		**Clemson (9-5)**	ESPNU	24	40	L
11/14/2009	Florida State		@		**Wake Forest (5-7)**	ESPNU	41	28	W
11/21/2009	Florida State		vs		**MARYLAND (2-10)**		29	26	W
11/28/2009	Florida State		@	#1	Florida (13-1)	CBS	10	37	L
1/1/2010	**Florida State**		vs	#17	**West Virginia (9-4)**	**CBS**	**33**	**21**	W
Coach: Bobby Bowden					**Season Record >>**		391	390	7-6

Schedule Source: Steve's Football Bible LLC

Selected game(s) highlights

MIAMI

Jacoby Harris threw for 386 yards, including a 40 yard pass over double coverage to Travis Benjamin that set up Graig Cooper's 3 yard touchdown run with 1:53 left and led the Hurricanes past #18 Florida State 38-34. It went down to the very last play, a pass that Florida State's Jarmon Fortson nearly scooped off the garnet-colored grass in the end zone as time expired. Harris completed 21 of 34 passes for two touchdowns and two interceptions. Markus White ran back an interception 31 yards for a 31-24 Florida State lead with 11:45 remaining. Christian Ponder completed 24 of 41 passes for a career-best 294 yards and two touchdowns. The Seminoles scored the first 13 points of the second half, with Ponder running in from 9 yards out to put Florida State back on top on the first drive following intermission. Ponder then threw to Taiwan Easterling for a 21 yard score for a 23-14 edge with 4:57 left in the third.

JACKSONVILLE STATE

Florida State needed two scores in the final 35 seconds Saturday night to avoid one of the most embarrassing upsets in school history. Ty Jones' 1 yard touchdown run with 35 seconds left put the

Seminoles ahead of lower-division Jacksonville State and teammate Kevin McNeil returned a fumble for a score 21 seconds later to seal the 19-9 victory. Trailing 9-7, Jones' TD rallied the Seminoles and McNeil scooped up Ryan Perrilloux's fumble and ran 33 yards for his score. McNeil also blocked a field goal try by Jacksonville's Patrick Tatum in the third quarter. Christian Ponder threw for a career high 324 yards, completing 22 of 35 passes without a touchdown or interception

Byu

      Christian Ponder threw for two touchdowns and ran for another, Ty Jones ran for 108 yards and a score and Greg Reid returned an interception 63 yards for a TD in a rout by the Seminoles. The Seminoles scored every time they got inside the 20 and forced five turnovers in a 54-28 win. Florida State (2-1) converted on its first nine third downs, pounced for 10 points in the final 24 seconds of the second quarter and added two touchdowns in the third, running away and spoiling the most anticipated home opener at BYU in years. The Seminoles out rushed the Cougars 313 yards to 108. FSU didn't punt until about a minute remained in the third quarter. Lonnie Pryor ran for two touchdowns on his first two college carries and Ponder was 21-for-26 and carried 11 times.

SOUTH FLORIDA

      B.J. Daniels dismantled the Seminoles' defense with one big play after another. Daniels ran for 126 yards, threw two touchdown passes and accounted for 341 of USF's 368 yards of offense. Florida State lost four fumbles, including a critical one by quarterback Christian Ponder that allowed USF to ice the game. South Florida stuffed Florida State's running game and sacked Ponder five times. Ponder completed 25 of 37 passes for 269 yards. Ty Jones ran 3 yards for FSU's lone touchdown.

Boston College

      Montel Harris broke free up the middle for a 42 yard touchdown run with 4:07 left, his second score of the game, and Boston College recovered after blowing an 18-point lead to beat Florida State 28-21. The Seminoles trailed 21-3 late in the second quarter before Christian Ponder led them to a pair of second-half touchdowns, tying the score 21-all when wide receiver Bert Reed hit Caz Piurowski for the 2 point conversion with 11 minutes left. Jeff Smith fumbled the ensuing kickoff and JaJuan Harley recovered at the Boston College 29, but Dustin Hopkins' 37 yard field goal attempt was wide right. Ponder finished 29-for-42 for 345 yards. Reed caught seven passes for 107 yards, and Richard Goodman caught nine for 105 yards.

GEORGIA TECH

      Josh Nesbitt ran for three touchdowns and threw for one more to lead the 22nd ranked Yellow Jackets to a 49-44 win at Florida State, handing the Seminoles their third straight loss. Marcus Wright's 19 yard touchdown run put the Yellow Jackets ahead for good at 42-38 late in the third quarter and Nesbitt iced the outcome with a 22 yard scoring run with 6:29 left in the game. At halftime, Florida State had rung up 403 yards of offense and 21 first downs behind Christian Ponder, who completed 18 of 21 passes for 267 yards and four touchdowns as the Seminoles led 35-28 at the break. Florida State managed just 156 yards offense in the second half. Ponder finished with 5 TD passes to five different receivers.

North Carolina

      Christian Ponder threw for a career-high 395 yards and three touchdowns to help Florida State rally from a big second-half deficit and beat North Carolina 30-27. Rod Owens added career-highs of nine catches for 199 yards, including a 98 yard score, for the Seminoles, who trailed 24-6 early in the third quarter. Ponder threw the go ahead 18 yard touchdown pass to a wide open Beau Reliford with 6:20 to play. Ponder completed 33 of 40 passes, including his final 16 attempts.

NC STATE

Receiver Bert Reed's 3 yard touchdown run on an inside reverse with 1:36 left and lifted Florida State to a 45-42 win over North Carolina State that produced 1,100 yards of offense. Reed had 44 yards on four runs and caught six passes for 66 yards. Jermaine Thomas ran for a career high 186 yards and a pair of touchdowns and Chris Thompson scored twice on short runs for the Seminoles. Christian Ponder threw for 277 yards. He completed 26 of 40, including a 6 yard touchdown pass to Rod Owens.

Clemson

C.J. Spiller had a career-high 165 yards rushing and his 20th touchdown of at least 50 yards to lead the Tigers to a 40-24 victory over Florida State. Along with his rushing TD, Spiller had a 58 yard scoring catch and finished with 312 all-purpose yards, surpassing his school record. Kyle Parker passed for 242 yards and threw 4 touchdown passes.

Wake Forest

E.J. Manuel threw for a touchdown and ran for another in his first career start. Jermaine Thomas helped out by rushing for 149 yards and a touchdown as the Seminoles beat Wake Forest 41-28. Manuel completed 15 of 20 passes for 220 yards and an interception. Manuel, Ty Jones and Thomas each had touchdown runs and Greg Reid a 68 yard punt return for a score to give Florida State a 31-14 halftime lead. Manuel's 7 yard touchdown pass to Jarmon Fortson made it 41-21 early in the fourth quarter.

MARYLAND

The Seminoles were only a couple minutes away from a loss to Maryland when Greg Reid ran 48 yards with a punt return that set up Lonnie Pryor's 3 yard run with 32 seconds left to give Florida State a 29-26 win that it needed to become bowl eligible for the 28th straight year. Pryor also scored on a 50 yard run in the second quarter. Manuel completed 17-of-27 passes for 206 yards. He ran for 49, including gains of 15 and 20 yards on the final drive. Maryland took its first lead at 19-14 on a 20 yard touchdown pass from Jamarr Robinson to Adrian Cannon early in the fourth quarter, but Florida State regained the lead when Bert Reed scored on a 42 yard end around.

Florida

Tim Tebow accounted for five touchdowns in his home finale, a triumphant farewell that included tears on the field and in the stands, and #1 ranked Florida thumped rival **Florida State** 37-10 Saturday for its sixth consecutive victory in the series. The Seminoles trailed 30-0 before Bowden opted for a field goal on fourth-and-goal from the 2 on the final play of the third. They added a touchdown with 6:03 remaining to make it 37-10. Tebow had two TD passes to Aaron Hernandez and another to Riley Cooper and added two rushing touchdowns.

2009 GATOR BOWL

Seminoles tailback Jermaine Thomas ran for two touchdowns, Florida State scored 20 straight points to take control and the Seminoles knocked off No. 18 West Virginia 33-21 in the final game of Bobby Bowden's storied 44-year career as a head coach. Bowden finished with a 389-129-4 record, and most importantly to him, a 33rd consecutive winning season. West Virginia took the opening kickoff and scored without much resistance, a 72 yard, eight-play drive capped by a 32 yard touchdown rush by starting quarterback Jarrett Brown, who was injured in the second quarter. The Mountaineers went up 14-3 on their second possession, after Noel Devine broke off a 70 yard run to get inside the Florida State 5, then wound up scoring from 1 yard out. After Jamie Robinson intercepted Brown early in the second quarter, Florida State got back into it on Thomas' first touchdown of the day, a 12 yard rush. Dustin Hopkins, who missed a 37 yard try earlier in the period, connected on a 42 yard field goal with 8 seconds left in the half, getting the Seminoles within 14-13 at the break.

After the second-half kickoff was taken 69 yards to the West Virginia 9, FSU kicked another field goal. Then a Jarmon Fortson ridiculous, leaping, one-handed, 29 yard catch, Thomas scored from 19 yards out later in the third to give Florida State a 23-14 lead entering the last 15 minutes of Bowden's career. Ryan Clarke plunged in from 5 yards away for West Virginia on the first play of the fourth quarter, but the Seminoles answered with a methodical drive to restore the nine-point lead, quarterback E.J.

Manuel's 2 yard touchdown burst putting Florida State up 30-21. West Virginia's school-record four-game bowl winning streak came to an end with the loss. Florida State won five of its final seven games of the season after a three-game losing streak. In his 33rd and presumably final bowl game, Bobby Bowden won again, bringing his career bowl record to 22-10-1. His .682 bowl winning percentage is the best in NCAA history among coaches to coach in at least 20 bowl games.

2010 Florida State Seminoles

The Seminoles were led by first-year head coach Jimbo Fisher. They finished the season 10–4, 6–2 in ACC play, and won the Atlantic Division to earn a spot in the ACC Championship Game where they were defeated by Virginia Tech. They were invited to the Chick-fil-A Bowl where they defeated South Carolina. The 2010 season marked the Seminoles' first ten win season since 2003 and their first appearance in the ACC title game since 2005.

Rodney Hudson {G} was selected to the All-ACC first team and received the Jacobs Blocking Trophy. Hudson was selected as a Unanimous First team All-American. Brandon Jenkins {DE} was selected to the All-ACC first team. Xavier Rhodes {DB} was selected the Atlantic Coast Conference Defensive Rookie of the Year and was a Consensus First team Freshmen All-American. Christian Ponder {QB} {Minnesota}, Hudson {Kansas City} and Markus White {DE} {Washington} were selected in the 2011 NFL draft. Ponder was a #1 pick.

FINAL RANK: #17 AP, #16 CP

Home games were played at Doak Campbell Stadium

Date	Team	Rank		Opp Rank	Opponent	TV	PF	PA	W/L
9/4/2010	Florida State	#20	vs		SAMFORD	ESPNU	59	6	W
9/11/2010	Florida State	#17	@	#10	Oklahoma (12-2)	ABC	17	47	L
9/18/2010	Florida State		vs		BYU (7-6)	ESPNU	34	10	W
9/25/2010	Florida State		vs		WAKE FOREST (3-9)	ABC	31	0	W
10/2/2010	Florida State		@		Virginia (4-8)	ACC	34	14	W
10/9/2010	Florida State	#23	@	#13	Miami (7-6)	ABC	45	17	W
10/16/2010	Florida State	#16	vs		BOSTON COLLEGE (7-6)	ESPN	24	19	W
10/28/2010	Florida State	#16	@		NC State (9-4)	ESPN	24	28	L
11/6/2010	Florida State	#24	vs		NORTH CAROLINA	ABC	35	37	L
11/13/2010	Florida State		vs		CLEMSON (6-7)	ABC	16	13	W
11/20/2010	Florida State		@		Maryland (9-4)	ABC	30	16	W
11/27/2010	Florida State	#22	vs		FLORIDA (8-5)	ABC	31	7	W
12/4/2010	Florida State	#20	vs	#12	Virginia Tech (11-3)	ESPN	33	44	L
12/31/2010	Florida State	#23	vs	#19	South Carolina (9-5)	ESPN	26	17	W
Coach: Jimbo Fisher					Season Record >>		439	275	10-4

Schedule Source: Steve's Football Bible LLC

Selected game(s) highlights

SAMFORD

The first points of the game came on a 4 yard pass from Christian Ponder to fullback Lonnie Pryor. Florida State put 35 points on the board in the second quarter, thanks to three TD passes by Ponder (B. Reed, L. Pryor, T. Easterling), a 4 yard run by Jermaine Thomas, and a 74 yard punt return by Greg Reid. Samford kicked a FG as time expired to make the score 42–3 heading into halftime. The 'Noles were on cruise control this game and in the second half FSU's backups hung another 17 on Samford, and only allowed 3 points.

Oklahoma

Christian Ponder threw for just 113 yards and two interceptions. Backup EJ Manuel had 108 yards and one touchdown. Jermaine Thomas posted a touchdown on FSU's initial drive. The Sooners Landry Jones threw for 380 yards and four scores. Ryan Broyles grabbed 12 of those passes for 124 yards and one touchdown. FSU's other points came on a 52 yard field goal by kicker Dustin Hopkins early in the final quarter. Manuel found Taiwan Easterling on a 47 yard touchdown pass on the game's final play.

BYU

The Seminoles run game accounted for 278 yards and 3 TD's. Christian Ponder completed 66% of his passes, throwing zero interceptions, and adding 50 yards rushing. Chris Thompson ran for 123 yards, 83 of which came on one touchdown run. Ty Jones added another 95 and a touchdown. The FSU defense dominated most of the game by only allowing 191 yards and 10 points.

WAKE FOREST

The Seminoles opened ACC play at home with a 31-0 thumping of Wake Forest. FSU held the Demon Deacons to 185 yards of offense. Christian Ponder passed for over 200 yards for the first time all season. Ponder tossed two touchdown passes, both to Willie Haulstead, with 24 completions and 243 yards. He also added a rushing touchdown. EJ Manuel threw to Kenny Shaw for a 23 yard touchdown pass in the 4th quarter.

Virginia

Jermaine Thomas and Chris Thompson combined for nearly 200 yards rushing as Florida State pulled away early from Virginia to win 34-14. Thomas ran for two touchdowns and Thompson ran for one. Greg Reid finished with a career-best two interceptions while the defense recorded six sacks.

Miami

After the Hurricanes missed their opening field goal chance, the first half became the Jermaine Thomas show as he scored three touchdown, one on a pass from Christian Ponder and the other two using his own legs, as Florida State took a 24-7 lead into the locker room at the half. Lonnie Pryor got things started in the third quarter with a touchdown run, but Miami scored 10 unanswered points to cut the deficit to 10 points and start to make things worrisome for the fans in Garnet and Gold who invaded what was then called Sun Life Stadium. In the fourth, FSU put it away with a pass from Ponder to Rodney Smith and a 90 yard touchdown run by Chris Thompson – just one play after he had a 50 yard run taken away due to a holding penalty. The victory would be the third biggest win over Miami in FSU football history

BOSTON COLLEGE

Bert Reed's 42 yard touchdown run on a reverse lifted the Seminoles to a 24-19 win as they survived four turnovers by quarterback Christian Ponder to win their fifth straight. Boston College took a 19-17 lead early in the fourth quarter on Nate Freese's fourth field goal of the game that followed a Ponder fumble at the Eagles' 44. Ponder completed 19 of 31 passes for 170 yards and a pair of touchdowns, 3 yards to Lonnie Pryor and 10 yards to Beau Reliford.

NC State

Russell Wilson led the way as North Carolina State rallied from a big halftime deficit against #16 Florida State. Wilson threw a fourth-down touchdown pass to George Bryan with 2:40 left, then Nate Irving recovered a fumble in the final minute on the Seminoles' final drive to give NC State a 28-24. Christian Ponder, who ran for a pair of scores and threw for one, nearly rallied the Seminoles, driving Florida State all the way to the NC State 4 yard line in the final minute. But on the fake, Ponder extended the ball too far as tailback Ty Jones ran by. Jones bumped the ball with his hip, knocking it free and to the turf where Irving recovered.

NORTH CAROLINA

T.J. Yates threw for a school-record 439 yards, Casey Barth kicked his third goal, a 22 yarder, with 55 seconds left and the Tar Heels beat No. 24 Florida State 37-35. Dustin Hopkins missed two field goals in the fourth quarter, including a 40 yard try with 7 seconds left. Yates threw three touchdown passes and took the Tar Heels 72 yards on the winning drive to set up Barth's decisive kick. Florida State took a 35-34 lead with 5:49 left on Lonnie Pryor's second touchdown. Jermaine Thomas' 18 yard run set up a 5 yard touchdown pass from Ponder to Willie Haulstead as Florida State tied it midway through the first period. Ponder's 27 yard touchdown throw to Rodney Smith tied the game at 14 and Taiwan Easterling scooted 7 yards with a short pass from Ponder to give the Seminoles a short-lived 21-14 lead. Ponder completed 24 of 34 passes for 264 yards and three touchdowns and Haulstead had a career game with 10 catches for 154 yards.

CLEMSON

Dustin Hopkins booted a career-best 55 yard field goal as time expired to give Florida State a 16-13 victory over Clemson. EJ Manuel scored Florida State's only touchdown on an 8 yard run with 10:08 left to give the Seminoles a 13-10 lead. Jamie Harper ran for a career high 126 yards and Clemson's lone touchdown and caught nine passes, a school record for a running back.

Maryland

Christian Ponder threw for 170 yards and a touchdown, and Florida State beat Maryland 30-16. Clinging to a one-score lead in the final minute, FSU safety Nick Moody intercepted a Danny O'Brien pass attempt and ran untouched for a 90 yard game clinching score. The Seminoles took advantage of four Maryland turnovers, including two interceptions and a fumble in the fourth quarter after FSU took a 20-16 lead. Chris Thompson ran for 95 yards, including a 70 yard touchdown, Ponder completed 16 of 26 passes and Bert Reed had six catches for 93 yards and a touchdown for the Seminoles.

FLORIDA

Florida State capped its regular season with a 31-7 win to Florida in front of 82,324 fans that snapped the Gators' six-game winning streak in the series and its three-game streak at Doak Campbell Stadium. The Gators led 7-3 early in the second quarter but were unable to overcome four turnovers as the Seminoles scored 28 unanswered points to take control. The Gators outrushed the Seminoles 212-112. Florida State regained the lead by capitalizing on a second quarter fumble by Rainey, who appeared to be on his way to picking up a first down, when he lost the ball at Florida's 17 yard line. Seminole running back Lonnie Pryor found the end zone two plays later from nine yards out to put FSU in front 10-7. On the Gators' next possession, a Jordan Reed 12 yard run was followed by three plays that left them five yards short of a first down. On fourth down, senior punter Chas Henry attempted to run for a first down on a fake punt and was stopped a yard shy of the marker. It was the first time in nine fake punt attempts during Urban Meyer's tenure that the Gators failed to pick up a first down. Christian Ponder hit Rodney Smith for a 39 yard touchdown on the next play from scrimmage, giving the Seminoles a 17-7 edge. After a Florida three-and-out the following drive, the Seminoles embarked on a 12-play, 73 yard drive that culminated in a 15 yard strike from Ponder to Taiwan Easterling that extended FSU's lead to 24-7 that completed the first half scoring. Coming out of intermission, the Florida offense went three-and-out and Florida State put together a 10-play, 71 yard drive that ended with Ponder's third touchdown pass, a 29 yarder to Willie Haulstead, as the Seminoles went ahead by 24.

2010 ACC CHAMPIONSHIP

The 2010 game began slowly, as Florida State scored only a field goal on its opening possession and Virginia Tech was held scoreless on its first try. On the second play of Florida State's second possession, Virginia Tech defender Jeron Gouveia-Winslow intercepted a pass by Florida state quarterback E. J. Manuel and returned it for a touchdown, giving the Hokies a 7–3 lead. They did not relinquish the advantage the rest of the game. The teams traded field goals and touchdowns through the remainder of the first and second quarters and entered halftime with Tech leading 21–17. In the third quarter, Tech scored 14 points to Florida State's seven, establishing the winning margin. In the final quarter, each team scored nine points, and the Hokies won with the most points ever scored by one team in an ACC championship game. In recognition of his winning performance, Virginia Tech quarterback Tyrod Taylor was named the game's most valuable player. By winning, Virginia Tech earned a spot in the 2011 Orange Bowl football game, and Florida State was selected for the 2010 Chick-fil-A Bowl.

2010 CHICK-FIL-A BOWL

E.J. Manuel came on in relief for injured starting quarterback Christian Ponder and helped guide the #23 Florida State football to a 26-17 win over #20 South Carolina in the 2010 Chick-fil-A Bowl. Manuel threw a 7 yard touchdown pass to Taiwan Easterling to put a halt to a South Carolina rally. Dustin

Hopkins kicked four field goals for the Seminoles, who reached 10 victories for the first time since 2003. Hopkins tied his own school record for a bowl, and the four field goals also matched the Chick-fil-A Bowl record. Michael Harris, Kendall Smith, and Xavier Rhodes each had interceptions of Gamecocks quarterback Stephen Garcia. Garcia recovered to lead two long touchdown drives that trimmed Florida State's lead to 19-17 before Manuel answered with his TD pass to Easterling.

2011 Florida State Seminoles

The Seminoles were led by second-year head coach Jimbo Fisher. Despite starting the season with a 2–3 record, the Seminoles finished the season 9–4, 5–3 in ACC play, to finish in a tie for second place in the Atlantic Division. They were invited to the Champs Sports Bowl where they defeated Notre Dame.

Dustin Hopkins {K}, Shaun Powell {P} and Zebrie Sanders {T} were selected to the All-ACC first team. Powell was selected as a Consensus First team All-American. Nigel Bradham {LB} {Buffalo}, Sanders {Buffalo}, Mike Harris {CB} {Jacksonville} and Andrew Darko {OL} {Green Bay} were selected in the 2012 NFL draft.

FINAL RANK: #23 AP, #23 CP

Home games were played at Doak Campbell Stadium

9/3/2011	Florida State	#6	vs		LOUISIANA-MONROE (4-8)	ESPNU	34	0	W
9/10/2011	Florida State	#5	vs		CHARLESTON SOUTHERN		62	10	W
9/17/2011	Florida State	#5	vs	#1	OKLAHOMA (10-3)	ABC	13	23	L
9/24/2011	Florida State	#11	@	#21	**Clemson (10-4)**	ESPNU	30	35	L
10/8/2011	Florida State	#23	@		**Wake Forest (6-7)**	ACC	30	35	L
10/15/2011	Florida State		@		**Duke (3-9)**		41	16	W
10/22/2011	Florida State		vs		**MARYLAND (2-10)**	ABC	41	16	W
10/29/2011	Florida State		vs		**NC STATE (8-5)**	ESPNU	34	0	W
11/3/2011	Florida State		@		**Boston College (4-8)**	ESPN	38	7	W
11/12/2011	Florida State		vs		**MIAMI (6-6)**	ABC	23	19	W
11/19/2011	Florida State	#23	vs		**VIRGINIA (8-5)**	espn2	13	14	L
11/26/2011	Florida State		@		Florida (7-6)	espn2	21	7	W
12/29/2011	**Florida State**	**#25**	**vs**		**Notre Dame (8-5)**	**ESPN**	**18**	**14**	**W**
Coach: Jimbo Fisher					**Season Record >>**		**398**	**196**	**9-4**

Schedule Source: Steve's Football Bible LLC

Selected game(s) highlights

LOUISIANA-MONROE

EJ Manuel threw for 252 yards and two touchdowns and backup quarterback Clint Trickett threw a touchdown pass on his first college play as #6 Florida State beat Louisiana-Monroe 34-0. Manuel connected with Bert Reed on a 9 yard TD pass to get the Seminoles on the scoreboard in the opening quarter and hit Greg Dent in full stride on a 50 yard scoring play just before the half. Trickett fired a 28 yard touchdown pass to Rashad Greene, on his first collegiate play. Dustin Hopkins kicked a pair of short field goals and freshman Devonta Freeman added a 1 yard touchdown run in the third quarter.

CHARLESTON SOUTHERN

EJ Manuel threw for a career-best 329 yards and four touchdowns while Charleston Southern didn't complete its first pass and get a first down until the third quarter. Florida State amassed 29 first downs and 647 yards offense while holding Charleston Southern to three first downs and 84 yards in a 62-10 blowout victory. Clint Trickett completed 6 of 7 passes for 148 yards and two touchdowns and ran 4 yards for a third. Both TD throws were to freshman Rashad Greene on plays covering 29 and 69 yards. Manuel hit Bert Reed on two short TD passes while the Seminoles' defense limited Charleston Southern to 84 total yards. Lonnie Pryor scored on a 14 yard pass from Manuel and Chris Thompson added a 2 yard touchdown run.

OKLAHOMA

Kenny Stills reached high to grab a 37 yard touchdown pass from Landry Jones midway through the fourth quarter for the tiebreaking score, and Oklahoma's defense made the last stand as the top-ranked Sooners beat #5 Florida State 23-13. Javon Harris picked off two passes for the Sooners, who forced three turnovers and had six sacks against two Florida State quarterbacks. Clint Trickett kept the Seminoles in it. He hooked up with freshman Rashad Greene for a 56 yard touchdown on a third-and-28 with 9:32 left in the fourth quarter to tie the game at 13.

Clemson

#21 Clemson knocked off a ranked opponent for the second straight week as Tajh Boyd threw for three touchdowns and ran for another in a 35-30 victory over #11 Florida State. Boyd had 344 yards on 23 of 37 passing. Freshman Sammy Watkins had eight catches for 141 yards and his fifth and sixth touchdown catches of 24 and 62 yards. Andre Ellington added 71 yards rushing.

Wake Forest

Tanner Price threw three scoring passes and Josh Harris rushed for 136 yards and Wake Forest upset the 23rd ranked Seminoles 35-30. Price was 21 of 35 for 233 yards with touchdowns covering 22 yards to Chris Givens, 2 yards to Tommy Bohanon and 8 yards to Terence Davis. EJ Manuel replaced Clint Trickett late in the first half and finished 19 of 35 for 286 yards with two touchdowns and two interceptions. His 2 yard scoring pass to Kenny Shaw made it a five-point game with 54 seconds left. Manuel also threw a 46 yard touchdown pass to Rashad Greene. James Wilder Jr. and Ty Jones had 3 yard touchdown runs. But Florida State turned it over five times -- four interceptions and a fumble -- and Wake Forest turned those giveaways into 17 points.

Duke

EJ Manuel threw for 239 yards and two touchdowns to help Florida State beat Duke 41-16. Manuel had three completions of at least 50 yards in the first quarter, including a 50 yard scoring toss to Rodney Smith. Manuel followed with a 51 yard throw out of his own end zone to Kenny Shaw on the next drive, which ended with Devonta Freeman's 10 yard touchdown run that helped the Seminoles jump ahead 24-3, barely a minute into the second quarter. Manuel also ran for 62 yards and a pair of touchdowns. His 3 yard scoring pass to Nick O'Leary midway through the third quarter gave Florida State its largest lead at 34-3, then he answered a pair of touchdowns from the Blue Devils by scoring on a 6 yard keeper with 9:49 left.

MARYLAND

EJ Manuel passed for 264 yards and a touchdown, and freshman Devonta Freeman ran for 100 yards as Florida State routed Maryland 41-16. Jermaine Thomas chipped in with 86 yards and a 35 yard rushing score for the Seminoles. Dustin Hopkins added a pair of field goals. Florida State built its largest lead at 41-10 on Debrale Smiley `s 1 yard TD run with 47 seconds left in the game. Freeman's 41 yard TD with 5:57 left had put the Seminoles into a 34-10 lead.

NC STATE

EJ Manuel threw for 321 yards and two touchdowns Saturday to lead Florida State to a 34-0 win over North Carolina State. Florida State led 24-0 at halftime and intercepted N.C. State quarterback Mike Glennon twice on the way to its first shutout of the season. Manuel completed 25 of 34 passes and connected on scoring plays of 20 yards to Kenny Shaw and 26 yards to Greg Dent. Lonnie Pryor and Devonta Freeman scored on short runs and Dustin Hopkins chipped in with two field goals for the Seminoles.

Boston College

EJ Manuel threw for one touchdown and ran for another to lead Florida State to a 38-7 victory over Boston College. Manuel completed 12 of 16 passes for 180 yards and ran 16 times for 37 yards to help Florida State open a 28-0 halftime lead. Devonta Freeman ran for 62 yards and two touchdowns, and Nick O'Leary caught three passes for 87 yards

MIAMI

Special teams were the key as the Florida State football team beat Miami 23-19. Clinging to the 23-19 advantage with just 1:24 left, Nick O'Leary leapt into the air and snagged the onside kick attempt to secure the win for the Seminoles. Dustin Hopkins converted three field goals and Greg Reid's 83 yard punt return gave the 'Noles a 17-7 lead. EJ Manuel threw for 196 yards on 17-of-23 passing with one touchdown. His favorite target on the night was Christian Green, who caught 4 for 55 yards. Bert Reed also grabbed three passes for 45 yards and Rodney Smith had a 21 yard touchdown reception.

VIRGINIA

In the final 38 seconds, a costly facemask penalty gave Florida State a crucial first down and a replay ruling gave the Seminoles a few extra seconds to attempt a potential game winning kick, but Dustin Hopkins' missed a 43 yard potential game winner in with 3 seconds left in the game. FSU lost to Virginia 14-13. Kevin Parks gave Virginia the one-point lead, by running 10 yards for a touchdown with 1:16 left.

Florida

On senior night at the Swamp, the University of Florida had little to celebrate. Florida State took advantage of short fields and costly turnovers to defeat Florida at Ben Hill Griffin Stadium for the first time since 2003, taking a 21-7 decision. The Seminoles capitalized four Florida interceptions and won despite amassing just 95 yards of total offense. Florida State got all 21 points off of turnovers, returning one for a touchdown and driving just 20 and 4 yards for their two other scores.

2011 CHAMPS SPORTS BOWL

The Seminoles rallied from a 14-point second-half deficit and used a pair of touchdown passes by EJ Manuel and two field goals from Dustin Hopkins to earn their fourth straight bowl win over Notre Dame, 18-14. The Irish's Zeke Motta returned a fumble 29 yards for a touchdown and Michael Floyd caught a 5 Yard TD Pass from Tommy Rees for 14-0 lead. Dustin Hopkins kicked a 42 yard field, and the Seminoles went into halftime trailing 14-3. Still trailing 14-3 going into the 4th quarter, EJ Manuel threw two touchdown passes, one to Bert Reed (18 yards) and Rashad Greene (15 yards) to rally the Seminoles to a 15-14 lead. Hopkins added a 29 yard field goal to cap the scoring.

2012 Florida State Seminoles {ACC Champions}

The Seminoles were led by third-year head coach Jimbo Fisher. Florida State won its first ACC title since 2005, advancing to their first BCS bowl since that season as well, and won ten regular season games for the first time since the 2003 season. The Seminoles also won their first BCS game since the 2000 Sugar Bowl.

Dustin Hopkins (K) and Bjorn Werner (DE) were selected as first team All-Americans. Werner was selected as ACC Defensive Player of the Year. E.J. Manuel {QB} {Buffalo}, Bjorn Werner {Indianapolis}, Xavier Rhodes {CB} {Minnesota}, Tank Carradine {DE} {San Francisco}, Menelik Watson {OL} {Oakland}, Chris Thompson {RB} {Washington}, Brandon Jenkins {DE} {Washington}, Dustin Hopkins {K} {Buffalo}, Nick Moody {LB} {San Francisco}, Vince Williams {LB} {Pittsburgh} and Everett Dawkins {DT} {Minnesota} were selected in the 2013 NFL Draft. Werner (Indianapolis), E.J. Manual (QB) (Buffalo) and Xavier Rhodes (DB) (Minnesota) were all #1 picks.

ACC CHAMPIONS					FINAL RANK: #10 AP, #8 CP				
					Home games were played at Doak Campbell Stadium				
9/1/2012	Florida State	#7	vs		MURRAY STATE		69	3	W
9/8/2012	Florida State	#6	vs		SAVANNAH STATE		55	0	W
9/15/2012	Florida State	#5	vs		**WAKE FOREST**	ESPN	52	0	W
9/22/2012	Florida State	#5	vs	#10	**CLEMSON**	ABC	49	37	W
9/29/2012	Florida State	#4	@		South Florida	ESPN	30	17	W
10/6/2012	Florida State	#3	@		**NC State**	espn2	16	17	L
10/13/2012	Florida State	#12	vs		**BOSTON COLLEGE**	espn2	51	7	W
10/20/2012	Florida State	#12	@		**Miami**	ABC	33	20	W
10/27/2012	Florida State	#11	vs		**DUKE**	ESPNU	48	7	W
11/8/2012	Florida State	#8	@		**Virginia Tech**	ESPN	28	22	W
11/17/2012	Florida State	#10	@		**Maryland**	ESPNU	41	14	W
11/24/2012	Florida State	#10	vs	#6	FLORIDA	ABC	26	37	L
12/1/2012	**Florida State**	#13	vs		**Georgia Tech**	**ESPN**	21	15	W
1/1/2013	**Florida State**	#13	vs	#16	**Northern Illinois**	**ESPN**	31	10	W
Coach: Jimbo Fisher					Season Record >>		550	206	12-2

Schedule Source: Steve's Football Bible LLC

Selected game(s) highlights

MURRAY STATE

The Seminoles opened the season ranked #7 with a home game vs **Murray State**. Florida State dominated the Racers throughout the game, winning 69–3. Florida State opened the scoring and scored 14 points in the first quarter, with Rashad Greene returning a 47 yard punt return from kicker Dustin Hopkins and a 1 yard touchdown run from Lonnie Pryor. Florida State added another fourteen points in the second quarter as the result of an 18 yard touchdown run from Lonnie Pryor and a 6 yard touchdown pass from EJ Manuel to Kenny Shaw. In the third quarter, Florida State scored 20 points. James Wilder, Jr. had a 9 yard touchdown run, Dustin Hopkins kicked a 23 yard field goal, Lonnie Pryor had a 1 yard touchdown run, and Dustin Hopkins kicked another 30 yard field goal. Florida State scored another 21 points in the fourth quarter with a 7 yard touchdown run from James Wilder, Jr. and two 1 yard touchdown runs from Debrale Smiley. E.J. Manuel led the team in passing with 188 yards and one touchdown; James Wilder, Jr. led the team in rushing with 12 carries for 106 yards and two touchdowns; Kenny Shaw led the team in receiving with 4 receptions for 82 yards and one touchdown. Xavier Rhodes recorded one interception and Karlos Williams returned a punt for a touchdown.

SAVANNAH STATE

Ranked #6, FSU hosted **Savannah State**. The Seminoles were installed as 67 point favorites, reportedly making Savannah State the biggest underdogs in any college football game ever. Florida State held the Tigers scoreless, winning 55–0. Florida State opened the scoring and scored 35 points in the first quarter, with a 61 yard touchdown pass from EJ Manuel to Rodney Smith, a 6 yard touchdown run from Chris Thompson, an 8 yard touchdown pass from E.J. Manuel to Greg Dent, a 9 yard touchdown pass from E.J. Manuel to Kelvin Benjamin, and a 5 yard touchdown run from Devonta Freeman. Florida State added another thirteen points in the second quarter as the result of a 19 yard touchdown run from James Wilder, Jr. and another 1 yard touchdown run from James Wilder, Jr. with a subsequent failed point-after-attempt from kicker Dustin Hopkins, ending his streak of 145 consecutive extra point attempts. Florida State scored another seven points in the third quarter as the result of a 19 yard touchdown pass from Jacob Coker to Kelvin Benjamin. E.J. Manuel led the team in passing with 161 yards and three touchdowns; Devonta Freeman led the team in rushing with 7 carries for 69 yards and one touchdown; Rodney Smith led the team in receiving with 3 receptions for 77 yards and one touchdown.

WAKE FOREST

#5 Florida State shutout a team for the second week in a row by holding Wake Forest scoreless for the second time in three years and winning 52–0. Despite a sluggish start, Florida State scored first with a 16 yard rushing touchdown from EJ Manuel late in the first quarter. Another touchdown in the first quarter came from Rashad Greene with a 60 yard punt return. After a fourteen point first quarter, the Seminoles scored twenty-four more points in the second with a 74 yard touchdown run and an 80 yard touchdown run from Chris Thompson, a field goal from Dustin Hopkins, and a 20 yard touchdown pass from E.J. Manuel to Rodney Smith. Florida State dominated the second half of the game as well. The Seminoles added seven points in the third quarter with a 17 yard touchdown pass from E.J. Manuel to Kenny Shaw. They finished off the game with seven points in the fourth quarter courtesy of an 18 yard touchdown run from Debrale Smiley. E.J. Manuel led the team in passing with 176 yards and two touchdowns; Chris Thompson led the team in rushing with 9 carries for 197 yards and two touchdowns; Kelvin Benjamin

CLEMSON

The #4 ranked **Florida State** Seminoles used a 35-3 run in a 20-minute span of the second half Saturday night to remain unbeaten with a 49-37 over the #10 Clemson. The two teams combined for 1,093 yards offense as Clemson put up 426 yards against the nation's top-ranked defense. Tajh Boyd completed 20 of 36 passes for 237 yards and three touchdowns for Clemson.

South Florida

In the first road game of the season, the #4 ranked Seminoles traveled to Tampa to take on the **South Florida** Bulls. Florida State won the game 30–17 despite a sluggish start. USF got on the board first with a 32 yard field goal from Maikon Bonani. Florida State took the lead with a 10 yard touchdown run from Rashad Greene. At the end of the first quarter, the Seminoles held a slim four point lead. They extended their lead in the second quarter with two field goals from Dustin Hopkins, a 6 yard field goal and a 23 yard field goal, after previously missing a field goal in the first quarter. Florida State carried a ten point lead into the half. At the start of the second half, South Florida closed the gap with a 1 yard touchdown run from B.J. Daniels. Florida State responded with a 1 yard touchdown pass from EJ Manuel to tight end Kevin Haplea and later extended their lead again with a 23 yard field goal from Hopkins. At the end of the third quarter, the Seminoles capitalized on a South Florida turnover when Christian Jones had a 12 yard fumble return to give the Seminoles their largest lead of the game. The Bulls scored again in the fourth quarter with B.J. Daniels 3 yard touchdown run, but Florida State was able to preserve a 13 point victory. Quarterback E.J. Manuel gave another impressive performance. Manuel led the team in passing with 242 yards and one touchdown; Chris Thompson led the team in rushing with 17 carries for 74 yards; Rashad Greene led the team in receiving with 2 receptions for 71 yards.

NC State

    #3 Florida State traveled to Raleigh for their first ACC road game against the **NC State** Wolfpack. Florida State lost to the Wolfpack, 17–16. Florida State dominated the first half of the game, building a 16–0 lead by halftime. The Seminoles scored first with a 49 yard field goal from kicker Dustin Hopkins which put FSU up by three in the first quarter. They followed that up in the second quarter with a 4 yard touchdown pass from EJ Manuel to Nick O'Leary to give them a ten point lead. Two more field goals of 45 and 20 yards respectively extended that lead to sixteen. NC State scored their first points of the game with a 27 yard field goal. This was followed by a 24 yard touchdown pass from Mike Glennon to put the Wolfpack within six points. A subsequent drive by the Seminoles ended with a sack that put them out of field goal range. North Carolina State State blocked the punt and were able to score on a fourth down touchdown to give them the lead with just sixteen seconds remaining in the game. E.J. Manuel led the team in passing with 218 yards and one touchdown; Chris Thompson led the team in rushing with 25 carries for 141 yards; Rashad Greene led the team in receiving with 6 receptions for 60 yards.

BOSTON COLLEGE

    After two straight road games, the #12 ranked Seminoles returned home to face the **Boston College** Eagles. Florida State rebounded from a loss and defeated Boston College, 51–7. The Seminoles dominated the game from start to finish. They scored first early in the game with a 77 yard touchdown pass from EJ Manuel to Kenny Shaw. This was followed by a 2 yard touchdown run from Lonnie Pryor to give FSU a 14–0 lead at the end of the first quarter. Scoring was opened in the second quarter with a 7 yard touchdown run from James Wilder, Jr. on a pass from E.J. Manuel. They built a four possession lead with 6 yard touchdown pass from E.J. Manuel to Kelvin Benjamin. The Eagles got on the board with an 18 yard touchdown pass from Chase Rettig to Bobby Swiggert. Florida State extended the lead with a 51 yard field goal from kicker Dustin Hopkins, giving the Seminoles a twenty-four point lead at the half. E.J. Manuel led the team in passing with 439 yards and four touchdowns; Devonta Freeman led the team in rushing with 8 carries for 70 yards; Kenny Shaw led the team in receiving with 2 receptions for 125 yards and one touchdown. The Defense held BC to 225 yards of offense.

Miami

    #12 Florida State beat **Miami** for a third straight time, 33–20. Miami struck first, scoring the first ten points of the game, the first seven off a Florida State fumble and the other three on a botched punt. Florida State then went on to score 13 unanswered points in the first half, courtesy of a 33 yard field goal from Dustin Hopkins, a 17 yard run from James Wilder, Jr. to tie the game, and another 46 yard field goal as time expired. The Seminoles carried a three point lead into halftime. Florida State opened the second half with a 35 yard field goal to increase their lead to six. Miami responded with a 27 yard field goal of their own to cut the lead back down to three. The Seminoles then took control of the game in the fourth quarter with a 3 yard touchdown run from Devonta Freeman, a 48 yard field goal from Dustin Hopkins, and another 5 yard touchdown run from Devonta Freeman. The Hurricanes scored the final points of the game with an 8 yard touchdown pass from Stephen Morris to Rashawn Scott. Florida State got the ball back and ran the clock to maintain a thirteen point win over their rival. EJ Manuel led the team in passing with 229 yards; Devonta Freeman led the team in rushing with 10 carries for 70 yards and two touchdowns; Rashad Greene led the team in receiving with 7 receptions for 49 yards. Tyler Hunter recorded one interception. Dustin Hopkins successfully attempted four out of five field goals.

DUKE

    #11 Florida State returned home for a homecoming game against the **Duke** Blue Devils. Florida State kept their unbeaten streak against Duke going with a 48–7 win over the Blue Devils. Florida State led the game from start to finish. The first score came from a 13 yard touchdown pass from EJ Manuel to Rashad Greene to give the Seminoles the early lead. They then scored on a 75 yard punt returned for a touchdown by Tyler Hunter and then added to that lead with a 26 yard field goal from Dustin Hopkins. Florida State continued their control of the game in the second quarter with a 1 yard touchdown run from James Wilder, Jr. capping a three play drive and a 9 yard touchdown run from Devonta Freeman. Duke got on the board with their first score of the game courtesy of a 3 yard touchdown run from Jela Duncan. The Seminoles had a twenty-four point lead at the half. E.J. Manuel led the team in passing with 282 yards and two touchdowns; Devonta Freeman led the team in rushing with 12 carries for 104 yards and two touchdowns; Rodney Smith led the team in receiving with 3 receptions for 112 yards. On special teams, Tyler Hunter returned a punt for a touchdown and Dustin Hopkins successfully attempted two field goals.

Virginia Tech

#8 Florida State rallied to defeat **Virginia Tech** by a score of 28–22. Florida State opened the scoring with a 52 yard field goal from Dustin Hopkins to put the Seminoles up by three. Virginia Tech responded with a 35 yard field goal of their own to tie the game. In the second quarter, Florida State settled for another 45 yard field goal to give them a three point lead once again. Late in the quarter, Virginia Tech took the lead for the first time with a 4 yard touchdown pass from Logan Thomas to Corey Fuller. The Seminoles scored again on a 25 yard touchdown pass from EJ Manuel to Rashad Greene to take back the lead. Florida State led by three points at the half. Florida State struck first in the second half as well courtesy of a 10 yard touchdown from Greg Dent on a pass from E.J. Manuel to give the Seminoles their largest lead of the game. The Hokies then scored a touchdown of their own with a 5 yard run from Logan Thomas to get back within three. Florida State entered the final quarter with a slim lead. The lead slimmed even more as a penalty called on Devonta Freeman in the end zone resulted in a safety which cut the lead to one. The Hokies took the lead on a 21 yard touchdown run from Cody Journell with two minutes left. Trailing by two, the Seminoles, led by their quarterback, put together an 8-play, 68 yard game-winning drive that resulted in a 39 yard touchdown pass from E.J. Manuel to Rashad Greene and a subsequent two point conversion. The drive gave Florida State a six point lead with forty seconds left in the game. The game ended with Virginia Tech driving down the field with just seconds remaining on the clock. Tyler Hunter made a key interception in the red zone to prevent Tech from scoring and secure a victory for the Seminoles. E.J. Manuel led the team in passing with 326 yards and three touchdowns while also recording one interception; Rashad Greene led the team in receiving with 6 receptions for 125 yards and two touchdowns.

Maryland

#10 Florida State ended conference play with a 41–14 win over the Terrapins. Florida State routed **Maryland** during the first half of the game. On their first possession, the Seminoles drove down the field and scored with a 5 yard touchdown run from Devonta Freeman. Immediately after, they capitalized on a Maryland fumble to go up by two scores with a 10 yard touchdown pass from EJ Manuel to Nick O'Leary. In the second quarter, Florida State extended their lead with two field goals from Dustin Hopkins, a 26 yard field goal and a 40 yard field goal, and a 30 yard touchdown pass to Rashad Greene from E.J. Manuel to make it a four score lead. The Seminoles led by twenty-seven points at halftime while the Terps remained scoreless at the half. E.J. Manuel led the team in passing with 144 yards and two touchdowns while also recording one interception. Devonta Freeman led the team in rushing with 16 carries for 148 yards and two touchdowns; Rashad Greene led the team in receiving with 4 receptions for 50 yards and one touchdown. Dustin Hopkins successfully attempted two field goals, making him the all-time NCAA scoring leader with 448 points.

FLORIDA

Sixth-ranked Florida ran roughshod over the rival Florida Seminoles and the nation's #1-ranked defense in the fourth quarter Saturday, erupting for 24 points in the final period for a 37-26 victory at Doak Campbell Stadium. Senior tailback Mike Gillislee became the first UF player to reach the 1,000 yard milestone in a season since 2004, carrying 24 times for a 140 yards and two scores, including a 37 yard touchdown blast in the fourth quarter that gave the Gators the lead for good. Freshman running back

Matt Jones added 81 yards on 10 carries, with a 32 yard scoring run late to ice the game. The best defense on the field turned out to be Florida's, which forced five turnovers in the game, four by Seminoles senior quarterback E.J. Manuel, who rushed for a touchdown on the game's final play to make the score closer than it really was.

2012 ACC CHAMPIONSHIP

#13 Florida State captured the ACC title with a 21–15 win over **Georgia Tech**. Florida State built up an early lead and never relinquished it. The Seminoles forced Georgia Tech to punt on the first possession of the game and then went on to score on their own first possession with a 3 yard touchdown run from Devonta Freeman. This was followed by a 16 yard touchdown run from James Wilder, Jr. in the second quarter. Georgia Tech put their first points on the board with a 27 yard field goal from Chris Turner to cut the Seminoles lead to eleven. Florida State scored again courtesy of another 1 yard touchdown run from James Wilder, Jr. Before halftime, Georgia Tech kicked a 47 yard field goal to give the Yellow Jacekets three more points. The Seminoles went into the half with a 21–6 lead. After dominating the first two quarters, Florida State was held scoreless during the last two quarters. Georgia Tech added more points in the third quarter with a 36 yard field goal from Chris Tanner and in the fourth quarter with a 1 yard touchdown run from Tevin Washington.

2013 ORANGE BOWL

#13 Florida State went to a bowl game for the 31st straight season. The Seminoles faced the #16 **Northern Illinois** Huskies of the MAC. The Seminoles won their first Orange Bowl in twelve years with a 31–10 win over the Huskies of Northern Illinois. Florida State never trailed in the game. The Seminoles scored in the first quarter with a 60 yard touchdown run from eventual MVP Lonnie Pryor to give them an early seven to zero lead. Northern Illinois responded later in the first quarter with a 25 yard field goal from Matthew Sims to cut the lead to four. Late in the second quarter, Florida State built up their lead with a 6 yard touchdown pass from EJ Manuel to Rashad Greene. Florida State led by eleven at the half.

After halftime, Florida State made it a two possession game with a 25 yard field goal from Dustin Hopkins. The Huskies pulled to within one possession with an 11 yard touchdown pass from Jordan Lynch to Martel Moore. Going into the final quarter, the Seminoles held a seven point lead. Florida State scored fourteen points in the fourth quarter courtesy of a 9 yard touchdown run from E.J. Manuel and a 37 yard touchdown run from Lonnie Pryor. E.J. Manuel led the team in passing with 291 yards and a touchdown. Lonnie Pryor led the team in rushing with 5 carries for 134 yards and two touchdowns.

2013 Florida State Seminoles {National Champions}

The Seminoles were led by fourth-year head coach Jimbo Fisher. Led by eventual Heisman Trophy winner Jameis Winston, Florida State finished the season with a school-record fourteen wins and completed the school's third undefeated season. The Seminoles captured their seventeenth conference title and third national championship, earning the Grantland Rice Award, the MacArthur Trophy, the Associated Press Trophy and the AFCA National Championship Trophy. In addition to the Heisman, Jameis Winston won the Walter Camp Award, the Davey O'Brien Award, and the Manning Award. Roberto Aguayo won the Lou Groza Award as the nation's best placekicker; Bryan Stork won the Rimington Trophy awarded to the nation's top center. **Winston set new single season team records with 40 touchdown passes, 4,276 yards of total offense and 44 total touchdowns. Kelvin Benjamin tied the team record for touchdown receptions with 15.**

Roberto Aguayo (K), Kelvin Benjamin (WR), Terrance Brooks (DB), Cameron Irving (OL), Timmy Jernigan (DT), Lamarcus Joyner (DB), Bryan Stork (OL) and Jameis Winston (QB) were all selected first team All-Americans. Benjamin {Carolina}, Joyner {St. Louis Rams}, Jernigan {Baltimore Ravens}, Brooks {Baltimore Ravens}, Devonta Freeman {RB} {Atlanta}, Stork {New England} and Telvin Smith {LB} {Jacksonville} were selected in the 2014 NFL Draft. Kelvin Benjamin (Carolina) was a #1 pick.

NATIONAL CHAMPIONS					FINAL RANK: #1 AP, #1 CP				
Home games were played at Doak Campbell Stadium									
9/2/2013	Florida State	**#11**	@		**Pittsburgh**	ESPN	41	13	**W**
9/14/2013	Florida State	**#10**	vs		*NEVADA*	ESPN	62	7	**W**
9/21/2013	Florida State	**#8**	vs		*BETHUNE-COOKMAN*		54	6	**W**
9/28/2013	Florida State	**#8**	@		**Boston College**	ABC	48	34	**W**
10/5/2013	Florida State	**#8**	vs	#25	**MARYLAND**	ESPN	63	0	**W**
10/19/2013	Florida State	**#5**	@	#3	**Clemson**	ABC	51	14	**W**
10/26/2013	Florida State	**#3**	vs		**NC STATE**	ABC	49	17	**W**
11/2/2013	Florida State	**#3**	vs	#7	**MIAMI**	ABC	41	14	**W**
11/9/2013	Florida State	**#3**	@		**Wake Forest**	ABC	59	3	**W**
11/16/2013	Florida State	**#2**	vs		**SYRACUSE**	ABC	59	3	**W**
11/23/2013	Florida State	**#2**	vs		*IDAHO*	ESPNU	80	10	**W**
11/30/2013	Florida State	**#2**	@		*Florida*	ESPN	37	7	**W**
12/7/2013	**Florida State**	**#1**	vs	#20	**Duke**	**ABC**	**45**	**7**	**W**
1/6/2014	**Florida State**	**#1**	vs	#2	**Auburn**	**ESPN**	**34**	**31**	**W**
Coach: Jimbo Fisher					**Season Record >>**		**723**	**166**	**14-0**

Schedule Source: Steve's Football Bible LLC

Selected game(s) highlights

Pittsburgh

Florida State opened the season ranked #11 and traveled to **Pittsburgh**. The Seminoles had to overcome an early deficit to defeat the Panthers, 41–13. After Pitt scored on their first possession to take a touchdown lead, Florida State quickly responded on their first drive with a touchdown pass from Winston to Nick O'Leary to tie the game. Winston and O'Leary would connect twice for touchdowns in a game where the offense rolled. The Seminoles would extend their lead with a rushing touchdown from Jameis Winston and a pass to Rashad Greene following an interception to give Florida State an eighteen point lead at halftime. The third quarter was mostly uneventful with a pair of field goals from Florida State and a single field goal from Pittsburgh. The Seminoles held a three score lead going into the fourth quarter. Winston would add another touchdown in the final quarter.

NEVADA

In their home opener, #10 Florida State faced the **Nevada** Wolf Pack. After a slow start and another early deficit, the Seminoles would go on to defeat the Wolf Pack in dominating fashion, 62–7, after scoring 59 unanswered points. The Seminoles would strike first courtesy of a field goal from Roberto Aguayo, which would serve as the only score of the first quarter. Going into the second quarter, the Seminoles held a three point lead, but they would eventually trail after Nevada scored the first touchdown of the game to take a four point lead. However, this would be the only points allowed by the Seminole defense. Florida State scored touchdowns on two consecutive drives with two passes from quarterback Jameis Winston to Kenny Shaw and Rashad Greene to take a ten point lead into the half. Florida State rolled during the second half of the game, scoring thirty-one points in the third quarter and fourteen more points in the fourth quarter while holding Nevada scoreless. Despite allowing a touchdown early in the game, the Florida State defense allowed only 214 yards while the Florida State offense tallied up 617 yards of total offense.

BETHUNE-COOKMAN

#8 Florida State defeated the **Bethune–Cookman** Wildcats on a rainy night in their first meeting by a final score of 54–6. Florida State jumped out to a quick lead by scoring the first 40 points of the game. Telvin Smith opened the scoring for The Seminoles with an interception returned for a touchdown followed up by a 45 yard field goal from Roberto Auayo. A safety, caused by a penalty in the endzone by the Wildcats, gave the Seminoles an early twelve point lead. Florida State then scored three straight touchdowns courtesy of Kelvin Benjamin, James Wilder Jr., and Devonta Freeman to carry a thirty-three point lead into halftime. Bethune–Cookman scored their first points at the start of the third quarter with a seven yard touchdown run; they subsequently missed the extra point kick. Florida State would then score the final fourteen points of the game with two touchdown runs from newly converted RB Karlos Williams.

Boston College

#8 Florida State hit the road to face the **Boston College** Eagles. Florida State mounted a comeback to defeat Boston College, 48–34. Boston College took the early lead with a touchdown pass from BC quarterback Chase Rettig. Florida State responded with a seven play drive that ended in a field goal to cut the lead to four. The Eagles would then go on to score the next ten points of the game to take a fourteen point lead and seemingly seize control of the game. However, the Seminoles rattled off twenty-one unanswered points including a "Hail Mary" pass, with no time remaining, at the end of the second quarter to take a seven point lead at the half. On the first drive of the second half, Boston College mustered up a drive that resulted in a field goal to close the gap and make it a four point game. Florida State then completed two drives ending in touchdowns to take an eighteen point lead. Boston College added another touchdown at the end of the third quarter. Entering the fourth quarter, Florida State held an eleven point lead. In the final quarter, Florida State would extend their lead with a field goal. Boston College then began a promising drive, but P.J. Williams intercepted the ball and returned it for a touchdown to put the Noles up 48–27 late in the game.

MARYLAND

The #8 Seminoles returned home to face the #25 **Maryland** Terrapins. Florida State earned their first shutout of the season with a rout of the Terrapins, 63–0, setting a record for the most lop-sided victory against a ranked opponent in school history as well as the first shut-out of a ranked opponent in sixteen years. Florida State struck first on offense and defense, forcing a three-and-out on the opening possession of the game and scoring a touchdown on their first possession. Maryland's defense held Florida State scoreless for the rest of the first quarter. However, Florida State would score another fourteen points in the second quarter courtesy of two five yard touchdown runs from Devonta Freeman and Kelvin Benjamin. At halftime, Florida State held a 21–0 lead. The Seminoles opened the second half with another scoring drive capping off with an eight yard pass from Jameis Winston to tight end Nick O'Leary to extend the lead to twenty eight. The second half was an offensive explosion for Florida State as the Seminoles went on a forty-two point scoring spree. With a twenty-one yard pass to Kenny Shaw and a twelve yard pass to Nick O'Leary, Florida State carried a forty-two point lead into the final quarter. Florida State continued to score in the fourth with another twenty-one point quarter that consisted of touchdowns from Kelvin Benjamin and Karlos Williams along with backup QB Jacob Coker.

Clemson

#5 Florida State traveled to "Death Valley" to face the #3 **Clemson** Tigers in a top five matchup. Florida State stunned Clemson, 51–14, becoming the first team in history to score 50 points at Memorial Stadium. Florida State struck early, capitalizing on a Clemson turnover on the first play from scrimmage. The Seminoles scored a touchdown on their third play as Winston threw a touchdown on his first pass of the game. Florida State added a field goal on their second series of the game. With a ten point lead, Mario Edwards, Jr. returned a fumble for a touchdown that put the Seminoles up 17–0. Clemson scored their first points of the game near the end of the first quarter with a touchdown pass from Tajh Boyd to Sammy Watkins to cut the lead back down to ten. Florida State doubled their lead with a touchdown and a field goal in the second quarter while Clemson failed to score. The Seminoles went into the half holding a twenty point advantage. Florida State continued to control the game in the second half, scoring twenty-four straight points, courtesy of a passing touchdown to Rashad Greene, rushing touchdowns from Devonta Freeman and Jameis Winston, and a field goal from Roberto Agauyo. Clemson would not make it into the endzone again until the end of the fourth quarter, securing a thirty-seven point win for the Noles.

NC STATE

#3 Florida State avenged last season's upset loss to **NC State**, riding on a huge first quarter to defeat the Wolfpack, 49–17. The Seminoles took control of the game early, scoring the first thirty-five points. The first score of the game came from an 18 yard run from Karlos Williams following an interception by Brandon Mitchell. The next score came courtesy of a 39 yard touchdown pass from Jameis Winston to Kelvin Benjamin to give the Noles an early fourteen point advantage. Devonta Freeman scored on an 11 yard rush for a touchdown. After a forced fumble by Terrence Brooks, Florida State converted the turnover into points with a 14 yard pass to Nick O'Leary. The Seminoles ended the first quarter with another receiving touchdown from Rashad Greene. The scoring continued in the second quarter when Devonta Freeman ran four yards for a touchdown. Florida State scored a total of 42 points in the first half while holding NC State scoreless. NC State put their first points on the board in the third quarter by scoring ten unanswered points with a field goal and a 72 yard touchdown. The Wolfpack added seven more points in the fourth with another rushing touchdown. Florida State scored their final points of the game with a 31 yard rushing touchdown from Levonte Whitfield.

MIAMI

In front of a record crowd at Doak Campbell Stadium, #3 Florida State defeated their rival, #7 **Miami** for the fourth straight time, 41–14. The Seminoles scored the first points on the opening drive of the game when Devonta Freeman ran the ball into the endzone to give Florida State an early seven point lead. Miami then drove the ball down the field only to be stopped in the red zone; the Hurricanes then attempted a field goal that sailed wide left. As the Seminoles were once again going down the field, Jameis Winston threw his first interception of the season that led to a Miami touchdown five plays later to tie the game at 7. The first quarter ended in a tie game. Florida State responded by scoring the fourteen unanswered points courtesy of a rushing touchdown from James Wilder, Jr. and a receiving touchdown from Devonta Freeman. Looking to go up by more before the half, Jameis Winston made his second mistake of the game with an interception that led to another Miami score, to make the score 21–14 at halftime. The Seminoles went on to dominate the second half, scoring twenty points while holding Miami scoreless. James Wilder, Jr. and Devonta Freeman each scored a touchdown in the third quarter to give Florida State a fourteen point lead heading into the final quarter.

Wake Forest

#3 Florida State traveled to face the **Wake Forest** Demon Deacons. The defense totaled a school record seven turnovers in a rout of Wake Forest, 59-3. Florida State scored on their first possession to take the lead. Following their opening drive, Terrence Smith intercepted Tanner Price's pass and set up Devonta Freeman to score on a one yard touchdown run. Price was then picked off again by Mario Edwards, Jr. to set up another rushing touchdown from Karlos Williams. In the second quarter, the Florida State defense continued their impressive performance when Nate Andrews returned an interception for a touchdown. On the next play, Jalen Ramsey returned a fumble for a touchdown. The offense put together another drive to go up by 42 points before halftime. Another interception would lead to a touchdown at the start of the second half. A field goal extended the lead to 52 going into the final quarter. Wake Forest's only points of the game came courtesy of a field goal in the fourth. Florida State would add a score on special teams with a sixty-two yard punt return.

SYRACUSE

#2 Florida State faced the **Syracuse** Orange at Tallahassee. The Seminoles dominated by defeating Syracuse 59-3. The Seminoles seized control of the game, scoring on the first drive of the game with a six-play drive culminating in a three yard touchdown run from James Wilder, Jr. to put the Seminoles up early. Florida State went on to score on three straight possessions, with touchdown runs from Levonte Whitfield and Devonta Freeman and a touchdown throw from Jameis Winston to Rashad Greene, to put the Seminoles up by twenty-eight going into the second quarter. Florida State scored on their first possession in the second as well courtesy of a Jameis Winston pass to Kelvin Benjamin. The Seminoles extended their lead with a 53 yard field goal from Roberto Aguayo to go into halftime with a 38-0 lead. To open the third quarter, Florida State forced Syracuse to punt. James Wilder, Jr. then ran for a touchdown to put the Seminoles up by forty-five. The Seminoles scored on their next possession with a seventeen yard pass from Sean Maguire to Nick O'Leary. After forcing a fumble, Chris Casher returned the ball thirty-one yards for a touchdown.

IDAHO

For their final home game of the season, #2 Florida State faced the independent **Idaho** Vandals. In the first meeting between the two, Florida State set a school record for points scored with an 80-14 victory over the Vandals. The Seminoles dominated the game from the start, scoring the game's first thirty-five points. Florida State's first score came courtesy of a rushing touchdown from Devonta Freeman. This was followed up by a touchdown run from Kelvin Benjamin. Telvin Smith returned an interception seventy-one yards for another touchdown to put the Noles up by three scores at the end of the first quarter. Florida State built on their lead in the second quarter with a passing touchdown from Jameis Winston to Kenny Shaw and a rushing touchdown from James Wilder, Jr. to give the Seminoles a commanding lead. Idaho got on the board with a ten-play drive that ended with a passing touchdown. In the final seconds of the first half, Florida State scored with a passing touchdown to Kenny Shaw. The Seminoles went into halftime, leading 42-7. Florida State scored on the opening drive of the second half with a pass to Kelvin Benjamin. Karlos Williams rushed for a touchdown on the Seminole's next possession. A 42 yard field goal from Roberto Aguayo extended the lead going into the fourth. In the final quarter, Florida State scored two more touchdowns, a rush from Karlos Williams and a pass from backup Sean Maguire to Ryan Green.

Florida

#2 Florida State traveled to Gainesville for their annual rivalry game with the **Florida** Gators. Florida State defeated their archrival, 37-7, marking the Seminoles' third win in the last four games against the Gators. The Seminoles started off sluggish against the Gators, scoring only three points in the first quarter. The offense was more productive in the second quarter, scoring their first touchdown of the game when Jameis Winston completed a 45-yd pass to Kelvin Benjamin to put them up by ten. Just before the half, Winston completed a 29-yd pass to Kelvin Benjamin for a touchdown to give the Noles a seventeen point lead at halftime. Despite the offensive struggles, the defense held the Gators scoreless in the first half. Early in the third quarter, Florida State capitalized on a Florida fumble, scoring three more points on a 40-yd field goal. Florida State extended their lead when Devonta Freeman rushed 11 yards for a touchdown to give the Seminoles a twenty-seven point advantage. Florida scored their first points of the game in the fourth quarter courtesy of a 5-yd pass from third-string quarterback Skyler Mornhinweg to Hunter Joyer. Florida State responded with a 4-yd pass from Winston to Benjamin. The final score of the game would come from Roberto Aguayo who kicked 28-yd field goal to give the Seminoles a thirty point win over the rival Gators. Because of their victory over Florida, along with their earlier victory over Miami, the Seminoles were awarded the Florida Cup.

2013 ACC CHAMPIONSHIP

The #1 Seminoles won the ACC title, defeating the #20 **Duke** Blue Devils, 45-7, earning a spot to play in the BCS National Championship Game as the only undefeated team left in the country. Florida State was held scoreless in the first quarter for the first time all season. The Seminoles scored the first points of the game with a fourteen yard pass to Kelvin Benjamin to put the Noles up by a touchdown. After being forced to punt on their next possession, Florida State scored with a rushing touchdown from Karlos Williams. A field goal before the half put Florida State up by seventeen. Florida State began to seize control of the game in the second half. An interception turned into points with a pass to Kenny Shaw. The Seminoles scored on their next drive courtesy of a pass to Kelvin Benjamin. Nate Andrews forced a fumble which the Seminoles converted into points when Winston rushed seventeen yards for a touchdown. In the fourth quarter, Devonta Freeman rushed for a touchdown while Duke scored their only points of the game in the final minute with a five yard rushing touchdown.

2014 BCS CHAMPIONSHIP GAME

Florida State scored first on a 35 yard field goal to take an early 3–0 lead. Auburn responded with a touchdown in the first quarter and two in the second to storm out to a 21–3 lead. After a successful punt fake, the Seminoles managed a touchdown late in the second quarter, making it a 21–10 game in Auburn's favor going into halftime. Both teams dominated on defense in the third quarter with the Seminoles hitting a field goal to cut  Auburn's lead to eight. In the fourth quarter, Florida State scored a touchdown early to make it a one point game. Auburn extended its lead to 24–20 on a field goal, but Florida State took the lead 27–24 when Levonte Whitfield took the ensuing kickoff 100 yards for a touchdown. Auburn then retook the lead 31–27 with 1:19 remaining in the game, but Florida State was able to respond, winning the game 34–31 with a Kelvin Benjamin touchdown with 13 seconds left on the clock. Jameis Winston was 20 for 35 for 237 yards and two fourth-quarter touchdown passes. Rashad Greene caught 9 passes for 147 yards. For their performances in the game, quarterback Jameis Winston and defensive back P. J. Williams were named the game's most valuable players.

2014 Florida State Seminoles {ACC Champions}

The Seminoles were led by fifth-year head coach Jimbo Fisher. The Seminoles ended the regular season as the only team from a power conference without a loss but finished the season with a 13–1 record. The Seminoles won the ACC Atlantic Division for the sixth time, advancing to their fifth conference championship game, where they defeated Georgia Tech to win their fifteenth conference title. Florida State was selected to play in the inaugural College Football Playoff, losing to Oregon in the semifinal at the Rose Bowl and snapping the Seminoles' 29 game win streak. Nick O'Leary won the John Mackey Award. **Rashad Greene set a new single season record with 99 receptions. Roberto Aguayo tied a single season record for field goals made with 27.**

Roberto Aguayo (K), Cameron Erving (C), Eddie Goldman {DT}, Tre' Jackson {OG}, Nick O'Leary {TE} and Jalen Ramsey {LB} were selected as first team All-Americans. Winston {Tampa Bay}, Erving {Cleveland}, Mario Edwards Jr. {DE} {Oakland}, Goldman {Chicago}, Ronald Darby {DB} {Buffalo}, P.J. Williams {DB} {New Orleans}, Jackson {New England}, Rashad Greene {WR} {Jacksonville}, Karlos Williams {RB} {Buffalo}, O'Leary {Buffalo} and Bobby Hart {T} {New York Giants} were selected in the 2015 NFL Draft. Jameis Winston {Tampa Bay} was the #1 overall pick and Cameron Erving (Cleveland) was a #1 pick.

ACC CHAMPIONS				FINAL RANK: #10 AP, #8 CP				
Home games were played at Doak Campbell Stadium								
8/30/2014	Florida State	#1	vs		Oklahoma State	ABC	37	31	W
9/6/2014	Florida State	#1	vs		THE CITADEL		37	12	W
9/20/2014	Florida State	#1	vs	#22	CLEMSON	ABC	23	17	W
9/27/2014	Florida State	#1	@		NC State	ABC	56	41	W
10/4/2014	Florida State	#1	vs		WAKE FOREST	ABC	43	3	W
10/11/2014	Florida State	#1	@		Syracuse	ESPN	38	20	W
10/18/2014	Florida State	#2	vs	#5	NOTRE DAME	ABC	31	27	W
10/30/2014	Florida State	#2	@		Louisville	ESPN	42	31	W
11/8/2014	Florida State	#2	vs		VIRGINIA	ESPN	34	20	W
11/15/2014	Florida State	#2	@		Miami	ABC	30	26	W
11/22/2014	Florida State	#1	vs		BOSTON COLLEGE	ABC	20	17	W
11/29/2014	Florida State	#1	vs		FLORIDA	ESPN	24	19	W
12/6/2014	Florida State	#2	vs	#12	Georgia Tech	ABC	37	35	W
1/1/2015	Florida State	#2	vs	#3	Oregon	ESPN	20	59	L
Coach: Jimbo Fisher					Season Record >>		472	358	13-1

Schedule Source: Steve's Football Bible LLC

Selected game(s) highlights

Oklahoma State

Florida State opened the season ranked #1. Two fourth quarter defensive stops and a back-breaking 50 yard touchdown pass from Jameis Winston to Rashad Greene delivered the Seminoles a 37-31 season opening victory over **Oklahoma State** in the AdvoCare Cowboys Classic. Winston pass for 370 yards and one TD pass and ran for a touchdown. Roberto Aguayo kicked three field goals. Greene caught 11 passes for 203 yards and a TD reception. Nate Andrews returned an interception 9 yards for a touchdown.

THE CITADEL

Ranked #1, Florida State hosted **The Citadel**. The Noles raced to a 34-0 lead on the way to a 37-12 victory. Four different Seminoles scored touchdowns and Roberto Aguayo kicked three field goals. Jameis Winston passed for 256 yards and threw two TD passes.

CLEMSON

Quarterback Sean Maguire hung in with an up-and-down effort as Winston's replacement and #1 **Florida State** escaped with a 23-17 overtime victory Saturday night over #22 Clemson. Maguire completed 21 of 39 passes for 305 yards with two interceptions and a 74 yard touchdown to Rashad Greene to tie it at 17 with 6:04 left in the fourth. Clemson's DeShaun Watson was 19-28 for 286 yards.

NC State

Still ranked #1, Florida State traveled to Raleigh to play **NC State**. NC State hung the first 24 point first quarter on the Seminoles in the 769-game history of the program, building a 24-7 lead. Jameis Winston's 4 yard touchdown pass to Rashad Greene with 3:24 remaining in the third quarter – set up when freshmen defensive ends Lorenzo Featherston and Jacob Pugh collaborated on a sack and a fumble recovery – that the Seminoles had their first lead, 42-38. Karlos Williams ran for 126 yards and three touchdowns. Rashad Greene caught 11 passes for 125 yards and a TD reception. Jesus Wilson caught 6 passes for 109 yards and two TD receptions. Jameis Winston passed for 365 yards and four TD passes.

WAKE FOREST

The #1 ranked Seminoles welcomed **Wake Forest** to Doak Campbell Stadium. Roberto Aguayo matched a Florida State single-game school record with five field goals and linebacker Reggie Northrup stripped Demon Deacons tailback Isaiah Robinson of the ball and returned it 31 yards for a touchdown as the Seminoles scored 43 unanswered points in a 43-3 victory. Jameis Winston passed for 297 yards and ran for one touchdown.

Syracuse

The Tribe, ranked #1, traveled to **Syracuse** to play the Orangemen. Senior receiver Rashad Greene notched the 213th catch of his career, surpassing Ron Sellers for the most receptions in school history. Greene finished with a team-high 107 yards on six catches. Dalvin Cook rushed for 122 yards and a touchdown. Mario Pender ran for a TD and caught a pass for a TD. Jameis Winston passed for 317 yards and three TD passes.

NOTRE DAME

Dropping to #2 in the polls, Florida State returned home for a showdown with #5 **Notre Dame**. The Seminoles survived in a thriller vs the Fighting Irish. The Irish apparently threw a go ahead touchdown pass with 13 seconds left but were flagged for offensive pass interference. Jacob Pugh interception on the next play sealed the 31-27 victory. Karlos Williams scored on two short touchdown runs. Rashad Greene 8 passes for 108 yards and a TD reception. Jameis Winston passed for 273 yards and two TD passes.

Louisville

Ranked #2, Florida State traveled to **Louisville** to play the Cardinals. The Seminoles fell behind 21-0 in the first half, but a furious 4th quarter rally helped the Noles to a comeback 42-31 victory. Dalvin Cook rushed for 110 yards on 9 carries and two touchdowns. Jameis Winston passed for 401 yards and three TD passes but threw 3 interceptions.

VIRGINIA

The #2 Seminoles returned home to play **Virginia**. Florida State overcame three turnovers and another early deficit before rallying to a 21 point second quarter and a 34-20 victory over Virginia. Karlos Williams ran for two touchdowns. Rashad Greene caught 13 passes for 136 yards and a TD reception. Jameis Winston passed for 261 yards and one TD pass. Winston added a 4 yard touchdown run.

Miami

For the first 30 minutes of action, things couldn't get much worse for the Seminoles. It started when freshman quarterback Brad Kaaya hit Phillip Dorsett for the first touchdown of the game, followed not long after by a score on the ground from Duke Johnson. Florida State trailed by 16 before a true freshman from Miami got them on the board as Dalvin Cook ran one in from 44 yards out. Miami would add another touchdown pass and the Seminoles were treading water as they trailed 23-10 at the half. As was the story for most of 2014, FSU football turned things on in the second half, starting with a tipped pass from Jameis Winston, who had another 300 yard game, that fell into the arms of Karlos Williams, who took it in for a score. The Seminoles would get two more field goals from Roberto Aguayo in the fourth quarter and trail by three when Cook rumbled in for the 26 yard touchdown and the lead. It was the defense's turn to step up when Jalen Ramsey intercepted a Kaaya pass with less than a minute to go.

BOSTON COLLEGE

Back to #1 in the polls, Florida State hosted **Boston College**. Roberto Aguayo's 26 yards field goal with 3 seconds left in the game, vaulted the Seminoles to a 20-17 victory over the Eagles. Dalvin Cook rushed for 76 yards and Rashad Greene caught 8 passes for 106 yards. Jameis Winston passed for 281 yards and one TD pass. His one interception was the only turnover in the game.

FLORIDA

Jameis Winston threw two touchdowns passes in the second quarter after linebacker Terrence Smith returned an interception 94 yards for a momentum changing touchdown, as the Seminoles wiped out an early nine point deficit and went on to defeat the Gators 24-19 in their annual rivalry at Doak Campbell Stadium. The Seminoles overcame a career-worst four interceptions by Winston, but from those four picks, three of which placed the Gators in Seminoles' territory, Florida managed just six points. The Florida defense was terrific in holding the potent Florida State offense to just 306 total yards, with 176 of those coming on the Seminoles lone touchdown drives, both in the second quarter. Offensively, though, the Gators managed only 282 yards and turned to placekicker Austin Hardin to finish drives with field goals of 52, 39, 43 and 32 yards on his first four attempts.

2014 ACC CHAMPIONSHIP

The Seminoles fell to #2 in the polls as they went ot Charlotte to play #12 **Georgia Tech** in the ACC Championship game. The Seminoles survived another wild affair in a season that's been full of them, beating the Ramblin' Wreck 37-35. Florida State is 13-0 for a second straight season and riding a school-record 29-game winning streak. Rashad Greene caught 7 passes for 123 yards and two TD receptions. Dalvin Cook rushed for 177 yards and a touchdown. Roberto Aguayo kicked three field goals and Jameis Winston passed for 309 yards and threw three TD passes.

2015 ROSE BOWL {CFP SEMIFINAL}

In the inaugural College Football Playoffs, #3 **Oregon** was matched against #2 Florida State in the 101st Rose Bowl game in Pasadena, CA. After a close first half with Oregon leading 18-13, the Ducks outscored the Seminoles 41-7 in the 2nd half for a 59-20 blowout victory and advancing to the CFP Championship game. Heisman Trophy winner, Marcus Mariotta, threw two TD passes to Darren Carrington and ran for another TD to spur the 2nd half scoring surge. Dalvin Cook rushed for 103 yards. Travis Rudolph caught 6 passes for 96 yards and a TD reception. Jameis Winston passed for 348 yards and a TD pass.

2015 Florida State Seminoles

The Seminoles were led by sixth-year head coach Jimbo Fisher. It was the Seminoles' 24th season as a member of the ACC and its 11th in the ACC Atlantic Division. Florida State came into the season after a two-year run (2013 and 2014) in which the Seminoles won 27 games with a pair of ACC Championships, a BCS National Title, an appearance in the College Football Playoff, a Heisman Trophy winner, and eighteen NFL Draft selections. They finished the season 10–3, 6–2 in ACC play, to finish in second place in the Atlantic Division. They were invited to the Peach Bowl where they lost to Houston. Florida State seniors – Giorgio Newberry, Derrick Mitchell, Nile Lawrence-Stample, Reggie Northrup, Terrance Smith, Tyler Hunter, Javien Elliott, Keelin Smith, Lamarcus Brutus and Cason Beatty – ended their college careers with 49 wins over the course of four seasons, becoming the winningest class in school history.

Roberto Aguayo {K}, Dalvin Cook {RB}, Roderick Johnson {OL} and Jalen Ramsey {DB} were selected to the Atlantic Coast Conference All-Conference 1st Team. Aguayo, Cook and Ramsey were selected at First team All-Americans. Ramsey was a Consensus All-American. Rmsey {Jacksonville} and Aguayo {Tampa Bay} were selected in the 2016 NFL draft. Ramsey was a #1 pick.

FINAL RANK: #14 AP, #14 CP

Home games were played at Doak Campbell Stadium

9/5/2015	Florida State	#10	vs		*TEXAS STATE*			59	16	W
9/12/2015	Florida State	#11	vs		*SOUTH FLORIDA*	ESPN		34	14	W
9/18/2015	Florida State	#9	@		**Boston College**	ESPN		14	0	W
10/3/2015	Florida State	#11	@		**Wake Forest**	ESPN		24	16	W
10/10/2015	Florida State	#12	vs		**MIAMI**	ABC		29	24	W
10/17/2015	Florida State	#11	vs		**LOUISVILLE**	ESPN		41	21	W
10/24/2015	Florida State	#9	@		**Georgia Tech**	espn2		16	22	L
10/31/2015	Florida State	#17	vs		**SYRACUSE**	ABC		45	21	W
11/7/2015	Florida State	#17	@	#3	**Clemson**	ABC		13	23	L
11/14/2015	Florida State	#19	vs		**NC STATE**	ACC		34	17	W
11/21/2015	Florida State	#16	vs		*TENNESSEE-CHATT.*			52	13	W
11/28/2015	Florida State	#14	@	#10	*Florida*	ESPN		27	2	W
12/31/2015	**Florida State**	#9	vs	#14	**Houston**	**ESPN**		24	38	L
Coach: Jimbo Fisher					**Season Record >>**			412	227	10-3

Schedule Source: Steve's Football Bible LLC

Selected game(s) highlights

TEXAS STATE

Everett Golson matched a career high with four touchdown passes and had the seventh 300 yard game of his career to help the #10 Seminoles beat Texas State 59-16. Jesus Wilson caught a 14 yard touchdown pass early in the fourth quarter to make it 42-10. Golson also threw a touchdown pass to Ryan Izzo before wrapping up his night with a 55 yarder to Ja'Vonn Harrison. Sean Maguire came in midway through the fourth quarter and directed two scoring drives, including a 24 yard touchdown pass to Johnathan Vickers. Dalvin Cook ran for 156 yards and two touchdowns, Mario Pender added 92 yards on 14 carries.

SOUTH FLORIDA

Dalvin Cook rushed for 266 yards on 30 carries with three touchdowns in the 11th ranked Seminoles 34-14 victory. Cook carried the Seminoles in the first half. The passing game had only six yards as it was tied 7-all at halftime. Cook's 74 yard touchdown in the first quarter started the scoring. Cook's 24 yard touchdown on the opening possession of the second half put the Seminoles ahead for good as they scored on all five second-half drives. Everett Golson finished 14 of 26 for 163 yards and a touchdown.

Boston College

Cornerback Jalen Ramsey returned a fourth-quarter fumble 36 yards for a touchdown, and #9 Florida State's defense shut down the Eagles in a 14-0 victory. Everett Golson completed 15 of 24 passes for 119 yards and a touchdown. Florida State had just 217 yards to 195 yards for Boston College.

Wake Forest

The Seminoles 24-16 victory over the Demon Deacons on Saturday wasn't secure until Tyler Hunter's diving interception in the end zone with 21 seconds to play. Dalvin Cook ran 94 yards for a touchdown before leaving with an injury. Johnathan Vickers added a 9 yard touchdown run, and Everett Golson was 20 of 31 for 202 yards with a 5 yard TD to Kermit Whitfield.

MIAMI

Dalvin Cook ran for 222 yards and three touchdowns, the last a 23 yarder around the right end with 6:44 remaining, to help #12 Florida State outlast Miami 29-24. Miami took a 24-23 lead on Brad Kaaya's 29 yard touchdown pass to Stacy Coley with 10:02 left. Everett Golson completed 25 of 33 passes for 291 yards and a touchdown. Cook opened the scoring on his first carry with a 72 yard run. After Michael Badgley's 30 yard field goal put Miami on the board, Cook extended the Seminoles' lead to 14-3 when he took Golston's screen pass 36 yards for a score.

LOUISVILLE

Behind 372 yards passing and three touchdowns from Everett Golson along with Dalvin Cook's fourth 100 yard game of the season, the 11th ranked Seminoles broke it open in the third quarter on the way to a 41-21 win over the Cardinals at Doak Campbell Stadium. Cook had a season-high four receptions for 60 yards. Cook had two touchdowns, including a 54 yard score.

Georgia Tech {Block Six}

Lance Austin scooped up the ball at his own 22 and took off the other way. He didn't stop running until he reached the end zone, his 78 yard return of a blocked field goal on the final play giving Georgia Tech a stunning 22-16 upset of the #9 Seminoles. It all started when Roberto Aguayo attempted a 56 yard field goal to win it for the Seminoles with 6 seconds remaining. But Patrick Gamble managed to get a hand on the ball.

SYRACUSE

The 17th ranked Seminoles had one of their best offensive displays of the season despite missing their top two playmakers. Sean Maguire passed for 348 yards and three touchdowns while Jacques Patrick added three scores on 162 yards rushing in FSU's 45-21 win over Syracuse. Maguire completed 23 of 35 passes. Travis Rudolph caught all 3 touchdown passes from Maguire.

Clemson

Trailing by three midway through the fourth quarter, the Seminoles went for a 1st down on 4th and 1. Clemson stopped Dalvin Cook short and shortly after, Wayne Gallman ran for a 25 yard touchdown that sealed #1 Clemson's 23-13 victory over 16th ranked FSU. Cook silenced the crowd with a 75 yard touchdown run on the game's second play. Cook finished with 194 yard on 21 carries. Roberto Aguayo kicked two field goals for the other Seminole points.

NC STATE

Dalvin Cook ran for two touchdowns and Sean Maguire threw for two more as FSU erased an early deficit and pulled away for a 34-17 victory over NC State on homecoming at Doak Campbell Stadium. After the Wolfpack turned three Everett Golson turnovers into a 17-7 lead, Fisher turned to Maguire to take the reins. The FSU offense heated up, striking for 20 points (two touchdowns, two field goals) in its next four drives. Cook started the rally with 30 yard touchdown run, then Roberto Aguayo made a 40 yard field goal to tie the game, 17-17, at halftime. Aguayo then reclaimed the lead with a 26 yard kick early in the third quarter, and Maguire put the Wolfpack away with back-to-back touchdown passes to Kermit Whitfield.

TENNESSEE-CHATTANOOGA

Dalvin Cook ran for two touchdowns, Sean Maguire threw for two more and FSU's senior class tied a school record for total wins (48) in a career after a 52-13, Senior Day romp over Chattanooga. Cook reached the end zone twice, on runs of 13 and two yards, and finished with 106 yards on 15 carries. Sean Maguire and Kermit Whitfield, meanwhile, hooked up for two touchdowns, one for 26 yards and one for 13 yards.

Florida

Dalvin Cook ran for 183 yards and two touchdowns, Roberto Aguayo kicked two long field goals and the #13 Seminoles upended 12th ranked Florida 27-2. Florida avoided its first shutout in the Swamp since 1988 when FSU quarterback Sean Maguire recovered a fumble in the end zone for a safety with 8:58 remaining. Cook scored on a 15 yard run with 6:17 to play -- sending many of the record crowd (90,916) to the exits -- and added a 29 yarder with 20 seconds left. Maguire completed 14 of 28 passes for 160 yards.

2015 CHICK-FIL-A BOWL

Greg Ward Jr. ran for two touchdowns and threw for another, leading Houston past turnover plagued Florida State 38-24 in the Peach Bowl. Florida State's Sean Maguire, who was carted off the field with a sprained left ankle in the first quarter, returned but threw four interceptions. Dalvin Cook was held to 33 yards rushing with a touchdown and a lost fumble. The #9 Seminoles, who trailed 21-3 at halftime, tried to rally with two fourth-quarter touchdown passes by Maguire. Ward threw for 238 yards and ran for 67 yards for #14 Houston who finished with 13 wins on the season. Maguire's 65 yard scoring pass to Travis Rudolph cut Houston's lead to 24-17 early in the fourth quarter. Maguire's last interception came with 25 seconds remaining. He completed 22 of 44 passes for 392 yards with two touchdowns and four interceptions.

2016 Florida State Seminoles

The Seminoles were led by seventh-year head coach Jimbo Fisher. Prior to the start of the 2016 season, Dalvin Cook, Derwin James, Roderick Johnson and DeMarcus Walker were named pre-season All-Americans. In the pre-season media poll, Florida State was picked to finish second in the ACC Atlantic and Dalvin Cook was picked as runner-up for ACC Player of the Year while Cook, Roderick Johnson, Travis Rudolph, DeMarcus Walker, and Derwin James were named to the pre-season All-ACC team. Florida State finished the regular season with nine wins and was picked to play in the Orange Bowl, a fifth straight appearance in a major bowl game, where they defeated Michigan to finish with double digit wins for the fifth straight season and secure a top ten finish in the polls. During the season, the Seminoles notched their seventh consecutive win over Miami and their fourth consecutive win over Florida, making this senior class the first to go unbeaten against their rivals. **Dalvin Cook set a new team record with 1,765 yards rushing in a season.**

Dalvin Cook {RB}, Roderick Johnson {OL}, Tarvarus McFadden {DB}, Derrick Nnadi {DT} and DeMarcus Walker {DE} were named to the Atlantic Coast Conference All-Conference 1st Team. Roderick Johnson was awarded the Jacobs Blocking Trophy. DeMarcus Walker was named the ACC Defensive Player of the Year. Defensive end DeMarcus Walker and running back Dalvin Cook were named consensus All-Americans. Cook {Minnesota}, Walker {Denver}, Johnson {Cleveland} and Marquez White {CB} {Dallas} were selected in the 2017 NFL draft.

FINAL RANK: #8 AP, #8 CP
Home games were played at Doak Campbell Stadium

Date	Team	Rank		Opp Rank	Opponent	Network			Result
9/5/2016	Florida State	#4	vs	#11	*Mississippi*	ESPN	45	34	W
9/10/2016	Florida State	#3	vs		*CHARLESTON SOUTHERN*		52	8	W
9/17/2016	Florida State	#2	@	#10	**Louisville**	ABC	20	63	L
9/24/2016	Florida State	#13	@		*South Florida*	ABC	55	35	W
10/1/2016	Florida State	#12	vs		**NORTH CAROLINA**	ESPN	35	37	L
10/8/2016	Florida State	#23	@	#10	**Miami**	ABC	20	19	W
10/15/2016	Florida State	#14	vs		**WAKE FOREST**	ESPN	17	6	W
10/29/2016	Florida State	#12	vs	#3	**CLEMSON**	ABC	34	37	L
11/5/2016	Florida State	#19	@		**NC State**	ESPNU	24	20	W
11/11/2016	Florida State	#20	vs		**BOSTON COLLEGE**	espn2	45	7	W
11/19/2016	Florida State	#17	@		**Syracuse**	ABC	45	14	W
11/26/2016	Florida State	#15	vs	#13	*FLORIDA*	ABC	31	13	W
12/30/2016	**Florida State**	#10	vs	#6	**Michigan**	**ESPN**	33	32	W
Coach: Jimbo Fisher					**Season Record >>**		456	325	10-3

Schedule Source: Steve's Football Bible LLC

Selected game(s) highlights

Mississippi

The rebels' quarterback Chad Kelly drove the Rebel offense to an early score on the first drive of the game, when Kelly found receiver Damorea'ea Stringfellow in the end zone from 3 yards out, taking only 1:46 off the clock. Deondre Francois led the Seminoles to the red zone, but the Seminoles settled for a 25-yd field goal as time expired in the first quarter. Ole Miss started off the second quarter when Kelly found D. K. Metcalf for his second touchdown pass of the game from three yards out with 12:42 remaining in the half to take a 14–3 lead. Ole Miss got the ball back and extended their lead to 21–3 when Kelly found Evan Engram from 21 yards out with 9:42 remaining in the half. On the ensuing FSU drive, the Seminoles reached the red zone and Francois found Dalvin Cook but Cook dropped the ball out of bounds short of the goal line and the Seminoles settled for a field goal from 21 yards out, cutting the lead to 21–6. Ole Miss scored again when Akeem Judd found the end zone from 11 yards out to increase the Rebel lead to 28–6 with a little more than 3:00 remaining in the first half. Francois gave the Seminoles momentum when he found Travis Rudolph from 16 yards out as time expired at the half, giving the Rebels a 28–13 lead at halftime. Florida State dominated the third quarter, beginning with a Ricky Aguayo field goal from 40 yards out. Following an interception thrown by Kelly, the Seminoles scored their first touchdown of the half with a Freddie Stevenson run from one yard out to cut the deficit to 28–23. On the next Rebel possession, Kelly fumbled the ball and it was recovered by Florida State, and they scored another touchdown on the following drive. Following a failed two point conversion attempt, the Seminoles had a 29–28 lead with 9:17 left in the third quarter. Following another fumble recovery by the Seminoles, FSU scored again when Deondre Francois passed to Ryan Izzo from two yards out, giving the Seminoles a 36–28 lead with 4:12 left in the third quarter. The following Ole Miss drive stalled; Florida State got the ball to begin the fourth quarter. The Seminoles were forced to settle for a field goal, which Aguayo made from 40 yards out, giving FSU a 39–28 lead. Kelly led the Rebels to their first touchdown since the first half, when he found Van Jefferson from 20 yards out. Following a failed two point conversion, Florida State led 39–34. Ole Miss got the ball back following two FSU field goals from Aguayo from 44 and 30 yards out. Kelly and the Rebel had one final opportunity to possibly win the game, but the game was sealed by an interception thrown by Kelly with roughly two and a half minutes left in the game, in what was the biggest comeback win in FSU football history. **Ricky Aguayo set a single game record for field goals made with 6.**

Louisville

Lamar Jackson ran for four touchdowns and threw for another as #10 Louisville poured it on for a 63-20 victory on Saturday, the most points ever allowed by Florida State. Jackson ran for 146 yards and four TDs and passed for 216 yards and a score to lead the Cardinals. Louisville's defense chipped in with five sacks. The Cardinals also held FSU to 284 yards and forced two turnovers. The Seminoles' only bright spot was 10 straight points to get within 14-10 before Jackson took over.

South Florida

Dalvin Cook rushed for a career-high 267 yards and two touchdowns Saturday, helping the 13th ranked Seminoles to a 55-35 rout of previously unbeaten USF. Cook scored on a 75 yard run on the Seminoles' first play from scrimmage after Quinton Flowers and Rodney Adams teaming on an 84 yard catch-and-run for a quick 7-0 lead. Deondre Francois threw for 169 yards, one touchdown and no interceptions. He added a 35 yard TD run midway through the fourth quarter. Freddie Stevenson caught two touchdown passes for the Seminoles.

NORTH CAROLINA

Nick Weiler kicked a career-best 54 yard field goal as time to expired to give North Carolina a 37-35 win and snap the Seminoles' 22-game home winning streak. Florida State took a late one point lead with the difference being a blocked extra point. But the Tar Heels were able to drive 38 yards in three plays to set up Weiler's game winner. Florida State (3-2, 0-2) trailed 21-0 in the second quarter but rallied to take a 35-34 lead in the final minute on an 8 yard touchdown run by Deondre Francois who was 20 of 32 for 372 yards. Dalvin Cook accounted for 256 yards of total offense -- 140 yards rushing and 106 receiving -- and three touchdowns. He is the first Florida State back to have a 100 yard rushing and receiving game.

Miami {Block at the Rock}

Miami entered the game unbeaten and ranked 10th in the country. Florida State, meanwhile, was coming off a crushing loss to North Carolina that ended its nation-leading 22-game home winning streak. The Hurricanes led 13-0 in the first half, but Florida State cut the lead with a 31 yard field goal just before halftime. Miami junior quarterback Brad Kaaya threw an interception in the end zone and lost a molar on a helmet-to-helmet hit in the third quarter as the Seminoles mounted a comeback. Florida State scored on three consecutive possessions, including a pair of touchdown catches from junior running back Dalvin Cook and senior wide receiver Kermit Whitfield in the third quarter, to take a 20-13 lead. The Hurricanes were in position to tie the game after Kaaya connected with senior wide receiver Stacy Coley on an 11 yard touchdown pass with 1:38 remaining, but FSU senior defensive end DeMarcus Walker pushed through the line and blocked Miami kicker Michael Badgley's point-after attempt. The game-sealing play was affectionately coined by fans as the "Block at the Rock." Walker went on to become the Atlantic Coast Conference defensive player of the year, and his 15 sacks tied for the national lead. FSU's 20-19 win was its seventh in a row against the Hurricanes.

WAKE FOREST

Florida State held the Demon Deacons out of the end zone and Travis Rudolph had the fourth highest receiving total in school history as the # 14 Seminoles downed Wake Forest, 17-6, in front of a homecoming crowd at Doak Campbell Stadium. Rudolph caught 13 passes for 238 yards. The Seminoles sacked John Wolford five times and got interceptions from Marquez White and Tarvarus McFadden. Deondre Francois ran for a touchdown and threw an 11 yard TD pass to Auden Tate.

CLEMSON

#4 Clemson traveled to Tallahassee, Florida to face #12 **Florida State**. Clemson pulled off yet another close win, pulling ahead late to win 37–34. It was their first win on the road against FSU in 10 years. Deshaun Watson responded with a 34 yard touchdown pass to Jordan Leggett, and the Tigers converted the two point attempt to secure a 37–34 lead with 2:06 remaining. Watson finished with 430 total yards of offense in the game.

NC State

With FSU trailing or tied for the first 56 plus minutes, quarterback Deondre Francois needed just five plays to march the offense 83 yards for a late touchdown that gave the Seminoles their only lead of the game. Francois' 19 yard touchdown pass to Travis Rudolph proved to be the difference in the Seminoles' 24-20 victory. The Seminoles rallied from deficits of 10-3 and 20-10, using a pair of touchdowns, one on a Dalvin Cook 10 yard run and Rudolph's touchdown, in the second half to complete their comeback.

BOSTON COLLEGE

The 18th ranked Seminoles grabbed the early lead and cruised to a 45-7 victory. The Seminoles took control by scoring on their first two drives and led 14-0 at the end of the first quarter. Dalvin Cook and Deondre Francois paced the offense. Cook rushed for 108 yards on 18 carries with a touchdown and Francois tied a season high with three touchdown passes. Auden Tate caught two touchdown passes and Sean Maguire threw two touchdown passes in the 2nd half, one to Tate and one to Freddie Stevenson.

Syracuse

Dalvin Cook ran for 227 yards and four touchdowns, three in the third quarter, as the #17 Seminoles raced past Syracuse for a 45-14 victory at the Carrier Dome. Deondre Francois threw for 315 yards and touchdowns on each of FSU's first two drives. The Defense sacked Syracuse quarterback Zack Mahoney seven times and Tarvarus McFadden had an interception, his 8th of the season.

FLORIDA

Dalvin Cook rushed for 153 yards and a touchdown, while quarterback Deondre Francois passed for a score and ran for another, which was enough for the #15 Seminoles to beat the 13th ranked Gators, 31-13, in their annual rivalry game at Doak Campbell Stadium. The Gators failed to score an offensive touchdown against the Seminoles for the second straight year. Florida finished with just 207 yards of total offense, with more than a quarter of those yards coming in the final 60 seconds after Francois dashed for an 8 yard touchdown run with exactly one minute remaining.

2016 ORANGE BOWL

The 11th ranked Florida State football team capped off a dramatic midseason turnaround with a 33-32 win over #6 Michigan in the Capital One Orange Bowl. Dalvin Cook ran for 145 yards and a touchdown on his way to Orange Bowl MVP honors, opened the scoring with a two yard run as the

Seminoles raced to a 17-3 lead after one quarter. The Wolverines chipped away at their deficit with three field goals – all of them within the red zone, then finally broke through for a touchdown when Mike McCray picked off Francois at the FSU 14 yard line and returned it for a touchdown. Michigan's two point conversion failed, and FSU led 20-15 after three quarters. Facing a third and 22 from their FSU's 13 yard line, Cook broke loose for a 71 yard run down the left sideline before stepping out at the 16 yard line. Four plays later, Francois ran into the end zone for a touchdown that put FSU up 27-15 with 11:38 to go in the game. A 30 yard scoring run by Michigan's Chris Evans gave the Wolverine a 30-27 lead. Deondre Francis threw a 12 yard TD pass to Nyqwan Murray with 36 seconds left to give the Seminoles a 33-30 lead. Murray caught a 92 yard TD pass from Francois in the 1st quarter. The Wolverines blocked the extra point and ran it back for two points to make the final score 33-32.

2017 Florida State Seminoles

The Seminoles were led by eighth-year head coach Jimbo Fisher until he left to coach at Texas A&M before the final game of the regular season. They were then coached by interim head coach Odell Haggins. In the pre-season media poll, Florida State was picked to finish first in the ACC Atlantic and win the conference title. In the opening game against Alabama, quarterback Deondre Francois suffered a season ending knee injury which resulted in true freshman James Blackman being named the starter for the remainder of the season, leading to the program's worst start since 1976 although the Seminoles went on to become bowl eligible for the 36th consecutive year. Following the game against Florida, Jimbo Fisher resigned as coach; associate coach Odell Haggins was named interim head coach for the remainder of the season.

Derwin James {S} was named to the Atlantic Coast Conference All-Conference 1st Team and was selected as a First team All-American by The Football Writers Association. James {Los Angeles Chargers}, Derrick Nnadi {DT} {Kansas City}, Rick Leonard {OT} {New Orleans}, Josh Sweat {DE} {Philadelphia}, Ryan Izzo {TE} {New England} and Auden Tate {WR} {Cincinnati} were selected in the 2018 NFL draft. James was a #1 pick.

Home games were played at Doak Campbell Stadium

9/2/2017	Florida State	**#3**	**vs**	#1	*Alabama*	ABC	7	24	L
9/23/2017	Florida State	**#12**	**vs**		**NC STATE**	ABC	21	27	L
9/30/2017	Florida State		**@**		**Wake Forest**	ABC	26	19	W
10/7/2017	Florida State		**vs**	#13	**MIAMI**	ESPN	20	24	L
10/14/2017	Florida State		**@**		**Duke**	espn2	17	10	W
10/21/2017	Florida State		**vs**		**LOUISVILLE**	ESPN	28	31	L
10/27/2017	Florida State		**@**		**Boston College**	ESPN	3	35	L
11/4/2017	Florida State		**vs**		**SYRACUSE**	ACC	27	24	W
11/11/2017	Florida State		**@**	#4	**Clemson**	ESPN	14	31	L
11/18/2017	Florida State		**vs**		*DELAWARE STATE*		77	6	W
11/25/2017	Florida State		**@**		*Florida*	ESPN	38	22	W
12/2/2017	Florida State		**vs**		*LOUISIANA-MONROE*		42	10	W
12/27/2017	**Florida State**		**vs**		**Southern Mississippi**	**ESPN**	**42**	**13**	**W**
Coach: Jimbo Fisher					**Season Record >>**		750	881	7-6

Schedule Source: Steve's Football Bible LLC

Selected game(s) highlights

Alabama

The first half was characterized largely as a defensive struggle for both teams. After a turnover on downs stop by the Alabama defense on fourth and 2, the offense would march down the field for a 36 yard Andy Pappanastos field goal (ALA 3 FSU 0) late in the first quarter. FSU would respond with a drive of their own culminating in a 3 yard pass to Auden Tate (ALA 3 FSU 7) which was matched by a 53 yard bomb from Alabama's Jalen Hurts to Calvin Ridley for a touchdown on Alabama's next drive (ALA 10 FSU 3). Both teams would hold the other's offense to minimal production for the rest of the half including a blocked FG attempt by FSU from Alabama's Minkah Fitzpatrick. Florida State would open the second half with a promising drive that stalled at midfield after an Alabama sack. After a few possession exchanges, Alabama would find itself in prime position to score after a punt attempt by Florida State was blocked and recovered by Alabama deep in FSU territory. This would culminate in an Andy Pappanastos FG for 25 yards (ALA 13 FSU 7). On the ensuing kick return, Alabama's Dylan Moses would force a fumble recovered by Alabama, and on the first play of Alabama's drive, Damien Harris would score on a rushing touchdown from 11 yards out. Alabama would come away with a successful two point conversion attempt after the touchdown to go up by two touchdowns (ALA 21 FSU 7). For the rest of the game, the Alabama defense would dominate FSU including picking off two passes by Deondre Francois. Alabama would kick one more field goal late in the game from 33 yards out (ALA 24 FSU 7) to seal the Alabama victory. The Alabama defense held the Seminoles to 40 yards rushing.

NC STATE

Ryan Finley threw for 230 yards and two touchdowns as North Carolina State got its first road win over a ranked team since 2008, defeating #12 Florida State 27-21. Jaylen Samuels had two touchdowns as the Wolfpack broke a 10-game losing streak to ranked teams. Finley completed 22 of 32 passes, had a 71 yard touchdown pass late in the second quarter to give the Wolfpack a 17-7 lead. James Blackman was 22 of 38 for 278 yards in his first start for the Seminoles. Auden Tate had nine receptions for 138 yards, including a 4 yard touchdown early in the second quarter that drew the Seminoles within 10-7. Ricky Aguayo made four field goals for FSU.

Wake Forest

James Blackman connected with Auden Tate on a 40 yard touchdown throw with 53 seconds left, helping Florida State rally past Wake Forest 26-19. Jacques Patrick ran for 120 yards and a score for FSU. Ricky Aguayo kicked four field goals for the Seminoles.

MIAMI

Miami entered the October 7 match-up in Tallahassee undefeated at 3–0; FSU entered 1–2, with a loss to future National Champions Alabama, a close loss at NC State, and a win against Wake Forest. The Canes, who hadn't beaten FSU since 2009, entered halftime trailing by three. Behind heroics from senior wide receiver Braxton Berrios, who finished with eight receptions for 90 yards and two touchdowns, the Canes led the Seminoles 17–13 with only 5:09 remaining. FSU, led by true freshman backup quarterback, James Blackman, drove into Miami territory and scored what seemed to be the game-winner via a 20 yard touchdown reception from junior wide receiver Auden Tate with 1:24 remaining. Miami quarterback Malik Rosier, though, methodically drove the Canes downfield and lobbed a 23 yard touchdown to senior wide receiver Darrell Langham, who made a back-shoulder catch and lunged past the pylon with 6 seconds remaining. The scoring play, following a five-minute review, stood. This game would end Miami's seven-year run of futility vs. FSU and against Coach Jimbo Fisher.

Duke

Cam Akers ran 42 yards for the go ahead touchdown with 8:23 to play, and Florida State held on to beat Duke 17-10. Akers finished with 115 yards while James Blackman threw a 20 yard touchdown pass to Auden Tate on the opening drive for the Seminoles. Blackman finished 18 of 21 for 197 yards passing with two interceptions. Ricky Aguayo kicked a 23 yard field goal to give FSU a 10-3 lead in the 3rd quarter.

LOUISVILLE

Blanton Creque kicked a 34 yard field goal with five seconds left that lifted the Cardinals to a 31-28 victory over FSU at Doak Campbell Stadium. The Cardinals took over on their own 24 with 2:05 remaining after Henry Famurewa recovered a James Blackman fumble. They then drove 59 yards in eight plays before Creque's kick. Lamar Jackson had 334 yards of total offense and accounted for two touchdowns. Florida State trailed 28-14 going into the fourth quarter before rallying on a pair of Nyqwan Murray touchdowns. James Blackman was 16 of 28 for 248 yards with two touchdowns but he also had all three FSU turnovers (two interceptions, one fumble).

Boston College

Boston College struck first with a reverse-pass from receiver Jeff Smith to Kobay White, and the Eagles never looked back on the way to a 35-3 victory over the Seminoles at Alumni Stadium. Nyqwan Murray caught three passes for 102 yards to lead FSU. Ricky Aguayo kicked a 36 yard field goal for the Seminoles points.

SYRACUSE

Cam Akers ran for touchdowns of 63 and 54 yards, and Nyqwan Murray caught a 51 yard touchdown pass from James Blackman as the Seminoles held on for a 27-24 victory over Syracuse at Doak Campbell Stadium. Syracuse drove to Florida State's 25 yard line with six seconds to play, but Cole Murphy's 43 yard kick sailed wide left as time expired. Akers carried 22 times for a career-high 199 yards. Ricky Aguayo kicked two field goals for the Seminoles.

Clemson

Travis Etienne ran for 97 yards and two touchdowns to lead the fourth ranked Tigers to a 31-14 victory over Florida State. Following Van Smith's key fourth -quarter interception, Etienne had a 25 yard run to the FSU 5. Two plays later, he burst through for a 1 yard score that made it 24-14 with 3:05 left. Trailing 17-0 in the 3rd quarter, the Seminoles rallied on Jacques Patrick's 3 yard TD run and a double-pitch back, flea-flicker pass from James Blackman that went for a 60 yard score to Ryan Izzo. Cornerback Trayvon Mullen knocked away Blackman's fourth-down pass with 2:13 left to end the Seminoles' comeback hopes.

DELAWARE STATE

The Seminoles used all three phases to score their first three touchdowns on the way to a 77-6 win over the Hornets in front of a Homecoming crowd of 70,599 at Doak Campbell Stadium. Jacques Patrick ran for a touchdown; Tarvarus McFadden returned a block kick for a score and Derwin James grabbed the first "pick-six" of his career as the Seminoles raced out to a school record-tying 56 points in the first half. FSU fell just three points short of the single game scoring mark of 80 set against Idaho in 2013. Ryan Green ran for two touchdowns and 96 yards. James Blackman passed for 179 yards and threw 3 TD passes.

Florida

It was a one-score game heading into the fourth quarter, but the visiting Florida State Seminoles took control with a pair of touchdowns in the final period for a 38-22 win over Florida. Florida outgained FSU 280-216 but the Seminoles capitalized on the Gators' mistakes, scoring 28 points off four Florida turnovers. Florida State's defense opened the scoring in the first quarter when defensive lineman Brian Burns got free in the Florida backfield and forced a fumble from quarterback Feleipe Franks. Seminoles linebacker Jacob Pugh recovered the ball and returned it 16 yards for a touchdown. Levonta Taylor's second interception of the day resulted in another touchdown for Florida State after he returned it 18 yards for a 24-7 lead with 3:46 to go before halftime.

LOUISIANA-MONROE

Jacques Patrick and Cam Akers each ran for two touchdowns, Ryan Green added another and FSU's defense limited ULM's high-powered offense to just 300 yards in a 42-10 victory in front of 58,750 fans at Doak Campbell Stadium. Patrick ran for 155 yards while Akers ran for 117 yards.

2017 INDEPENDENCE BOWL

Cam Akers broke FSU all-time leading rusher Dalvin Cook's school record for rushing yards by a freshman while James Blackman threw four touchdowns to earn Independence Bowl offensive MVP honors following FSU's 42-13 win over Southern Miss. Blackman completed 18 of 26 passes for 233 yards with three of his four touchdown passes thrown in the first half. Nate Andrews earned defensive MVP honors after the game. He had six tackles and one pass deflection. Auden Tate caught three TD passes from Blackman while Akers caught a TD pass from Blackman.

2018 Florida State Seminoles

The Seminoles were led by first-year head coach Willie Taggart. The Seminoles finished the season with a losing record for the first time since 1976, missing a bowl game for the first time since 1981. Taggart is the 10th full-time head coach in program history and just its third head coach since 1976, when the legendary Bobby Bowden first took over in Tallahassee.

Brian Burns {LB} was selected to the Atlantic Coast Conference All-Conference 1st Team. Burns {Carolina} and Demarcus Christmas {DT} {Seattle} were selected in the 2019 NFL draft. Burns was a #1 pick.

Home games were played at Doak Campbell Stadium

Date	Team				Opponent	Network			
9/3/2018	Florida State	#19	vs	#20	**VIRGINIA TECH**	ESPN	3	24	L
9/8/2018	Florida State		vs		*SAMFORD*	ACC	36	26	W
9/15/2018	Florida State		@		Syracuse	ESPN	7	30	L
9/22/2018	Florida State		vs		*NORTHERN ILLINOIS*	ESPNU	37	19	W
9/29/2018	Florida State		@		Louisville	espn2	28	24	W
10/6/2018	Florida State		@	#17	Miami	ABC	27	28	L
10/20/2018	Florida State		vs		**WAKE FOREST**	espn2	38	17	W
10/27/2018	Florida State		vs	#2	**CLEMSON**	ABC	10	59	L
11/3/2018	Florida State		@		**NC State**	ABC	28	47	L
11/10/2018	Florida State		@	#3	*Notre Dame*	NBC	13	42	L
11/17/2018	Florida State		vs	#22	**BOSTON COLLEGE**	espn2	22	21	W
11/24/2018	Florida State		vs		*FLORIDA*	ABC	14	41	L
Coach: Willie Taggart					**Season Record >>**		**263**	**378**	**5-7**

Schedule Source: Steve's Football Bible LLC

Selected game(s) highlights

VIRGINIA TECH

Josh Jackson threw two touchdown passes, one early and another late, and the 20th ranked Hokies handled #19 Florida State 24-3 in the rain to spoil Taggart's debut in Tallahassee. Florida State finished with five turnovers, a blocked punt that was returned for a touchdown and a missed field goal. Jackson completed 16 of 26 passes for 207 yards.

SAMFORD

Deondre Francois threw for 320 yards and three touchdowns, including the game winning score to Tre' McKitty with 4:03 to go, as Florida State held off Samford 36-26. Trailing 26-21, Francois led the Seminoles on an 11-play, 82 yard drive that put them ahead. Francois connected with McKitty for the 5 yard touchdown, and he then found Nyqwan Murray for the two-point conversion pass as Florida State went ahead 29-26. Samford's Devlin Hodges threw for 475 yards and a pair of touchdown passes to Kelvin McKnight but tossed four interceptions. Levonta Taylor returned the last one 63 yards for a touchdown with 2:23 to go.

Syracuse

Quarterback Tommy DeVito scored on a 3 yard run and hit tight end Ravian Pierce with a 3 yard score in a span of just over 3 minutes in the third quarter, and Syracuse beat Florida State 30-7 in the sweltering heat of the Carrier Dome. Syracuse recorded four sacks, deflected a couple of passes, and constantly harassed quarterback Deondre Francois, who finished 18 of 36 for 178 yards passing with one interception while leading an offense that gained just 240 yards. Florida State prevented the shutout on a 2 yard run by Francois with 6:16 to play.

NORTHERN ILLINOIS

Deondre Francois threw for a season-high 352 yards and two touchdown passes as Florida State used an efficient first-half offense on the way to a 37-19 win over Northern Illinois. Francois had his seventh career 300 yard day, completing 23 of 31 passes. Francois had a 78 yard touchdown pass to Tamorrion Terry and an 8 yard TD pass to Jacques Patrick. Ricky Aguayo connected on three field goal, from 50 yards and twice from 42 yards.

Louisville

Louisville was up by three with the ball at the Seminoles 21 and the clock running under 2:00, decided to pass the ball instead of run, and A.J. Westbrook stepped in front to get the interception the Seminoles desperately needed. Five plays later, Deondre Francois connected with Nyqwan Murray on a 58 yard touchdown pass with 1:13 left to give the Seminoles a 28-24 come-from-behind victory. Francois completed 16-of-27 passes for 294 yards and a career-best four touchdowns. Murray caught six for 114 yards and two scores.

Miami {Wide Left II}

Florida State came into the game as 14 point underdogs against Miami. After two TD passes to tight end receiver Keith Gavin and wide receiver Tammorrion Terry, with two field-goal kicks from the foot of Ricky Aguayo, the Seminoles finished the first half leading 20–7 over the Hurricanes. Florida State extended the lead in the 2nd half as wide receiver D.J. Matthews executed a 74 yard punt return for a touchdown, putting the Noles in front 27–7 over the Canes. Miami's defense then caused two turnovers followed up with two touchdown passes by freshman quarterback N'Kosi Perry to cut the score to 27–21. With 11:52 left in the 4th Quarter, Perry threw a pass to receiver Brevin Jordan for a touchdown, taking a 28–27 lead over FSU, erasing a 20 point deficit and claiming victory after a wide left field goal attempt by Aguayo. This game would mark Miami's first win at home against Florida State since 2004

WAKE FOREST

Cam Akers had two touchdown runs, including a 58 yarder, and Deondre Francois threw for a season-high 353 yards as Florida State bounced back from an early 10-0 deficit and scored 38 straight points in a 38-17 win over Wake Forest. Francois completed 29 of 40 passes and had two touchdown passes, including a 33 yard scoring toss to Nyqwan Murray. Murray caught eight passes for 131 yards, both of which are season highs.

CLEMSON

Both offenses were held scoreless in the first quarter. Early in the second quarter, Trevor Lawrence opened the scoring for the Tigers with a seven yard touchdown pass to Tee Higgins. The next Clemson drive ended the same way, with a three yard touchdown pass from Lawrence to Higgins. Later in the quarter, Clemson lined up on the goal-line in a "Fridge Package" with defensive linemen Christian Wilkins and Dexter Lawrence in the backfield. Wilkins received the handoff and scored his first career rushing touchdown. Clemson scored another touchdown via a two yard run by tight end Garrett Williams to bring the score to 28–0 before the half. In Clemson's first drive of the second half, Trevor Lawrence connected with Amari Rodgers for a 58 yard touchdown pass. The two connected again later in the quarter for a 68 yard score, after which it was 45–0 Clemson. Florida State kicker Ricky Aguayo completed a 35 yard field goal in the third quarter to break up the shutout. In the fourth quarter, Clemson running back Adam Choice scored on a 15 yard run. Florida State's final points came via a 73 yard pass from quarterback James Blackman to Keyshawn Helton with 4:43 left to go in the game. The final score of 59–10 was Florida State's worst home loss in program history.

NC State

NC State raced to a 17-0 lead and the Seminoles tried to play catch-up the rest of the game as the Wolfpack went on to a 47-28 victory. James Blackman threw for 421 yards and four touchdown passes. Tammorion Terry caught 5 passes for 142 yards and two touchdown passes, one from 35 yards and one from 10 yards out. The Seminoles never got closer than 10 points after they scored their first touchdown.

Notre Dame

Brandon Wimbush's three-touchdown performance led the Fighting Irish to a 42-13 victory over Florida State on Senior Night in frosty Notre Dame Stadium. Wimbush finished 12 of 25 for 130 yards with the scoring passes to fellow seniors -- a 3 yarder to wide receiver Miles Boykin and 6- and 15 yard tosses to tight end Alize Mack. Dexter Williams ran for a career-high 202 yards and Notre Dame's defense came up with two first-quarter turnovers by the Seminoles, which led to a 17-0 1st quarter lead. Cam Akers had two touchdown runs for Florida State, his second on a 7 yard run following Stanford Samuels' interception early in the third quarter.

BOSTON COLLEGE

Deondre Francois threw a 74 yard touchdown pass to Tamorrion Terry with 1:49 left and the Seminoles beat #22 Boston College 22-21 to keep their bowl hopes alive. Francois was 19 of 39 for 322 yards, shaking off two first-half interceptions for his fourth 300 yard game of the season. Cam Akers had 19 carries for 110 yards for the Seminoles. Florida State got the ball back with 2:45 left and needed to drive 87 yards to score a touchdown. Anthony Brown completed 18 of 33 passes for 297 yards, a touchdown and two interceptions for BC.

FLORIDA

Feleipe Franks threw three touchdown passes and #13 Florida used a punishing ground attack to end a five-game losing streak to Florida State, defeating the Seminoles 41-14. Lamical Perine had a 74 yard touchdown run as Florida rushed for 278 yards. Perine ran for 129 yards. Florida racked up 536 yards on offense. Franks completed 16 of 26 passes for 254 yards. He threw touchdown passes to Van Jefferson, Trevon Grimes and Josh Hammond. Grimes led the Gators with five receptions for 118 yards.

2019 Florida State Seminoles

Florida State was initially led by second-year head coach Willie Taggart. On November 3, 2019, Taggart was fired after losing to Miami (FL) and falling to 4–5 on the season and 9–12 overall. Defensive line coach Odell Haggins was named interim head coach for the remainder of the season, for the second time during his tenure with the program. The Seminoles ultimately finished the season with a 6–7 record, completing consecutive losing seasons for the first time since the 1975 and 1976 seasons. This was the first season since 1976 that Florida State was not ranked in either of the major polls.

Marvin Wilson {DT} was selected to the Atlantic Coast Conference All-Conference 1st Team. Cam Akers {RB} {Los Angeles Rams} was selected in the 2020 NFL Draft.

Home games were played at Doak Campbell Stadium

8/31/2019	Florida State	vs		*Boise State*	ESPN	31	36	L
9/7/2019	Florida State	vs		*LOUSIAIANA-MONROE*	ACC	45	44	W
9/14/2019	Florida State	@	#25	**Virginia**	ACC	24	31	L
9/21/2019	Florida State	vs		**LOUISVILLE**	ESPN	35	24	W
9/28/2019	Florida State	vs		**NC STATE**	ACC	31	13	W
10/12/2019	Florida State	@	#2	**Clemson**	ABC	14	45	L
10/19/2019	Florida State	@		**Wake Forest**	ACC	20	22	L
10/26/2019	Florida State	vs		**SYRACUSE**	espn2	35	17	W
11/2/2019	Florida State	vs		**MIAMI**	ABC	10	27	L
11/9/2019	Florida State	@		**Boston College**	ACC	38	31	W
11/16/2019	Florida State	vs		*ALABAMA STATE*	ACC	49	12	W
11/30/2019	Florida State	@	#8	*Florida*	SEC	17	40	L
12/31/2019	**Florida State**	**vs**		**Arizona State**	**CBS**	**14**	**20**	**L**
Coach: Willie Taggart				**Season Record >>**		363	362	6-7

Schedule Source: Steve's Football Bible LLC

Selected game(s) highlights

Boise State

Hank Bachmeier tossed a third quarter TD pass and Robert Mahone had a 1 yard touchdown run in the fourth and Boise State rallied from an 18 point deficit to knock off Florida State 36-31. Florida State squandered a 31-13 lead and lost its season opener for the third straight time. Bachmeier was pounded early by Florida State's defensive front for five sacks and eight hurries. But he threw for 407 yards as Boise State defeated a Power 5 team for the sixth time since the 2014 season. James Blackman had three touchdown passes in the first half as Florida State took a 24-6 lead with 10:53 left. Blackman finished completing 23 of 33 passes for 327 yards but the Seminoles were held scoreless after halftime. His third touchdown pass, a 58 yard toss to Keyshawn Helton, put the Seminoles up 31-13 with 4:07 left in the second quarter.

LOUISIANA-MONROE

Cam Akers had a record 36 carries, the final one a 4 yard touchdown, as Florida State defeated Louisiana Monroe 45-44 in overtime. Caleb Evans had a 5 yard touchdown run just moments later and the Warhawks went for the one-point conversion that would force a second overtime period, but Jacob Meeks missed the kick. Akers ran for a career high 193 yards and scored two rushing touchdowns. He also had a 44 yard TD reception for Florida State. James Blackman completed 30 of 40 passes for 282 yards, three touchdowns and two interceptions for the Seminoles. He connected with nine receivers, throwing touchdowns to D.J. Matthews, Tre'Shaun Harrison, and Akers.

Virginia

The Cavaliers stopped Cam Akers on a final play run from the 4 yard line and barely hung on for a 31-24. Akers took a direct snap and was met by a host of Cavalier defenders. UVA's Wayne Taulapapa ran for three touchdowns, the last with 2:34 remaining, to cap a rally that seemed doomed after the Cavaliers were poised to tie it with 6:02 remaining until Brian Delaney was wide right on his extra point try, keeping the Seminoles ahead, 24-23. FSU went three and out, then Bryce Perkins led Virginia down the field. It took them just six plays to travel 72 yards when Taulapapa scored his third touchdown to give UVA the lead.

LOUISVILLE

Cam Akers scored three touchdowns and Alex Hornibrook came off the bench and threw a 60 yard touchdown pass in the fourth quarter as Florida State defeated Louisville 35-24. Akers ran 29 times for 112 yards for Florida State, which had a season-high 522 offensive yards. His final score, a 1 yard touchdown run with 1:37 to go, secured a win for the Seminoles. The Seminoles raced to a 21-0 first quarter lead, only to let the Cardinals storm back to take a 24-21 lead in the 4th quarter. Hornibrook put the Seminoles ahead for good, 28-24, on a touchdown pass to Tamorrion Terry with 7:25 left in the game. Hornibrook completed 15 of 20 passes for 255 yards and two touchdowns.

NC STATE

Alex Hornibrook threw for a career-high 316 yards, tossing three touchdown passes in the Seminoles' 31-13 win over North Carolina State. Hornibrook was often pressured and was sacked eight times. But he completed 29 of 40 passes and had two touchdown passes to Tamorrion Terry and another to Ontaria Wilson. NC State had more sacks (eight) than points (six) through three quarters. Defensive tackle Darrell Murchison had 3.5 sacks in three quarters. But the Wolfpack weren't very effective on offense. They fumbled twice, turned it over on downs twice and punted six times. Cam Akers had 17 carries for 83 yards but nearly half of them came on a 41 yard touchdown run in the fourth quarter.

Clemson

Trevor Lawrence threw three touchdown passes, two to Justyn Ross, as Clemson pounded Florida State 45-14 to extend its program record with its 21st straight victory. Travis Etienne ran for 127 yards and caught Lawrence's other TD. The Tigers' defense collected four turnovers and limited the Seminoles to season lows with 253 yards and 103 rushing yards. Lawrence completed 17 of 25 passes for 170 yards, including 10 and 8 yard TD throws to Ross. Lawrence also ran for a touchdown. The Seminoles broke the shutout with Blackman's 64 yard TD pass to Tamorrion Terry late in the third quarter.

Wake Forest

Nick Sciba kicked a 25 yard field goal, his school-record tying fifth of the game, with 4:18 remaining to give Wake Forest the lead. Ricky Aguayo attempted a go ahead, 50 yard field goal with 2:17 to play, but the kick missed wide left, and the Demon Deacons held on for a 22-20 victory. After the Seminoles forced a stop and got the ball back with 35 seconds left, Blackman fumbled the final two snaps. Cade Carney had a 3 yard touchdown run on the second play of the fourth quarter, Sam Hartman was 21 of 38 for 308 yards in his first start of the season and Sage Surratt had seven catches for 170 yards for Wake. James Blackman put the Seminoles up 20-19 with his 36 yard touchdown pass to Tamorrion Terry with 11:22 to play. Cam Akers rushed for 157 yards and scored two touchdowns, rushing 2 yards for a score, then catching pass from Blackman 19 yards for another TD for the Seminoles. Blackman finished 27 of 43 for 280 yards with the two scores.

SYRACUSE

Cam Akers ran for 144 yards and tied a school record with four touchdown runs as Florida State routed Syracuse 35-17 on homecoming. Akers also took some snaps out of the wildcat formation and completed two passes for 26 yards. Akers' 26 total points, which included a 2-point conversion run, was the second highest in school history. Alex Hornibrook completed 15 of 26 passes for 196 yards for the Seminoles, who led 35-3 going into the third quarter.

MIAMI

Florida State cut a 14-point deficit to seven early in the third quarter but could get no closer. Miami's Jarren Williams then made the result official with a 56 yard touchdown pass midway through the fourth quarter that helped the Hurricanes to a 27-10 victory in front of 63,995 fans at Doak Campbell Stadium. Paced by first half passing plays of 42, 39 and 34 yards, the Hurricanes built a 17-3 lead at halftime. The Seminoles answered with a six play, 62 yard drive that ended in an 18 yard touchdown pass from Alex Hornibrook to Cam Akers. Hornibrook was sacked eight times, and the Hurricanes finished the contest with nine sacks and 16 tackles for loss. The Seminoles were outgained 353-203.

Boston College

D.J. Matthews' 60 yard touchdown catch from James Blackman gave the Seminoles a late lead, then a 66 yard scoring run from Jordan Travis put the finishing touches on a 38-31 win over Boston College. Trailing 14-3 late in the second quarter, the Seminoles used a big-play offense and a bend-but-don't-break defense to upset the Eagles. Florida State rolled up a season-high 524 yards of offense. Tamorrion Terry set new career highs for catches (seven) and receiving yards (156), and his 74 yard scoring strike late in the second quarter helped turn things in Florida State's favor. James Blackman completed 18-of-26 passes for 346 yards and two touchdowns.

ALABAMA STATE

James Blackman threw for three touchdowns, Khalan Laborn ran for two more and Hamsah Nasirildeen chipped in with an 80 yard interception return for a score as the Seminoles rolled to a 49-12 victory. Deonte Sheffield scored the first touchdown of his career to provide the final margin with 18 seconds to play. Blackman passed for 246 yards.

Florida

Quarterback Kyle Trask passed for 343 yards and three touchdowns, and the Florida defense sacked FSU quarterbacks eight times, three by senior linebacker Jonathan Greenard, during Saturday's 40-17 rout of the Seminoles at Spurrier/Florida Field. The Gators scored 23 unanswered points spanning the first and second quarters to take a 30-7 halftime lead and roll to the win. Trask completed 30 of his 41 passes and did not turn the ball over. Freddie Swain and Van Jefferson each caught two touchdown passes for the Gators.

2019 SUN BOWL

Florida State closed out their 2019 season with a 20-14 loss to Arizona State in the Tony the Tiger Sun Bowl. Tamorrion Terry caught a 91 yard touchdown pass, Ontaria Wilson ran for a three yard score, and the Seminoles outgained the Sun Devils by nearly 200 yards, 470-282. Florida State was undone by six turnovers that Arizona State converted into 14 points, including a game winning interception return for a touchdown by ASU's Willie Harts midway through the fourth quarter. It was the Sun Devils' only touchdown of the game. The Seminoles trailed 9-0 at halftime but rallied in the 3rd quarter to take a 14-9 lead, only to be undone by tunrovers. Arizona State kicker Christian Sendejas tied a Sun Bowl record for the most field goals in a game with four.

2020 Florida State Seminoles

The Seminoles were led by head coach Mike Norvell, in his first season. The Seminoles finished the season with a losing record (3-6) for the third consecutive season for the first time since the 1974–1976 seasons and their worst record since 1975. Florida State had games scheduled against Boise State, Florida, Samford, and West Virginia, which were all canceled due to the COVID-19 pandemic, which resulted in the ACC playing a ten-game conference schedule with one non-conference opponent and reduced stadium capacity. Florida State ended up playing nine games as the result of further cancelations. This was the first season since 1957 that the Seminoles did not play Florida.

Asante Samuel {DB} was selected to the Atlantic Coast Conference All-Conference 1st Team.

Home games were played at Doak Campbell Stadium

9/12/2020	Florida State		vs		**GEORGIA TECH**	ABC	13	16	**L**
9/26/2020	Florida State		@	#12	**Miami**	ABC	10	52	**L**
10/3/2020	Florida State		vs		*JACKSONVILLE STATE*		41	24	**W**
10/10/2020	Florida State		@	#5	**Notre Dame**	NBC	26	42	**L**
10/17/2020	Florida State		vs	#5	**NORTH CAROLINA**	ESPN	31	28	**W**
10/24/2020	Florida State		@		**Louisville**	ACC	16	48	**L**
11/7/2020	Florida State		vs		**PITTSBURGH**	ACC	17	41	**L**
11/14/2020	Florida State		@		**NC State**	ACC	22	38	**L**
12/12/2020	Florida State		vs		**DUKE**	ACC	56	35	**W**
Coach: Mike Norvell					**Season Record >>**		**232**	**324**	**3-6**

Schedule Source: Steve's Football Bible LLC

Selected game(s) highlights

GEORGIA TECH

Georgia Tech outscored Florida State by a 16-3 margin in the second half and earned a hard fought 16-13 win over the Seminoles in the season opener for both teams at Doak Campbell Stadium. Despite three blocked kicks by the Seminoles' special teams unit, the debut of first year head coach Mike Norvell was spoiled by the Yellow Jackets' come from behind effort. Georgia Tech outgained Florida State 438-307 in total yards including a 175-123 margin the second half. The Yellow Jackets scored the final nine points of the game. James Blackman was 23 of 43 passing for 198 yards and one touchdown. Marvin Wilson blocked both field goal attempts and Asante Samuel had two interceptions for the Seminoles. Keyshawn Helton caught a 3 yard TD pass from Blackman for the lone Seminole touchdown.

Miami

Florida State lost for only the second time in nine games at Hard Rock Stadium as #12 Miami gained a 52-10 victory over the Seminoles. James Blackman completed 16-of-26 passes for 120 yards with one touchdown and one interception. Camren McDonald caught a 12 yard TD pass from Blackman for the lone Seminoles touchdown.

JACKSONVILLE STATE

Jordan Travis directed five consecutive touchdown drives in the second and third quarters to lead Florida State to a come-from-behind 41-24 victory over Jacksonville State at Doak Campbell Stadium. The Seminoles outscored the Gamecocks by 24 points in the second half after trailing by a 21-14 margin at halftime. Travis completed 12 of 17 passes for a career high 210 yards and one touchdown. Lawrance Toafili had 12 rushes for 99 yards and one touchdown while Ontaria Wilson caught a career high seven passes for 86 yards. Five different Seminoles scored at least one touchdown in the victory - Keyshawn

Helton (one receiving touchdown), Travis (one rushing), La Damian Webb (two rushing), Toafili (one rushing) and Jashaun Corbin (one rushing).

Notre Dame

Jordan Travis threw for 204 yards and ran for a career high 96 yards in the first start of his career, but #5 Notre Dame outscored Florida State by a 42-26 margin. Florida State scored three touchdowns by three different players, scored on three touchdowns on four trips into the red zone and committed only one turnover. Tamorrion Terry caught a season-high nine passes for a season-high 146 yards and a TD reception.

NORTH CAROLINA

The Seminoles took a 31-7 halftime lead and earned a hard fought 31-28 win over #5 North Carolina. Jordan Travis completed eight passes for 191 yards and one touchdown and ran 16 times for a career high 107 yards and two touchdowns. Running back La'Damian Webb rushed 12 times for a career best 109 yards. The defense stopped North Carolina on downs on its final drive of the game to secure the victory. Travis scored on a 23 yard keeper on their first play from scrimmage after blocking a Tar Heel punt. Florida State extended its lead to 10-0 on a 24 yard field goal by Ryan Fitzgerald. Florida State moved to a 17-0 on a 1 yard rushing touchdown by Travis. Joshua Kaindoh intercepted a Sam Howell pass and returned it for a touchdown and a 24-0 Seminole lead. Camren McDonald caught a 12 yard TD pass from Jordan Travis to make it 31-7 Seminoles and FSU had to withstand a Tar Heel rally for the victory.

Louisville

Louisville scored on its first five possessions of the game and held Florida State under 26 points scored for the first time in four games as the Cardinals took a 48-16 win over the Seminoles at Cardinal Stadium. Florida State limited Louisville to just 17 second half points but was unable to recover from a 31-14 halftime deficit. Jordan Travis threw for 118 yards and one touchdown. Florida State scored a touchdown on its first drive on a Jordan Travis 15 yard run. Travis threw a 4 yard TD pass to Ontaria Wilson to cut the lead to 28-14, but that was as close as the Seminoles would get.

PITTSBURGH

Florida State showed flashes of brilliance early in taking a 14-3 first quarter lead, but Pitt outscored the Seminoles by a 38-3 margin over the final three quarters and took a 41-17 win at Doak Campbell Stadium. Jordan Travis scored a rushing touchdown and completed 11-of-18 passes for 106 yards and totaled 83 yards on 14 rushes before leaving with an injury. Camren McDonald caught seven passes for 61 yards to lead nine different Seminoles caught at least one pass. Pitt's defense was credited with seven sacks, five quarterback hurries and three interceptions as they pressured the Seminoles quarterbacks all game long.

NC State

Chubba Purdy threw for 181 yards and two touchdowns in his first career start and wide receiver Ontaria Wilson caught a career high seven passes for 117 yards and a 69 yard TD pass from Purdy, but Florida State fell to NC State, 38-22, at Carter Finley Stadium. Jashaun Corbin scored on a 28 yard run and Warren Thompson caught a 24 yard TD pass from Corbin to wrap up the Seminoles scoring.

DUKE

Putting up 324 yards on the ground, Florida State Football got back to its winning ways as it ran past Duke, 56-35, in its final home game of the season at Doak Campbell Stadium. The Seminoles delivered 524 yards of total offense, as quarterback Jordan Travis led the way with 192 yards passing along with two TDs while adding 90 yards on the ground and another rushing score. Lawrance Toafili led FSU's ball carriers with 117 yards rushing, which was highlighted by a 73 yard touchdown run in the second half. Six of FSU's eight touchdowns scored came on the ground, with running back Jashaun Corbin running for three scores along with 72 rushing yards. Treshaun Ward added another rushing TD.

2021 Florida State Seminoles

The Seminoles were led by head coach Mike Norvell, in his second season. The Seminoles finished the season with a losing record (5-7) for the fourth consecutive season. The Seminoles outscored their opponents by 331 to 318. The Seminoles missed going to a Bowl Game for the 3rd time in 4 seasons.

Jermaine Johnson II and Jammie Robinson were selected to the All-ACC first team. Johnson was a #1 pick of the New York Jets in the 2022 NFL Draft.

Home games were played at Doak Campbell Stadium

9/5/2021	Florida State		**vs**	#9	*NOTRE DAME*	ABC	38	41	L
9/11/2021	Florida State		**vs**		*JACKSONVILLE STATE*	ACC	17	20	L
9/18/2021	Florida State		@		**Wake Forest**	ABC	14	35	L
9/25/2021	Florida State		**vs**		**LOUISVILLE**	espn2	23	31	L
10/2/2021	Florida State		**vs**		**SYRACUSE**	ACC	33	30	W
10/9/2021	Florida State		@		**North Carolina**	ESPN	35	25	W
10/23/2021	Florida State		**vs**		*MASSACHUSETTS*	ACC	59	3	W
10/30/2021	Florida State		@		**Clemson**	ESPN	20	30	L
11/6/2021	Florida State		**vs**	#22	**NC STATE**	ACC	14	28	L
11/13/2021	Florida State		**vs**		**MIAMI**	ESPN	31	28	W
11/20/2021	Florida State		@		**Boston College**	ACC	26	23	W
11/27/2021	Florida State		@		*Florida*	ESPN	21	24	L
Coach: Mike Norvell					**Season Record >>**		331	318	5-7

Schedule Source: Steve's Football Bible LLC

Selected game(s) highlights

NOTRE DAME

Notre Dame survived Florida State backup quarterback McKenzie Milton's unlikely comeback on an emotional night when the Seminoles honored Bobby Bowden. Jonathan Doerer made a 41-yard field goal in overtime and No. 9 Notre Dame escaped with a 41-38 victory after Florida State overcame an 18-point deficit. Ryan Fitzgerald's 37-yard attempt sailed wide left on the first overtime possession, allowing Notre Dame to run a few plays and set up Doerer's kick. Milton fired a 22-yard strike to Ja'Khi Douglas on his first pass. Treshaun Ward completed that drive by scoring on a 2-yard run, and Fitzgerald tied it with a 43-yard field goal with 40 seconds left. Florida State started the comeback with Jordan Travis connecting with Andrew Parchment on an 8-yard touchdown strike. Milton entered the game when Travis' helmet popped off, and he then found Douglas to keep things going. Jack Coan completed 26 of 35 passes for 366 yards and four touchdowns in his Notre Dame debut. Coan threw touchdown passes to Michael Mayer, Kyren Williams, Kevin Austin and Joe Wilkins. Notre Dame led 38-20 with 4:37 to go in the third quarter. Travis threw two touchdown passes and ran for another score. But he also threw three interceptions — two to Notre Dame star safety Kyle Hamilton. The Fighting Irish capitalized all three times by scoring touchdowns. Jashaun Corbin had an 89-yard touchdown run for Florida State. Corbin finished with 15 carries for 144 yards, pacing the Seminoles' 264 yards on the ground.

SYRACUSE

Ryan Fitzgerald made a 34-yard field-goal as time expired to lift Florida State to its first win of the season, 33-30 over Syracuse. Jordan Travis had runs of 33 and 25 on a drive in the final minute to set up Fitzgerald's kick. Travis had 19 rushes for 113 yards for the Seminoles. Travis completed 22 of 32 passes for 131 yards, including touchdown passes to Camren McDonald and Keyshawn Helton. Florida State's defense bent but held Syracuse to just 2 of 12 on third-down conversions. The Orange were also 0 for 3 on fourth-down conversions, including linebacker Kalen DeLoach's goal-line stop in the third quarter.

North Carolina

Jordan Travis threw three touchdown passes and rushed for two more scores as Florida State upset North Carolina for the second year in row, winning 35-25. Travis ran for 121 yards on 14 carries and completed 11 of 13 passes for 145 yards. Two of his touchdown throws went to Ontaria Wilson and another to Malik McClain. Sam Howell hit Kamari Morales in the end zone on a 21-yard play on North Carolina's first possession of the second half to close within 21-17. Florida State responded with Travis' 1-yard sneak. The Seminoles scored again on Travis' 6-yard toss to Wilson. Travis ran 53 yards for a second-quarter touchdown as the Seminoles took a 14-10 lead. He had 87 yards on the ground in the first half. Travis threw 32 yards to Wilson for a touchdown on Florida State's next possession to stretch the lead with 53 seconds left in the half.

MIAMI

Jordan Travis completed a fourth-and-14 pass to Andrew Parchment and two plays later ran it in from 1 yard out with 26 seconds to go as Florida State defeated Miami 31-28. Trailing 28-23 and taking over at the Seminoles' 20-yard line, Travis dropped back and connected with Ja'Khi Douglas on a 59-yard catch-and-run. After two incompletions and a false start, Travis connected with Parchment on the 24-yard reception to the goal line. Travis completed 18 of 26 passes for a career-high 274 yards and he ran 22 times for 62 yards and two touchdowns for Florida State. Tyler Van Dyke threw four touchdown passes as Miami rallied from a 17-point deficit. After a shaky first half, Van Dyke regrouped and completed touchdown passes to Key'Shawn Smith, Mike Harley, Will Mallory and Jaylan Knighton for the Hurricanes. Jermaine Johnson forced a fumble that set up Florida State with a short field, setting up Jashaun Corbin's 12-yard touchdown run that put the Seminoles up 14-0. Johnson, a defensive end, had three sacks — giving him 11 on the season.

BOSTON COLLEGE

Jordan Travis threw for three touchdowns and 251 yards and Florida State stopped the Eagles in its own territory in the final two minutes for a 26-23 victory. Travis completed 20-of-34 passes with no interceptions, connecting with three different receivers for scores. The Seminoles led 19-3 at halftime and scored on the initial drive of the second half when Malik McClain made a leaping grab of Travis' pass in the back of the end zone. BC then scored two TDs — failing on a two-point conversion on the first — in just over 3 ½ minutes early in the fourth, slicing it to 26-23 on Phil Jurkovec's 36-yard TD pass to Zay Flowers. BC converted a fourth-and-2 from their 43 with just over 4 ½ minutes left, but Akeem Dent picked off Jurokvec's desperation pass as the QB was falling to the ground under pressure at the Seminoles' 25 on a fourth-and-9 with 1:42 left.

Florida

Anthony Richardson came off the bench and led the Gators to a 24-21 victory over rival Florida State. Richardson replaced turnover-prone Emory Jones early in the third quarter and completed 5 of 7 passes for 55 yards, including a 5-yard touchdown to Justin Shorter. Dameon Pierce took over from there, going untouched for a 2-yard score after running around and through the Seminoles. The Seminoles scored to make it close in the final minutes, but they badly botched an onside kick. Parker Grothaus essentially whiffed trying to hit the top of the ball, barely brushing it and knocking it off the tee. Florida took over and ran out the clock for their third straight victory in the series.

2022 Florida State Seminoles

The Seminoles were led by head coach Mike Norvell, in his third season. The Seminoles finished the regular season with a 9-3 record and were invited to the Cheez-It Bowl to play Oklahoma from the Big XII conference. The Seminoles knocked off the Sooners, 35-32 for their first win vs Oklahoma since 1965.

Dillan Gibbons, Jared Verse, and Jammie Robinson were selected to the first team All-Conference ACC team.

FINAL RANK: #11 AP, #10 CP

Home games were played at Doak Campbell Stadium

8/27/2022	Florida State		vs		*DUQUESNE*	ACC	47	7	**W**
9/4/2022	Florida State		vs		*Lsu {@ New Orleans}*	ABC	24	23	**W**
9/16/2022	Florida State		@		**Louisville**	ESPN	35	31	**W**
9/24/2022	Florida State		vs		**BOSTON COLLEGE**	ACC	44	14	**W**
10/1/2022	Florida State	**#23**	vs	#21	**WAKE FOREST**	ABC	21	31	**L**
10/8/2022	Florida State		@	#14	**NC State**	ACC	17	19	**L**
10/15/2022	Florida State		vs	#4	**CLEMSON**	ABC	28	34	**L**
10/29/2022	Florida State		vs		**GEORGIA TECH**	ACC	41	16	**W**
11/5/2022	Florida State		@		**Miami**	ABC	45	3	**W**
11/12/2022	Florida State	**#25**	@		**Syracuse**	ACC	38	3	**W**
11/19/2022	Florida State	**#20**	vs		*LOUISIANA*	ACC	49	17	**W**
11/26/2022	Florida State	**#16**	vs		*FLORIDA*	ABC	45	38	**W**
12/29/2022	**Florida State**		vs		**Oklahoma**	ESPN	**35**	**32**	**W**
Coach: Mike Norvell					**Season Record >>**		**469**	**268**	**10-3**

Schedule Source: Steve's Football Bible LLC

Selected game(s) highlights

LSU

Shyheim Brown's deflection of Damian Ramos' kick sent the ball into the crossbar and gave Florida State a 24-23 victory over LSU. LSU's improbable comeback bid came despite a slew of mistakes, including a muffed punt with 2:15 left. Florida State's Treshaun Ward fumbled at the LSU 1 with 1:20 to go, and Tigers quarterback Jayden Daniels drove LSU for a touchdown on a 2-yard pass to Jaray Jenkins with no time left. With LSU fans celebrating an apparent two-touchdown comeback in the final 4:07 - and Florida State fans bracing for what could have gone down as an infamous implosion - Brown's block sent the Seminoles streaming triumphantly onto the field. Jordan Travis' scoring passes came on a 39-yard throw to Ontaria Wilson on a flea flicker and a 27-yard pass that Wilson corralled with one hand. Noah Cain scored LSU's first TD from a yard out on fourth down late in the third quarter to make it 17-10. Travis marched the Seminoles right back to the end zone, highlighted by a 15-yard completion to Johnny Wilson as the elusive QB jumped away from closing defenders. DJ Lundy finished the drive with a 1-yard TD run to make it 24-10 with 9:04 to go.

Louisville

The Seminoles didn't need a blocked extra point with no time left to win as they did two weeks ago against LSU. Instead, they relied on their backup quarterback Tote Rodemaker to lead the way in a 35-31 come-from-behind victory over Louisville. The sophomore came in after Jordan Travis suffered a lower left leg injury with a little more than four minutes left in the second quarter and Florida State down 21-14. All Rodemaker did was lead the Seminoles to three, 75-yard second-half scoring drives. The last came with 7:54 left with a sensational 2-yard catch in the end zone by Johnny Wilson that put the Seminoles up for good. Florida State gained 260 of its 455 yards with Rodemaker taking the snaps. Treshaun Ward added 126 yards rushing on 10 carries for the Seminoles. Wilson finished with seven catches for 149 yards and both touchdowns from Rodemaker. Hindering the Cardinals' effort were three turnovers, including a second-quarter fumble by Malik Cunningham on a botched handoff at the Seminoles 12 early in the second quarter. Louisville, which held four leads in the game, also committed 11 penalties for 81 yards. The Cardinals had a chance to win the game after Ryan Fitzgerald missed a 36-yard field goal with 1:44 left, but Kevin Knowles II picked off a Cunningham pass at the Florida State 38 with 37 seconds left.

CLEMSON

DJ Uiagalelei threw for 203 yards and three touchdowns and No. 4 Clemson forced a momentum-turning takeaway to hold off Florida State 34-28 on Saturday night. Clemson scored on six straight drives and surpassed the 30-point mark for a seventh straight game to open the season. Will Shipley had 20 carries for 121 yards and six catches for 48 yards to help the Tigers to their seventh straight victory over the Seminoles. Florida State kept up with Clemson for the first 20 minutes, but defensive end Myles Murphy's sack of Jordan Travis forced a fumble, and the Tigers were set up with a short field. Three plays later, Uiagalelei's 5-yard TD run put Clemson up 24-14. Uiagalelei then had a 31-yard TD pass to Davis Allen, and B.T. Potter added a 34-yard field-goal attempt to give Clemson what appeared to be a commanding 34-14 lead with 7:32 left in the third quarter. But Travis led Florida State on a pair of touchdown drives in the fourth quarter, the second a 94-yard march that culminated in a 25-yard TD pass to Kentron Poitier with 2:17 left and cut Clemson's lead to 34-28. But the Tigers recovered the onside kick and were able to put the game away.

Miami

Jordan Travis threw three touchdown passes, Trey Benson ran for 128 yards and two scores and Florida State became bowl-eligible with a 45-3 rout over Miami on Saturday night. The Seminoles outgained the Hurricanes 456-188 and were never threatened after a 31-3 lead at halftime. Travis completed 10 of 12 passes for 202 yards before being removed early in the fourth quarter. Florida State exceeded 200 yards rushing for the fourth straight game with 225. The Seminoles ended their first two drives on Travis' touchdown passes to Ontaria Wilson and DJ Lundy. Travis connected with Wilson for 56 yards 1:38 into the game, then found Lundy open in the end zone for a 2-yard score. Lundy, a linebacker, was utilized in the short-yardage situation. Benson's touchdown runs from 13 yards and 1 yard in the second quarter made it 28-3. The Hurricanes drove to the Florida State 2-yard line late in the third quarter, but freshman quarterback Jacurri Brown failed to retrieve a poor snap from center that lost 23 yards with Jarred Verse recovering the ball for the Seminoles. Travis threw his third touchdown pass, an 8-yard completion to Camren McDonald on the first play of the fourth quarter. Andres Borregales capped the Hurricanes' opening drive of the game with a season-high 47-yard field goal.

FLORIDA

Trey Benson had a 17-yard touchdown run with 4:06 left to give No. 16 Florida State a 45-38 win over Florida on Friday. Benson had 111 yards rushing and three touchdowns, and Jordan Travis ran for 83 yards and two touchdowns. Florida drove the field in the final minutes but Anthony Richardson's fourth-down pass over the middle fell incomplete with 39 seconds to go. It was the highest scoring game in the Florida State-Florida rivalry, which dates to 1958. Travis also completed 13 of 30 passes for 270 yards as Florida State completed a sweep of its state rivals for the first time under Mike Norvell. Florida State trailed 24-21 at the half but opened the second half with scores on the next three drives (Fitzgerald field goal, Benson touchdown run, Jordan touchdown pass to Poitier) to jump in front 38-24. The Gators answered back with a pair of touchdowns, one each by Montrell Johnson and Trevor Etienne, to tie the game with 7:41 left.

2022 CHEEZE-IT BOWL

The No. 13 Seminoles used a 32-yard field goal from kicker Ryan Fitzgerald with 55 seconds left to defeat the Sooners, 35-32, at Camping World Stadium in Orlando on Thursday. With the victory, FSU now has its first 10-win season since 2016. Quarterback Jordan Travis went 27 of 38 for a career-high 418 yards and two touchdowns with an interception. Wide receiver Johnny Wilson recorded a career-high 202 receiving yards on eight catches.

Florida State began the game with fury. On the third play of its opening possession, quarterback Jordan Travis scrambled for 16 yards. The Florida State quarterback then hit wide receiver Johnny Wilson for a 26-yard completion, which was immediately followed by a 22-yard run from running back Treshaun Ward, putting the ball at the Oklahoma 5-yard line. However, Oklahoma's defense made a stand, keeping Florida State out of the end zone and forcing a field goal. Oklahoma came down the field and scored the game's first touchdown. A 13-play drive ended with quarterback Dillon Gabriel hitting wide receiver Jalil Farooq for a 22-yard touchdown, giving the Sooners a 7-3 lead. Oklahoma's Marvin Mims gained 23 yards on a Florida State punt, putting the ball at the Florida State 49-yard line. Nine plays later, Gabriel ran an 8-yard touchdown. The score gave Oklahoma a 14-3 lead. After Oklahoma missed a 45-yard field goal, Florida State scored its first touchdown. Travis, running to his left, hit wide receiver Ontaria Wilson for a 16-yard score. The Seminoles then converted a two-point conversion on a trick play, as tight end Wyatt Rector hit fellow tight end Brian Courtney for the conversion. Oklahoma got a field goal before halftime, taking a 17-11 lead into the break.

Florida State methodically moved the ball down the field in the middle of the third quarter, going on a 15-play, 94-yard drive to take the lead. The Seminoles capped off the drive with Ward working as the QB in the wildcat formation, running the ball in for a 1-yard score that helped put FSU in front, 18-17. Gavin Sawchuk scored his first college touchdown on a 15-yard run, helping the Sooners go up 23-18. A successful two-point conversion on a pass from Gabriel to Brayden Willis extended their lead to 25-18. Treshaun Ward hit another gear on a 38-yard run that resulted in a touchdown, leaving Oklahoma defenders in the dust to tie the game at 25-25. After forcing a fumble, FSU took over and took care of business. Travis finished off the six-play, 68-yard drive by connecting with Markeston Douglas on a 17-yard score that put the 'Noles up 32-25 halfway through the fourth. The Sooners Jovantae Barnes had nothing but green in between him and the end zone on his touchdown run that evened the game up at 32-32 with less than four minutes left. Ontario Wilson looked like he had one hand being held, but that didn't stop him from making a huge 58-yard grab that put FSU in field-goal territory. The Seminoles took a 35-32 lead with 55 seconds remaining. Oklahoma got the ball back with hopes of tying the game or taking the lead. However, Florida State's defense stepped up, sacking Gabriel on the final play and securing a 35-32 victory.

2023 Florida State Seminoles

The Seminoles were led by Mike Norvell in his fourth year as their head coach. Despite finishing the regular season with a 13−0 record, including winning the 2023 ACC Championship Game, Florida State became the first undefeated Power Five conference team not to make the College Football Playoff. The Seminoles were invited to the Orange Bowl to play #6 ranked Georgia from the SEC. It is the 11th appearance in the Orange Bowl for the Seminoles. The Seminoles were 5-5 in their prior 10 appearances.

Jordan Travis was voted the ACC Player of the Year and Offensive Player of the Year. Ryan Fitzgerald was voted the ACC Specialist of the Year and Mike Norvell was voted the ACC Coach of the Year. Trey Benson was voted the ACC Running Back of the Year. Jaheim Bell was voted the ACC Tight End of the Year; Darius Washington was voted the ACC Offensive Lineman of the Year and Keon Coleman was voted ACC Newcomer of the Year. All made the ACC First team All-Conference in addition to D'Mitri Emmanuel {G}, Bless Harris {OT}. Braden Fiske {DT} was voted ACC Interior Lineman of the Year and Jarrian Jones was voted ACC Cornerback of the Year. Both made the ACC All-Conference team in addition to Kalen DeLoach {LB} and Renardo Green {CB}. Jared Verse {DL} was voted ACC Defensive Lineman of the Year as was selected as a First team All-American by the Football Writers Association of America.

FINAL RANK: #6 AP, #6 CP

Home games were played at Doak Campbell Stadium

9/3/2023	Florida State	#8	vs	#5	*Lsu {@ Orlando}*	ABC	45	24	W
9/9/2023	Florida State	#4	vs		*SOUTHERN MISS*	ACC	66	13	W
9/16/2023	Florida State	#3	@		**Boston College**	ABC	31	29	W
9/23/2023	Florida State	#4	@	#23	**Clemson**	ABC	31	24	W
10/7/2023	Florida State	#5	vs		**VIRGINIA TECH**	ABC	39	17	W
10/14/2023	Florida State	#4	vs		**SYRACUSE**	ABC	41	3	W
10/21/2023	Florida State	#4	vs	#18	**DUKE**	ABC	38	20	W
10/28/2023	Florida State	#4	@		**Wake Forest**	ABC	41	16	W
11/4/2023	Florida State	#4	@		**Pittsburgh**	ESPN	24	7	W
11/11/2023	Florida State	#4	vs		**MIAMI**	ABC	27	20	W
11/18/2023	Florida State	#4	vs		*NORTH ALABAMA*	CW	58	13	W
11/25/2023	Florida State	#5	@		*Florida*	ESPN	24	15	W
12/2/2023	**Florida State**	**#4**	**vs**	**#15**	**Louisville**	**ABC**	**16**	**6**	**W**
12/30/2023	**Florida State**	**#5**	**vs**	**#6**	**Georgia**	**ESPN**	**3**	**63**	**L**
Coach: Mike Norvell					**Season Record >>**		**484**	**270**	**13-1**

Schedule Source: Steve's Football Bible LLC

Selected game(s) highlights

Lsu

Jordan Travis accounted for five touchdowns, including three to Michigan State transfer Keon Coleman, and the eighth-ranked Seminoles throttled No. 5 LSU 45-24. The Seminoles delivered a dominant second half to extend their winning streak to seven and established themselves as an early season favorite to make the College Football Playoff. FSU stopped the Tigers twice on fourth down in the first half, including once at the goal line, and scored the go-ahead touchdown one play after Travis connected with Lawrance Toafili for 41 yards on fourth-and-2. Travis ran in on the ensuing play to put the Seminoles ahead 24-17. Coleman finished with nine catches for 122 yards, including scoring plays of 40, 21 and 7 yards. Johnny Wilson added seven receptions for 104 yards. Travis completed 23 of 31 passes for 342 yards and four TDs. He and Coleman hooked up for a 40-yarder to start the scoring, added a 21-yarder late in the second to tie the game at 14 and then connected on a 7-yard fade in the fourth.

Boston College

After blowing most of a 21-point lead, No. 3 Florida State escaped with a 31-29 victory over Boston College. DJ Lundy intercepted a pass to set up his own 1-yard touchdown run as the Seminoles scored four unanswered touchdowns to make it 31-10 before surviving a late BC charge for their ninth straight victory. Boston College set a school record for penalties, missed an extra point, went for 2 after another touchdown and failed, and opted not to kick a field goal from the Seminoles 5 when trailing by 15 points early in the fourth quarter. But the Eagles still trailed by only 2 points, with the ball, in the final three minutes before Kalen DeLoach sacked Thomas Castellanos on third down to stall BC's last possession. Jordan Travis completed 16 of 24 passes for 212 yards and two touchdowns and ran for 38 yards for the Seminoles. Kye Robichaux scored from 1 yard out for BC to cut the deficit to 31-16 with a minute left in the third quarter, but Connor Lytton's kick failed. BC recovered a squib kick and advanced to the FSU 5 before getting stopped on fourth down. Khari Johnson recovered Toafili's fumble and ran it in to pull the Eagles within nine points; BC went for 2 and failed, then stopped FSU for the third straight time — the Eagles did that only once in the entire first half. They drove to the 7 before Castellanos froze the defense with a stutter step and ran it in on a fourth-and-2 to make it 31-29. But BC's last possession stalled after Castellanos was sacked.

Clemson

Keon Coleman caught a 24-yard TD pass from Jordan Travis in overtime and the Seminoles followed up with a defensive stand to snap a seven-game losing streak to Clemson with a 31-24 win that touched off a Death Valley celebration. Travis also threw for another TD and ran for a score for the Seminoles, who had not beaten Clemson since an overtime victory in 2014. FSU linebacker Kalen DeLoach forced a fumble by Cade Klubnik and scooped it up for a 56-yard TD return to tie things at 24-all with 31 seconds left in the third quarter. Clemson had a chance to take a late lead with 1:47 left in the fourth quarter, but Jonathan Weitz missed a 29-yard try wide left. Travis lofted a high-arching pass that Coleman caught in stride and hushed the raucous Death Valley crowd on the first extra possession. Clemson couldn't get a first down on its possession when Klubnik's fourth-and-2 pass sailed wide of the target and Florida State's players sprinted to celebrate on the field where the program hadn't won since 2013.

MIAMI

Trey Benson ran for two touchdowns, Keon Coleman hauled in a score and No. 4 Florida State held off the rival Hurricanes 27-20. Miami controlled both lines of scrimmage and played turnover-free football for most of the game. It still wasn't enough to overcome FSU, which has won three in a row in the series and 10 of the last 14. Jordan Travis threw for 265 yards and his 20th TD pass of the season, a 6-yard fade to Coleman that gave the 'Noles a little breathing room in the final quarter. Miami answered when Emory Williams found Jacolby George down the sideline for an 85-yard score.

Florida

Trey Benson ran for three touchdowns, including a 26-yarder on third down with less than three minutes to play, and No. 5 Florida State beat rival Florida 24-15. Benson finished with 95 yards on 19 carries. The 'Noles trailed 12-0 in the second quarter but were dominant in the second half, holding Florida to 48 yards in the final 30 minutes and minus-15 yards in the fourth quarter. FSU finished with six sacks, including 2 1/2 by standout Jared Verse. Kalen DeLoach squashed any thoughts of a late-game miracle when he intercepted Max Brown's pass.

2023 ACC CHAMPIONSHIP

The Seminoles started freshman third-stringer Brock Glenn at quarterback, and he finished 8 of 21 for 55 yards. Their offense gained just 3.4 yards per play. Lawrance Toafili ran for 118 yards and a touchdown for the Seminoles. Trailing 10-6 in the fourth quarter, the Cardinals (10-3) had a chance to take the lead after they tackled Seminoles punter Alex Mastromanno before he could get the kick away. Louisville took over at the Seminoles 11, but three plays later, Tatum Bethune picked off Jack Plummer's pass in the end zone. After a 33-yard field goal by Ryan Fitzgerald put Florida State ahead 13-6 with 3:11

left, the Cardinals had one more shot. But Braden Fiske sacked Plummer on a fourth down, giving the Seminoles the ball at the Louisville 20 with 2:35 remaining. Fitzgerald made it a two-possession game with his third field goal of the game from 40 yards. Fiske finished with three sacks. The game was tied 3-3 in the third quarter when the Seminoles finally took the ball out of Glenn's hands, going to the wildcat formation with Toafili in the backfield. Toafili received the direct snap from center and raced around right end for a 73-yard gain and then scored from 2 yards out on the next play, from the same formation. Toafili was named MVP of the game.

2023 ORANGE BOWL

The No. 5 Florida State Seminoles took on the No. 6 Georgia Bulldogs in the Capital One Orange Bowl on December 30. Georgia won the matchup, 63-3. The Seminoles were forced to rely on backups at multiple position groups. They were down to true freshman Brock Glenn, who started his second career at quarterback as Heisman Finalist Jordan Travis was out due to injury. Backup quarterback Tate Rodemaker entered the transfer portal before the game. Overall, 20 freshmen were listed on the three deep for the game, and the 'Noles had to start backups at over 15 positions as over 25 players were out due to injury, the NFL Draft, and the transfer portal. The Seminoles got the ball first and were backed up on their own ten-yard line. Running back Caziah Holmes and wide receiver Kentron Poitier moved the chains, but the drive ended with a three-and-out on their first possession. Georgia running back Kendall Milton got the ball moving for the Bulldogs. Quarterback Carson Beck found Dominic Lovett, defensive end Patrick Payton made his presence known with a strip sack, and linebacker Omar Graham Jr. made a tackle for loss. On a 3rd and 22, Beck found Lovett again, and on 4th and three, the Bulldogs turned the ball over on downs. The Seminole offense stalled on their second drive, forcing the defense back on the field. From the 48-yard line, defensive back Shyheim Brown batted down Beck's pass and found Marcus Rosamary-Jacksaint moving UGA into the FSU red zone, and Milton gave Georgia its first score of the game. Florida State went with a wild cat formation, which they found success with during the ACC Championship. A quick pass to wide receiver Ja'Khi Douglas gave them some momentum, but the drive stalled, and the 'Noles were forced to punt. Georgia moved the ball down the field, and Milton got the Bulldogs in scoring range. From 1st and 10, Milton scored again making the score 14-0. Glenn found Poitier for a 17-yard pass and, on the next play, found him again for 55. The 'Noles were unable to punch it in, and kicker Ryan Fitzgerald gave Florida State its first points from 22 yards. UGA wide receiver Dillon Bell made a play of his own with a 33-yard reception, and Georgia scored its third touchdown of the half off a 15-yard run by Daijun Edwards. On the kickoff, Georgia's Chazz Chambliss forced a fumble, and the Bulldogs scored on the following play on a 27-yard run by Ladd McConkey.

Returning to the wildcat, Douglas rattled off a 30-yard run that put FSU at midfield. On fourth and one, wide receiver Darion Williamson took a handoff from Glenn to move the chains. The 'Noles were put in another 4th down situation at the 38-yard line; this time, they were unable to convert. Freshman defensive back Quindarrius Jones made back-to-back tackles but made a costly pass interference mistake that gave the Bulldogs a new set of downs. Freshman defensive back Conrad Hussey saved a touchdown reception, but UGA found the endzone again on the next play with a touchdown pass to wide receiver Arian Smith. FSU freshman wide receiver Hykeem Williams had his name called, and Glenn converted a set of downs on a 5-yard scramble. Williamson got the 'Noles in the red zone with a 26-yard pass. But the bad turnover luck continued for FSU. Georgia defensive lineman Mykell Williams forced and recovered a fumble. The Bulldogs would score again on the next play. Florida State turned the ball over three times in the first half and couldn't get anything going on offense or defense. At the start of the second half, UGA got the ball moving into the red zone. Freshman Ashlynd Barker was able to save a touchdown run by Cash Jones, and after a second attempt, FSU freshman Justin Cryer forced a third down. Edwards scored again, making the score 49-3. Georgia pulled its starting quarterback, Carson Beck, and backup, Gunner Stockton. The Bulldog's second scoring drive of the second half came from a 4-yard touchdown pass to tight end Lawson Luckie. As seconds dwindled in the third quarter, the Seminoles had their fourth turnover on an interception by defensive back Daylen Everette thrown by Glenn. The Seminoles continued to fight despite such a large deficit, but by the start of the fourth quarter, there seemed no gas was left in the tank. Georgia would go on to score one more time, leaving the final score 63-3. With FSU not having its entire starting roster, it was no contest for Georgia, who didn't suffer as much roster attrition.

2024 Florida State Seminoles

The Seminoles were led by Mike Norvell, who was in his fifth year as their head coach. The Seminoles finished with a 2-10 record {1-7 ACC}. Despite high pre-season expectations, including a top ten ranking in the polls, the Seminoles finished with their worst record in a season since 1974, becoming the first team in the CFP era to go from double-digit wins to double-digit losses the following year as well as the first team in college football history to start the season in the top ten and finish with double-digit losses.

Alex Mastromanno {P} was selected as a First Team All-American.

Home games were played at Doak Campbell Stadium

8/24/2024	**#10**	**vs**		**Georgia Tech {Dublin, IRE}**	ESPN	21	24	L
9/2/2024	**#10**	**vs**		**BOSTON COLLEGE**	ESPN	13	28	L
9/14/2024		**vs**	#25	*MEMPHIS*	ESPN	12	20	L
9/21/2024		**vs**		**CALIFORNIA**	espn2	14	9	W
9/28/2024		**@**		**Smu**	ACC	16	42	L
10/5/2024		**vs**	#15	**CLEMSON**	ESPN	13	29	L
10/18/2024		**@**		**Duke**	espn2	16	23	L
10/26/2024		**@**	#6	**Miami**	ESPN	14	36	L
11/2/2024		**vs**		**NORTH CAROLINA**	ACC	11	35	L
11/9/2024		**@**	#8	*Notre Dame*	NBC	3	52	L
11/23/2024		**vs**		*CHARLESTON SOUTHERN*	ACC	41	7	W
11/30/2024		**vs**		*FLORIDA*	espn2	11	31	L
Coach: Mike Norvell				**Season Record >>**		185	336	**2-10**

Schedule Source: Steve's Football Bible LLC

Selected game(s) highlights

Georgia Tech

Aidan Birr made a 44-yard field goal as time expired, and Georgia Tech upset No. 10 Florida State 24-21. Jamal Haynes ran for 75 yards and two touchdowns for Georgia Tech, while Haynes King threw for 146 yards and ran for 54 yards. the Seminoles tied the game with 6:33 left in the fourth quarter on a 15-play touchdown drive that included two fourth-down conversions by DJ Uiagalelei. Florida State never touched the ball again. Birr came on with 5 seconds left to hit the winner that just stayed inside the left upright. Uiagalelei completed 19 of 27 passes for 193 yards. Ryan Fitzgerald made a 59-yard field goal, a career long and the second longest in school history, just before halftime to tie the game at 14. Fitzgerald had a 52-yarder earlier.

CALIFORNIA

Ja'Khi Douglas had a 36-yard touchdown reception in the fourth quarter and Florida State defeated Cal 14-9. Patrick Payton had three of Florida State's seven sacks, the last when Marvin Jones Jr. and Edwin Joseph combined to sack Cal's Fernando Mendoza on fourth down with 54 seconds left. Lawrance Toafili had a 2 yard touchdown run for the Seminoles.

Duke

Chandler Rivers scored on an interception return, Todd Pelino kicked three field goals, and the Blue Devils beat Florida State for the first time in 23 all-time meetings, winning 23-16. With a chance to pull even, the Seminoles drove to the Duke 37-yard line before a first-down fumble at the 5:18 mark. Florida State's final possession ended on a fourth-down play that lost yards. Florida State quarterback Brock Glenn committed turnovers on three consecutive first-half snaps, with two interceptions sandwiched around a fumble. He finished 9-for-19 passing for 110 yards. Florida State's Samuel Singleton Jr. returned the second-half kickoff 95 yards for a touchdown.

#6 Miami

Cam Ward passed for 208 yards and caught a touchdown pass; Damien Martinez ran for 148 yards and two touchdowns and No. 6 Miami remained unbeaten by beating rival Florida State 36-14. Mark Fletcher Jr. rushed for a score and Andres Borregales kicked three field goals to help Miami snap a three-game losing streak against the Seminoles. Caziah Holmes ran 1 yard for a touchdown getting FSU within 14-7 midway through the second quarter. But the Seminoles didn't score again until 18 seconds remained, when Brock Glenn found Malik Benson with a 5-yard pass.

FLORIDA

Montrell Johnson ran for 99 yards, including a 65-yard touchdown, and Florida recovered five fumbles in a 31-11 win over Florida State. Florida recorded eight sacks, 14 tackles for loss and grabbed four fumbles — a fifth came on a muffed Florida State punt. The Gators scored a touchdown after recovering a fumble at the Florida State 14 and tacked on a field goal after recovering a fumble at the Seminoles' 12. DJ Lagway completed 14 of 22 passes for 133 yards, including a 4-yard touchdown pass to Marcus Burke and an 8-yard pass to Tony Livingston. Lawrance Toafili had a 1-yard touchdown run late in the fourth quarter for Florida State and Ryan Fitzgerald kicked a 39 yard field goal.

2025 Florida State Seminoles

The **2025 Florida State Seminoles football team** entered the season after arguably the worst season in the program's history. The Seminoles were led by Mike Norvell, who was in his sixth year as their head coach. Florida State began the season with an upset win over the eighth-ranked Alabama Crimson Tide as a double digit underdog. The Seminoles set the school record for largest margin of victory with a win over the East Texas A&M Lions. The Seminoles suffered four consecutive defeats, starting a season 0–4 in conference play for the first time. The Seminoles ended their season with a loss to their rival Florida Gators, compiling a losing record for the fourth time in the last six seasons, finishing winless on the road for the second consecutive season, and leaving them ineligible for a bowl game. Due to a lack of available bowl teams, Florida State was offered a spot in the Birmingham Bowl due to a high academic progress rate score but the school turned down the bid.

Home games were played at Doak Campbell Stadium

8/30/2025	Florida State		vs	#8	*ALABAMA*	ABC	31	17	**W**
9/6/2025	Florida State	**#14**	vs		*EAST TEXAS A&M*	ACC	77	3	**W**
9/20/2025	Florida State	**#7**	vs		*KENT STATE*	ACC	66	10	**W**
9/26/2025	Florida State	**#8**	@		Virginia	ESPN	38	46	**L**
10/4/2025	Florida State	**#18**	vs	#3	MIAMI	ABC	22	28	**L**
10/11/2025	Florida State	**#25**	vs		PITTSBURGH	ESPN	31	34	**L**
10/18/2025	Florida State		@		Stanford	ESPN	13	20	**L**
11/1/2025	Florida State		vs		WAKE FOREST	ACC	42	7	**W**
11/8/2025	Florida State		@		Clemson	ACC	10	24	**L**
11/15/2025	Florida State		vs		VIRGINIA TECH	ACC	34	14	**W**
11/21/2025	Florida State		@		NC State	ESPN	11	21	**L**
11/29/2025	Florida State		@		*Florida*	espn2	21	40	**L**
Coach: Mike Norvell					**Season Record >>**		396	264	**5-7**

Schedule Source: Steve's Football Bible LLC

Selected game(s) highlights

#8 ALABAMA

Florida State upset No. 8 Alabama 31–17 at Doak Campbell Stadium. The victory was a massive turnaround for a Seminoles program coming off a 2–10 season and snapped Alabama's 23-game winning streak in season openers. Alabama took an early 7–0 lead with a methodical 16-play opening drive. However, FSU answered immediately and rattled off 17 unanswered points. Castellanos sparked the comeback with his legs, while kicker Jake Weinberg added a career-long 45-yard field goal to give the Seminoles a 17–7 halftime lead. FSU extended the lead to 24–7 early in the third quarter following a 4-yard touchdown run by Caziah Holmes. Alabama attempted a comeback in the fourth quarter, cutting the deficit to 24–17 with 11 minutes remaining. Florida State responded with a 10-play, 75-yard drive capped by a 14-yard Gavin Sawchuk touchdown run to seal the 31–17 win.

#3 MIAMI

In a classic rivalry game that started as a blowout and ended in a nail-biter, No. 3 Miami defeated No. 18 Florida State 28–22. The Hurricanes dominated for three quarters, building a massive 28–3 lead, before withstanding a furious 19-point fourth-quarter rally by the Seminoles. Miami's Georgia transfer quarterback, Carson Beck, put on a clinic for most of the night. After FSU took an early 3–0 lead on a field goal, Beck took over, throwing four touchdown passes to effectively silence the Tallahassee crowd. Freshman wideout Malachi Toney was the breakout star, catching two touchdowns (44 yards and 40 yards) in the first three quarters. FSU quarterback Tommy Castellanos threw two critical interceptions in the first half, both of which Miami turned into touchdowns. By the end of the third quarter, Miami seemed to have the game in hand, leading 28–3 and out-gaining the Seminoles significantly. Castellanos found Lawayne McCoy for an 8-yard touchdown (and a successful 2-point conversion) to make it 28–11. FSU then orchestrated a massive 19-play, 96-yard drive that chewed up over five minutes, ending in a Randy Pittman Jr. touchdown catch to cut the lead to 28–19. After another stop, FSU added a field goal with just 20 seconds remaining to pull within six. However, Miami recovered the ensuing onside kick to survive the scare.

VIRGINIA TECH

In their 2025 home finale, Florida State delivered a methodical and disciplined performance to defeat Virginia Tech 34–14. The victory was significant as it marked the 600th win in program history. After a scoreless first quarter that saw both teams miss field goals, the Seminoles' offense found its rhythm, scoring on six consecutive possessions to pull away from the Hokies. Florida State broke the deadlock with a 26-yard field goal from Jake Weinberg. Virginia Tech briefly took the lead, 7–3, on a 4-yard touchdown run by quarterback Kyron Drones. However, FSU regained the lead just before halftime when Tommy Castellanos connected with Duce Robinson for a 50-yard touchdown strike, making it 10–7 at the break. The Seminoles dominated the second half, opening with a 13-play touchdown drive capped by a 1-yard Castellanos run. Following a Virginia Tech fumble, FSU scored again on a 1-yard plunge by Randy Pittman Jr. to extend the lead to 24–7. Virginia Tech cut the lead to 10 points early in the fourth quarter, but Castellanos answered with a 15-yard touchdown run—his third total score of the night. A late Weinberg field goal provided the final 34–14 margin.

Florida

In a dominant finish to a difficult season, Florida defeated Florida State 40–21. The victory denied the Seminoles bowl eligibility. The game was a historic performance from sophomore running back Jadan Baugh, who carried the ball 38 times for 266 yards and two touchdowns. Florida jumped out to a 10–0 lead in the first quarter following a Trey Smack field goal and a 5-yard touchdown pass from DJ Lagway to J. Michael Sturdivant. FSU responded with a touchdown to cut the lead to 10–7, but Florida extended it back to 17–7. A late 4-yard scramble by FSU quarterback Tommy Castellanos made it a 17–14 game at halftime. The Gators broke the game open in the third quarter. Lagway threw his third touchdown pass of the night—a 3-yarder to Hayden Hansen—and Baugh added a 22-yard scoring run to push the lead to 31–14. The Exclamation Point: After FSU pulled within 34–21 late in the fourth, Florida leaned on Baugh to seal the win. On a 4th-and-3 with less than a minute remaining, Baugh took a wildcat snap 12 yards for a touchdown.

www.ingramcontent.com/pod-product-compliance
Lightning Source LLC
Chambersburg PA
CBHW060558120726
48002CB00010B/2732